INTRODUCTORY

NETWORK
THEORY

INTRODUCTORY

NETWORK THEORY

AMAR G. BOSE

KENNETH N. STEVENS

MASSACHUSETTS INSTITUTE OF TECHNOLOGY

Department of Electrical Engineering

HARPER & ROW, Publishers

New York

To Students of Students

of PROFESSOR E. A. GUILLEMIN

Contents

Preface

With the rapid expansion of scientific knowledge in the past decade, considerable attention has been devoted to the problems and objectives of scientific education. One result of this attention has been a much needed updating of classroom subjects. With this updating came the realization that, within the four years of an undergraduate education, it is increasingly difficult, if not impossible, to reach the frontiers of knowledge even in rather restricted areas. However, even if this were possible, we would question the desirability of such an objective, as it does not necessarily provide the best preparation for absorbing and developing the new horizons that the students will encounter during their careers. We feel, therefore, that it is more important to develop the student's ability to reason clearly and to think critically in a few areas than to provide him with a wide but shallow collection of presently useful techniques. Thus, an education should give the student the experience of deriving results that are new to him, and the thought processes leading to these results are perhaps even more important than the results.

Let us now briefly discuss our attempts to realize these objectives in the context of a sophomore course in network theory. Basic to our entire development of the subject is the concept of complementary roles for the teacher, the text, and the homework. We believe the student should receive motivation and insight from the teacher, fundamentals from the text, and the experience of developing new results for himself from the homework.

A text is often judged by how completely it covers the subject. However, the more completely it does so, the more redundant the function of the teacher becomes and the more the homework is reduced to the routine application

of the text material. In the extreme such a text becomes a strait jacket
rather than a foundation for an education. If we agree that often the
thought process leading to a result is at least as important as the result,
then we must appreciate that it is valuable for the student to establish for
himself many of the basic concepts of a subject. The homework is a natural
vehicle for enabling the student to develop these concepts and thereby to
obtain experience in extending his own frontiers of knowledge—experience
that will be helpful in his future career regardless of his field of endeavor.
With these thoughts in mind, we have introduced many topics solely in the
homework. The convolution integral, the relation between the impulse
response and the frequency response of a network, the concept of analogue
simulation, and the ideas of feedback and oscillation are just a few of the
topics that are developed by the student in the homework and do not appear
in the text. The function of the text is to present some of the fundamentals
and to expand on them in a way that should be helpful to the student when
he proceeds to unfold the subject further through the medium of the problems.

Having mentioned the roles of the text and the homework, we come now
to that of the teacher. Again the concept of complementary roles for each
medium of instruction demands that the teacher do more than repeat the
text, or, in other words, that the text not dwell on the material that is best
presented by the teacher. We believe the teacher can most effectively contribute motivation, interest, and insight by way of the discussion of examples of current interest. The text should provide flexibility for the teacher to
modify, develop, and augment the homework in order to reflect his individual view of the relative importance of different topics and approaches.

If we expect the student to develop basic concepts of the subject in the
homework, it is essential that his work be checked and that he have the
opportunity to discuss questions raised by the homework. By far the most
effective means that we have tried for accomplishing this is to assign a
teaching assistant, in addition to a professor or instructor, to each class of
twenty-four students. The teaching assistant has been so effective that we
feel it is worthwhile to describe in detail the functioning of the teaching-
assistant program as it has evolved in the teaching of network theory at the
Massachusetts Institute of Technology during the past four years.

The teaching assistant is usually a first-term graduate student who carries
a load of two graduate courses in addition to his teaching duties. He
arranges his schedule in order to be available to each student for up to one
hour a week. The specific function of the teaching assistant is to discuss
the homework with the student and to try to locate and remedy the root of
any difficulty that the student may have. This one-to-one meeting between

teacher and student has significantly improved the motivation and performance of many poorer students, and has provided the opportunity to explore the subject in greater depth with the better students. With all students it has been effective in shaping their attitude toward study and their approach to problems to an extent that the benefits of this sophomore program are observable throughout the junior and senior years. The students' reaction to this meeting can be appreciated by noting that, although the meeting is entirely optional, they all attend it regularly and report that it constitutes one of the most valuable hours of the week. In addition to the benefits to the students, we have observed that this program provides an effective way of launching a teaching career. The basic principles of teaching are brought into sharp focus in a one-to-one meeting. In addition, after the teaching assistant becomes acquainted with his students, he is given opportunities to teach the class under the supervision of the section instructor.

We turn now to a few specific comments on the organization of the text. Chapter 1 is concerned primarily with the constraints that comprise the network model; questions of selecting variables for the efficient formulation of equilibrium equations are deferred until Chapter 5. This sequence is selected for two reasons. First, we wish to emphasize in Chapter 1 that Kirchhoff's laws and the voltage-current relations of the elements are the fundamental constraints on the network model. The choice of convenient variables, such as loop currents and node voltages, is analogous to the choice of a coordinate system and should not be confused with the basic constraints on the model. Second, the treatment of the loop and node methods involves a development of network topology that can provide a significant motivation problem if taught before a student has any insight into the behavior of simple networks. The problems that the student is called on to solve before studying Chapter 5 have sufficiently simple topology that they can be handled directly in terms of the element variables.

Chapter 2 is intended to provide the mathematical background for the development of the remaining chapters. The mathematics is presented separately because it is basic to many disciplines in which the models are governed by linear differential equations and because it is essential that the insight and interpretations of network behavior, developed in the following chapters, not be hindered by a simultaneous attempt to learn the necessary mathematics. The emphasis on exponential signals as building blocks and on the roles of the homogeneous solution and particular integral for linear differential equations with exponential excitations is intended also to establish the background for a course in signal analysis and linear systems that would follow this course.

As taught at the Massachusetts Institute of Technology, the course for which this book serves as the text occupies about twenty weeks of the sophomore year and represents approximately one-fourth of the academic load for students during this period. About two-thirds of those who take the course are in the Department of Electrical Engineering, and the remainder are from other areas of engineering and science.

A number of our colleagues in the Department of Electrical Engineering have participated in the planning and teaching of this course. In particular, we wish to thank Alan Oppenheim and Ralph Alter, who provided many valuable suggestions with regard to the material for the text and worked closely with us in the development of the problems. They have prepared a teacher's guide for this text, and the care with which this guide examines the issues raised in the text and in the problems reflects the depth of their concern for excellence in teaching. We also wish to thank Thomas Huang and Jonny Andersen for their significant contributions to the development of the text and the problems.

Finally we wish to acknowledge the support of the Ford Foundation in the development of the teaching program of which this text forms a part. A Ford Foundation grant to the School of Engineering of the Massachusetts Institute of Technology supported experiments in the teaching of this subject, and some of the innovations resulting from these experiments have since been adopted in the teaching of this and other subjects at M.I.T.

AMAR G. BOSE
KENNETH N. STEVENS

INTRODUCTORY

NETWORK
THEORY

1

The Network Model
and Equilibrium Equations

Introduction

A physical problem is never analyzed exactly. This is a consequence both of our inability to describe a physical situation completely and of the increasing complexity of the analysis as greater accuracy is demanded. A problem that involves events in the real world is always approached by making simplifying assumptions that hold only approximately, thereby forming a *model* of the events under study. The problem then reduces to that of analyzing the model. If the assumptions by means of which the physical situation was reduced to the model are reasonable, then our analysis should produce results that correspond to observed events, and the same type of analysis should be useful in predicting the behavior for other similar physical situations.

The study of network theory arises from the consideration of physical events that result from a given interconnection of electrical devices. In many cases such devices can be considered to be connected to their environment through sets of terminals, and the behavior of the devices can be approximately characterized by a set of currents and voltages associated with the terminals, along with constraints, dictated by the devices, that relate these currents and voltages. Furthermore, constraints on the voltages and currents at the terminals of the devices are introduced by their interconnection. The latter constraints are approximately expressed by two laws known as *Kirchhoff's laws*.

The approach to obtaining approximate solutions to such problems consists of two steps:

1. We idealize the physical devices by defining a set of basic elements with their associated ideal voltage-current constraints, which alone or in combination can be made to approximate the actual characteristics of the physical devices within the ranges of voltages and currents that are of interest.

2. We form an interconnection of these basic elements in much the same way that the devices are connected in the real problem, and we assume Kirchhoff's laws are satisfied exactly for the voltages and currents existing in this interconnection of idealized elements.

By this procedure we evolve a model for the physical problem, including a set of rules, Kirchhoff's laws, that govern the voltage and current variables. By applying the rules, we can proceed to determine values for the voltage and current variables. The solution so obtained approximates the solution to the real problem with which we started. The degree of approximation is determined by the extent to which Kirchhoff's laws applied to the original problem and by the degree to which we approximated the device characteristics.

Thus, for example, there are no physical devices for which the voltage-current relations are identical with the voltage-current relations that we shall define for ideal resistance, inductance, or capacitance elements. It may be that the voltage v associated with a particular device is very closely proportional to the current i for the device for modest values of v and i, but the plot of v versus i departs from a straight line as v or i becomes large. Hence over a limited range of v and i this device could be approximated by an ideal resistance for which v is defined to be proportional to i over all ranges of v and i. It may also happen that, for high frequencies, the current at one terminal of a device is not identical with the current at the other terminal. In this case, the device could not be modeled as a single two-terminal element of the type that we shall define, although it may be possible to approximate its performance with an interconnection of several such ideal elements to form a model with more than two terminals. If, however, the ranges of v and i and their time derivatives are appropriately restricted, it is possible to represent, with a high degree of accuracy, many physical devices by single ideal resistances, inductances, or capacitances, or by simple interconnections of these ideal elements. Likewise, sources of energy in a physical electric network can very frequently be modeled by so-called ideal voltage or current sources, often in combination with ideal elements.

Network theory is a discipline concerned with the study of models, i.e., ideal elements and sources and their interconnections. As such it does not encompass the problems of proceeding from the physical devices to the network models, or, for that matter, the problems of providing a physical interpretation for the voltage and current variables that describe the behavior of the network models. The latter problems require the application of electromagnetic field concepts and a study of the properties of materials. It is only after such studies that we shall be able to justify properly when and why our network models yield useful solutions in the analysis of physical problems.

Network elements

A large class of electrical devices can be modeled in terms of one or more two-terminal elements. Associated with each element is a voltage variable $v(t)$ and a current variable $i(t)$. Since in the physical situation we measure voltages across the terminals of devices and currents flowing through the devices, it is customary to symbolize the voltage and current variables associated with each two-terminal element in the manner shown in Fig. 1-1; that is, in our network model it is convenient, but not necessary, to think of voltage as existing across an element and current as flowing

FIG. 1-1. Symbol for a general network element with two terminals, showing the convention for assigning signs to the voltage v and the current i.

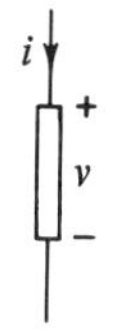

through the element. By definition, the current $i(t)$ flowing into one terminal of the network element is identical to the current flowing out of the other terminal, and there is a constraint between $v(t)$ and $i(t)$, known as the voltage-current (v-i) characteristic of the element.[1] A reference sense is assigned to current by means of an arrow; by convention, i is positive if the current flows in the direction of the arrow, and negative if it flows in the opposite direction. Likewise, the plus and minus signs at either end of the box assign a reference sense to voltage; v is positive if the terminal labeled $+$ is positive relative to the terminal labeled $-$, and negative if the terminal labeled $+$ is negative relative to the terminal labeled $-$. It is customary to place the arrow in a direction pointing into the $+$ terminal

---

[1] For convenience in writing equilibrium equations and in drawing figures, we shall usually write v for $v(t)$ and i for $i(t)$, with the understanding that all the voltages and currents are regarded as functions of time unless stated to be constant.

of the element. If we observe this convention, then it is not necessary to specify the reference sense of both v and i, since, by this convention, the specification of the reference sense for either quantity implies that of the other. It should be clearly understood that the assignment of reference senses for v and i in no way restricts the currents and voltages associated with the element. It simply supplies reference directions with respect to which voltages and currents of any magnitude and sense can be expressed.

Three elements that are used very frequently to model physical devices are shown in Fig. 1-2. The resistance element has a terminal voltage that

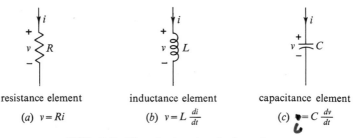

resistance element   inductance element   capacitance element

(a) $v = Ri$ (b) $v = L\frac{di}{dt}$ (c) $i = C\frac{dv}{dt}$

FIG. 1-2. Three basic network elements.

is proportional to the current flowing through it. The proportionality constant is called the resistance of the element. In the case of the inductance element, the voltage-current characteristic is

$$v = L\frac{di}{dt},\qquad(1\text{-}1)$$

where L is the inductance of the element. Integration of both sides of this equation yields an integral relation for the current:

$$i(t) = \frac{1}{L}\int_{t_0}^{t} v(\tau)\,d\tau + i(t_0),\qquad(1\text{-}2)$$

where t_0 is any instant of time. For the capacitance element the voltage-current characteristic is

$$i = C\frac{dv}{dt},\qquad(1\text{-}3)$$

where C is the capacitance of the element. Integration of this equation leads to the integral relation

$$v(t) = \frac{1}{C} \int_{t_0}^{t} i(\tau)\, d\tau + v(t_0), \tag{1-4}$$

where t_0 is any instant of time.[1]

Sources

The excitations of many physical networks can be modeled in terms of two types of ideal sources: voltage sources and current sources. As in the case of elements, the current flowing into one terminal of a source is by definition equal to that flowing out through the other terminal. However, the two types of sources are distinguished from the general element that we have defined by the fact that the v-i characteristic for a source fixes one of the terminal variables independently of the other, whereas the v-i characteristic for an element is a constraint involving both terminal variables.

A *voltage source* has by definition a prescribed voltage across its terminals independent of the current flowing through it. The general symbol used to represent a voltage source of value v_s is shown in Fig. 1-3a. When the

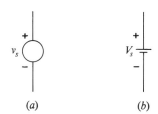

(a)   (b)

FIG. 1-3. Symbols representing voltage sources.

value v_s of the voltage source does not change with time, i.e., is a constant V_s, the symbol in Fig. 1-3b is sometimes employed. Under certain conditions, such an ideal voltage source is a good model for a battery, although the voltage across a physical battery does change slightly as the terminal current is varied. A plot of the voltage at the terminals of a voltage source versus the current flowing through the source is shown in Fig. 1-4. If the source voltage v_s is zero, then the voltage across the two terminals of the source is, of course, constrained to be zero at all times. In this case the source is equivalent to, and hence can be replaced by, a short circuit

---

[1] When the units of i, v, and t are amperes, volts, and seconds, respectively, then the units of R, L, and C are ohms, henries, and farads, respectively.

FIG. 1-4. The diagram at the right gives the voltage-current characteristic at the terminals of the voltage source shown at the left.

that by definition has the property that no voltage can appear across it regardless of the current flowing through it.

A *current source* has a prescribed current through it independent of the voltage appearing across it. Figure 1-5 shows the symbol used for a

FIG. 1-5. Symbol representing a current source.

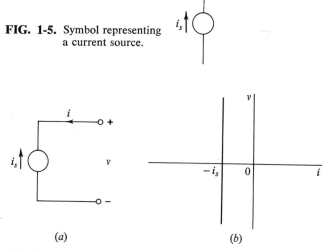

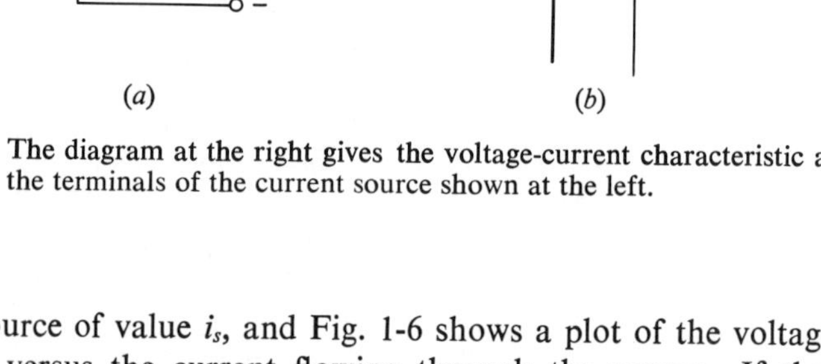

(a)   *(b)*

FIG. 1-6. The diagram at the right gives the voltage-current characteristic at the terminals of the current source shown at the left.

current source of value i_s, and Fig. 1-6 shows a plot of the voltage at the terminals versus the current flowing through the source. If the source current i_s is zero, then the current flowing through it is, of course, constrained to be zero at all times. In this case the source is equivalent to, and hence can be replaced by, an open circuit that by definition has the property that no current can flow through it regardless of the voltage that appears across it.

Basic equilibrium equations for networks

Any interconnection of elements and sources is called a *network*. The voltages and currents in a network must satisfy three basic types of constraints. The constraints of the first type are the voltage-current relations for the elements. These relations are properties of the elements alone and have nothing to do with how they are connected in the network. The remaining two types of constraints are concerned only with how the elements and sources are interconnected and have nothing to do with the properties of the elements. One type of constraint is imposed upon the currents as a result of the interconnection of various elements and sources and is known as Kirchhoff's current law (KCL). The other type of constraint is imposed upon the voltages as a result of the interconnection of various elements and sources and is known as Kirchhoff's voltage law (KVL).

In Chap. 2 we shall introduce the concept of a complex time function in order to facilitate the analysis of networks. In anticipation of this extension to complex time functions, we define the basic equilibrium equations for networks to apply to complex as well as real time functions $v(t)$ and $i(t)$. However, since measurable voltages and currents are real time functions, only the real time functions in our network model have direct physical counterparts.

Kirchhoff's laws. Kirchhoff's current law states that the algebraic sum of the currents entering a connection point (or, alternatively, the sum of the currents leaving a connection point) is zero. A connection point is a point in the network at which one or more elements or sources terminate. If, for example, KCL is applied to the currents entering the connection point shown in Fig. 1-7, we obtain

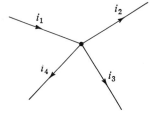

FIG. 1-7. Illustrating the application of Kirchhoff's current law at a connection point.

$$i_1 - i_2 - i_3 - i_4 = 0. \tag{1-5}$$

It follows from the statement of KCL and from the fact that the currents entering and leaving any element or source are identical that the algebraic sum of the currents entering any closed surface in the network must be zero.[1]

Kirchhoff's voltage law states that the algebraic sum of the voltage drops around a closed path (or, alternatively, the sum of the voltage rises around a closed path) is zero. If, for example, KVL is applied to the voltage drops

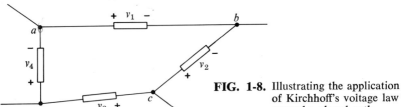

FIG. 1-8. Illustrating the application of Kirchhoff's voltage law around a closed path.

in a clockwise direction around the closed path *abcda* indicated in Fig. 1-8, we obtain

$$v_1 - v_2 + v_3 + v_4 = 0. \tag{1-6}$$

The terms in this equation can be rearranged to give

$$v_1 - v_2 = -v_4 - v_3; \tag{1-7}$$

i.e., the sum of the voltage drops between *a* and *c* along path *abc* is equal to the sum of the voltage drops between *a* and *c* along path *adc*. By the same reasoning, the sum of the voltage drops between two points in a network must be the same for any path if KVL is satisfied for all closed paths in the network. Therefore, KVL allows us to define a voltage between any two points in a network as the sum of the voltage drops (rises) along any path in the network joining the two points.

Problem 1-1

A portion of a network is shown within the dashed line in Fig. 1-9. The remainder of the network is indicated by the shaded area. Using the fact that KCL is satisfied at each of the connection points *a*, *b*, *c*, and *d*, show

[1] See Prob. 1-2.

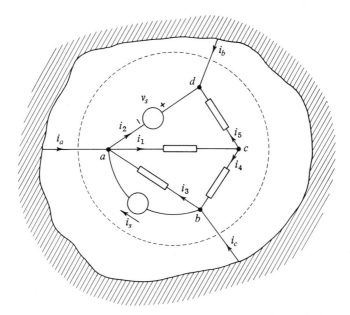

FIG. 1-9. Network used in Prob. 1-1 to illustrate the extension of KCL to closed surfaces.

that the sum of the currents entering the portion of the network enclosed by the dashed line is zero.

Problem 1-2

A network N with n terminals is shown in Fig. 1-10. Each of the n terminals connects to one of the connection points inside N. The currents i_1, i_2, ..., i_n result from the interconnection of network N with any external network by means of the n terminals.

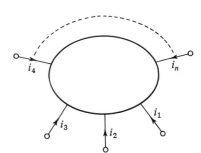

FIG. 1-10. An n-terminal network (Prob. 1-2).

In Prob. 1-1 we observed that a current in an element or source appears in the two KCL equations written at the two points to which the element or source is connected. Using this result, and the fact that KCL is satisfied at every connection point inside N, generalize the solution of Prob. 1-1 to show that

$$i_1 + i_2 + \cdots + i_n = 0.$$

Problem 1-3

a. Consider the two-terminal network shown in Fig. 1-11. Currents i_1 and

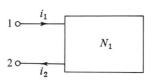

FIG. **1-11.** A two-terminal network (Prob. 1-3).

i_2 result from the connection of this network to another network by means of the terminals 1 and 2. Use the result of Prob. 1-2 to show that, regardless of what is connected to the terminals, the current i_1 entering terminal 1 is equal to the current i_2 leaving terminal 2.

b. What relation exists among the currents i_1, i_2, i_3, and i_4 in Fig. 1-12a?

c. Network N_1 is now connected to two networks, N_2 and N_3, as shown in Fig. 1-12b. What is the relation between currents i_1 and i_2?

d. Does the result obtained in (c) necessarily apply to currents i_1 and i_2 in the connection of Fig. 1-12a? Explain.

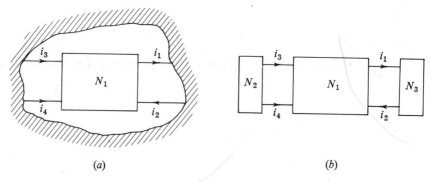

(a)   (b)

FIG. **1-12.** Two possible ways of connecting a four-terminal network (Prob. 1-3).

Problem 1-4

Show that it is sufficient to impose the KCL constraint at all but one of the connection points in a network in order to guarantee that KCL is satisfied at all connection points in the network.

Problem 1-5

a. Show that, if KVL is satisfied for each of the closed paths A, B, and C separately in Fig. 1-13, then KVL is satisfied for all closed paths in the network.

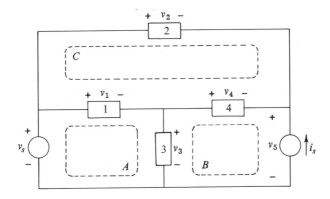

FIG. 1-13. Network for the study of Kirchhoff's voltage law in Prob. 1-5.

b. A planar network is a network that can be drawn on a plane without any elements crossing each other. Generalize the argument of (a) to show that, in a planar network, it is sufficient to impose KVL for all the closed paths that have no elements or sources intersecting them in order to guarantee that KVL is satisfied for all closed paths in the network.

Problem 1-6

a. For the network of Fig. 1-14, write a set of equations that imposes on

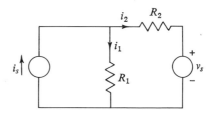

FIG. 1-14. Network for Prob. 1-6.

the element and source voltages and currents all of the constraints inherent in the network model.

b. Solve the equations obtained in (*a*) to determine i_1.

The basic network. We stated above that there are only three types of constraints on the network voltages and currents: the *v-i* relations for the elements, KVL constraints on the voltages, and KCL constraints on the currents. Therefore, we could obtain a set of simultaneous equations that govern the voltages and currents in the network model by writing the *v-i* relation for each element, a KVL equation around each closed path in the network, and a KCL equation at every connection point. Since this procedure expresses all the constraints inherent in our model, it must yield the desired equilibrium equations governing the voltages and currents in the network. However the writing of this set of equations is often a lengthy procedure as well as an unenlightening one from the point of view of understanding the relative roles played by the sources, elements, and their interconnections in determining the network response, i.e., in determining the voltages and currents in the network.

In order to gain some insight into the relative roles played by the sources and elements, we shall first formulate the Kirchhoff-law equations for the closed paths and connection points in the network when all sources are set to zero. These equations, of course, impose certain constraints on the voltages and currents in the elements. We shall then show that these equations, appropriately modified by the presence of the sources, are sufficient to impose all the Kirchhoff-law constraints on the element voltages

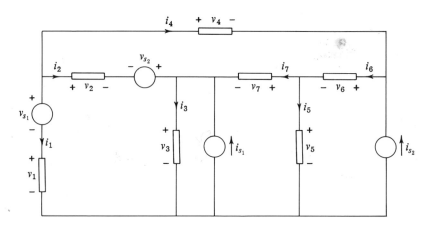

FIG. 1-15. Example of a network with current and voltage sources.

and currents in the network when the sources are included; that is, it is not necessary to write any more Kirchhoff-law equations even though the network with the sources contains more closed paths and more connection points than the network without the sources.

Let us consider any network containing sources. We shall choose the network of Fig. 1-15 as an example to aid in our discussion. It should be clear, however, that our arguments apply to any network and are in no way limited by the choice of this example. Suppose we set all the sources to zero in the network of Fig. 1-15. Then the voltage sources can be replaced by short circuits and the current sources by open circuits, resulting in the network shown in Fig. 1-16.

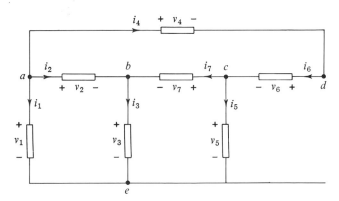

FIG. 1-16. Network of Fig. 1-15 with sources set to zero.

The network with all the sources set to zero will be called the *basic network*. The basic network is sufficiently important in the study of network theory to warrant terminology that distinguishes its components from those of the network containing sources. In the basic network, elements will be called *branches*, and the branches terminate in *nodes*. We define a node as the collection of all points that are joined to each other by short circuits. In the case of a planar network, i.e., a network that can be mapped on a plane without any elements crossing each other, a closed path in the basic network that does not enclose other closed paths is known as a *mesh*. For example, in Fig. 1-16 the path *abea* is a mesh, whereas the path *abcea* is not.

Formulation of KVL and KCL equations. Assume now that the Kirchhoff-law constraints have been imposed on the branch voltages and currents in the basic network. A typical KCL equation for the basic network in Fig. 1-16 is

$$i_2 - i_3 + i_7 = 0, \qquad (1\text{-}8)$$

which is an expression of KCL for node b. An equation of this type must be satisfied for every node in the basic network. Likewise, a typical KVL equation is

$$v_2 + v_3 - v_1 = 0, \qquad (1\text{-}9)$$

which is an expression of KVL for mesh $abea$. An equation of this type must be satisfied for every closed path in the basic network.

Let us now reinsert the sources into the network and observe how the set of KVL equations written for each closed path of the basic network and KCL equations written for each node of the basic network must be modified by the reinsertion of the sources.

Consider first the way in which the KVL equations for the basic network must be modified when the sources are reinserted. For each of the closed paths in the basic network there exists a corresponding closed path in the total network with sources. Such a path can be identified by noting the elements traversed in the basic network and finding the path in the total network in which the same elements are traversed. Voltage sources may now appear in addition to the elements in these closed paths.[1] Consequently new source terms must be included in the KVL equations for certain of the closed paths, but the remaining terms, corresponding to voltage drops in the elements, remain unchanged. For example, after the voltage sources are reinserted in the basic network of Fig. 1-16, in the manner shown in Fig. 1-15, the KVL equation (1-9) which was written for path $abea$ of the basic network must be modified to read

$$v_2 - v_{s_2} + v_3 - v_1 - v_{s_1} = 0. \qquad (1\text{-}10)$$

It is always possible, of course, to shift the source terms to the right-hand sides of such equations. In the present example, such a shift would lead to the equation

$$v_2 + v_3 - v_1 = v_{s_2} + v_{s_1}. \qquad (1\text{-}11)$$

Thus with the reinsertion of sources the KVL equations for the basic network can be revised in such a way that the left-hand sides remain unchanged and voltage-source terms are added to the right-hand sides.

---

[1] But current sources cannot appear, since a current source is replaced by an open circuit when the basic network is formed and hence cannot lie in a closed path defined from the basic network.

The reintroduction of current sources into the network creates new closed paths in addition to those in the basic network, and hence it would appear that new KVL equations must be written for these paths. Let us imagine the current sources to be reinserted into the basic network one at a time. If we now reinsert one current source and apply KVL around any closed path that includes this source, we can express the voltage across the source as the sum of the voltage drops across elements (and voltage sources if they are present) that form a path from one terminal of the source to the other. The equation so obtained can be considered to define the voltage across the current source, since the v-i characteristic of a current source places no constraint on its voltage. Now when we write the KVL equation for any other closed path including the current source, we can insert this derived value for the voltage across the source, and we immediately obtain an equation that is identical to an equation for a closed path that existed in the network before the current source was reinserted, i.e., an equation of the type already considered in the previous paragraph. For example, after i_{s_1} is reinserted across nodes eb of the basic network of Fig. 1-16, we can, by application of KVL, express the voltage drop v across it in the direction of its current as $v = -v_3$. If we now applied KVL around the closed path defined by elements 1 and 2, voltage sources v_{s_1} and v_{s_2} and current source i_{s_1}, we could insert this derived value of v for the voltage drop across the current source and obtain an equation identica to (1-10), which is an equation for a closed path that does not traverse the current source. A similar procedure can be followed as each current source in turn is reinserted into the basic network. In effect, therefore, as far as the KVL equations are concerned, the reinsertion of any current source simply introduces one new equation defining the voltage across the source and does not give rise to any new constraints on the element voltages. Thus if our concern is simply to solve for the element voltages and currents, it is sufficient to write KVL equations around the set of closed paths dictated by the basic network.

We next consider how the KCL equations for the basic network must be modified when the sources are reinserted. Surrounding each node in the basic network we can imagine a closed surface that intersects each element current that flows into (or away from) the node. In the full network with sources a similar closed surface can be imagined to intersect the same element currents as those identified with the node in the basic network. For the network of Fig. 1-15, for example, the closed surfaces corresponding to the nodes of the basic network of Fig. 1-16 take the form shown in Fig. 1-17. One or more currents from current sources may be intersected by such a surface in the full network, since the basic network was formed

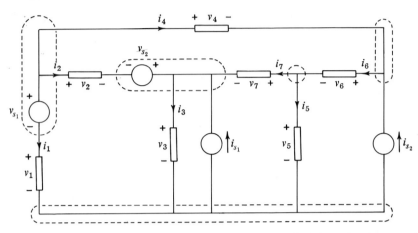

FIG. 1-17. Illustrating the selection of closed surfaces (dashed lines) for the network of Fig. 1-15 corresponding to the nodes of the basic network of Fig. 1-16.

originally by open-circuiting current sources. Voltage sources, however, must lie within the surfaces, since the basic network was found originally by short-circuiting such sources. If we now write KCL for each of the closed surfaces selected in this manner, current-source terms may appear in the equations, but the terms involving the element currents that flow into the surfaces are the same as those in the KCL equations for the nodes in the basic network. Thus, for example, the KCL equation (1-8) for node *b* of the basic network of Fig. 1-16 must be modified when the full network of Fig. 1-17 is formed, and becomes a KCL equation for the closed surface that encloses v_{s_2}, i.e.,

$$i_2 - i_3 + i_{s_1} + i_7 = 0 . \qquad (1\text{-}12)$$

The source term can be shifted to the right-hand side, to give

$$i_2 - i_3 + i_7 = -i_{s_1} . \qquad (1\text{-}13)$$

Thus with the reinsertion of current sources the KCL equations for the basic network can be revised in such a way that the left-hand sides remain unchanged and current-source terms are added to the right-hand sides.

Since in our model we require that KCL be satisfied at all connection points in a network, we must examine the KCL equations for connection points that are not included in the procedure just described, namely, the connection points at either end of each voltage source. We shall imagine the voltage sources to be reinserted into the basic network one at a time. If we now reinsert one voltage source and write the KCL equation for the connection point at one end of the source, we can express the current through the source in a direction entering the connection point as the sum of all other currents leaving the connection point through elements (and current sources, if they are present) that are attached to the connection point. The equation so obtained can be considered to define the current through the voltage source, since the v-i relation for a voltage source places no constraint on its current. Now when we write the KCL equation for the connection point at the other end of the voltage source, we can insert this derived value for the current through the source, and we immediately obtain an equation that is identical to the KCL equation for a closed surface surrounding the voltage source, i.e., an equation of the type already considered in the previous paragraph. For example, after v_{s_2} is reinserted in the basic network of Fig. 1-16 in the position shown in Fig. 1-17, we can express the current i through the source in the direction of its voltage drop as $i = -i_2$ by application of KCL at the point connecting the source and element 2. If we now applied KCL for the connection point at the right-hand side of the source, we could insert this derived value of i for the current in the voltage source and obtain an equation identical to (1-13), which is a KCL equation for a closed surface surrounding the voltage source. A similar procedure can be followed as each voltage source in turn is reinserted into the basic network. In effect, therefore, as far as the KCL equations are concerned, the reinsertion of any voltage source simply introduces one new equation defining the current through the source and does not give rise to any further constraints on the element currents. Thus if our concern is simply to solve for the element currents and voltages, it is sufficient to write KCL equations for the set of closed surfaces derived from the nodes of the basic network.

In summary, then, we can guarantee that the Kirchhoff-law constraints for the element variables are satisfied if we first formulate the Kirchhoff-law equations for the nodes and closed paths in the basic network and then modify these equations to account for the sources. These modified Kirchhoff-law equations can be written in such a way that their left-hand sides are characteristic of the basic network and their right-hand sides reflect the sources in the network. In practice, it is convenient to bypass the first step, involving the writing of the Kirchhoff-law equations for the basic network, and to use the basic network simply for the purpose of identifying suitable sets of closed paths and closed surfaces for which to apply KVL and KCL respectively in the total network. These KVL and KCL equations, together with the voltage-current relations for the elements, express all the constraints inherent in our network model and hence yield the equilibrium equations for the element voltages and currents. Additional KVL equations associated with closed paths through current sources or KCL equations associated with connection points at the terminals of voltage sources serve simply to define the voltages across the current sources or the currents through the voltage sources and do not play a role in the solution for the element voltages and currents in the network.

The question remains, what closed paths and what nodes should we select in the basic network in order to guarantee that Kirchhoff's laws are satisfied? From Prob. 1-5 we can conclude that KVL will be satisfied throughout the basic network if we impose the KVL constraint around each mesh in the network. (We are at present restricting our attention to planar networks.) Similarly, from Prob. 1-4 we can conclude that it is sufficient to impose KCL at one less than the total number of nodes in order to guarantee that KCL is satisfied at all the nodes of the basic network.[1] Thus in order to obtain a set of Kirchhoff-law equations for a complete network, it is sufficient to write, for that network, a KVL equation around the closed path defined by each mesh in the basic network and a KCL equation for the closed surface derived from each node but one in the basic network.

In order to clarify this procedure for writing equilibrium equations, let us consider the network shown in Fig. 1-18. When the voltage and current sources are set equal to zero (short and open circuits respectively), we obtain the basic network shown in Fig. 1-19. Note that, according to our definition of branches and nodes, the two points labeled *a* are *not* separate nodes. The basic network has three nodes and two meshes, and hence we shall write two KCL equations and two KVL equations.

Following our established procedure we return to the original network (Fig. 1-18) and identify the two closed paths corresponding to the two meshes of the basic network and the two closed surfaces corresponding to two of the three nodes of the basic network, say *a* and *b*. These surfaces are identified by dashed lines in Fig. 1-18. The KVL equations can be written with source terms on the right-hand sides as follows:

---

[1] Both Probs. 1-4 and 1-5 were concerned with networks containing sources. However, it should be immediately clear that the results are applicable to basic networks as well.

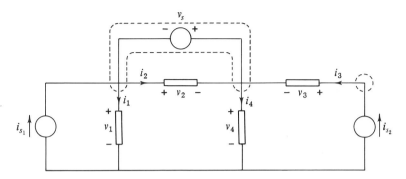

FIG. 1-18. Network used to illustrate the formulation of equilibrium equations. The dashed lines depict closed surfaces derived from nodes of the basic network and used to write KCL equations.

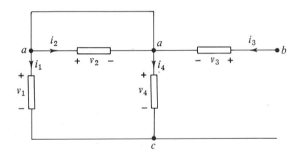

FIG. 1-19. The basic network for the network of Fig. 1-18.

$$v_2 = -v_s, \qquad (1\text{-}14)$$

and
$$-v_1 + v_2 + v_4 = 0. \qquad (1\text{-}15)$$

The KCL equations for the closed surfaces corresponding to nodes a and b are, respectively,

$$i_1 - i_3 + i_4 = i_{s_1}, \qquad (1\text{-}16)$$

and
$$i_3 = i_{s_2}. \qquad (1\text{-}17)$$

The Kirchhoff-law equations that we have written, together with the $v\text{-}i$ characteristics for the four elements, are sufficient to guarantee that all the constraints on the element variables inherent in the network model are satisfied. Hence these equations form the desired equilibrium equations for the element voltages and currents. We note again that the left-hand sides of the Kirchhoff-law equations are identical to those which could be written for the basic network, and the right-hand sides contain the sources.

The procedure of setting all the sources in a network to zero in order to identify the branches, nodes, and meshes may at first glance seem cumbersome and unnecessary. However, if we wish to solve only for element voltages and currents, it has the advantage that it indicates which closed surfaces in the original network should be selected for writing KCL equations and which closed paths in the original network should be selected for writing KVL equations. If the equations are written with the source voltages and currents placed on the right-hand sides, a clear distinction is then made between terms in the equilibrium equations that depend on the basic network and terms that depend on the way in which the network is excited by sources.

Suppose, for example, we are given several networks that all reduce to the same basic network when the sources are set to zero. When the Kirchhoff-law equations are written in the way we have proposed, the left-hand sides will be the same for all these networks, and the right-hand sides will be different. We shall see later that, when the only elements in the networks are resistances, inductances, and capacitances, the behavior of all these networks will have much in common. It will be shown that certain aspects of the response of such networks are related to the structure of the basic network and that other aspects are related to the manner in which the basic network is excited.

Problem 1-7

a. (1) Draw the basic network corresponding to the network of Fig. 1-20*a*. (2) Identify the closed paths in the total network that correspond to meshes in the basic network. (3) Identify the closed surfaces in the total network that correspond to nodes in the basic network.

b. Repeat (*a*) for the network of Fig. 1-20*b*.

c. Repeat (*a*) for the network of Fig. 1-20*c*.

Problem 1-8

a. Draw the basic network for the network of Fig. 1-21.[1]

---

[1] Unless otherwise stated, numerical values for current, voltage, resistance, inductance, and capacitance on network diagrams are in amperes, volts, ohms, henries, and farads, respectively.

b. Write a set of equilibrium equations sufficient to guarantee that all the constraints on the network element variables are satisfied. Indicate which type of constraint is expressed by each equation; i.e., indicate whether the constraint is a statement of KVL or KCL, or is a *v-i* relation.

c. Solve these equations for all the element voltages and currents.

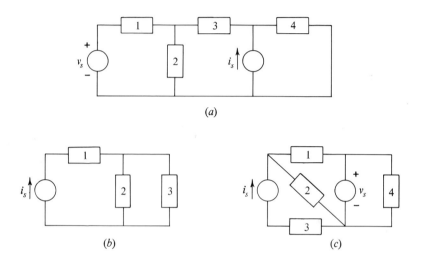

(a)

(b)   (c)

FIG. 1-20. Three planar networks for which the basic networks are to be determined in Prob. 1-7.

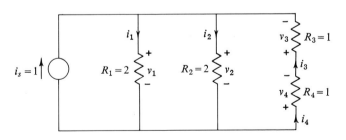

FIG. 1-21. Network for Prob. 1-8.

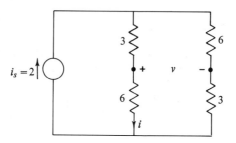

FIG. 1-22. Network for Prob. 1-9.

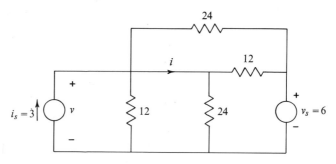

FIG. 1-23. Network for Prob. 1-10.

Problem 1-9

Determine v and i in the network shown in Fig. 1-22.

Problem 1-10

Determine v and i in the network shown in Fig. 1-23.

Problem 1-11

A particular network contains one current source, an unknown number of voltage sources, and three elements. The basic network contains three nodes. The KCL equations written at two of the closed surfaces corresponding to nodes are

$$i_1 + i_2 - i_s = 0,$$

and

$$-i_2 - i_3 + i_s = 0,$$

where i_1, i_2, and i_3 are the element currents and i_s is the current-source value. These KCL equations sum the currents entering the closed surfaces.

a. Write the KCL equation for the closed surface corresponding to the third node.

b. Draw the basic network corresponding to the KCL equations above.

c. Determine the location of the current source such that the given KCL equations result.

d. Determine the possible locations of voltage sources in the network.

e. Write the KVL equations governing the element voltages, assuming the voltage sources are set to zero.

f. When the three elements are 1-ohm resistances, the currents i_1, i_2, and i_3 are all found to be 1 amp. Determine the value of the current source i_s, and determine a possible distribution of voltage sources in the network such that all the constraints governing network equilibrium are satisfied.

Formulation of equilibrium equations for two-terminal networks. There are many situations in which one portion of a network is connected to the remainder of the network through only two terminals. Such configurations are of sufficient importance in network theory that it is appropriate to examine generally the manner in which a two-terminal network exerts an influence on the currents and voltages in any network to which it is connected.

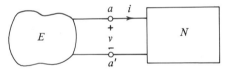

FIG. 1-24. A two-terminal network N connected to an external network E.

Figure 1-24 shows a network of the type we shall consider: a two-terminal network N is joined to an external network E by connections at terminals a and a'. We denote the voltage across terminals a-a' by v and the current flowing into terminal a by i. As demonstrated in Prob. 1-3, it is a consequence of KCL that the current entering one terminal of a two-terminal network is equal to the current leaving the other terminal. Our objective is to determine the constraint that the network N imposes on its terminal variables v and i. In finding such a constraint, we will have demonstrated that a two-terminal network has the properties of an element or source; i.e., associated with it is a voltage variable v, a current variable i, and a constraint on the variables v and i.*

---

* In the special case where network N is simply a source, this constraint will, of course, involve only one of the variables.

Suppose that the Kirchhoff-law equations and voltage-current relations for the elements have been applied to the complete network consisting of both E and N in Fig. 1-24. For convenience we select terminal a' as the connection point that is omitted in writing the KCL equations. Let us now examine all the equations that involve voltages and currents associated with elements and sources in N. Some of these equations involve only voltages and currents in N; these include v-i relations for the elements in N and Kirchhoff-law equations for closed paths and connection points (or closed surfaces) that lie within N. In KCL and KVL equations involving voltages and currents both in E and in N, we can substitute i for the sum of the currents entering terminal a from network E and v for the sum of the voltage drops through any path in network E from terminal a to terminal a'. We are left, therefore, with a subset of equations involving only voltages and currents in N, together with the variables v and i, and these are the only equations among the equilibrium equations for the complete network that involve voltages and currents in N. Consequently the constraints imposed on v and i by N are given by this subset of equations, which can be considered to constitute the equilibrium equations for the two-terminal network N.

As a result of the discussion in the previous paragraph, it is evident that the equilibrium equations for a two-terminal network N, such as that shown in Fig. 1-25, can be formulated directly without reference to the external network by the following procedure:

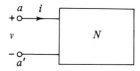

FIG. 1-25. A two-terminal network N.

1. Write a set of KVL equations for closed paths in network N corresponding to those which exist when all the sources in N are set equal to zero, including an external closed path through the terminal voltage drop v and returning through elements and sources within N. (In the case of planar networks we can use the reasoning given in the previous section to show that it is sufficient to write a KVL equation around the closed path defined by each mesh, including the external closed path.)

2. Write a set of KCL equations for closed surfaces in N corresponding to the nodes obtained by setting all the sources in N equal to zero and considering the current i to flow into one such closed surface from terminal a. (Again by the reasoning of the previous section it is sufficient to write

a KCL equation for the closed surface derived from each node but one; it is usually convenient to exclude the node corresponding to terminal a'.)

3. Write a set of v-i relations for the elements in N.

As an illustration, let us consider network N to consist of the interconnection of resistances shown in Fig. 1-26. We write KVL equations

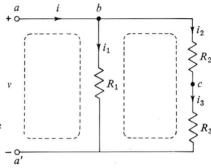

FIG. 1-26. Network used to illustrate the formulation of equilibrium equations for a two-terminal network.

for the internal closed path through R_1, R_2, and R_3 and for the closed path through R_1 and the terminals a' and a, as shown by the dashed lines in the figure. Likewise we write KCL equations for connection points b and c. The Kirchhoff-law equations are

$$v_1 = v, \qquad (1\text{-}18)$$

$$-v_1 + v_2 + v_3 = 0, \qquad (1\text{-}19)$$

$$i_1 + i_2 = i, \qquad (1\text{-}20)$$

and
$$-i_2 + i_3 = 0. \qquad (1\text{-}21)$$

Combination of Eqs. (1-18) to (1-21) with the voltage-current relations for the three resistance elements and elimination of all variables except v and i from the total set of equations lead to the relation

$$v = i \cdot \frac{R_1(R_2 + R_3)}{R_1 + R_2 + R_3}. \qquad (1\text{-}22)$$

In this example, therefore, the combination of resistances in the two-terminal network N can be replaced by a single resistance of value

$$R = \frac{R_1(R_2 + R_3)}{R_1 + R_2 + R_3} \qquad (1\text{-}23)$$

as far as the voltage and current at the terminals of N are concerned.

Problem 1-12

Determine and sketch the v-i relation for the two-terminal network shown in Fig. 1-27.

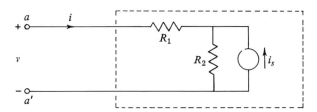

FIG. 1-27. Network for which v-i relation is to be determined in Prob. 1-12.

Problem 1-13

Two two-terminal networks N_1 and N_2 are connected as shown in Fig. 1-28. The v-i relations at the terminals of networks N_1 and N_2 are, respectively,

$$v_1 = 2i_1 + 8,$$

and

$$v_2 = 6i_2.$$

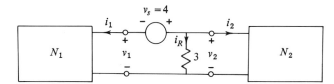

FIG. 1-28. Interconnection of two two-terminal networks N_1 and N_2 (Prob. 1-13).

Write and solve the equations necessary to determine the variables v_1, v_2, i_1, i_2, and i_R. For each equation, specify whether it is a consequence of KCL, KVL, or a v-i relation.

Solution of equilibrium equations for simple networks

In the previous section we established procedures for formulating equilibrium equations for networks, including networks with one terminal pair. These procedures are quite general, since they apply to interconnections of elements and sources but place no restrictions on the properties of the elements. The elements may be resistances, inductances, and capacitances, or they may be characterized by any voltage-current relations. We shall now formulate and solve the equilibrium equations for some simple networks in which the *v-i* characteristics of the elements have been specified. In the process of working out examples, we shall point out certain techniques that can be applied through direct inspection of the networks, in order to shorten the formal equation-writing procedures discussed above. These techniques will be sufficient for handling the simple networks with which we shall be concerned during the early stages of our study. When more complex networks are introduced, a general approach to the formulation and solution of network equilibrium equations will be developed (Chap. 5). In order to obtain algebraic equilibrium equations, we shall confine our attention in this chapter to networks containing resistance elements. The introduction of inductances and capacitances gives rise to differential equations, which will be discussed in the next chapter. First we shall compute terminal-pair relations for some simple combinations of resistances and then show how some more general networks can be analyzed by both graphical and algebraic methods.

Simple combinations of resistances. One of the simplest combinations consists of two resistances connected in series, as shown in Fig. 1-29. The

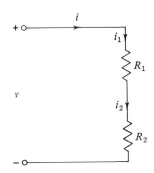

FIG. 1-29. Series combination of two resistances.

KCL and KVL equations in this case are

$$i_1 - i_2 = 0 \,, \tag{1-24}$$

$$i_1 = i \,, \tag{1-25}$$

and

$$v_1 + v_2 = v \,. \tag{1-26}$$

Substituting the voltage-current relations for the two elements into Eq. (1-26) and using Eqs. (1-24) and (1-25), we obtain

$$i(R_1 + R_2) = v, \qquad (1\text{-}27)$$

or
$$\frac{v}{i} = R_s = R_1 + R_2. \qquad (1\text{-}28)$$

Thus, from the point of view of the terminal pair, the two resistances in series appear like a resistance R_s equal to the sum of the two resistances. This result can easily be extended to several resistances in series. In this case the equivalent resistance seen at the terminals of the series combination is the sum of the individual resistances.

Another useful result for the simple network of Fig. 1-29 expresses the voltage across one of the resistances, say v_2, in terms of the voltage v across the combination. Since $v_2 = i_2 R_2 = i R_2$, then from Eq. (1-27) we have

$$v_2 = \frac{R_2}{R_1 + R_2} v. \qquad (1\text{-}29)$$

Likewise, a similar relation for v_1 can be written as follows:

$$v_1 = \frac{R_1}{R_1 + R_2} v. \qquad (1\text{-}30)$$

Equations (1-29) and (1-30), sometimes known as *voltage-divider* relations, indicate how the voltage across a series combination of resistances is distributed between the resistances.

For the case in which two resistances are connected in parallel in the manner shown in Fig. 1-30 the KCL and KVL equations are

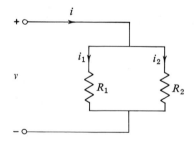

FIG. 1-30. Parallel combination of two resistances.

$$i_1 + i_2 = i, \qquad (1\text{-}31)$$

$$v_1 - v_2 = 0, \qquad (1\text{-}32)$$

and
$$v_1 = v. \qquad (1\text{-}33)$$

Again we substitute the voltage-current relations for the two elements into Eq. (1-31), and combining this with Eqs. (1-32) and (1-33), we obtain

$$v\left(\frac{1}{R_1} + \frac{1}{R_2}\right) = i, \tag{1-34}$$

or

$$\frac{v}{i} = R_p = \frac{1}{1/R_1 + 1/R_2} = \frac{R_1 R_2}{R_1 + R_2}. \tag{1-35}$$

If we define the conductance G_p as the reciprocal of the resistance R_p of the parallel combination, and G_1 and G_2 as the reciprocals of R_1 and R_2, respectively, then

$$\frac{i}{v} = G_p = G_1 + G_2. \tag{1-36}$$

Seen from the terminal pair, the parallel combination of the two resistances appears like a resistance R_p equal to $R_1 R_2/(R_1 + R_2)$. Alternatively, the conductance of the parallel combination is equal to the sum of the individual conductances. Extension of this analysis to several conductances in parallel leads to the result that the equivalent conductance is equal to the sum of the individual conductances. For this reason, it is often convenient to compute the v-i characteristic of resistances in parallel directly in terms of their conductances.

For the network of Fig. 1-30, expressions for i_1 and i_2 in terms of i can be derived from Eq. (1-34), using the voltage-current relations for R_1 and R_2. These expressions are

$$i_1 = \frac{R_2}{R_1 + R_2} i, \tag{1-37}$$

and

$$i_2 = \frac{R_1}{R_1 + R_2} i. \tag{1-38}$$

Equations (1-37) and (1-38), sometimes known as *current-divider* relations, indicate how the current flowing into a parallel combination of resistances is distributed between the resistances.

In order to illustrate the application of the above methods to more complicated networks, let us compute the equivalent resistance at the terminal pair of the network shown in Fig. 1-31, i.e., the v-i relation at the terminal pair. The formal procedure for finding the v-i relation would be to write the three KVL and two KCL equations together with the four voltage-current relations for the elements and eliminate all variables except v and i. With the results for simple series and parallel combinations of

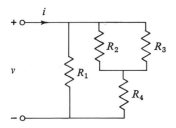

FIG. 1-31. Resistance network used to illustrate the calculation of the equivalent resistance at a terminal pair.

resistances available, however, the cumbersome procedure of writing and solving this set of simultaneous equations can be avoided in this case. The parallel combination of R_2 and R_3 is equivalent to a resistance R_5 given by $1/R_5 = 1/R_2 + 1/R_3$, as shown in Fig. 1-32a. Now R_5 can be

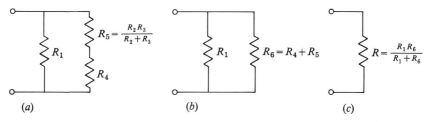

FIG. 1-32. Steps in the reduction of the combination of resistances in Fig. 1-31 to a single equivalent resistance R.

combined with R_4 to give an equivalent resistance $R_6 = R_4 + R_5$ (Fig. 1-32b), and this in parallel with R_1 yields the equivalent resistance $R = R_1R_6/(R_1 + R_6)$. The value of R is thus

$$R = \frac{R_1[R_4 + R_2R_3/(R_2 + R_3)]}{R_1 + R_4 + R_2R_3/(R_2 + R_3)}. \tag{1-39}$$

Problem 1-14

Determine the equivalent resistance at the terminals of each of the networks in Fig. 1-33, and determine the v-i characteristics of the networks. You may use any results derived in the text.

Problem 1-15

a. Determine the voltage v in the network of Fig. 1-34.

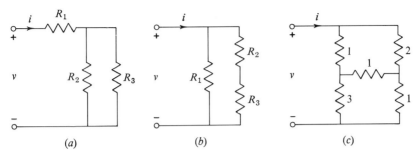

FIG. 1-33. Networks for which the equivalent resistances and *v-i* characteristics
      are to be determined (Prob. 1-14).

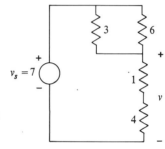

FIG. 1-34. Network for which the voltage
      v is to be determined
      (Prob. 1-15).

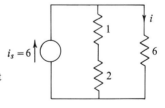

FIG. 1-35. Network for which the current
      i is to be determined
      (Prob. 1-15).

b. Determine the current i in the network of Fig. 1-35.

Problem 1-16

The network of Fig. 1-36 consists of n resistances in parallel.
a. Determine the terminal current i as a function of the terminal voltage v.
b. Determine the equivalent resistance at terminals a-a'.

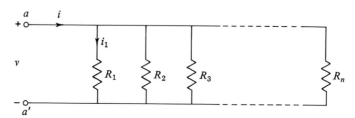

FIG. 1-36. Parallel connection of n resistances (Prob. 1-16).

c. Determine the current i_1 as a function of the terminal current i.

Problem 1-17

a. Determine the v-i relation at the terminals of each of the networks of Fig. 1-37, and replace each network by an equivalent network.

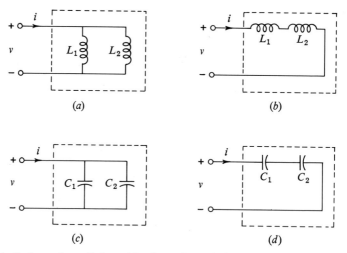

(a)   (b)

(c)   (d)

FIG. 1-37. Series and parallel combinations of two inductances or two capacitances (Prob. 1-17).

b. Determine the v-i relation at the terminals of the network of Fig. 1-38, and replace the network by an equivalent network containing a single resistance and a single capacitance. Find the values of the equivalent resistance and capacitance in terms of R_1, R_2, C_1, and C_2.

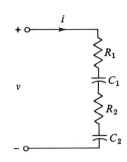

FIG. 1-38. Series combination of two resistances and two capacitances for which the equivalent resistance and capacitance are to be determined (Prob. 1-17).

Problem 1-18

We observed in Prob. 1-12 that the v-i relation at the terminals of the network consisting of two resistances and a current source was a straight line. Such a straight-line v-i relation is obtained in general for all networks composed only of resistances and sources, as suggested by the following heuristic reasoning: The equations we write in order to determine such a v-i characteristic are the KVL and KCL equations and the element v-i relations. These equations contain the variables to the first power only and do not contain products of variables. The operations that we perform on these equations to solve for the terminal v-i relation are multiplication by constants and addition of the equations. During the process of eliminating variables by means of these operations, products of the remaining variables cannot result. Hence, when all variables but the terminal variables v and i are eliminated, the resulting equation must be of the form

$$v = K_1 i + K_2 . \tag{1-40}$$

The constant K_1 depends on the resistances in the network, and K_2 is a linear combination of the source values. (If the sources are functions of time, then K_2 will, of course, be a function of time also.) This result is a special case of Thevenin's theorem, which will be proved in Chap. 6.

a. Find values for the resistance R_1 and the voltage source v_s in terms of K_1 and K_2 such that the network of Fig. 1-39 has a v-i relation that is the same as that given in Eq. (1-40).

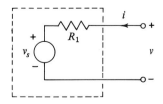

FIG. 1-39. Thevenin equivalent network having the v-i characteristic of Eq. (1-40). R_1 and v_s are to be determined in terms of K_1 and K_2 (Prob. 1-18).

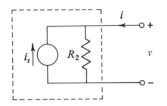

FIG. 1-40. Norton equivalent network having the v-i characteristic of Eq. (1-40). R_2 and i_s are to be determined in terms of K_1 and K_2 (Prob. 1-18).

b. Find values for the resistance R_2 and the current source i_s in terms of K_1 and K_2 (assuming that K_1 is not zero) such that the network of Fig. 1-40 has a v-i relation that is the same as that given in Eq. (1-40).

In (a) we saw that, for any given network containing only resistances and sources, the values for a resistance R_1 and a voltage source v_s could be found so that the network of Fig. 1-39 has the same v-i terminal relation as the given network. An equivalent network in the form of Fig. 1-39, consisting of a resistance in series with a voltage source, is called a *Thevenin* equivalent network. Similarly, an equivalent network consisting of a current source in parallel with a resistance was found in (b); this form of an equivalent network is called a *Norton* equivalent network.

c. Consider a two-terminal network containing only sources and resistances, as shown in Fig. 1-41. When its terminals are short-circuited, the

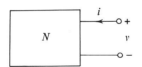

FIG. 1-41. Two-terminal network N containing only sources and resistances (Prob. 1-18).

current i through the short circuit is $i = i_{sc}$. When the terminals are open-circuited, the voltage v at the terminals is $v = v_{oc}$. Assuming that both v_{oc} and i_{sc} are not zero, find the Thevenin and Norton equivalent networks.

d. Suppose in the network of Fig. 1-41 both i_{sc} and v_{oc} are zero for all time. From these measurements can you draw an equivalent network? If not, what additional measurements would you make at the terminals?

Problem 1-19

Using each of the following methods, find a value for the resistance R in the network of Fig. 1-42 such that $i_1 = 2$:

1. Write all the equilibrium equations governing the element variables and solve for R.

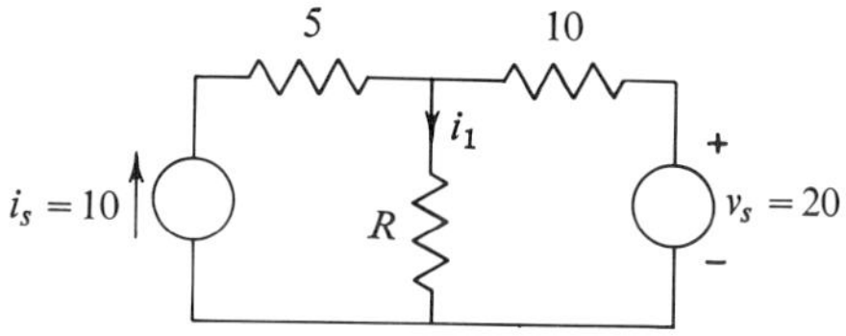

FIG. 1-42. Network for
Prob. 1-19.

$i_s = 10$

5   10

i_1

R

$v_s = 20$

2. Replace the part of the network seen from the terminals of the resistance R by a Thevenin or Norton equivalent network; take advantage of the current- and voltage-divider relations.

Problem 1-20

A network N_1, as shown in Fig. 1-43, has the v-i relation

$$v_1 = 3i_1 + 7$$

when $i_s = 2$.

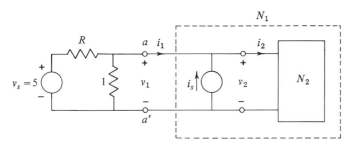

N_1

R

a i_1

i_2

$v_s = 5$

1

v_1

i_s

v_2

N_2

a'

FIG. 1-43. Network for Prob. 1-20.

a. With $i_s = 2$, determine R such that $i_1 = -1$.
b. The current source i_s is now set equal to zero. Determine the new value of i_1 if R has the value found in (a).

Graphical analysis of simple networks. Frequently the v-i characteristics at the terminals of elements or two-terminal networks may be given in graphical rather than analytical form.[1] Examples of graphical representations of the v-i characteristic at a terminal pair are those given previously in Figs. 1-4 and 1-6 for voltage and current sources. Other examples are

----

[1] A plot of v versus i can be given in graphical form when the value of v at a given time is a function only of i at the same time. This is the case for a resistance, for example, but not for an inductance or a capacitance.

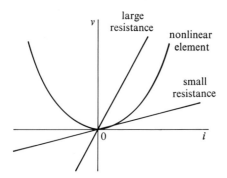

FIG. 1-44. Voltage-current characteristics for resistances and for a nonlinear element.

given in Fig. 1-44, which shows plots of the *v-i* relations for different values of resistance and for a nonlinear element for which $v = ai^2$, where a is a constant.

When one or more of the elements in a network are specified in graphical form, it is usually convenient to analyze the network by graphical means. In order to illustrate the concepts involved in such a graphical analysis, let us consider a simple example.

Consider two networks N_1 and N_2, whose *v-i* characteristics are given in Fig. 1-45. We shall determine the terminal voltages and currents resulting from interconnection of the two networks in the manner shown in Fig.

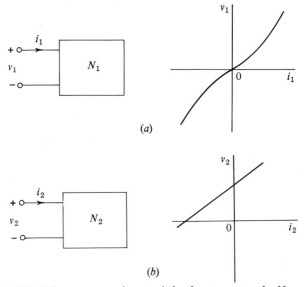

FIG. 1-45. Voltage-current characteristics for two networks N_1 and N_2.

FIG. 1-46. Illustrating the Kirchhoff-law constraints introduced by a particular interconnection of networks N_1 and N_2.

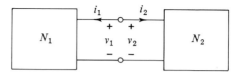

1-46. The Kirchhoff-law equations constraining the terminal voltages and currents for this interconnection are

$$\text{KVL: } v_1 = v_2 ,$$

and
$$\text{KCL: } i_1 = -i_2 .$$

In terms of the graphs of the v-i relations for the two networks, the KVL equation is satisfied for points where the ordinate on one graph is equal to the ordinate on the other. The KCL equation, on the other hand, is satisfied when the abscissa on one graph is equal to the negative of the abscissa on the other. Thus if either one of the graphs is plotted with the i axis reversed—say the graph for network N_2, as shown in Fig. 1-47—then both of the Kirchhoff-law equations are satisfied at points on the two graphs (Figs. 1-45a and 1-47) that have the same abscissas and ordinates. Hence the equilibrium voltage and current can be obtained by superposing these graphs, as shown in Fig. 1-48, and observing the values of v and i at the point of intersection P.

The important feature of graphical solutions, illustrated by the example

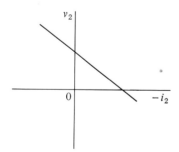

FIG. 1-47. Voltage-current characteristic of network N_2 (Fig. 1-45b) plotted with the current axis reversed.

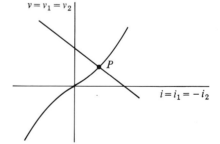

FIG. 1-48. Superposition of the graphs of Figs. 1-45a and 1-47 gives the point P that defines the equilibrium voltage and current when the two networks are connected in the manner shown in Fig. 1-46.

just given, is that Kirchhoff's laws dictate how the graphs must be oriented so that a solution corresponds to a point of intersection of the curves when the graphs are superposed.

Graphical procedures can also be applied to simple situations in which the v-i relation for a two-terminal network consisting of an interconnection of elements is to be determined. For a series connection of two elements, for example, KCL requires that the current at the terminals is the same as that flowing through each of the elements, and KVL states that the terminal voltage is the sum of the two element voltages. Thus the terminal voltage corresponding to a particular value of terminal current can be determined graphically by finding the voltage corresponding to this current from the v-i graph for each element separately and then adding the results. If this procedure is followed for each value of current, a complete v-i relation can be constructed for the series combination of the two elements. Again we see that the KCL and KVL equations for the interconnection of elements dictate the way in which the v-i graphs for the individual elements must be manipulated.

Problem 1-21

Two networks N_1 and N_2 have the v-i characteristics shown in Fig. 1-49a and b.

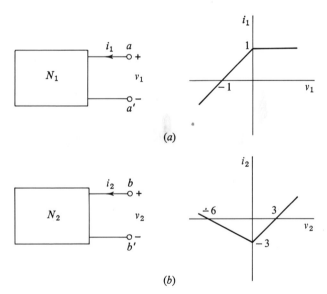

(a)

(b)

FIG. 1-49. Two two-terminal networks and their v-i characteristics (Prob. 1-21).

a. Determine graphically the values of the four variables v_1, v_2, i_1, and i_2 for the connection of Fig. 1-50.

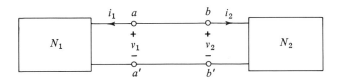

FIG. 1-50. Interconnection of the two-terminal networks of Fig. 1-49 (Prob. 1-21).

b. Networks N_1 and N_2 are now connected with the terminals of N_2 reversed; i.e., terminal a of N_1 is connected to terminal b' of N_2, and terminal a' of N_1 is connected to terminal b of N_2, as shown in Fig. 1-51. Determine graphically the values of the variables v_1, v_2, i_1, and i_2.

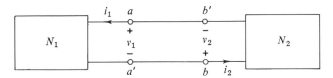

FIG. 1-51. Interconnection of the two-terminal networks of Fig. 1-49 with the terminals reversed (Prob. 1-21).

Problem 1-22

Using the v-i characteristic of element A, as shown in Fig. 1-52, determine

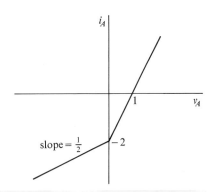

FIG. 1-52. The v-i characteristic of element A in Prob. 1-22.

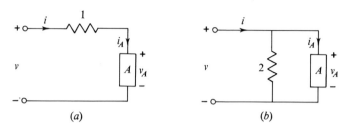

FIG. 1-53. Two two-terminal networks containing the element A. The v-i characteristics of each are to be determined (Prob. 1-22).

by graphical methods the v-i characteristics at the terminals of each of the networks shown in Fig. 1-53.

Problem 1-23

Two two-terminal networks are connected as shown in Fig. 1-54. The v-i relations for the two networks N_1 and N_2 are given in Fig. 1-55a and b respectively. Determine the current i_R.

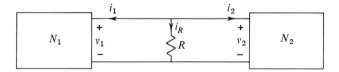

FIG. 1-54. Interconnection of two two-terminal networks N_1 and N_2 (Prob. 1-23).

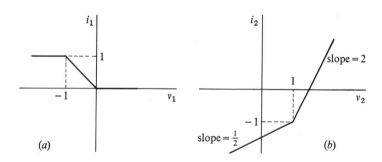

FIG. 1-55. The v-i relations for networks N_1 and N_2 of Fig. 1-54 (Prob. 1-23).

Problem 1-24

The v-i relations of three elements A, B, and C are shown in Fig. 1-56a to c respectively. Use graphical methods to determine the v-i relation at the terminals of the network in Fig. 1-57.

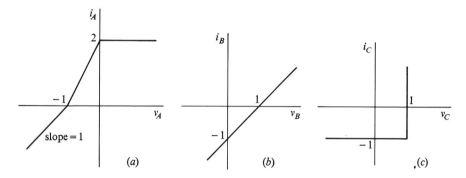

FIG. 1-56. The v-i relations for elements A, B, and C in Prob. 1-24.

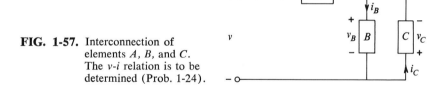

FIG. 1-57. Interconnection of elements A, B, and C. The v-i relation is to be determined (Prob. 1-24).

Simple procedures for writing and solving network equilibrium equations. We have seen that three sets of equations must be solved in order to find the voltages and currents for the elements in a network: KCL equations, KVL equations, and v-i relations. Frequently the solution of these equations may be a cumbersome procedure, even for networks with only a few elements. The solution can always be shortened by the introduction of so-called loop currents and node voltages, as will be discussed in Chap. 5. For the present, however, we shall focus our attention upon "inspection" procedures that are useful in cases in which the basic network has only a small number of nodes and meshes. (Most of the networks with which we shall be immediately concerned will have no more than two meshes or no more than three nodes.) The basic approach is to eliminate some of the variables by inspection, leaving only a small number of equations to be solved formally.

To illustrate this approach, we consider a network consisting of two resistances R_1 and R_2 connected in series and excited by a voltage source, as shown in Fig. 1-58. The problem is to find the currents and voltages

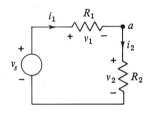

FIG. 1-58. Resistance network used to illustrate the short method of writing equilibrium equations.

for all the elements, i.e., to find v_1, i_1, v_2 and i_2. The formal procedure we have specified is to write down and solve the following three sets of equations:

1. KCL equation at point a:

$$i_1 - i_2 = 0 ;$$

2. KVL equation for the closed path:

$$v_1 + v_2 = v_s ;$$

3. v-i relations:

$$v_1 = i_1 R_1 ,$$

and

$$v_2 = i_2 R_2 .$$

We shall now describe two procedures for bypassing this formal approach.

One procedure consists of the following steps:

1. When possible, eliminate some of the current variables by inspection, using the KCL constraints.

2. By inspection introduce the v-i relations in order to express the voltage drops in the branches in terms of the remaining current variables.

3. Write the KVL equations, expressing the branch voltages in terms of the currents as in (2).

In the example of Fig. 1-58, we apply KCL by inspection at connection point a by assigning the current i_1 to both elements, thus eliminating i_2. We then eliminate v_1 and v_2 by designating the voltage drops in the elements

R_1 and R_2 as $i_1 R_1$ and $i_1 R_2$, respectively. The KVL equation can then be written as

$$i_1 R_1 + i_1 R_2 = v_s, \qquad (1\text{-}41)$$

which is one equation in the unknown i_1. Once a solution for i_1 is obtained, the values of i_2, v_1, and v_2 can be written down by inspection.

Similar methods can be applied to find the solution for a network such as the one shown in Fig. 1-59. From the basic network we select two nodes and two meshes for the writing of KCL and KVL equations. For the complete network of Fig. 1-59 connection points a and b correspond to two nodes, and the dashed lines designate closed paths corresponding to the two meshes. We can apply KCL at connection points a and b by inspection and hence eliminate i_2 and i_4, expressing all branch currents in terms of i_1 and i_3, as shown in Fig. 1-60. We now express the voltage across each element in terms of the current, using the v-i relations for the resistances, and we finally write KVL equations for the two closed paths as follows:

$$i_1 R_1 + (i_1 - i_3)R_2 = v_s, \qquad (1\text{-}42)$$

and

$$i_3 R_3 + i_3 R_4 - (i_1 - i_3)R_2 = 0. \qquad (1\text{-}43)$$

Thus we have reduced the problem to that of formally solving two equations in the two unknowns i_1 and i_3, rather than eight equations in the eight element currents and voltages.

The procedure just described consists basically of eliminating some of the current variables by applying KCL by inspection and then writing KVL equations. In the KVL equations the element voltages are expressed in terms of the remaining current variables using the v-i relations of the

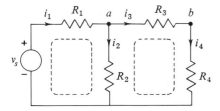

FIG. 1-59. Network used to illustrate the short method of solving equilibrium equations.

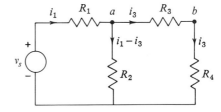

FIG. 1-60. All currents in the network of Fig. 1-59 are expressed in terms of i_1 and i_3 in a way that satisfies KCL at connection points a and b.

elements. This procedure of imposing KCL by inspection is not always applicable and is recommended only for the very simple networks with which we shall be immediately concerned. If in any network it is not apparent how to apply KCL by inspection at a given connection point or closed surface (as might happen if all element currents entering a connection point had been previously expressed in terms of other currents by applying KCL at other connection points), then we should return to our formal approach of writing the KCL constraints at that connection point or closed surface. The important point is that we must impose the KCL constraints at the connection points or closed surfaces corresponding to all but one of the nodes in the basic network. How we accomplish this is just a matter of convenience.

A second procedure for bypassing the formal approach is to eliminate some of the voltage variables by applying KVL by inspection and then to write KCL equations. This procedure is often the more convenient one to apply to the solution of networks in which there are several parallel connections of elements, since for such networks there are often fewer nodes than meshes, and hence fewer KCL equations than KVL equations. The steps in the application of this method are as follows:

1. When possible, eliminate some of the voltage variables by inspection, using the KVL constraints.

2. By inspection introduce the *v-i* relations in order to express the currents in the elements in terms of the remaining voltage variables.

3. Write the KCL equations, expressing the element currents in terms of the voltages as in (2).

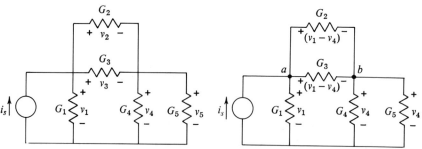

FIG. 1-61. Network used to illustrate the short method of solving equilibrium equations by applying KVL and the *v-i* relations for the elements by inspection and then writing KCL equations.

FIG. 1-62. Network of Fig. 1-61 with voltages across all elements expressed in terms of v_1 and v_4.

To illustrate this procedure, consider the network shown in Fig. 1-61. Application of KVL around the closed path defined by G_1, G_3, and G_4 enables us to write v_3 as $v_1 - v_4$, as indicated in Fig. 1-62. Likewise, application of KVL around the closed path defined by G_1, G_2, and G_4 enables us to write v_2 as $v_1 - v_4$. Finally, application of KVL around the right-hand closed path permits us to replace v_5 by v_4. The result is that all the element voltages can be expressed in terms of v_1 and v_4, as shown in Fig. 1-62. From the v-i relations, the current in each element is the product of the conductance (reciprocal of resistance) of the element and the voltage across it. Since the basic network has three nodes, two KCL equations are required. These can now be written at connection point a:

$$v_1 G_1 + (v_1 - v_4)G_2 + (v_1 - v_4)G_3 = i_s ; \qquad (1\text{-}44)$$

and at connection point b:

$$-(v_1 - v_4)G_2 - (v_1 - v_4)G_3 + v_4 G_4 + v_4 G_5 = 0 . \qquad (1\text{-}45)$$

These two equations in the two voltage variables can be solved in a straight-forward manner, and all other voltages and currents can then be expressed in terms of v_1 and v_4. The comments about the applicability of the previous procedure, illustrated by Figs. 1-59 and 1-60, also apply to this inspection method of accounting for the KVL constraints. It is recommended only for very simple networks, and when it is not apparent how to apply it, one should return to the formal approach of writing the KVL equations around the closed paths.

Another procedure that is sometimes useful in network analysis is to reduce the complexity of a network through the use of equivalent networks, following methods discussed previously on pages 27 to 30. Where pos-sible, groups of resistances in series or in parallel are replaced by single equivalent resistances, and the network is thus simplified to the point where one of the currents or voltages in the original network can be found by inspection. All the other currents and voltages can then (by inspection of the original network) be expressed in terms of this particular current or voltage.

Applying this procedure to the network of Fig. 1-59, for example, we might first reduce the series combination of R_3 and R_4 to a single resistance $R_5 = R_3 + R_4$. The equivalent resistance R_5 can then be combined with the parallel resistance R_2 to obtain an equivalent resistance

$$R_6 = \frac{R_2 R_5}{R_2 + R_5} = \frac{R_2(R_3 + R_4)}{R_2 + R_3 + R_4} . \qquad (1\text{-}46)$$

Since this equivalent resistance is in series with R_1, the current flowing in R_1 is given by

$$i_1 = \frac{v_s}{R_1 + R_6} = \frac{v_s}{R_1 + \dfrac{R_2(R_3 + R_4)}{R_2 + R_3 + R_4}} . \qquad (1\text{-}47)$$

The currents i_2 and i_3 of Fig. 1-59 can then be obtained by the current-divider relation [Eqs. (1-37) and (1-38)], giving

$$i_2 = \frac{R_3 + R_4}{R_2 + (R_3 + R_4)} i_1 , \qquad (1\text{-}48)$$

and
$$i_3 = \frac{R_2}{R_2 + (R_3 + R_4)} i_1 . \qquad (1\text{-}49)$$

The values of i_1 and i_3 will, of course, be the same as those obtained by solving Eqs. (1-42) and (1-43), as can be readily verified.

We have discussed just a few procedures for shortening the solution of simple networks. Experience in solving such networks will, however, lead one to the formulation of various other short cuts; the available approaches are limited only by one's ingenuity and experience. Formal procedures that are applicable to all networks regardless of complexity will be developed in Chap. 5.

Problem 1-25

The voltage v_1 in the network of Fig. 1-63 is known to be 1 volt. Determine

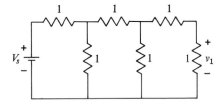

FIG. 1-63. Ladder network for Prob. 1-25.

the value V_s of the voltage source by each of the following three methods:
1. Apply KCL by inspection so that all element currents are expressed in terms of just three element currents. Then write the KVL equations in terms of these three element currents by incorporating the v-i relations.
2. Apply KVL by inspection so that all element voltages are expressed in terms of just three element voltages. Then write the KCL equations in terms of these three element voltages by incorporating the v-i relations.
3. Work "backward" from the right-hand resistance toward the source through repeated application of KCL, KVL, and the v-i relations for the

resistances. The reasoning begins as follows: "1 volt across 1 ohm gives a current of 1 amp, which also flows through the series 1-ohm resistance," etc. In this way the problem can be solved by inspection.

Problem 1-26

Determine the current i in the network of Fig. 1-64.

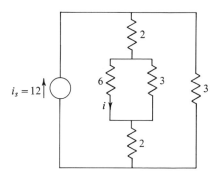

FIG. 1-64. Network for Prob. 1-26.

Problem 1-27

a. Determine the Thevenin equivalent network at terminals a-a' of the network shown in Fig. 1-65.

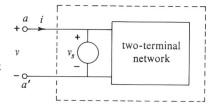

FIG. 1-65. Parallel connection of a current source with a two-terminal network (Prob. 1-27).

b. Determine the Norton equivalent network at terminals a-a' of the network shown in Fig. 1-66.

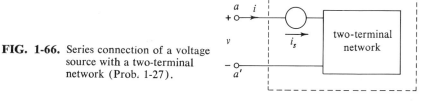

FIG. 1-66. Series connection of a voltage source with a two-terminal network (Prob. 1-27).

c. Determine $v_L(t)$ and $i_C(t)$ for the network of Fig. 1-67 in terms of $v_s(t)$, $i_s(t)$, and the element values.

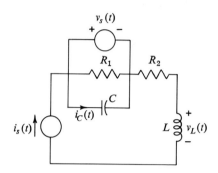

FIG. 1-67. *RLC* network in which $v_L(t)$ and $i_C(t)$ are to be determined (Prob. 1-27).

d. For the network of Fig. 1-67, determine $i_C(t)$ and $v_L(t)$ if $v_s(t) = Ve^t$ and $i_s(t) = Ie^t$, where V and I are constants.

Problem 1-28

Using the *v-i* relations for capacitances and inductances in any convenient form, write (but do not solve) a set of equations expressing the constraints on the element voltages and currents for the network of Fig. 1-68.

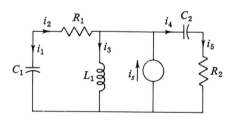

FIG. 1-68. *RLC* network for which the equilibrium equations are to be written (Prob. 1-28).

2

Exponential Signals
and Linear Differential Equations

Introduction

We have seen that the equations governing the behavior of a network are derived from Kirchhoff's voltage law, Kirchhoff's current law, and the voltage-current relations for the elements. When the elements in a network are all resistances, which have voltage-current relations of the form $v = Ri$, the network equations are all algebraic equations. If, however, the network contains any inductances or capacitances (often called energy-storage elements for reasons we shall see later), the equations contain derivatives or integrals of the voltage or current variables, since the voltage-current relations of these elements involve such derivatives or integrals.

As a first example of a network with an energy-storage element consider the series RL network shown in Fig. 2-1. The excitation is the time-varying voltage source $v_s(t)$, and we wish to find the response of the network,

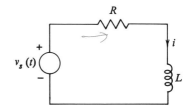

FIG. 2-1. Series RL network excited by a time-varying voltage source $v_s(t)$.

say the current $i(t)$ in this case. From Kirchhoff's laws and the voltage-current characteristics for the resistance and inductance, we obtain

$$L \frac{di}{dt} + Ri = v_s(t), \qquad (2\text{-}1)$$

which is to be solved for the dependent variable $i(t)$.

Equation (2-1) is an example of the type of equation that is obtained from KCL, KVL, and the v-i relations for the elements for a situation in which a network containing resistances, capacitances, and inductances is excited by one or more sources. An equation of this type, in which the dependent variable and its derivatives appear only to the first power and in which there are no products of the derivatives or the variable, is called a *linear differential equation*. If in addition the coefficients of the variable and its derivatives are constants (as they always are in a network with constant element values), the equation is called a constant-coefficient linear differential equation. The *order* of the differential equation is defined as the order n of the highest derivative d^n/dt^n of the dependent variable occurring in the equation. In our example, Eq. (2-1) is a first-order differential equation with the constant coefficients L and R; more complicated networks will, in general, lead to differential equations of higher order.

The right side of the differential equation may consist of a linear combination of derivatives of the excitation as well as the excitation itself. In our example the right side of Eq. (2-1) is simply the excitation or source function of the network. This function may in some cases be a constant (d-c) or may represent any function of time, such as the sinusoidal waveform (a-c) appearing at the home power outlet, the waveform of a pulsed radar signal, or the waveform at the antenna of a radio receiver.

We shall begin our study of network responses by considering exponential excitation functions of the form $Xe^{s_p t}$, where X and s_p are constants. In view of the discussion of the last paragraph one might think the choice of this class of excitations to be a very limited and uninteresting one. As we shall see, however, exponential functions have the important property that they yield exponential responses when they form the excitations of networks characterized by linear constant-coefficient differential equations. Furthermore, through a study of Fourier theory it is possible to demonstrate that any waveform can be expressed in terms of a sum or integral of exponential functions. A related property is that, for a network characterized by a linear constant-coefficient differential equation, a knowledge of the responses to exponential excitation functions is sufficient to determine the response to an arbitrary excitation.

In many cases the exponential building blocks $Xe^{s_p t}$ that are needed to construct a real signal may be characterized by complex rather than real values of X and s_p. For example, the sinusoid can be represented as the sum of two complex exponential functions.

In summary, then, the analysis of networks with inductances, capacitances, and resistances requires that we be able to find the solutions of linear differential equations with constant coefficients. The right-hand sides of the differential equations will contain exponential functions of the form Xe^{s_pt}, where X and s_p may be complex. In order to acquire the mathematical techniques necessary to solve such problems, we shall now digress briefly to present a review of pertinent mathematical concepts divorced from any reference to networks. We shall first summarize some properties of complex numbers and then discuss the nature of signals constructed from real and complex exponential functions. Finally we shall study the properties of solutions of linear differential equations with constant coefficients in which the excitation function is an exponential. Following this digression into mathematics we shall return to networks and relate the solutions of the differential equations to properties of the networks.

Review of complex numbers

Since the axioms of the real-number system imply that the square of a real number cannot be negative, there is no solution among the real numbers to a quadratic equation such as $x^2 + 1 = 0$. To provide solutions to such equations, an additional dimension is added to the real-number system by the introduction of complex numbers that are simply ordered pairs of real numbers. Thus, the pair (x,y) of real numbers x and y denotes a complex number.

Equality, addition, and multiplication of complex numbers are defined such that, if the second member of a complex number is zero, i.e., if a complex number is of the form $(x,0)$, we obtain the familiar results for real numbers. For this reason the first member of the complex number is often referred to as the real part of the complex number. To distinguish the second member, it is often called the imaginary part of the complex number. (It should be recalled, however, that both x and y are real numbers.)

Equality of two complex numbers (x_1,y_1) and (x_2,y_2) means $x_1 = x_2$ and $y_1 = y_2$. Thus an equation in terms of complex numbers is the equivalent of two equations in terms of real numbers. Addition is defined by the equation

$$(x_1,y_1)(x_2,y_2) = (x_1 + x_2,\ y_1 + y_2), \qquad (2\text{-}2)$$

and multiplication is defined by the equation

$$(x_1, y_1)(x_2, y_2) = (x_1 x_2 - y_1 y_2, x_1 y_2 + x_2 y_1) . \qquad (2\text{-}3)$$

In all cases we observe the usual result for real numbers when the imaginary parts of the complex numbers are zero. We observe further that the square of the complex number $(0, y_1)$ is

$$(0, y_1)(0, y_1) = -y_1^2 , \qquad (2\text{-}4)$$

which is a negative number. Thus by extending the dimension of the real-number system in the manner indicated, we can satisfy our objective of providing solutions to equations such as $x^2 + 1 = 0$.

There exists a very convenient representation for complex numbers that enables them to be manipulated according to the rules for real numbers and, therefore, makes it unnecessary to remember special relations like the product relation of Eq. (2-3). This representation consists of writing a complex number z as

$$z = x + jy , \qquad (2\text{-}5)$$

where j is defined to have the property $j^2 = -1$. As before, x is called the real part of z, written $\text{Re}(z)$, and y the imaginary part of z, written $\text{Im}(z)$. It is readily verified that all the rules for complex numbers are consistent with treating the quantity $x + jy$ according to the rules of real numbers and then substituting -1 for j^2. Thus, for example, following the rules for real numbers, we obtain

$$(x_1 + jy_1) + (x_2 + jy_2) = (x_1 + x_2) + j(y_1 + y_2)$$

for the sum of two complex numbers. Note that the real part of the sum is the sum of the real parts and the imaginary part of the sum is the sum of the imaginary parts, in accordance with the Eq. (2-2). Similarly, following the rules for real numbers and replacing j^2 by -1, we obtain

$$(x_1 + jy_1)(x_2 + jy_2) = (x_1 x_2 - y_1 y_2) + j(x_1 y_2 + x_2 y_1)$$

for the product of two complex numbers, which is consistent with the Eq. (2-3). In Prob. 2-2, similar rules are developed for subtraction and division of complex numbers.

From these definitions and the properties of real numbers it is easily verified that the commutative and associative laws hold for complex numbers and that multiplication is distributive with respect to addition. That is, for all complex numbers Q, R, and S the following formal laws are satisfied:

	Addition	Multiplication
Commutative law:	$Q + R = R + Q$	$QR = RQ$
Associative law:	$Q + (R + S) = (Q + R) + S$	$Q(RS) = (QR)S$
Distributive law:	$Q(R + S) = QR + QS$	

Problem 2-1

a. Determine the real values for the variables u and v such that

$$(1 - j2)u + (1 + j2)v = 2 + j4 .$$

b. Is the above equation sufficient to determine the variables u and v uniquely if they are permitted to have complex values?

Problem 2-2

a. Given a complex number $z_1 = a + jb$, find the complex number $z_2 = c + jd$ such that the sum $z_1 + z_2 = 0 + j0$. The complex number $0 + j0$ has the same properties as zero has in the real number system and hence is often written as 0. The complex number z_2 is referred to as the *negative* of z_1 and will be written as $-z_1$.

b. Given a nonzero complex number $z_1 = a + jb$, find the complex number $z_3 = e + jf$ such that the product $z_1 z_3 = 1 + j0$. The complex number $1 + j0$ has the same properties as unity has in the real number system and hence is often written as 1. The complex number z_3 is referred to as the *reciprocal* of z_1 and will be written as $1/z_1$.

Problem 2-3

Express each of the following complex numbers in the form $a + jb$ with a and b real:

1. $(-7 + j3) + (4 + j5)$.
2. $(2 + j3)(-5 + j7)$.
3. $(1 + j)^4$.
4. $\dfrac{1 + j}{1 - j}$.

Problem 2-4

Let $z = x + jy$ be a complex variable. Express the following functions in the form $u(x,y) + jv(x,y)$, where $u(x,y)$ and $v(x,y)$ are real functions of the real variables x and y:

1. $1 + z^2$.
2. $\dfrac{1 + z}{1 - z}$.

3. $(1 - jz)^2$.

Geometric interpretation. A complex number $z = x + jy$ is conveniently represented geometrically by a point in the xy plane or by a vector from the origin to the point (x,y) as shown in Fig. 2-2. In this context the xy plane is called the *complex plane*; the x axis is called the real axis and the y axis the imaginary axis.

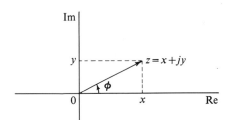

FIG. 2-2. Geometric representation of a complex number.

The *magnitude* or *absolute value* $|z|$ of a complex number z is equal to the length of the vector representing z in the complex plane. Therefore

$$|z| = \sqrt{x^2 + y^2} . \tag{2-6}$$

The *argument* of a complex number z, sometimes written as arg (z), is defined as the polar angle ϕ between the vector and the positive direction of the real axis, measured in a counterclockwise direction from the positive real axis, as shown in Fig. 2-2. We see from the geometric interpretation of ϕ in Fig. 2-2 that, for a given point (x,y), ϕ is determined only to within multiples of 2π. However, it is often convenient to define a unique angle for a complex number. This can be done by restricting ϕ to lie in the interval

$$-\pi < \phi \leq \pi ,$$

for example. In this case we speak of ϕ as the principal angle, and we define it to be the unique angle in that interval satisfying the conditions

$$x = |z| \cos \phi ,$$

and

$$y = |z| \sin \phi . \tag{2-7}$$

A complex number can therefore be specified either in rectangular coordinates by its real and imaginary parts or in polar coordinates by its magnitude and angle.

Complex exponentials. A very useful result emerges from the extension of the definition of e^x to the case of complex exponents. This extension can be made in various ways and is often done through the power series for e^x. However, it can also be accomplished by the following definition.[1] If $z = x + jy$, then we define e^z to be the complex number

$$e^z = e^x(\cos y + j \sin y). \qquad (2\text{-}8)$$

This definition is not made arbitrarily by any means. It is motivated by our desire that e^z agree with the usual exponential when z is real and our desire that the law of exponents

$$e^z e^w = e^{z+w} \qquad (2\text{-}9)$$

hold for all complex z and w.*

If in the above definition (2-8) we let $x = 0$ and $y = \phi$, we obtain the familiar Euler relation

$$e^{j\phi} = \cos \phi + j \sin \phi. \qquad (2\text{-}10)$$

From this relation, which is represented in the complex plane in Fig. 2-3, we see that $e^{j\phi}$ is a complex number with unit magnitude and argument ϕ.

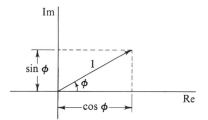

FIG. 2-3. Representation of $e^{j\phi}$ in the complex plane.

The expression $e^{j\phi}$ is convenient for representing complex numbers in terms of polar coordinates. From Eq. (2-7) and Euler's relation (2-10) we can express any complex number $z = x + jy$ in the form

$$z = x + jy = |z|e^{j\phi}. \qquad (2\text{-}11)$$

We shall call this the *polar form* of the complex number. An alternative notation that is sometimes used is

$$z = |z| \angle \phi. \qquad (2\text{-}12)$$

From Euler's relation we can also derive the following useful expressions for the cosine and sine functions in terms of complex exponentials:

[1] See, for example, T. M. Apostol, *Calculus*, Blaisdell, New York, 1962, vol. II, p. 381.
* See Prob. 2-5.

$$\cos \phi = \frac{e^{j\phi} + e^{-j\phi}}{2}, \tag{2-13}$$

and
$$\sin \phi = \frac{e^{j\phi} - e^{-j\phi}}{2j}. \tag{2-14}$$

Multiplication in polar form.   It is convenient to use the polar form when a product of complex numbers is to be computed. Suppose we are given two complex numbers

$$z_1 = |z_1|e^{j\phi_1},$$

and
$$z_2 = |z_2|e^{j\phi_2}.$$

Then
$$z_1 z_2 = |z_1|e^{j\phi_1}|z_2|e^{j\phi_2}$$
$$= |z_1|\,|z_2|e^{j(\phi_1+\phi_2)}. \tag{2-15}$$

Thus the magnitude of the product of two complex numbers is the product of the magnitudes of the numbers; the argument of the product is the sum of the arguments of the numbers.

The complex conjugate.   If $z = x + jy$, the complex conjugate of z is defined to be the complex number z^* whose imaginary part is the negative of that of z; i.e.,

$$z^* = x - jy. \tag{2-16}$$

If a complex number z is added to its conjugate z^*, the imaginary parts cancel, since they are equal in magnitude but opposite in sign, and the result is twice the real part of z; i.e.,

$$z + z^* = 2 \operatorname{Re}(z) = 2 \operatorname{Re}(z^*). \tag{2-17}$$

Graphically, the angle of the vector z is the negative of the angle of z^*, and thus the vector sum of z and z^* is a vector on the real axis, as shown in Fig. 2-4. Likewise, the difference between a complex number and its conjugate is $2j$ times the imaginary part; i.e.,

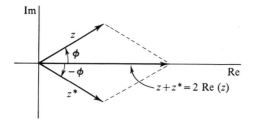

FIG. 2-4. Graphical illustration of the relation $z + z^* = 2 \operatorname{Re}(z)$.

$$z - z^* = 2j \operatorname{Im}(z). \tag{2-18}$$

We can easily verify (Prob. 2-6) that the conjugate of a complex number z has the same magnitude as that of z and an argument that is the negative of that of z. Thus if z is expressed in the polar form $z = |z|e^{j\phi}$, then

$$z^* = |z|e^{-j\phi}. \tag{2-19}$$

If we take the product of a complex number and its conjugate, we obtain

$$zz^* = |z|e^{j\phi}|z|e^{-j\phi} = |z|^2; \tag{2-20}$$

i.e., the product of a complex number and its conjugate is the square of the magnitude of the complex number.

Problem 2-5

a. Using the definition of the complex exponentials given in the text (Eq. 2-8), show that complex exponentials satisfy the law of exponents, i.e., that

$$e^z e^w = e^{z+w}$$

for all complex z and w.

b. Using Euler's relation, derive the following identities:

$$\cos \theta = \frac{e^{j\theta} + e^{-j\theta}}{2},$$

and

$$\sin \theta = \frac{e^{j\theta} - e^{-j\theta}}{2j},$$

where θ is any real number. These identities are often referred to as the exponential forms for the trigonometric functions $\cos \theta$ and $\sin \theta$.

c. Using the exponential forms for the trigonometric functions, derive each of the following identities:
1. $\cos^2 a = \frac{1}{2}(1 + \cos 2a)$.
2. $(\sin a)(\sin b) = \frac{1}{2}\cos (a - b) - \frac{1}{2}\cos (a + b)$.

Problem 2-6

a. Referring to Prob. 2-2, show that the reciprocal of a complex number z with magnitude $|z|$ and angle ϕ can be written in polar form as

$$\frac{1}{z} = \frac{1}{|z|} e^{-j\phi}.$$

b. Show that the complex conjugate of a complex number z with magnitude $|z|$ and angle ϕ can be written in polar form as

$$z^* = |z|e^{-j\phi} .$$

Problem 2-7

a. Sketch each of the following complex numbers in the complex plane. Indicate on your sketch the real and imaginary parts as well as the magnitude and angle of the complex number. Write the polar representation for each complex number:

1. $3 + j4$.
2. $-5 - j5$.
3. $1 - j\sqrt{3}$.
4. -5.

b. Sketch each of the following complex numbers in the complex plane. Indicate the real part, the imaginary part, the magnitude, and the angle in each case. Write the rectangular representation for each complex number:

1. $4e^{j(\pi/6)}$.
2. $6e^{-j(3\pi/4)}$.
3. $7e^{j\pi}$.
4. The complex number z described by $|z| = \sqrt{2}$, arg $(z) = -\pi/4$.

c. Express z in polar form in each of the following cases:

1. $z = (1 + \sqrt{-3})^2$.
2. $z = 3 + j4$.
3. $z = \dfrac{2 - j(6/\sqrt{3})}{2 + j(6/\sqrt{3})}$.
4. $z = (4 - j^3)(1 + j\frac{1}{2})$.
5. $z = 3e^{j\pi} + 4e^{j(\pi/2)}$.
6. $z = (\sqrt{3} + j) 2\sqrt{2}\, e^{-j(\pi/4)}$.
7. $z = \dfrac{6e^{-j(\pi/3)}}{1 - j\sqrt{3}}$.

Problem 2-8

a. Show that the product of any complex number and its complex conjugate is a real number.

b. Let $z = x + jy$, where x and y are real variables. Express each of the following functions in the form $u(x,y) + jv(x,y)$, where $u(x,y)$ and $v(x,y)$ are real for all values of x and y:

1. $f(z) = |z| + z^*$.
2. $f(z) = \dfrac{1}{zz^*}$.

Problem 2-9

Throughout the remainder of the text, many properties of complex variables will be used. The identities concerning the complex conjugate operation developed in this problem will be especially useful in later work.

In each of the following identities z, z_1, and z_2 represent complex variables.

a. Using either the polar or rectangular representation for each complex variable, show that:

1. $(z_1z_2)^* = z_1^* z_2^*$.
2. $(az)^* = a(z^*)$, where a is any real number.
3. $(z_1 + z_2)^* = z_1^* + z_2^*$.
4. $(e^z)^* = e^{(z^*)}$.
5. $(z^a)^* = (z^*)^a$, where a is any real number.
6. $\left(\dfrac{z_1}{z_2}\right)^* = \dfrac{z_1^*}{z_2^*}$.

b. Using the results of (a), show that

$$[P(z)]^* = P(z^*),$$

where $P(z)$ is a polynomial of nth order in z with real coefficients, of the form

$$P(z) = a_n z^n + a_{n-1} z^{n-1} + \cdots + a_1 z + a_0.$$

c. Using the results of (a) and (b), show that

$$[Q(z)]^* = Q(z^*),$$

where $Q(z)$ is the ratio of two polynomials with real coefficients, of the form

$$Q(z) = \frac{a_n z^n + a_{n-1} z^{n-1} + \cdots + a_1 z + a_0}{b_m z^m + b_{m-1} z^{m-1} + \cdots + b_1 z + b_0}.$$

Problem 2-10

Using the results obtained in Prob. 2-9, show that the complex roots of a polynomial with real coefficients occur in complex conjugate pairs; i.e., show that, if $P(z_1) = 0$, where P is a polynomial with real coefficients, then $P(z_1^*) = 0$.

Problem 2-11

In the study of RLC networks, a central role is played by the complex exponential time function $z(t) = Ae^{st}$, in which A and s are complex numbers. It is important that the effect of the parameters A and s on the behavior of this time function be understood.

We shall denote the angle of A by ϕ, the real part of s by σ, and the imaginary part of s by ω.

a. For $\sigma = 0$:

1. Sketch the locus of the point $z(t)$ in the complex plane as t increases from negative values through $t = 0$ to large positive values. Indicate the location of $z(0)$; i.e., $z(t)$ at $t = 0$. Describe the effect of ϕ and ω on the sketch.
2. Repeat (1) for $z^*(t)$.
3. Repeat (1) for $[z(t) + z^*(t)]$.
4. Sketch Re $[z(t)]$ versus t.
5. Repeat (4) for Im $[z(t)]$.

b. Repeat (*a*) for some negative value of σ. Show on all sketches how the locus of z changes when σ becomes larger or smaller in magnitude.

c. For all sketches in (*b*), state in words the effect of letting σ take on some positive rather than negative value. Include in your discussion the effect of making σ assume larger or smaller positive values.

Exponential functions

Let us now examine some of the properties of exponential time functions of the form $Xe^{s_p t}$ for various real and complex values of X and s_p. We shall call X the *complex amplitude* and s_p the *complex frequency* of the exponential function.

We consider first the case where X and s_p are real, and we put $s_p = \sigma$, where σ is a real number. In this case $Xe^{s_p t}$ is a real time function that may represent a voltage or current. For σ negative, the function is a decaying exponential, as shown in Fig. 2-5*a*; the rate of decay depends, of course, on the value of σ. For $\sigma = 0$, the function reduces to a constant whose value is X, as shown in Fig. 2-5*b*. The function becomes a rising exponential of the form shown in Fig. 2-5*c* when $\sigma > 0$.

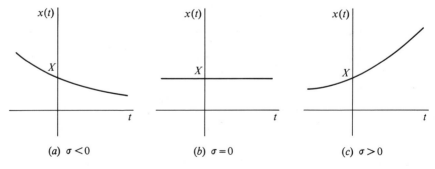

FIG. 2-5. Form of exponential function when X and s_p are real and $s_p = \sigma$.

A more general set of time functions can be represented by exponential functions for which X and s_p are allowed to be complex. In this case $Xe^{s_p t}$ is a complex time function that cannot by itself represent a real time function such as the waveform of a voltage or current. However, if we add to this complex exponential another exponential that is its complex conjugate, the sum is a real time function. (Recall that the sum of any complex quantity and its conjugate is real.) A simple example is the case in which $X = 1$ and $s_p = j\omega$, where ω is a real number. Addition of this exponential and its complex conjugate gives a cosine wave; i.e.,

$$e^{j\omega t} + e^{-j\omega t} = 2 \cos \omega t . \qquad (2\text{-}21)$$

More generally, however, both X and s_p are complex, and we can form a real time function $x(t)$ as follows:

$$x(t) = Xe^{s_p t} + X^* e^{s_p^* t} . \qquad (2\text{-}22)$$

We shall denote the real part of the complex frequency s_p by σ and the imaginary part by ω, thus writing $s_p = \sigma + j\omega$. If the complex amplitude X is expressed in the polar form $|X|e^{j\phi}$, then Eq. (2-22) becomes

$$x(t) = |X|e^{\sigma t}e^{j(\omega t+\phi)} + |X|e^{\sigma t}e^{-j(\omega t+\phi)}$$
$$= 2|X|e^{\sigma t} \cos (\omega t + \phi) . \qquad (2\text{-}23)$$

Note that, when we allow X to be a complex number, a phase shift equal to the angle of X is introduced in the argument of the cosine in Eq. (2-23). The rate of growth (or decay) of the amplitude of the cosine depends on σ. For $\sigma < 0$ we obtain a damped oscillatory signal, such as that shown in Fig. 2-6a; when $\sigma = 0$, $x(t)$ is a sinusoidal signal (Fig. 2-6b); for $\sigma > 0$,

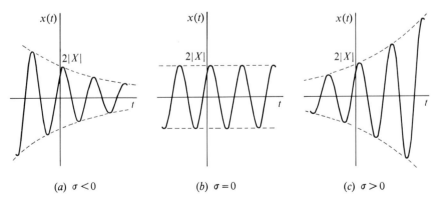

(a) $\sigma < 0$ (b) $\sigma = 0$ (c) $\sigma > 0$

FIG. 2-6. Waveforms constructed from conjugate complex exponential building blocks—Eq. (2-23)—for different ranges of values for σ.

$x(t)$ is an oscillatory signal whose amplitude rises exponentially with time, as shown in Fig. 2-6c. In the case $\sigma = 0$ the waveform is periodic, the number of cycles per unit of time being $\omega/2\pi$. (For constant-amplitude sinusoidal signals the term *frequency*, designated by the symbol f, is often used to denote the number of cycles per second, as distinguished from the complex number $s_p = \sigma + j\omega$, which we call the *complex frequency*.)

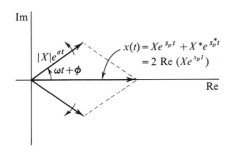

FIG. 2-7. Vector diagram showing how a real signal is constructed from two complex exponential functions $Xe^{s_p t}$ and $X^*e^{s_p * t}$, where $X = |X|e^{j\phi}$ and $s_p = \sigma + j\omega$.

It is sometimes convenient to interpret simple exponential functions as vectors in the complex plane, in the manner shown in Fig. 2-7. Thus at a given time t the exponential function $Xe^{s_p t} = |X|e^{j\phi}e^{(\sigma+j\omega)t}$ can be represented by a vector of length $|X|e^{\sigma t}$ at angle $\omega t + \phi$ with the positive real axis. As time proceeds, the angle increases, and the vector rotates in a counterclockwise direction. At the same time the amplitude $|X|e^{\sigma t}$ changes —it decreases if σ is negative and increases if σ is positive—and thus the tip of the vector traces out a spiral shape as t increases. The vector representing the complex conjugate of $Xe^{s_p t}$ can be written $X^*e^{s_p * t} = |X|e^{-j\phi}e^{(\sigma-j\omega)t}$. This vector, which is also shown in Fig. 2-7, has the same amplitude as the original vector, but forms an angle with the real axis that is exactly the negative of the angle of $Xe^{s_p t}$. As time increases, the conjugate vector rotates in a clockwise direction with changing amplitude, the amplitude being proportional to $e^{\sigma t}$. The figure shows, however, that the sum of the two vectors, given by $x(t) = Xe^{s_p t} + X^*e^{s_p * t}$, always lies on the real axis and is equal to twice the real part of either one of the component vectors.

In summary, then, we have seen that a complex exponential function $Xe^{s_p t}$, when added to the conjugate complex function, yields a real time function that can be visualized as a sinusoid with changing amplitude. The properties of the time function are defined completely by the two complex numbers X and s_p. Alternatively, if we set $X = |X|e^{j\phi}$ and $s_p = \sigma + j\omega$, then the properties of the time function can be said to be defined by the four real numbers $|X|$, ϕ, σ, and ω. The factor $|X|$ controls the amplitude of the signal; ϕ is the phase angle of the oscillatory signal at $t = 0$; σ controls the rate of growth (or decay) of the waveform; and ω determines how frequently the waveform oscillates back and forth through zero.

Problem 2-12

a. Let

$$f(t) = Ae^{(a+jb)t} + A^*e^{(a-jb)t},$$

where A is a complex constant with magnitude $|A|$ and angle θ, a and b are real constants, and t is a real variable. Write $f(t)$ in each of the following forms:

$$f(t) = e^{at}(C \cos bt + D \sin bt),$$

$$f(t) = e^{at} E \cos (bt + \phi),$$

where C, D, E, and ϕ are expressed in terms of $|A|$ and θ.

b. Write each function $f(t)$ below in each of the following three ways: (*i*) as the real part of a complex exponential function; (*ii*) as the imaginary part of a complex exponential function; (*iii*) as the sum of two complex exponential functions:

1. $f(t) = \cos 2t$.
2. $f(t) = e^{-t} \sin 3t$.
3. $f(t) = \cos \left(t + \dfrac{\pi}{4} \right)$.
4. $f(t) = \sin t$.
5. $f(t) = \cos 4(t - 2)$.

c. Express each of the following functions as a sum of complex exponential functions:

1. $f(t) = 3$.
2. $f(t) = e^{-2t} - e^t \cos 3t$.
3. $f(t) = \cos^2 t$.

The unit step function; signals starting at $t = 0$

In general it will be convenient to select $t = 0$ as the time at which the excitation of a network is turned on; i.e., we shall assume all sources to be zero prior to $t = 0$. All physical signals are, of course, turned on or started at some time, and we shall see in Chap. 3 that, for the networks we consider, there is no loss in generality if this time is selected at $t = 0$. Thus we shall be dealing with signals (or with building blocks of signals) that are zero for $t < 0$ and of the form Xe^{spt} for $t > 0$.

In order to provide a simple and convenient way of specifying signals that start at $t = 0$, we introduce a function $u_{-1}(t)$ called the *unit step function*. This function is defined to be zero for $t < 0$ and unity for $t > 0$; a plot of $u_{-1}(t)$ is given in Fig. 2-8. At the discontinuity at $t = 0$ the

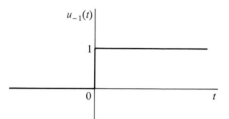

FIG. 2-8. The unit step function $u_{-1}(t)$.

function may take on any finite value. If the origin is approached from positive values of t, the value of $u_{-1}(t)$ is unity in the limit as $t \to 0$; if, on the other hand, the origin is approached from negative values of t, the value of $u_{-1}(t)$ is zero in the limit as $t \to 0$. The product $u_{-1}(t)f(t)$ of the unit step function with any analytic function $f(t)$ is then zero for $t < 0$ and $f(t)$ for $t > 0$.

Thus in our study of the response of networks to exponential excitations, we can use the step function to express the excitation in the form $u_{-1}(t)Xe^{s_p t}$ when X and s_p are real or in the form $u_{-1}(t)\left(Xe^{s_p t} + X^* e^{s_p^* t}\right)$ when X and s_p are complex. In the latter case we shall need to find the solution to a differential equation having a sum of two functions on the right-hand side. However, if the excitation is constructed from more than one function, we shall show that it is sufficient to solve the differential equation for the cases in which each function appears separately on the right side and to add the solutions. We shall turn now, therefore, to examine the properties of the solutions of linear differential equations with constant coefficients, in which the right-hand side is zero prior to $t = 0$ and is a single exponential function for $t > 0$.

Solution of linear differential equations with constant coefficients

A simple example of a linear differential equation with constant coefficients, in which the right-hand side is an exponential function of time for $t > 0$, is the first-order equation

$$a_1 \frac{dy}{dt} + a_0 y = u_{-1}(t)Xe^{s_p t}, \qquad (2\text{-}24)$$

where the coefficients a_1 and a_0 are real constants. More generally, we can write an nth-order linear constant-coefficient differential equation (with the same excitation function) as

$$a_n \frac{d^n y}{dt^n} + a_{n-1} \frac{d^{n-1} y}{dt^{n-1}} + \cdots + a_1 \frac{dy}{dt} + a_0 y = u_{-1}(t) X e^{s_p t}, \quad (2\text{-}25)$$

where the coefficients a_k are real constants. For purposes of illustration we shall take the complex amplitude X and the complex frequency s_p to be real, so that we can plot the excitation function $x(t)$ in the manner shown in Fig. 2-9. Our task is to find a solution $y(t)$ that is valid for all values of t.

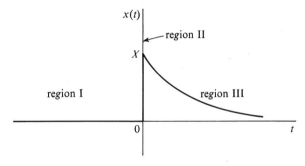

FIG. 2-9. Graph of a typical excitation function for differential equation (2-24) or (2-25), showing the three regions of time within which the solutions of the equation are examined separately.

In view of the fact that a discontinuity in the excitation occurs at $t = 0$, it is appropriate at the outset to divide the time scale into the regions $t < 0$ and $t > 0$ (designated regions I and III, respectively, in Fig. 2-9) and to examine the solution of the differential equation separately in each region. Within each of these regions the excitation function and its derivatives are continuous, and we expect, therefore, that the solutions within each region are similarly well behaved. Our general approach will be to find solutions to the equation in each of the two regions separately and then to select from these the solutions that satisfy certain conditions of continuity when they are joined at the boundary $t = 0$. Thus we shall need to examine the solution of the equation as we pass through the point $t = 0$ (region II in Fig. 2-9). These solutions for regions I, II, and III together form the complete solution to the differential equation for all time.

Since there is a discontinuity in the excitation function, its value at the origin depends on the direction from which we approach $t = 0$. That is, the value of the function depends on whether we approach the origin from region I or region III. When we are considering solutions in region III, we shall use the notation $t = 0+$ to designate the origin, thus indicating that we have approached it from positive values of t. Likewise the notation $t = 0-$ will be used to designate the origin for region I.

Solution for region III, $t > 0$. Let us first find a solution of the first-order differential equation (2-24) in this region. Our procedure is to select a trial solution and then to check the initial choice by substituting it into the differential equation. Since the right-hand side of the equation is an exponential function of time with complex frequency s_p, the left-hand side, i.e., the sum $a_1 \dfrac{dy}{dt} + a_0 y$, must, of course, be the same exponential function of time. We note that an exponential function of time has the property that any of its derivatives is simply the same exponential function multiplied by a constant. Hence if y is an exponential function with complex frequency s_p, then the sum $a_1 \dfrac{dy}{dt} + a_0 y$ is an exponential function with the same complex frequency. A solution proportional to $e^{s_p t}$ is suggested, therefore, and thus we write

$$y = Y e^{s_p t}, \tag{2-26}$$

where the proportionality constant Y is to be determined. Substitution of this trial solution into Eq. (2-24) gives

$$(a_1 s_p + a_0) Y e^{s_p t} = X e^{s_p t},$$

which is satisfied if $Y = X/(a_1 s_p + a_0)$. Hence

$$y(t) = \frac{X}{a_1 s_p + a_0} e^{s_p t} \tag{2-27}$$

We shall call this solution the *particular integral* or the *particular solution* of the differential equation.

The particular integral, as defined above, is not the most general solution of the differential equation. A more general solution can be obtained by adding to the particular integral a solution of the differential equation with the right-hand side set to zero, i.e., a solution of the equation

$$a_1 \frac{dy}{dt} + a_0 y = 0, \tag{2-28}$$

which is known as the *homogeneous equation*. The solution of the homogeneous equation is called the *homogeneous solution* or the *complementary function*. In order to show that the sum of the particular integral (which we shall designate as y_p) and the homogeneous solution (designated as y_h) is a solution of Eq. (2-24), we first write the separate equations

$$a_1 \frac{dy_p}{dt} + a_0 y_p = X e^{s_p t}$$

and

$$a_1 \frac{dy_h}{dt} + a_0 y_h = 0 .$$

Adding both sides of these equations gives

$$a_1 \frac{dy_p}{dt} + a_1 \frac{dy_h}{dt} + a_0 y_p + a_0 y_h = X e^{s_p t} ,$$

which can be written

$$a_1 \frac{d}{dt}(y_p + y_h) + a_0(y_p + y_h) = X e^{s_p t} .$$

Thus the sum $y = y_p + y_h$ is a solution of the differential equation, and consequently we are justified in adding to the particular integral the solution of the homogeneous equation.[1]

To find the homogeneous solution, we observe that the terms $a_0 y_h$ and $a_1(dy_h/dt)$ must be equal in magnitude but opposite in sign for all t. Recognizing again that the derivative of an exponential function is proportional to the function, we select the following trial solution for the homogeneous equation:

$$y_h = A e^{st} , \qquad (2\text{-}29)$$

where A and s are constants. Substitution of (2-29) into the homogeneous equation (2-28) gives

$$a_1 A s e^{st} + a_0 A e^{st} = 0 ,$$

or

$$(a_1 s + a_0) A e^{st} = 0 .$$

This equation is satisfied if

$$a_1 s + a_0 = 0 , \qquad (2\text{-}30)$$

---

[1] Our use of the term *particular integral* differs from the usual mathematical one, which includes our particular integral plus any homogeneous solution. Our choice of terminology is motivated by the fact that in network theory we frequently need to make a clear distinction between the two components y_p and y_h.

independent of the value of A. Equation (2-30) is known as the *characteristic equation.* In this case, its solution is

$$s = - \frac{a_0}{a_1}. \tag{2-31}$$

The exponential function (2-29), with any constant A, is therefore a solution of the homogeneous equation provided that s has the value given in (2-31).

The general solution of the original first-order differential equation (2-24) for $t > 0$ is the sum of the particular integral (2-27) and the homogeneous solution (2-29)[1]:

$$y(t) = Ae^{-(a_0/a_1)t} + \frac{X}{a_1 s_p + a_0} e^{s_p t}. \tag{2-32}$$

This solution is the sum of two exponential functions of time: the complex frequency associated with the homogeneous solution $(-a_0/a_1$ in this case) is determined solely by the homogeneous equation; the complex frequency s_p associated with the particular integral is identical with the complex frequency of the excitation function on the right-hand side of the differential equation.[2]

As an example we shall examine the general solution (2-32) for the simple case in which $s_p = 0$ and X is real. In this case

$$y(t) = Ae^{-(a_0/a_1)t} + \frac{X}{a_0} \quad \text{for } t > 0. \tag{2-33}$$

Depending on the value of A, $y(t)$ may take several forms, as shown in Fig. 2-10. There are, in effect, an infinite number of solutions of the differential equation for $t > 0$ corresponding to different values of A. If, however, the value of y is known at some point in time, then only one of the possible solutions satisfies this constraint, and a particular value of A must be selected. Such a condition on y is known as an *initial condition.* For example, suppose the condition on y is imposed at $t = 0+$, such that $y(0+) = B$. Then substitution in (2-33) gives $B = A + (X/a_0)$, or $A = B - (X/a_0)$. Thus the constant A is determined from the initial condition.

---

[1] It can be shown that this sum forms the most general solution of the differential equation for $t > 0$.

[2] For the special case in which s_p is equal to the root of the characteristic equation, i.e., $s_p = -a_0/a_1$, the general solution takes the form $y(t) = Be^{-(a_0/a_1)t} + Xte^{-(a_0/a_1)t}$, where B is an arbitrary constant, as can be verified by substitution into the differential equation (2-24). Unless otherwise stated, we shall assume throughout the text that the complex frequency of the excitation function does not coincide with a root of the characteristic equation.

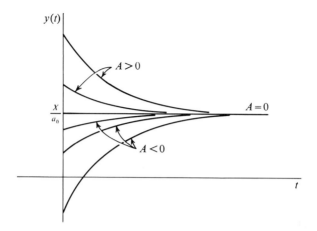

FIG. 2-10. Form of the solution (2-33.) of the first-order differential equation for $t > 0$ for several values of the constant A. The complex frequency s_p of the excitation function is zero.

The approach used to obtain the solution of the first-order differential equation in region III can also be applied to differential equations of higher order. Consider, for example, a second-order differential equation with the same right-hand side as before:

$$a_2 \frac{d^2y}{dt^2} + a_1 \frac{dy}{dt} + a_0 y = u_{-1}(t) X e^{s_p t} . \qquad (2\text{-}34)$$

As discussed in the case of the first-order differential equation, since the right-hand side is an exponential with complex frequency s_p, an appropriate trial solution of Eq. (2-34) is also an exponential with complex frequency s_p. Thus we try

$$y_p = Y e^{s_p t}$$

as the particular integral for $t > 0$. Substitution into the differential equation gives

$$a_2 s_p^2 Y e^{s_p t} + a_1 s_p Y e^{s_p t} + a_0 Y e^{s_p t} = X e^{s_p t} ,$$

from which we obtain the complex amplitude

$$Y = \frac{X}{a_2 s_p^2 + a_1 s_p + a_0} . \qquad (2\text{-}35)$$

Thus the particular integral for Eq. (2-34), for $t > 0$, is

$$y_p(t) = \frac{X}{a_2 s_p{}^2 + a_1 s_p + a_0} e^{s_p t} . \qquad (2\text{-}36)$$

Again we can add to the particular integral any solution of the homogeneous equation

$$a_2 \frac{d^2 y}{dt^2} + a_1 \frac{dy}{dt} + a_0 y = 0 . \qquad (2\text{-}37)$$

As before, we select a homogeneous solution (i.e., a solution of the homogeneous equation) of the form

$$y_h = A e^{st} .$$

When this exponential function is substituted into the homogeneous equation, we find that the equation is satisfied if s is a root of the characteristic equation

$$a_2 s^2 + a_1 s + a_0 = 0 . \qquad (2\text{-}38)$$

The characteristic equation is now a second-order algebraic equation and has, in general, two roots, i.e., $s = s_1, s_2$. Thus if s_1 and s_2 are distinct roots,[1] the homogeneous equation has two solutions, which we shall write as $A_1 e^{s_1 t}$ and $A_2 e^{s_2 t}$, where A_1 and A_2 are arbitrary constants. Since each of these exponential functions is a solution of the homogeneous equation, their sum is also a solution, as will be seen in the discussion of linearity later in this chapter. The general homogeneous solution is, therefore,

$$y(t) = A_1 e^{s_1 t} + A_2 e^{s_2 t} . \qquad (2\text{-}39)$$

The general solution of the second-order equation (2-34) for $t > 0$ is the sum of the particular integral and the homogeneous solution; i.e.,

$$y(t) = A_1 e^{s_1 t} + A_2 e^{s_2 t} + \frac{X}{a_2 s_p{}^2 + a_1 s_p + a_0} e^{s_p t} , \qquad (2\text{-}40)$$

as can be readily verified by substitution into the differential equation. As in the first-order case, the solution is a sum of exponential functions. The homogeneous solution now contains two exponentials with two different complex frequencies s_1 and s_2, since the characteristic equation is of the second order. As before, the complex frequency of the exponential in

---

[1] For the special case in which $s_1 = s_2$, the solution of the homogeneous equation is $y_h(t) = B_1 e^{s_1 t} + B_2 t e^{s_1 t}$ where B_1 and B_2 are arbitrary constants, as can be verified by direct substitution into the homogeneous equation (2-37). In this text we shall not in general be concerned with the case in which roots of the characteristic equation coincide.

the particular integral is identical with the complex frequency of the exponential on the right-hand side of the differential equation.

Unless additional information concerning the solution for $t > 0$ is given, $y(t)$ can take a variety of forms, depending on the values of the two arbitrary constants A_1 and A_2. Both constants can be determined if two independent conditions or constraints are imposed on the solution. For example, A_1 and A_2 can be determined if $y(t)$ is specified at two appropriate values of t or if the initial conditions (the solution and its first derivative at some instant of time) are known.

To illustrate the application of initial conditions to the solution of the second-order differential equation, let us assume that

$$\left. \begin{array}{l} y = B \\ \dfrac{dy}{dt} = C \end{array} \right\} \quad \text{at } t = 0+ \, ,$$

where B and C are constants. The general solution, given previously as Eq. (2-40), and its derivative are

$$y(t) = A_1 e^{s_1 t} + A_2 e^{s_2 t} + \frac{X}{a_2 s_p^2 + a_1 s_p + a_0} e^{s_p t} , \qquad (2\text{-}41)$$

and $$\frac{dy}{dt} = A_1 s_1 e^{s_1 t} + A_2 s_2 e^{s_2 t} + \frac{X s_p}{a_2 s_p^2 + a_1 s_p + a_0} e^{s_p t} . \qquad (2\text{-}42)$$

When we set $t = 0$ in Eqs. (2-41) and (2-42) and apply the initial conditions, we obtain the two equations

$$A_1 + A_2 + \frac{X}{a_2 s_p^2 + a_1 s_p + a_0} = B \, ,$$

and $$s_1 A_1 + s_2 A_2 + \frac{X s_p}{a_2 s_p^2 + a_1 s_p + a_0} = C \, .$$

These equations can be solved for A_1 and A_2, and the solution satisfying the given initial conditions is then completely determined.

Let us now apply the approach developed above to a linear constant-coefficient differential equation of nth order. As we have seen, the general form of such an equation is

$$a_n \frac{d^n y}{dt^n} + a_{n-1} \frac{d^{n-1} y}{dt^{n-1}} + \cdots + a_1 \frac{dy}{dt} + a_0 y = u_{-1}(t) X e^{s_p t} . \qquad (2\text{-}43)$$

Again we consider the case in which the right-hand side of the equation is an exponential function for $t > 0$, and, for the present, we consider solutions that are valid for $t > 0$, i.e., for region III of Fig. 2-9. As before, the particular integral is an exponential function $Ye^{s_p t}$ having the same complex frequency as the excitation. By substituting $Ye^{s_p t}$ for $y(t)$ in (2-43), we determine the complex amplitude of the particular integral to be

$$Y = \frac{X}{a_n s_p{}^n + a_{n-1} s_p{}^{n-1} + \cdots + a_1 s_p + a_0}. \tag{2-44}$$

The homogeneous solution is a sum of exponentials whose complex frequencies are solutions of the nth-order characteristic equation

$$a_n s^n + a_{n-1} s^{n-1} + \cdots + a_1 s + a_0 = 0. \tag{2-45}$$

In general this equation has n roots, given by

$$s = s_1, s_2, \ldots, s_{n-1}, s_n.$$

(We should recall[1] that, when the coefficients of an nth-order polynomial are real, the roots either are real or occur in conjugate complex pairs. This result is of importance in network theory, since most networks that are of interest are characterized by differential equations with coefficients that are real constants.) When the n roots are distinct and do not coincide[2] with s_p, the general solution of the differential equation for $t > 0$ is, therefore,

$$y(t) = A_1 e^{s_1 t} + A_2 e^{s_2 t} + \cdots + A_n e^{s_n t} + \left[\frac{X}{a_n s_p{}^n + a_{n-1} s_p{}^{n-1} + \cdots + a_1 s_p + a_0}\right] e^{s_p t}$$

$$\tag{2-46}$$

or, in more compact form,

$$y(t) = \sum_{k=1}^{n} A_k e^{s_k t} + \left[\frac{X}{a_n s_p{}^n + a_{n-1} s_p{}^{n-1} + \cdots + a_1 s_p + a_0}\right] e^{s_p t}, \tag{2-47}$$

where the A_k are arbitrary constants. The constants can be determined if the solution is constrained to satisfy n conditions that yield n independent equations for the A_k. A typical set of conditions would, for example, be the initial conditions specifying y and its first $n - 1$ derivatives at $t = 0+$.

The existence and uniqueness theorems for linear differential equations guarantee that there is one and only one function y which satisfies the differential equation and for which y and its first $n - 1$ derivatives

---

[1] Problem 2-10.
[2] See footnotes, pages 68 and 70.

satisfy a prescribed set of initial conditions.[1] The uniqueness theorem is very useful, since it guarantees that, if, by any means, we find *a* solution that satisfies the differential equation and the initial conditions, then it must be the only solution.

For this general case of an *n*th-order differential equation the properties of the two parts of the solution are again clearly in evidence: the homogeneous solution is characterized by complex frequencies that are determined from the homogeneous equation, and it does not involve the complex frequency of the excitation function on the right-hand side of the equation; the particular integral is characterized by a complex frequency that is identical with that of the excitation function appearing on the right-hand side of the equation.

Solution for region I, t < 0. We have indicated that we are interested in finding the solution of a linear differential equation with constant coefficients, in which the right-hand side is of the form $u_{-1}(t)Xe^{s_p t}$. Thus for $t < 0$ the differential equation is simply the homogeneous equation, and in the case of the *n*th-order equation (2-43) the solution is of the form

$$y(t) = \sum_{k=1}^{n} B_k e^{s_k t} \qquad \text{for } t < 0, \qquad (2\text{-}48)$$

where the B_k are arbitrary constants and the s_k are roots of the characteristic equation.

There are an infinite number of solutions in region I, depending on the values of the constants B_k. We shall be concerned initially with differential equations related to networks in which the voltages and currents are zero before the excitation is applied. Such systems are said to be at rest prior to application of the excitation. These considerations lead us to select the solution for which $y(t)$ and all its derivatives are zero in region I. This solution corresponds to the case in which all $B_k = 0$ in Eq. (2-48). Systems that are not at rest prior to application of the excitation will be considered in Chap. 3.

Solution for region II, t = 0, and the resulting solution for all t. We have established the solution of the differential equation for region I and determined the solution, to within arbitrary constants, for region III. In order to determine the solution for all time, it remains to find the solution at $t = 0$ and to evaluate the arbitrary constants in the solution for region

---

[1] See, for example, T. M. Apostol, *Calculus*, Blaisdell, New York, 1962, vol. II, p. 342. We shall assume without proof that these theorems are valid even though the excitation functions with which we shall be concerned may not be well behaved at $t = 0$.

III. Our approach to finding the solution in region II will be a heuristic one. (A more rigorous approach would be to consider the discontinuous excitation function of the differential equation as the limit of an appropriate sequence of functions.)

Let us consider initially the first-order differential equation discussed previously, i.e.,

$$a_1 \frac{dy}{dt} + a_0 y = u_{-1}(t) X e^{s_p t} . \qquad (2\text{-}49)$$

The right-hand side of this equation is equal to zero for $t < 0$ and is equal to X at $t = 0+$; i.e., there is a jump from zero to X at $t = 0$. If the differential equation is to be satisfied for all t, then the left-hand side must exhibit the same jump from zero to X at $t = 0$. We might expect a discontinuity to occur in the derivative term $a_1 \frac{dy}{dt}$ and not in the term $a_0 y$, since if $a_0 y$ had a discontinuity, then the derivative of y would be infinite at $t = 0$, and the differential equation would not be satisfied. With this motivation let us try to account for the discontinuity entirely by the highest-order term in the differential equation. If $a_0 y$ does not have a discontinuity, then $y(t)$ must be continuous at the origin. Thus if we select the solution in region I for which y and all its derivatives are zero, corresponding to a physical system at rest for $t < 0$, then $y(0-) = y(0+) = 0$. We can now apply this initial condition to the solution originally found for $t > 0$, which was

$$y(t) = A e^{-(a_0/a_1)t} + \frac{X}{a_1 s_p + a_0} e^{s_p t} . \qquad (2\text{-}50)$$

To satisfy the initial condition, the constant A must be

$$A = - \frac{X}{a_1 s_p + a_0} .$$

The final solution of (2-49) is

$$y(t) = \begin{cases} 0 & \text{for } t \le 0 \\ \dfrac{X}{a_1 s_p + a_0} [e^{s_p t} - e^{-(a_0/a_1)t}] & \text{for } t \ge 0 . \end{cases}$$

Since this function is finite at the origin, we can make use of the step function to express it in the more compact form

$$y(t) = u_{-1}(t) \frac{X}{a_1 s_p + a_0} [e^{s_p t} - e^{-(a_0/a_1)t}] . \qquad (2\text{-}51)$$

The same type of reasoning can be applied to find the solution, valid for all t, to the nth-order differential equation

$$a_n \frac{d^n y}{dt^n} + a_{n-1} \frac{d^{n-1} y}{dt^{n-1}} + \cdots + a_1 \frac{dy}{dt} + a_0 y = u_{-1}(t) X e^{s_p t} . \qquad (2\text{-}52)$$

Again the value of the right-hand side of this equation jumps from zero to X at $t = 0$, and consequently the left-hand side must also exhibit such a jump. By using an argument involving a limiting set of functions, one can reason that there cannot exist a jump in y or any of its first n − 1 derivatives, since such a jump would cause the higher derivatives on the left-hand side, and $d^n y/dt^n$ in particular, to have infinite value at $t = 0$, and the equation could not be satisfied. Thus the discontinuity must occur in the highest-order term $a_n(d^n y/dt^n)$, and we conclude that y and its first $n - 1$ derivatives are all continuous across region II. If the solution is to apply to a physical system that is at rest for $t < 0$, then y and all its derivatives must be zero for $t < 0$, and the initial conditions at $t = 0+$ are

$$y = \frac{dy}{dt} = \frac{d^2 y}{dt^2} = \cdots = \frac{d^{n-1} y}{dt^{n-1}} = 0 . \qquad (2\text{-}53)$$

These conditions provide a set of equations that can be solved for the n arbitrary constants $A_1, A_2, \ldots, A_n$ in the solution that was found for $t > 0$, namely

$$y(t) = \sum_{k=1}^{n} A_k e^{s_k t} + \left[\frac{X}{a_n s_p{}^n + a_{n-1} s_p{}^{n-1} + \cdots + a_1 s_p + a_0} \right] e^{s_p t} , \qquad (2\text{-}54)$$

where the s_k are the roots of the characteristic equation. Once the A_k have been found, then the solution[1] that is valid for all t is the $y(t)$ in Eq. (2-54) multiplied by $u_{-1}(t)$.

---

[1] The uniqueness theorem guarantees that there is no more than one solution that satisfies the differential equation and a given set of initial conditions. We shall assume without proof that the uniqueness theorem applies even when the excitation function is not well behaved at the origin. We can regard the statement that the system is initially at rest as being equivalent to a set of initial conditions at $t = 0-$, and hence we can conclude that the response of a system that is governed by a linear constant-coefficient differential equation and is initially at rest is unique.

Problem 2-13

Determine the solution of each of the following equations for $t > 0$, subject to the initial conditions specified. Carefully separate the steps in your procedure according to the following guide:

i. Find the characteristic equation.

ii. Determine the homogeneous solution, and verify that it contains the correct number of arbitrary constants.

iii. Determine the particular integral of the equation.

iv. Write down the general solution for $t > 0$, and evaluate the constants such that the solution satisfies the specified initial conditions.

1. $\dfrac{dy}{dt} + 2y = e^{-t}$, $\qquad y(0+) = 0$.

2. $\dfrac{d^2y}{dt^2} + 3\dfrac{dy}{dt} = -2e^{-2t}$, $\qquad y(0+) = 0$,

$$\dfrac{dy}{dt}(0+) = -2.$$

3. $\dfrac{dy}{dt} + 3y = e^{(3-j)t}$, $\qquad y(0+) = 1$.

4. $\dfrac{d^2y}{dt^2} + 4y = 1$, $\qquad y(0+) = \frac{1}{2}$,

$$\dfrac{dy}{dt}(0+) = 0.$$

Problem 2-14

Determine the solution for all time to each of the following differential equations, subject to the condition that the response be zero for $t < 0$:

1. $\dfrac{dy}{dt} + 2y = u_{-1}(t)e^{-t}$.

2. $\dfrac{d^2y}{dt^2} - y = u_{-1}(t)$.

3. $\dfrac{d^2y}{dt^2} + 5\dfrac{dy}{dt} + 4y = u_{-1}(t)20e^{t}$.

Problem 2-15

a. Determine from the following set of differential equations a single differential equation relating $y_1(t)$ and $x(t)$:

$$\frac{dy_1}{dt} + 2y_1 - y_2 = x,$$

$$\frac{dy_2}{dt} + 2y_2 - y_1 = -\frac{dx}{dt}.$$

b. In the above set of equations, let $x(t) = 3u_{-1}(t)$. Find $y_1(t)$ for all time, subject to the condition that $y_1(t) = 0$ for $t < 0$.

Problem 2-16

a. Consider the differential equation

$$\frac{dy(t)}{dt} + ay(t) = x(t),$$

where a is a positive real constant:
1. Determine the characteristic equation and plot its root in the complex plane.
2. From (1) determine the form of the homogeneous solution $y_h(t)$.
3. Assuming that $y_h(t)$ is real, sketch $y_h(t)$, indicating on this sketch, and on the sketch in (1), the effect of increasing and decreasing the parameter a.

b. Consider the differential equation

$$\frac{d^2y(t)}{dt^2} + \omega_0^2 y(t) = x(t),$$

where ω_0 is a positive real constant, and $x(t)$ is a real time function:
1. Determine the characteristic equation and plot its roots in the complex plane.
2. From (1) determine the form of the homogeneous solution $y_h(t)$.
3. Assuming that $y_h(t)$ is real, show that the two arbitrary constants in $y_h(t)$ must be complex conjugates. Sketch $y_h(t)$ for this case, indicating on this sketch, and on the sketch in (1), the effect of increasing and decreasing the parameter ω_0.

Problem 2-17

a. The equation

$$3s(s + 1) = 0$$

is the characteristic equation for a linear differential equation with constant coefficients. Determine the differential equation in as much detail as possible.

b. For $t > 0$, the homogeneous solution to a linear constant-coefficient differential equation is of the form

$$y_h(t) = A_1 e^{-3t} + A_2 e^{2t},$$

where A_1 and A_2 are arbitrary constants. Determine the differential equation in as much detail as possible.

c. The function

$$y(t) = A_1 e^t + A_2 - 2X e^{2t},$$

where A_1 and A_2 are arbitrary constants, is the general solution for $t > 0$ to a linear differential equation with constant coefficients. The right-hand side of the differential equation is $X e^{2t}$ for $t > 0$. Determine the differential equation.

Problem 2-18

a. Consider the nth-order linear constant-coefficient differential equation

$$a_n \frac{d^n y}{dt_n} + a_{n-1} \frac{d^{n-1} y}{dt^{n-1}} + \cdots + a_0 y = x(t). \qquad (2\text{-}55)$$

The excitation function $x(t)$ has a finite discontinuity at $t = t_0$. Determine the behavior of $y(t)$ and its first n derivatives as t passes through t_0.

b. The differential equation

$$\frac{dy}{dt} + 3y = x(t)$$

has the excitation function $x(t)$ shown in Fig. 2-11. The response $y(t)$ is zero for $t < 0$. Determine the response for all time.

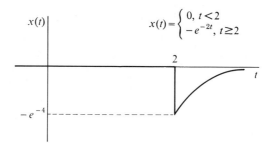

FIG. 2-11. Excitation waveform for Prob. 2-18b.

c. The excitation function $x(t)$ in Eq. (2-55) is known to be the exponential $e^{s_p t}$ in the interval $t_1 < t < t_2$ and is unknown outside that interval. Assuming that the characteristic equation corresponding to Eq. (2-55) does not have s_p as a root, describe the response in the time interval $t_1 < t < t_2$ in as much detail as possible.

d. The differential equation

$$\frac{dy}{dt} + 2y = x(t)$$

has the excitation function $x(t)$ shown in Fig. 2-12. The response $y(t)$ is zero for $t < 0$. Determine the response for all time.

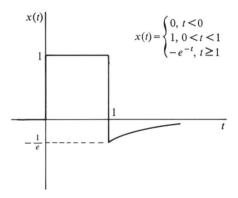

$$x(t) = \begin{cases} 0, & t < 0 \\ 1, & 0 < t < 1 \\ -e^{-t}, & t \geq 1 \end{cases}$$

FIG. 2-12. Excitation waveform for Prob. 2-18d.

Linear operations and linear systems

Systems which are characterized by linear differential equations with constant coefficients and which are initially at rest have several general properties that provide useful aids to the solution of network problems. These properties, however, also apply to a broader class of systems called linear systems, of which the systems characterized by constant-coefficient linear differential equations form only a subclass. The study of linear systems is of importance in many fields, since linear models are appropriate for the analysis of many physical systems, and useful mathematical techniques have been developed to facilitate the analysis of such systems. In order to preserve generality in our discussion, therefore, we shall consider some of the properties of linear systems before we examine these properties in the more restricted context of systems characterized by linear constant-coefficient differential equations.

At the outset we shall introduce the mathematical concept of a *linear operation*, since linear systems are defined in terms of linear operations. Consider an operation T which, when applied to a time function $x(t)$, yields a unique time function $T[x(t)]$. Then T applied to the time function x_1 yields $T(x_1)$, and T applied to x_2 yields $T(x_2)$. *The operation T is linear if and only if*

$$T(ax_1 + bx_2) = aT(x_1) + bT(x_2) \qquad (2\text{-}56)$$

for all complex time functions x_1 and x_2 and for all complex constants a and b. A linear operation thus has the following two properties: (1) applying it to a constant times a function x is equivalent to applying it to x and then multiplying the result by the constant; and (2) applying it to the sum of two functions is equivalent to applying it to each function separately and then adding the results.

We shall define a *linear system* as one whose excitation x and response y are related by a linear operation $T(x) = y$. Hence a linear system has the following properties: (1) the response of a linear system to any given excitation is unique; (2) multiplying the excitation by a constant multiplies the response by the same constant; and (3) the response to the sum of two or more excitations can be computed by finding the response for each excitation acting separately and then adding these responses. The latter property is commonly called the *superposition* property of linear systems. It provides the justification for considering different excitations separately and also for breaking up an excitation into a sum of building blocks that are then treated separately, the total response being obtained as a sum of the responses to the individual building blocks.

Let us consider a few simple operations and test them for linearity.

EXAMPLE 1. The operation $T(x) = cx$. We can then write $T(x_1) = cx_1$ and $T(x_2) = cx_2$. Applying the operation T to $ax_1 + bx_2$, we obtain

$$\begin{aligned} T(ax_1 + bx_2) &= c(ax_1 + bx_2) \\ &= acx_1 + bcx_2 \\ &= aT(x_1) + bT(x_2)\,, \end{aligned}$$

which satisfies the definition (2-56) of a linear operation. Thus a system whose response $y(t)$ is related to its excitation $x(t)$ by the equation $y(t) = cx(t)$ is a linear system.

EXAMPLE 2. The operation $T(x) = cx + d$. We can then write $T(x_1) = cx_1 + d$ and $T(x_2) = cx_2 + d$. Applying the operation T to $ax_1 + bx_2$, we obtain

$$T(ax_1 + bx_2) = c(ax_1 + bx_2) + d\,,$$

which is not equal to $aT(x_1) + bT(x_2)$, and hence this operation is not linear. Thus we could not apply the principle of superposition to a system whose excitation and response are related by such an operation. (We must be careful not to confuse a linear operation with a linear equation such as $y = cx + d$.)

EXAMPLE 3. The operation $T(x) = x^2$. Thus $T(x_1) = x_1^2$ and $T(x_2) = x_2^2$ and

$$T(ax_1 + bx_2) = (ax_1 + bx_2)^2$$
$$= a^2x_1^2 + b^2x_2^2 + 2abx_1x_2 ,$$

which is clearly not equal to $aT(x_1) + bT(x_2)$. Hence this operation is not linear.

EXAMPLE 4. The operation $T(x) = \dfrac{d}{dt}(x)$. Thus $T(x_1) = \dfrac{d}{dt}(x_1)$ and $T(x_2) = \dfrac{d}{dt}(x_2)$. Now we apply this operation to $ax_1 + bx_2$. We recall from the limiting definition of the derivative in calculus that the derivative of a finite sum of terms is the sum of the derivatives of each term and that the derivative of a constant times a function is the constant times the derivative of the function. As can be seen below, these are the two properties that are necessary for the derivative operation to satisfy the definition of linearity (2-56):

$$T(ax_1 + bx_2) = \frac{d}{dt}(ax_1 + bx_2)$$
$$= \frac{d}{dt}(ax_1) + \frac{d}{dt}(bx_2)$$
$$= a\frac{d}{dt}(x_1) + b\frac{d}{dt}(x_2)$$
$$= aT(x_1) + bT(x_2) .$$

Similarly it can be verified that the same result applies to a derivative of any order; i.e., the operation $T(x) = d^q x/dt^q$ is a linear operation.

Problem 2-19

Using the definition of a linear operator, determine whether each of the following operations is linear:

1. $T(x) = \text{Re}(x)$.

2. $T(x) = \sin x$.

3. $T[x(t)] = \int_{t_0}^{t} x(\tau)d\tau$, where t_0 is a constant.

4. $T[x(t)] = tx(t)$.

5. $T[x(t)] = x(t - \delta)$, where δ is a constant.

6. $T(x) = T_1(x) + T_2(x)$, where T_1 and T_2 are linear operations.

7. $T(x) = e^x$.

Problem 2-20

From the definition of linearity, prove that for a linear system the response is identically zero if the excitation is zero for all time.

Problem 2-21

In any physical system, the response at any instant of time cannot depend on the future of the excitation. A system that has this property is called a *realizable* system.

a. Consider a realizable system which is not necessarily linear but for which the response for any given excitation is unique. For an excitation $x_1(t)$, the response is $y_1(t)$, and for an excitation $x_2(t)$, the response is $y_2(t)$. The excitations $x_1(t)$ and $x_2(t)$ are chosen such that they are identical for $t < 0$ and are different for $t > 0$. What statement can be made about the relationship between $y_1(t)$ and $y_2(t)$ for $t < 0$?

b. Apply the result in (a), with $x_1(t) = 0$ for all time and $x_2(t) = 0$ for $t < 0$, to show that if a *linear* realizable system has an excitation that is zero for $t < 0$, then the response must be zero for $t < 0$.

Some properties of linear differential equations

In order to apply the results of the previous section to systems characterized by linear constant-coefficient differential equations we shall first demonstrate that a system that is initially at rest and whose excitation and response are related by such a differential equation is a linear system. We shall first show this result for the case of a system governed by a first-order differential equation relating an excitation $x(t)$ and a response $y(t)$, namely

$$a_1 \frac{dy}{dt} + a_0 y = x. \tag{2-57}$$

We assume that $x(t) = 0$ for $t < 0$ and that the solution $y(t)$ is zero for $t < 0$; i.e., the system is initially at rest. It has already been mentioned that such a solution $y(t)$ is unique, and hence the uniqueness requirement of a linear system is satisfied. In order to test for linearity, we first consider an excitation $x_1(t)$ to be applied. The response $y_1(t)$ is a solution of the differential equation

$$a_1 \frac{dy_1}{dt} + a_0 y_1 = x_1 . \tag{2-58}$$

Likewise the response $y_2(t)$ to an excitation $x_2(t)$ is a solution of the differential equation

$$a_1 \frac{dy_2}{dt} + a_0 y_2 = x_2 . \tag{2-59}$$

In both Eq. (2-58) and Eq. (2-59) the excitations are assumed to be zero for $t < 0$, and $y_1(t)$ and $y_2(t)$ are the unique responses that are zero for $t < 0$.

Multiplying both sides of Eq. (2-58) by a constant a and both sides of Eq. (2-59) by another constant b, and adding the resulting equations, we obtain

$$aa_1 \frac{dy_1}{dt} + aa_0 y_1 + ba_1 \frac{dy_2}{dt} + ba_0 y_2 = ax_1 + bx_2 , \tag{2-60}$$

which can be rearranged to give

$$a_1 \frac{d}{dt}(ay_1 + by_2) + a_0(ay_1 + by_2) = ax_1 + bx_2 . \tag{2-61}$$

Hence $ay_1 + by_2$ is a response corresponding to the excitation $ax_1 + bx_2$. Since both $y_1(t)$ and $y_2(t)$ are zero for $t < 0$, then $ay_1 + by_2$ is also zero for $t < 0$. As a consequence of the uniqueness property of the differential equation, $ay_1 + by_2$ is the only solution that satisfies this initial rest condition. Consequently a system which is at rest for $t < 0$ and whose excitation and response are related by Eq. (2-57) is a linear system.

A similar argument can be applied[1] to show that a system which is initially at rest and whose response y and excitation x are related by the nth-order differential equation

$$a_n \frac{d^n y}{dt^n} + a_{n-1} \frac{d^{n-1} y}{dt^{n-1}} + \cdots + a_1 \frac{dy}{dt} + a_0 y = x \tag{2-62}$$

is also a linear system. It follows, therefore, that the superposition property applies to any system characterized by a linear constant-coefficient differential equation of the form (2-62) when the system is initially at rest.

---

[1] See Prob. 2-22.

Another useful property of such systems states that if y is the response to an excitation x for initial rest conditions, then $d^q y/dt^q$ is the response to an excitation $d^q x/dt^q$, again for initial rest conditions. To establish this result, we start with the differential equation relating x and y, i.e., Eq. (2-62). If we introduce the notation

$$L_1(y) = a_n \frac{d^n y}{dt^n} + a_{n-1} \frac{d^{n-1} y}{dt^{n-1}} + \cdots + a_1 \frac{dy}{dt} + a_0 y, \qquad (2\text{-}63)$$

where L_1 represents a differential operator of order n, then the differential equation (2-62) can be written more compactly as

$$L_1(y) = x. \qquad (2\text{-}64)$$

We assume, as before, that the system is initially at rest; i.e., $x(t)$ and $y(t)$ are both zero for $t < 0$. We now differentiate both sides of Eq. (2-64) q times. Since the operation of differentiation is linear and has the commutative property

$$\frac{d^q}{dt^q} \left[\frac{d^r y}{dt^r} \right] = \frac{d^r}{dt^r} \left[\frac{d^q y}{dt^q} \right] \qquad (2\text{-}65)$$

and since the coefficients in the differential equation are constants, we can write[1]

$$\frac{d^q}{dt^q} L_1(y) = L_1 \left[\frac{d^q y}{dt^q} \right]. \qquad (2\text{-}66)$$

It follows, therefore, that

$$L_1 \left[\frac{d^q y}{dt^q} \right] = \frac{d^q x}{dt^q}. \qquad (2\text{-}67)$$

We observe that, if x and y are zero for $t < 0$, then $d^q x/dt^q$ and $d^q y/dt^q$ are also zero for $t < 0$, and hence $d^q y/dt^q$ is the unique response to the excitation $d^q x/dt^q$ for initial-rest conditions. A similar result holds with respect to integration of the excitation and response.[2]

---

[1] In establishing this property we have implicitly required that all the derivatives indicated in the expressions exist. However, this requirement is in general not satisfied at $t = 0$ for the excitations we consider. In such cases the property must be established by considering the excitation as a limit of a sequence of functions for which the required derivatives exist. We shall assume without proof that the properties derived in the text and in the problems on the assumption of well-behaved excitation functions hold for all the excitations that we shall encounter.

[2] See Prob. 2-24d.

Two other useful properties of the linear differential equation with (real) constant coefficients, for initial-rest conditions, are:[1] (1) if $y(t)$ is the response for a complex excitation function $x(t)$, then the real (imaginary) part of $y(t)$ is the response for an excitation function equal to the real (imaginary) part of $x(t)$; (2) if $y(t)$ is the response for a complex excitation function $x(t)$, then the conjugate of $y(t)$ is the response for an excitation function equal to the conjugate of $x(t)$. The latter result can be applied to the case in which a real excitation function is constructed by adding two conjugate complex exponential building blocks; i.e., the excitation function is $Xe^{st} + X^*e^{s^*t}$. If we determine the response $y(t)$ for an excitation equal to one of these building blocks, say Xe^{st}, then using the superposition property we can immediately write down the response for the total excitation function as $y(t) + y^*(t)$. This result shows, incidentally, that the response to an excitation Re $[Xe^{st}]$ is Re $[y(t)]$, which is the first of the two properties just stated.

Problem 2-22

a. Consider a system which is initially at rest and which is described by a linear differential equation of the form

$$L_1(y) = x,$$

where x is the excitation, y is the response, and L_1 is an nth-order linear differential operator. Show that the system is a linear system.

b. Consider a system which is initially at rest and which is described by a linear differential equation of the form

$$L_1(y) = L_2(x),$$

where x is the excitation, y is the response, and L_1 and L_2 are nth- and mth-order linear differential operators respectively. Show that the system is a linear system.

Problem 2-23

Prove that any system for which the excitation and response are related by an nth-order linear differential equation but which is not initially at rest (i.e., not at rest prior to the application of the excitation) is not a linear system.

---

[1] See Prob. 2-24a, b, c.

Problem 2-24

Consider a system which is initially at rest and for which the excitation $x(t)$ and response $y(t)$ are related by a differential equation of the form

$$L_1(y) = x,$$

where L_1 is an nth-order linear differential operator with real coefficients. If $y_1(t)$ is the response of the system when $x_1(t)$ is the excitation, show that:

a. Re (y_1) is the response when Re (x_1) is the excitation.

b. Im (y_1) is the response when Im (x_1) is the excitation.

c. The complex conjugate of y_1 is the response when the complex conjugate of x_1 is the excitation.

d. $\int_{-\infty}^{t} y_1(\tau)d\tau$ is the response when $\int_{-\infty}^{t} x_1(\tau)d\tau$ is the excitation. To show this you may make use of the following relations proved in calculus:

$$\frac{d}{dt}\left[\int_{-\infty}^{t} f(\tau)d\tau\right] = f(t);$$

$$\int_{-\infty}^{t}\left[\frac{df(\tau)}{d\tau}\right]d\tau = f(t) - f(-\infty).$$

(Since the system is initially at rest, $x_1(t)$, $y_1(t)$, and the first $n - 1$ derivatives of $y_1(t)$ are zero at $t = -\infty$.)

e. $y_1(t')$ is the response when $x_1(t')$ is the excitation, where $t' = t - t_0$, and t_0 is a constant.

Problem 2-25

Consider a system which is described by a linear differential equation with real, constant coefficients and which is initially at rest. When the excitation $x(t)$ is given by

$$x(t) = u_{-1}(t)\, e^{s_p t},$$

the response is

$$y(t) = \frac{1}{s_p + 2}(e^{s_p t} - e^{-2t})u_{-1}(t).$$

Without reconstructing the differential equation, find the system response for each of the following three excitations:

1. $x(t) = u_{-1}(t)\cos 2t$.

2. $x(t) = u_{-1}(t)\sin 2t$.

3. $x(t) = u_{-1}(t)\cos\left(2t - \dfrac{\pi}{4}\right)$.

Solution of linear constant-coefficient differential equations with a sum of derivative terms on the right-hand side

In the solution of many problems we shall encounter differential equations in which the right-hand side is not a single function $x(t) = u_{-1}(t)Xe^{sp}$ but is a sum of such a function and one or more of its derivatives. The general form of such equations is

$$a_n \frac{d^n y}{dt^n} + a_{n-1} \frac{d^{n-1}y}{dt^{n-1}} + \cdots + a_1 \frac{dy}{dt} + a_0 y \qquad (2\text{-}68)$$

$$= b_m \frac{d^m x}{dt^m} + b_{m-1} \frac{d^{m-1}x}{dt^{m-1}} + \cdots + b_1 \frac{dx}{dt} + b_0 x,$$

where the a_k and the b_k are real constants. Equation (2-68) can be written more compactly as

$$L_1(y) = L_2(x), \qquad (2\text{-}69)$$

where L_1 is defined in (2-63) and

$$L_2(x) = b_m \frac{d^m x}{dt^m} + b_{m-1} \frac{d^{m-1}x}{dt^{m-1}} + \cdots + b_1 \frac{dx}{dt} + b_0 x. \qquad (2\text{-}70)$$

The solution to Eq. (2-68) under initial-rest conditions can be found by making use of the properties discussed above in connection with the simpler differential equation

$$L_1(y) = x. \qquad (2\text{-}71)$$

The procedure is first to find the solution $y_1(t)$ to Eq. (2-71) under initial-rest conditions, using methods we have already described. Since the system characterized by Eq. (2-71) is linear, multiplication of the solution $y_1(t)$ by b_0 gives the solution for the case in which the right-hand side of the equation is $b_0 x$. As a consequence of the derivative property (2-67), the solution to the equation

$$L_1(y) = b_1 \frac{dx}{dt},$$

under initial-rest conditions, is given by $b_1 \frac{dy_1}{dt}$. In a similar manner, solutions corresponding to other derivative terms on the right-hand side of Eq. (2-68) can be written down. Application of the principle of superposition enables us to add these individual results to obtain the complete solution

$$y(t) = b_m \frac{d^m y_1}{dt^m} + b_{m-1} \frac{d^{m-1} y_1}{dt^{m-1}} + \cdots + b_1 \frac{dy_1}{dt} + b_0 y_1 . \qquad (2\text{-}72)$$

Thus the solution to the more general equation (2-68) can be written down directly once the solution to Eq. (2-71) has been found.

It can readily be shown that a system which is initially at rest and whose excitation and response are characterized by the differential equation

$$L_1(y) = L_2(x) \qquad (2\text{-}73)$$

is a linear system. We conclude, therefore, that the principle of super-position can be applied to such a system.

The impulse and other singularity functions

In the previous section we presented methods for obtaining the solution to a linear constant-coefficient differential equation when the right-hand side contains terms that are derivatives of the excitation function. When the excitation function has a discontinuity at $t = 0$, a problem arises, because the derivatives of this function, defined as for analytic functions, do not exist at $t = 0$. In order to be able to speak of such derivatives, we define a series of so-called *singularity functions*. When the proper restrictions are observed with respect to their manipulation, singularity functions provide useful artifices for obtaining simple solutions to many problems. The properties we shall define for singularity functions are justified in terms of arguments involving the limiting forms of continuous functions.[1] If doubt were to arise as to whether a manipulation is valid, we should have to resort to such limiting arguments to resolve the question.

On page 64 we have already defined one singularity function—the unit step function $u_{-1}(t)$. We shall now define the *unit impulse*, denoted by $u_0(t)$. The unit impulse has the property that its integral is $u_{-1}(t)$; i.e.,

$$\int_{-\infty}^{t} u_0(\tau)\, d\tau = u_{-1}(t) . \qquad (2\text{-}74)$$

Thus the area under the unit impulse $u_0(t)$ is zero for $t < 0$, has a discontinuity at $t = 0$, and is unity for all $t > 0$. The unit impulse $u_0(t)$ therefore has the following properties:
1. It is zero everywhere except at $t = 0$.
2. It is infinite at $t = 0$.
3. It has unit area.

---

[1] See, for example, Prob. 2-28.

FIG. 2-13. Graphical representation of unit impulse $u_0(t)$. The symbol beside the impulse (1 in this case) denotes the area under the impulse function.

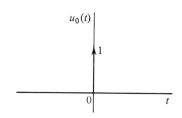

The unit impulse $u_0(t)$ is usually represented graphically in the manner shown in Fig. 2-13. Since the unit step function is the integral of the unit impulse, we shall regard the impulse as the derivative of the step; i.e.,

$$u_0(t) = \frac{d}{dt}[u_{-1}(t)].$$ (2-75)

Such an equation must, however, be interpreted with caution, since the derivative of a discontinuous function does not exist in the usual sense.

If the unit impulse is multiplied by a constant A, then the product $Au_0(t)$ has the property

$$\int_{-\infty}^{t} Au_0(\tau)\, d\tau = A\int_{-\infty}^{t} u_0(\tau)\, d\tau = Au_{-1}(t).$$ (2-76)

Thus $Au_0(t)$ is zero everywhere except $t = 0$, is infinite at $t = 0$, and has area A. This product is called an impulse of area A.

The product $f(t)u_0(t)$, where $f(t)$ is a continuous time function, is also zero everywhere except at $t = 0$. Its integral is $f(0)$ for $t > 0$, as can be shown by integration by parts, and hence $f(t)u_0(t)$ can be written as $f(0)u_0(t)$, which is an impulse of area $f(0)$ occurring at $t = 0$. If $f(t)$ is zero at $t = 0$, then the product $f(t)u_0(t)$ has zero area. An impulse of zero area will be defined to be identically zero.

We shall define the derivative of the product of the unit step function and an analytic function $g(t)$ by applying the usual rule for differentiating a product of analytic functions, but with the derivative of $u_{-1}(t)$ interpreted as $u_0(t)$, as discussed above. Thus

$$\frac{d}{dt}[u_{-1}(t)g(t)] = u_{-1}(t)g'(t) + u_0(t)g(t)$$

$$= u_{-1}(t)g'(t) + u_0(t)g(0).$$ (2-77)

Just as we define the unit impulse to have the property that its integral is equal to the unit step, we can likewise define the singularity function

$u_1(t)$, sometimes called the unit doublet, to have the property that its integral is $u_0(t)$. In a similar manner we can define higher-order singularity functions $u_2(t)$, $u_3(t)$, ..., $u_k(t)$ .... All these functions (for $k \geq 0$) have the properties that they are zero everywhere except at $t = 0$ and the integral of $u_k(t)$ is equal to $u_{k-1}(t)$; i.e.,

$$\int_{-\infty}^{t} u_k(\tau)\, d\tau = u_{k-1}(t) . \tag{2-78}$$

In view of this property, we shall regard $u_k(t)$ as the derivative of $u_{k-1}(t)$.

In addition to the singularity functions $u_k(t)$, where $k \geq -1$, it is possible to define other so-called singularity functions by integrating $u_{-1}(t)$ one or more times. For example, the integral of $u_{-1}(t)$, written $u_{-2}(t)$, represents a function that is zero for $t < 0$ and is a "ramp" function of unit slope for $t > 0$. Likewise, the function $u_{-3}(t)$, obtained by integrating $u_{-2}(t)$, is equal to $t^2/2$ for $t > 0$, and $u_{-4}(t)$ represents the function $t^3/6$ for $t > 0$. In general, $u_{-j}(t)$ represents the function $t^{j-1}/(j-1)!$ for $t > 0$, when j is positive. Since these functions are defined in terms of the integral of the step, they are, of course, all zero for $t < 0$. Some of these singularity functions are sketched in Fig. 2-14. For a system that is initially at rest

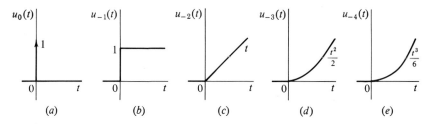

FIG. 2-14. Family of singularity functions obtained by successive integration of the unit impulse $u_0(t)$.

and characterized by a linear constant-coefficient differential equation whose excitation function is one of these singularity functions, say $u_{-j}(t)$ ($j \geq 1$), the response can be obtained by first finding the response for a unit step excitation function and then integrating the result $j - 1$ times.

Problem 2-26

In each case below, the excitation $x(t)$ and response $y(t)$ of a system, which is at rest for $t < 0$, are related by the given differential equation. For the excitation given, find the response for all t:

1. $\dfrac{dy}{dt} + y = \dfrac{dx}{dt}$; $x(t) = u_0(t)$.

2. $\dfrac{dy}{dt} + 2y = 3\dfrac{dx}{dt} - x$; $x(t) = 6u_{-1}(t)$.

3. $\dfrac{d^2y}{dt^2} - \dfrac{dy}{dt} = -12x$; $x(t) = (2e^{-t} - e^{-2t})u_{-1}(t)$.

4. $3\dfrac{dy}{dt} + 6y = \dfrac{dx}{dt} + x$; $x(t) = (1 + e^{-t})u_{-1}(t)$.

5. $\dfrac{d^2y}{dt^2} - 3\dfrac{dy}{dt} + 2y = x$; $x(t) = u_{-2}(t)$.

Problem 2-27

The excitation $x(t)$ and the response $y(t)$ of a given system are related by the differential equation

$$\frac{dy}{dt} + 2y = \frac{dx}{dt} + 3x .$$

The response for $t > 0$ to an excitation $x_1(t)$ is observed to be

$$y(t) = 2e^{-t} + 5e^{-2t} + \text{Re}\left[\frac{(j\omega + 3)(1 + j)}{j\omega + 2} e^{j\omega t}\right].$$

It is not known whether the system was at rest prior to $t = 0$.
a. Determine $x_1(t)$ for $t > 0$.
b. Is there any time function that can be added to $x_1(t)$ without changing the specified response? How is this time function determined?

Problem 2-28

The heuristic reasoning used in the treatment of step functions and impulses can often be justified by considering the step or the impulse as the limit of a sequence of functions whose derivatives of all orders are defined for all time. One such sequence of functions is discussed in this problem.
a. Consider the sequence of functions

$$f_1, f_2, \ldots, f_n, \ldots,$$

where
$$f_n(t) = \frac{1}{\pi}(\tan^{-1}nt) + \tfrac{1}{2},$$

and the principal value of $\tan^{-1}nt$ is to be used, i.e., $-\dfrac{\pi}{2} \le \tan^{-1}nt \le \dfrac{\pi}{2}$.

Sketch $f_n(t)$ for several values of n, and observe its behavior as $n \to \infty$. What singularity function does it approach?

b. Observe that the function $f_n(t)$ of (a) is analytic; i.e., its derivatives of all orders exist for all t. Determine

$$f_n'(t) = \frac{df_n(t)}{dt}.$$

What is the area under the curve $f_n'(t)$? Sketch $f_n'(t)$ for several values of n, and observe its behavior as $n \to \infty$. Note that in the limit this function has the properties defined for a unit impulse.

Problem 2-29

a. Express $u_{-2}(t)$ as the product of $u_{-1}(t)$ and a polynomial in t.

b. Express $u_{-n}(t)$, $n \geq 1$, as the product of $u_{-1}(t)$ and a polynomial in t.

c. Express the following function as a linear combination of singularity functions with constant coefficients:

$$f(t) = \begin{cases} 0, & t < 0; \\ t^2 - t^3, & t > 0. \end{cases}$$

3

Response of Networks
to Suddenly Applied Excitations

Formal solution for networks initially at rest

Series RL network with real exponential excitation. Let us return now to the solution of the series RL network introduced previously on page 49 and shown again in Fig. 3-1. It is recalled that application of Kirchhoff's

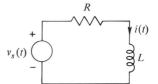

FIG. 3-1. Series RL network
with voltage source.

laws and introduction of the voltage-current relations for the elements yields a first-order differential equation for the current $i(t)$:

$$L\frac{di}{dt} + Ri = v_s(t).$$ (3-1)

We consider an excitation $v_s(t)$ that is zero for $t < 0$ and is a real exponential function of time or is the sum of two conjugate complex exponential functions for $t > 0$. It is assumed that the network is at rest for $t < 0$; i.e., $i(t) = 0$ for $t < 0$.

We shall examine first the case of a real exponential excitation, such that $v_s(t) = u_{-1}(t)V_s e^{s_p t}$, where V_s and s_p are real. As discussed previously, the solution for $t > 0$ consists of a particular integral and a homogeneous solution.

The homogeneous equation corresponding to Eq. (3-1) is

$$L \frac{di}{dt} + Ri = 0. \tag{3-2}$$

This equation describes the equilibrium conditions for the network with the source set to zero; i.e., it represents the equilibrium equation for the basic network. The solution of the homogeneous equation is

$$i_h = A e^{s_1 t}, \tag{3-3}$$

where A is an arbitrary constant and s_1 is a root of the characteristic equation

$$Ls + R = 0. \tag{3-4}$$

In this case $s_1 = -R/L$, and the homogeneous solution is

$$i_h = A e^{-(R/L)t}. \tag{3-5}$$

This homogeneous solution represents the behavior of the network in the absence of the source, i.e., the behavior of the basic network. The complex frequency of the root of the characteristic equation, in this case $s_1 = -R/L$, is said to be the *natural frequency* of the network, since an exponential with this frequency can exist as a current in the network even with the sources set to zero and reflects, so to speak, the "natural" behavior of the network.

It can readily be verified for this network that the same characteristic equation and hence the same natural frequency is obtained for every element current or voltage in the network. Thus we are justified in speaking of the natural behavior of this network independent of which element variable is considered as the response. The result that the same natural frequencies are obtained for any element voltage or current in a network applies in most situations we shall encounter, and hence we shall be able to speak of natural frequencies of a network rather than natural frequencies associated with a given current or voltage response. A formal justification for this result will be given in Chap. 5, when we discuss general methods for examining all the natural frequencies of a network.

The particular integral of the solution of Eq. (3-1) is given by

$$i_p = \frac{V_s}{Ls_p + R} e^{s_p t}, \tag{3-6}$$

as we have seen in our discussion of the solution of differential equations. The general solution for $t > 0$ can be written as the sum of the homogeneous solution and the particular integral, giving

$$i = i_h + i_p = Ae^{-(R/L)t} + \frac{V_s}{Ls_p + R} e^{s_p t} . \qquad (3\text{-}7)$$

Since we have imposed the condition that $i = 0$ for $t < 0$ and since the excitation applied at $t = 0$ is finite, then we know from our study of differential equations (pages 74 and 75) that $i(0+) = i(0-) = 0$. From Eq. (3-7), therefore, we find

$$A = -\frac{V_s}{Ls_p + R} .$$

The total solution for the current is thus given by

$$i(t) = \begin{cases} 0 & \text{for } t \leq 0 \\ \dfrac{V_s}{Ls_p + R} (e^{s_p t} - e^{-(R/L)t}) & \text{for } t \geq 0 . \end{cases}$$

Since $i(t)$ is finite at $t = 0$, we can use the step function to form a single expression that is valid for all time, namely,

$$i(t) = u_{-1}(t) \frac{V_s}{Ls_p + R} (e^{s_p t} - e^{-(R/L)t}) . \qquad (3\text{-}8)$$

The solution for $t > 0$ contains two exponential functions: one exponential (the homogeneous solution), with complex frequency $-R/L$, represents the natural behavior of the network without sources, and the other exponential (the particular integral) has a complex frequency that is identical with the complex frequency s_p of the exponential source voltage. This result could, of course, have been written down directly from Eq. (2-51), given previously in connection with the general discussion of the solution of differential equations, but the steps in the solution have been repeated in this example in order to emphasize the significance of each term in the solution and to provide an interpretation of each term with respect to the network behavior.

For the case in which $s_p = 0$ the source voltage is a step of height V_s, and the solution is

$$i(t) = u_{-1}(t) \frac{V_s}{R} (1 - e^{-(R/L)t}) . \qquad (3\text{-}9)$$

A plot of this solution is shown in Fig. 3-2. In this case, the particular

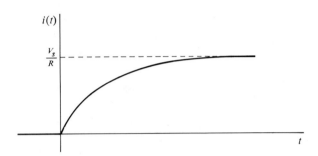

FIG. 3-2. Plot of the response $i(t)$ for the RL network of Fig. 3-1, for the case in which $v_s(t) = V_s u_{-1}(t)$.

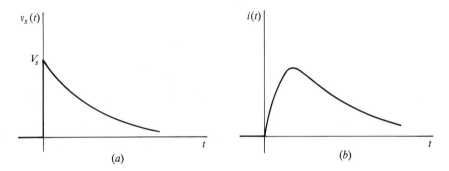

FIG. 3-3. (a) Source voltage applied to series RL network; (b) current response of network plotted to same time scale as (a), for the case $s_p = -(1/3)R/L$.

integral is a constant equal to V_s/R, and the homogeneous solution decays exponentially, approaching zero asymptotically.

When s_p is real and negative, the response (3-8) is the sum of two decaying exponentials (assuming $s_p \neq -R/L$) and has the form shown in Fig. 3-3. This figure also gives a plot of the source voltage $v_s(t)$ for comparison with the response. In the example for which the graphs are drawn, $s_p > -R/L$, and hence the particular integral predominates over the homogeneous solution when t becomes sufficiently large, since the latter decays more rapidly than the former. For the case in which $s_p < -R/L$, the particular integral would decay more rapidly than the homogeneous solution.

Series RL network with suddenly applied sinusoidal excitation. We shall now proceed to the problem of finding the current $i(t)$ in the series RL

network of Fig. 3-1 when the network is at rest for $t < 0$ and when the excitation can be represented as the sum of two complex exponential functions. We have shown previously that we can write

$$v_s(t) = u_{-1}(t)\tfrac{1}{2}[V_s e^{s_p t} + V_s^* e^{s_p^* t}]$$

$$= u_{-1}(t)|V_s|e^{\sigma t} \cos(\omega t + \phi),\qquad(3\text{-}10)$$

where $V_s = |V_s|e^{j\varphi}$ and $s_p = \sigma + j\omega$. Alternatively, $v_s(t)$ can be written in the form

$$v_s(t) = u_{-1}(t)\,\mathrm{Re}\,[V_s e^{s_p t}].\qquad(3\text{-}11)$$

As we have seen from our examination of the properties of differential equations, we find the solution for this excitation by first finding the solution for an excitation function $u_{-1}(t)V_s e^{s_p t}$. The total solution is then obtained either by taking one-half the sum of this solution and its conjugate or, equivalently, by taking the real part of this solution.

For the case of the series RL network, we shall consider the excitation to be a suddenly applied sinusoid of fixed amplitude, i.e.,

$$v_s(t) = u_{-1}(t)A \cos(\omega t + \phi).\qquad(3\text{-}12)$$

This can be written in the form of Eq. (3-11), where $V_s = Ae^{j\phi}$ and $s_p = j\omega$. The solution for an excitation function $u_{-1}(t)V_s e^{j\omega t}$ can be written from Eq. (3-8) by putting $s_p = j\omega$, yielding

$$u_{-1}(t)\frac{V_s}{j\omega L + R}\left(e^{j\omega t} - e^{-(R/L)t}\right).\qquad(3\text{-}13)$$

As in the examples discussed previously, the response for $t > 0$ is the sum of two terms: a particular integral and a homogeneous solution. The particular integral reflects the complex frequency of the excitation function, and the homogeneous solution is an exponential whose complex frequency is the natural frequency of the network. Taking the real part of (3-13), we obtain the desired solution for the current; i.e.,

$$i(t) = u_{-1}(t)\,\mathrm{Re}\left[\frac{V_s}{j\omega L + R}\left(e^{j\omega t} - e^{-(R/L)t}\right)\right]$$

$$= u_{-1}(t)\frac{|V_s|}{\sqrt{R^2 + \omega^2 L^2}}\left[\cos(\omega t + \phi - \theta) - e^{-(R/L)t}\cos(\phi - \theta)\right],$$

$$(3\text{-}14)$$

where $\theta = \tan^{-1}(\omega L/R)$. A plot of the response $i(t)$, shown in Fig. 3-4, demonstrates the two components of this response.

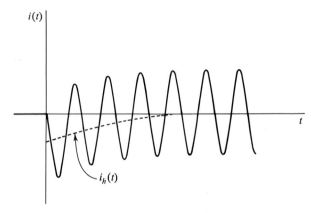

FIG. 3-4. Response of series RL network to suddenly applied sinusoid. Dashed line shows homogeneous solution.

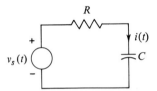

FIG. 3-5. Series RC network
with voltage source.

Series RC network with step excitation. As another example of a simple network with exponential excitation, let us consider the series RC network with a voltage source, shown in Fig. 3-5. Suppose we wish to find the current response $i(t)$ for the case in which $v_s(t)$ is a voltage step of value V_s, i.e.,

$$v_s(t) = V_s u_{-1}(t),$$

and in which the network is at rest for $t < 0$. The equation for the current is

$$Ri + \frac{1}{C} \int_{-\infty}^{t} i(\tau)\, d\tau = v_s, \qquad (3\text{-}15)$$

or, differentiating both sides to remove the integral, we obtain

$$R\frac{di}{dt} + \frac{i}{C} = \frac{dv_s}{dt} = V_s u_0(t), \qquad (3\text{-}16)$$

which has an impulse on the right-hand side. In order to solve this equation, we shall make use of the result, derived on page 84, that, if $y(t)$ is the solution of a linear constant-coefficient differential equation in which the excitation function is $x(t)$, then $\dfrac{dy}{dt}$ is the solution for the excitation function $\dfrac{dx}{dt}$, assuming initial-rest conditions in both cases.

In the present example, we first find the response $i_1(t)$ when the right-hand side of Eq. (3-16) is a step of height V_s, assuming $i_1(t) = 0$ for $t < 0$; i.e., we find the solution to the differential equation

$$R \frac{di_1}{dt} + \frac{i_1}{C} = V_s u_{-1}(t) . \tag{3-17}$$

We then differentiate this solution to obtain the solution of Eq. (3-16), in which the excitation function is $V_s u_0(t)$. This will be the desired solution corresponding to initial-rest conditions in the network.

The solution of Eq. (3-17) for initial-rest conditions is

$$i_1(t) = u_{-1}(t) V_s C (1 - e^{-t/RC}) . \tag{3-18}$$

We obtain the solution to (3-16) simply by differentiating (3-18), giving

$$i(t) = u_{-1}(t) \frac{V_s}{R} e^{-t/RC} + u_0(t) V_s C (1 - e^{-t/RC}) . \tag{3-19}$$

Since the coefficient of $u_0(t)$ is zero at $t = 0$, the second term in Eq. (3-19) is an impulse of zero area, and hence the response reduces to

$$i(t) = u_{-1}(t) \frac{V_s}{R} e^{-t/RC} \tag{3-20}$$

We note that in the case of the RC network the root of the characteristic equation and hence the natural frequency of the network is $-1/RC$.

Impulse response of networks. In Chap. 2 we defined the unit impulse and listed its important properties. We shall now introduce the concept of an idealized voltage or current source for which the voltage or current is equal to an impulse, and we shall determine the response of simple networks to such excitations.

The ideal impulse source implies an infinite voltage or current, which cannot, of course, exist in practice. Short, pulselike voltage or current sources occur frequently in practice, however, and can be regarded as impulses without affecting the responses of certain networks. The impulse will assume added importance in our future work because any well-behaved function can be considered to be made up of a sequence of narrow pulses.

A consequence of this result is that, if we know the response of an *RLC* network to a unit impulse source, we can determine the response to an arbitrary source function.[1] The response of a network to a unit impulse source is often designated simply as "the impulse response" of the network.

The responses of networks in which the source or sources are impulses can always be determined by formal methods of solution of differential equations. As we have seen, the first step in the application of these methods is to set up the differential equation for the pertinent voltage or current response with all source terms transferred to the right-hand side of the equation. We then find a solution corresponding to each source term separately and add these solutions to give the total response. When the source voltages or currents are impulses, then the terms on the right-hand side of the differential equation will be impulses or possibly derivatives of impulses. The solution corresponding to a term of this type can be determined by first finding the response when the right-hand side of the differential equation is a unit step. This response is then differentiated an appropriate number of times and multiplied by the appropriate constant to yield the desired solution. A sum of such solutions, each corresponding to one of the terms on the right-hand side of the differential equation, gives the total response of the network.

To illustrate this formal procedure let us find the current $i(t)$ in the *RL* network shown in Fig. 3-6 when the voltage source is an impulse of area A.

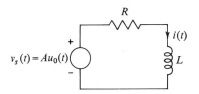

FIG. 3-6. Series *RL* network with impulse voltage source.

The differential equation for $i(t)$ is

$$L\frac{di}{dt} + Ri = Au_0(t).\qquad(3\text{-}21)$$

Since there is an impulse on the right-hand side of this equation, we first find the response with $u_{-1}(t)$ as the excitation function on the right-hand side. Assuming the network is at rest for $t < 0$, the solution of the differential equation with this step excitation function is, as we have seen,

---

[1] See Prob. 3-23.

$$i_1(t) = u_{-1}(t) \frac{1}{R} (1 - e^{-(R/L)t}). \tag{3-22}$$

Differentiation of this solution and multiplication by A give the response to an impulse of area A:

$$i(t) = u_{-1}(t) \frac{A}{R} \cdot \frac{R}{L} e^{-(R/L)t} + u_0(t) \frac{A}{R} (1 - e^{-(R/L)t}). \tag{3-23}$$

Since the second term is an impulse of area zero, this expression for the response reduces to

$$i(t) = u_{-1}(t) \frac{A}{L} e^{-(R/L)t}. \tag{3-24}$$

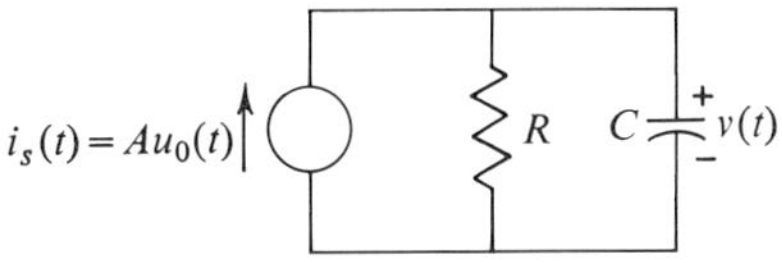

FIG. 3-7. Parallel RC network with impulse current source.

$i_s(t) = A u_0(t)$

As another example consider the parallel RC network with an impulse current source, shown in Fig. 3-7. The differential equation for the voltage response $v(t)$ is

$$C \frac{dv}{dt} + \frac{v}{R} = A u_0(t). \tag{3-25}$$

Again our first step is to find the solution of the equation with the right-hand side equal to $u_{-1}(t)$. This solution is $u_{-1}(t)R(1 - e^{-t/RC})$. We then differentiate this solution and multiply by A to obtain the response to an impulse of area A:

$$v(t) = u_{-1}(t) \frac{A}{C} e^{-t/RC}. \tag{3-26}$$

In each of the examples we have discussed, the impulse response of the network for $t > 0$ is simply an exponential function whose complex frequency is the natural frequency of the network. This result is to be expected, since the value of the impulse excitation is zero for $t > 0$, and hence the solution for $t > 0$ is the homogeneous solution. Thus the impulse response of an RLC network reflects the natural behavior of the network, since it brings into evidence the natural frequencies, which are determined by the basic network, and since it contains no particular integral for $t > 0$.

Problem 3-1

Determine the differential equation relating $v(t)$ and $i(t)$ at the terminals of the network shown in Fig. 3-8.

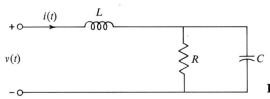

FIG. 3-8. Network for Prob. 3-1.

Problem 3-2

The network of Fig. 3-9 is initially at rest. Determine the voltage $v(t)$ for each of the excitations below:

1. $i_s(t) = u_{-1}(t)$.
2. $i_s(t) = u_{-1}(t) \sin t$.
3. $i_s(t) = u_{-2}(t)$.

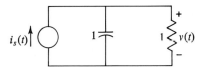

FIG. 3-9. Network for Prob. 3-2.

Problem 3-3

a. For the network of Fig. 3-10, write the differential equation relating $v_C(t)$ and $v_s(t)$.

b. Find $v_C(t)$ for all time if the network is at rest for $t < 0$ and $v_s(t) = u_{-1}(t)$.

c. Find $v_C(t)$ for all time if the network is at rest for $t < 0$ and $v_s(t) = 5u_0(t)$.

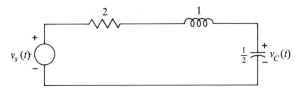

FIG. 3-10. Network for Prob. 3-3.

Problem 3-4

The network of Fig. 3-11 is at rest for $t < 0$. Determine $i(t)$.

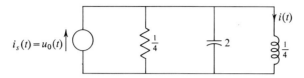

FIG. 3-11. Network for Prob. 3-4.

Problem 3-5

a. For the network of Fig. 3-12, write a differential equation relating the current $i(t)$ to the source values $i_s(t)$ and $v_s(t)$.

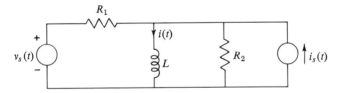

FIG. 3-12. Network for Prob. 3-5.

b. If we are only interested in solving for the current through the inductance, we can replace the part of the network external to the inductance by a Norton equivalent network, using the approach discussed in Prob. 1-18. The network of Fig. 3-12 takes the form shown in Fig. 3-13 with that substitution. Determine R_{eq} and $i_{eq}(t)$ in terms of R_1, R_2, $i_s(t)$, and $v_s(t)$. Verify that the differential equation relating $i(t)$ to $i_s(t)$ and $v_s(t)$, derived from this equivalent network, is the same as that found in (a).

FIG. 3-13. Network equivalent to the network of Fig. 3-12 with respect to the inductance terminals. The resistive portion external to the inductance has been replaced by a Norton equivalent network (Prob. 3-5).

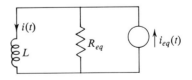

c. Determine $i(t)$ for all time if the network is at rest for $t < 0$ and if $v_s(t) = V_s u_{-1}(t)$ and $i_s(t) = I_s u_{-1}(t)$.

Problem 3-6

For the network of Fig. 3-14, determine the current $i(t)$ for all time. The network is at rest for $t < 0$.

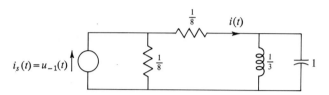

FIG. 3-14. Network for Prob. 3-6.

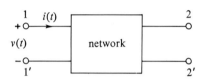

FIG. 3-15. Two-terminal-pair network for Prob. 3-7.

Problem 3-7

For the two-terminal-pair network of Fig. 3-15, the relation between $v(t)$ and $i(t)$ is

$$v(t) = 2i(t) + 2\frac{di(t)}{dt}$$

when the terminals 2 and 2' are open-circuited. The relation is

$$v(t) = i(t)$$

when the terminals 2 and 2' are short-circuited. Determine a possible network having these properties.

Problem 3-8

Consider the mechanical system shown in Fig. 3-16. From the laws of mechanics the equilibrium equation relating the force on the mass and the

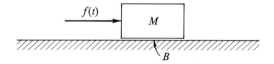

FIG. 3-16. Mechanical system with mass M, viscous resistance B, and applied force $f(t)$ (Prob. 3-8).

velocity of the mass in this system can be written as

$$M \frac{d\eta}{dt} + B\eta = f(t) \,,$$

where M is the mass of the body, B is the viscous resistance, $f(t)$ is an externally applied force, and η is the velocity in the direction of the force. The mechanical system is assumed to be at rest before a force is applied.

a. Synthesize an electrical network such that for a current excitation $i(t)$ numerically equal to the driving force $f(t)$, the resulting voltage response $v(t)$ is numerically equal to the velocity $\eta(t)$.

b. Synthesize an electrical network such that for a voltage excitation $v(t)$ numerically equal to the driving force $f(t)$, the resulting current response $i(t)$ is numerically equal to the velocity $\eta(t)$.

The electrical networks obtained in (a) and (b) are called electrical analogues of the mechanical system. They are often very useful in experimental studies, since it is much easier to realize a variety of electrical systems and electrical excitations than it is to realize the corresponding mechanical ones.

c. Suppose that we wish to make an experimental study of the mechanical system of Fig. 3-16 in terms of an electrical analogue. In particular, let us study how the response to a given excitation changes as we vary the mass M. How could this be done by changing parameters in the electrical system using (1) the electrical analogue obtained in (a); (2) the electrical analogue obtained in (b)?

Problem 3-9

a. For the network of Fig. 3-17, write the differential equation relating $v(t)$ to $i_s(t)$ and $v_s(t)$.

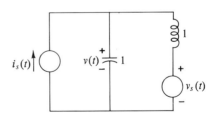

FIG. 3-17. Network for
Prob. 3-9.

b. If $i_s(t) = u_{-1}(t)$, $v_s(t) = u_{-1}(t)$, and the network is at rest for $t < 0$, find $v(t)$.

Problem 3-10

Consider a network whose excitation $x(t)$ is a complex exponential for $t > 0$ and whose response $y(t)$ is related to the excitation by a linear constant-coefficient differential equation that is of the nth order in y. We recall that, in general, the response is composed of two parts, viz.,

$$y(t) = y_h(t) + y_p(t) \qquad \text{for } t > 0, \tag{3-27}$$

where $y_h(t)$ and $y_p(t)$ are the homogeneous and the particular solutions, respectively. The homogeneous solution $y_h(t)$ contains constants whose values are determined by a set of initial conditions. The initial conditions usually specified are the values of $y(t)$ and its first $n - 1$ derivatives at $t = 0+$; i.e., $y^{(k)}(0+)$, $k = 0, 1, \ldots, (n - 1)$, where $y^{(k)}(t)$ denotes the kth derivative of $y(t)$.

We recall also that the particular solution is determined independently of the initial conditions and contains no undetermined constants. Thus, if the initial conditions that are specified are values other than those which the particular solution assumes at $t = 0+$, then the homogeneous solution must make up this difference. Hence, we may think of $y_h(t)$ as a "buffer," which supplies the discrepancy between the actual response $y(t)$ and the particular solution $y_p(t)$. In particular we have from Eq. (3-27)

$$y_h^{(k)}(0+) = y^{(k)}(0+) - y_p^{(k)}(0+) \qquad k = 0, 1, \ldots, (n - 1).$$

a. If the homogeneous solution is zero for $t > 0$, what relation must exist between the particular solution and the initial conditions?

b. If the relation between the particular solution and the initial conditions that was found in (a) does exist, is it necessary that the homogeneous solution be zero for $t > 0$? Explain.

c. Assume that the differential equation is of order 2 (i.e., $n = 2$). For each of the following cases, determine whether the homogeneous solution is zero for $t > 0$:

1. Initial conditions: $y(0+) = 1$; $\left. \dfrac{dy}{dt} \right|_{t = 0+} = 0$.

   Particular solution: $y_p(t) = e^{-3t}, t > 0$.

2. Initial conditions: $y(0+) = 0$; $\left. \dfrac{dy}{dt} \right|_{t = 0+} = 0$.

   Particular solution: $y_p(t) = 1 - e^{-t}, t > 0$.

Problem 3-11

In an RC network with a suddenly applied sinusoidal excitation the amplitude of the homogeneous solution depends on the phase of the excitation at $t = 0$. For some chosen phase the homogeneous solution is zero; that is, the total solution consists only of the particular integral. For the network of Fig. 3-18, determine a value for the phase angle ϕ of the voltage source such that the homogeneous solution for $v(t)$ is zero if the network is at rest for $t < 0$. (Give ϕ to the nearest degree.)

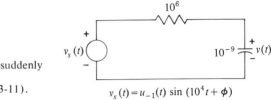

FIG. 3-18. RC network with suddenly applied sinusoidal excitation (Prob. 3-11).

$$v_s(t) = u_{-1}(t) \sin (10^4 t + \phi)$$

Problem 3-12

a. Determine the natural frequencies of each of the networks in Fig. 3-19.

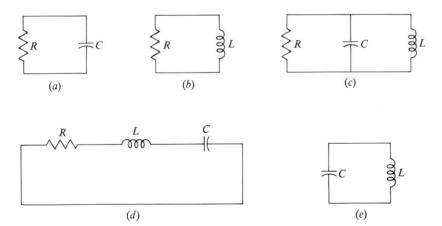

FIG. 3-19. Five basic network configurations for which the natural frequencies are to be determined (Prob. 3-12).

b. Using the results of (a), determine by inspection the natural frequencies of each of the networks of Fig. 3-20.

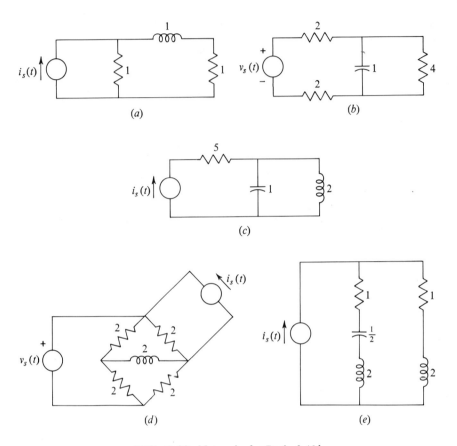

FIG. 3-20. Networks for Prob. 3-12*b*.

Inspection methods for determining the response of networks to step excitation

We have now developed formal procedures whereby the behavior of an *RLC* network can be determined directly from the differential equation when the network is initially at rest. This procedure has shown that, once we have established the differential equation for the network, we can then solve for the response formally, without further reference to the network. We shall often find it convenient, however, to determine the initial conditions and in some cases the total response for simple networks by an alternative procedure in which we reason by inspection of the network. This alternative method will help us to gain some insight into network behavior, although it will not enable us to obtain results that we could not have derived by the more formal methods already given.

Initial conditions for step excitation. We shall first develop a procedure for finding the value of any voltage or current in an RLC network at $t = 0+$ by direct inspection of the network when the network is at rest for $t < 0$ and when the excitation is characterized by a finite jump at $t = 0$; i.e., the excitation is of the form $u_{-1}(t)f(t)$, where $f(t)$ is continuous. Since the *v-i* relations for inductances and capacitances involve integrals and since the integral of a function with a finite jump cannot change instantaneously, we recognize that inductance and capacitance elements impose certain constraints on the changes that can occur in the voltages and currents in the network at $t = 0$.

For a capacitance the *v-i* relation is

$$v_C(t) = \frac{1}{C} \int_{t_0}^{t} i_C(\tau) \, d\tau + v_C(t_0), \tag{3-28}$$

which says that the voltage across a capacitance at any time t is equal to a constant plus a term that is proportional to the area under its current waveform from t_0 to t. Therefore as long as $i_C(t)$ is finite, $v_C(t)$ cannot change instantaneously; i.e., $v_C(t)$ must be continuous. A discontinuity in v_C can occur at a particular time only if i_C is infinite at that time. Of particular interest is the case in which a capacitance in a network is at rest for $t < 0$; i.e., v_C and i_C are zero for $t < 0$. If in this case i_C is finite at $t = 0$, then $v_C(0+) = 0$, and it follows that the state of the network at $t = 0+$; i.e., the distribution of currents and voltages in the network at $t = 0+$ is the same as if the capacitance were replaced by a short circuit.

Likewise for an inductance the *v-i* relation is

$$i_L(t) = \frac{1}{L} \int_{t_0}^{t} v_L(\tau) \, d\tau + i_L(t_0). \tag{3-29}$$

We now observe that $i_L(t)$ cannot change instantaneously at a given time unless $v_L(t)$ has an infinite value at that time. In particular, if an inductance in a network is at rest for $t < 0$, i.e., if v_L and i_L are zero for $t < 0$, and if v_L is finite at $t = 0$, then $i_L(0+) = 0$. It follows, therefore, that under these conditions the state of the network at $t = 0+$ is the same as if the inductance were replaced by an open circuit.

Let us now return to the problem of finding the initial conditions in a network at $t = 0+$. We shall consider the case in which the network is at rest for $t < 0$ and in which all source voltages and currents are finite at $t = 0$. In order to find the state of the network at $t = 0+$, we consider the resistive network formed by replacing all capacitances by short circuits and all inductances by open circuits, and we solve for the voltages and currents in this network. If these are finite, then the distribution of voltages and currents in the resistive network is identical to the distribution of voltages and currents that would be obtained if the capacitances and inductances were reinserted in the network, since, as we have seen, for finite currents through capacitances and finite voltages across inductances the $v\text{-}i$ relations of these elements over the time interval $t = 0-$ to $t = 0+$ are equivalent to those of short circuits and open circuits respectively. If, however, one or more of the voltages or currents in the resistive network are infinite, the procedure of replacing capacitances and inductances by short and open circuits respectively is not valid,[1] and we should resort to the formal methods of solution discussed earlier.

The assumption of finite voltages and currents is violated by two types of element configurations. If the replacing of all C's by short circuits causes a short circuit to exist across a voltage source, then the current through the short circuit is infinite. Infinite current can exist, therefore, if there are any paths from one terminal of a voltage source to the other that contain only capacitance branches. Likewise if the replacing of all L's by open circuits causes an open circuit to exist in series with a current source, then the voltage across the open circuit is infinite. Thus infinite voltage can exist if there is an inductance in all paths that can be drawn in the network from one terminal of a current source to the other.

As an example, let us find by inspection the initial values of $i(t)$ and $v(t)$ for the series RC network shown in Fig. 3-21. The source voltage is given by $v_s(t) = u_{-1}(t)V_s e^{s_p t}$, and we assume the network to be at rest for $t < 0$. Following the procedure just outlined, we replace the capacitance C by a

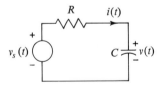

FIG. 3-21. Series RC network used to illustrate the finding of initial conditions by inspection. The network is at rest for $t < 0$, and the source voltage is $v_s(t) = u_{-1}(t)\, V_s e^{s_p t}$.

---

[1] It can be shown that an infinite current or voltage in the derived resistive network would imply an impulse in the corresponding current or voltage response in the original network at $t = 0$.

short circuit. From the network modified in this way, it is clear that all voltages and currents are finite, and we find that $i(0+) = V_s/R$ and $v(0+) = 0$.

As a further example, consider the series RL network shown in Fig. 3-22. The network is assumed to be at rest for $t < 0$, and the source voltage is $v_s(t) = u_{-1}(t)V_s e^{s_p t}$. To find the initial current $i(0+)$ and the initial voltage $v(0+)$ in this network, we first replace the inductance by an open circuit. By inspection of the resulting resistive network, we find that $v(0+) = v_s(0+)$ $= V_s$ and $i(0+) = 0$.

FIG. 3-22. Series RL network used to illustrate the finding of initial conditions by inspection. The network is at rest for $t < 0$, and the source voltage is $v_s(t) = u_{-1}(t)\, V_s e^{s_p t}$.

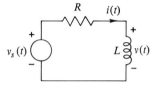

The procedure we have been discussing is valid for finding the initial voltages and currents in a network of arbitrary complexity. In certain practical problems it is useful to be able to make a rapid determination of the distribution of voltages and currents that result from a sudden change of excitation in a network, and the complete response of the network for all time may not always be required.

When the total solution for a network response is to be found, the procedure just presented provides a complete specification of the initial conditions for the case in which the response is governed by a first-order differential equation. For networks that give rise to differential equations of order higher than the first, we have seen that the initial conditions must include a specification of derivatives of the response as well as the response itself if a complete solution is to be found. In general, inspection procedures suitable for finding initial values of the derivatives of a voltage or current response would be more involved than the methods for finding the initial value of the response itself. However, we can use inspection procedures for the special cases in which we wish to find the initial value of the derivative of the voltage across a capacitance or the initial value of the derivative of the current through an inductance. These initial values for the derivatives can be written down immediately once the initial value of the current through the capacitance or the voltage across the inductance is known. In the case of a capacitance, if we apply the v-i relation at $t = 0+$, i.e.,

$$i_C(0+) = C\left.\frac{dv_C}{dt}\right|_{t=0+}, \qquad (3\text{-}30)$$

we see that the value of dv_C/dt at $t = 0+$ is given by $i_C(0+)/C$. Likewise, the $v\text{-}i$ relation for an inductance at $t = 0+$ is

$$v_L(0+) = L\left.\frac{di_L}{dt}\right|_{t=0+}, \qquad (3\text{-}31)$$

from which we observe that the value of di_L/dt at $t = 0+$ is $v_L(0+)/L$. Initial values of the derivatives of other voltages and currents in a network cannot, however, be determined so readily as the initial values of the derivatives of capacitance voltages or inductance currents. When the solution of a problem requires that such initial values be found, the formal procedures rather than the inspection procedures are recommended.

In order to determine initial values of the voltages and currents for the network of Fig. 3-23, the inspection procedure tells us to replace C_1 and

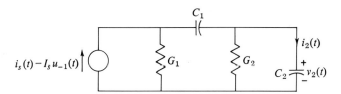

FIG. 3-23. Example of a more complex network, illustrating the finding of the initial value of the response $v_2(t)$ by inspection. The network is at rest for $t < 0$.

C_2 by short circuits. Since the currents and voltages in the resulting network are finite, we determine immediately that $v_2(0+)$ is zero. The response $v_2(t)$ is, however, the solution of a second-order differential equation (as can be readily verified), and hence two independent conditions must be specified—usually the initial conditions giving the values of v_2 and dv_2/dt at $t = 0+$. In this case the initial value of dv_2/dt can be obtained by finding $i_2(0+)$ and dividing by C_2. When we replace C_1 and C_2 by short circuits, we find that $i_2(0+) = i_s(0+) = I_s$, and hence

$$\left.\frac{dv_2}{dt}\right|_{t=0+} = \frac{I_s}{C_2}.$$

This condition, together with the condition $v_2(0+) = 0$, provides a complete specification of the initial conditions that must be imposed on the solution to the second-order differential equation in $v_2(t)$.

Total response for step excitation of networks characterized by a single natural frequency. We have just seen how inspection methods can be used to find the value of any voltage or current in an RLC network at $t = 0+$ when the excitation is finite at $t = 0$ and when the network is initially at rest. We shall now develop inspection methods for determining not only the initial value of the response but also the total response for some simple RL and RC networks when the excitation is a step function of the form $Au_{-1}(t)$. We shall restrict our attention to networks for which the basic network consists of an interconnection of one inductance or one capacitance with one or more resistances, and can be reduced to a parallel RL or RC network, as shown in Fig. 3-24. Such networks are characterized by a single natural frequency, and this natural frequency is real and negative if the element values are positive.

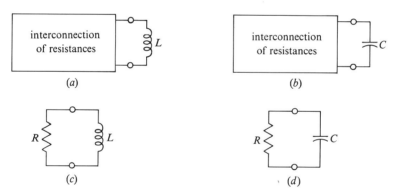

FIG. 3-24. The inspection method developed in the text applies to networks whose basic networks are of the type shown in the upper part of the figure. Replacing each resistance network by an equivalent resistance that has the same *v-i* relation at the terminals gives the equivalent networks shown in the lower part of the figure.

For step excitation of networks of this type, we have seen that the voltage or current in any element consists of a particular integral that is a constant, plus a homogeneous solution proportional to $e^{\sigma t}$, where σ is the natural frequency. Thus the response for $t > 0$ can always be written in the form

$$y(t) = B + Ce^{\sigma t}, \tag{3-32}$$

where B and C are constants and σ is the natural frequency of the network, i.e., is the root of the characteristic equation. The initial value of $y(t)$ at $t = 0+$ is $B + C$, and the particular integral is equal to B. Since σ is negative for the networks we are considering, the response approaches B as t becomes large. (Instead of referring to the complex frequency of an exponential function $e^{\sigma t}$ when σ is real and negative, we frequently speak of the *time constant* τ of the exponential, where $\tau = -1/\sigma$. The time constant can be interpreted as the time taken for an exponential function to decay to $1/e$ of its value at $t = 0$.)

The general approach we shall follow for obtaining the response by inspection is to find the initial value $B + C$, the final value B, and the time constant τ of the exponential. The entire response can then be sketched by joining the initial value to the final value by an exponential function of the form $e^{-t/\tau}$, in the manner shown in Fig. 3-25. Since we have already

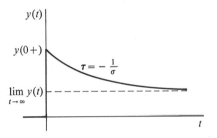

FIG. 3-25. General form of the response for step excitation of a network characterized by a single natural frequency; τ designates the time constant of the exponential component of the response.

shown how to determine the initial value of the response, it remains to establish inspection procedures for finding the final value of the response and the time constant of the network.

In order to determine the final value of the response, we make use of the fact that the voltage or current in any element of a network of the type we are considering approaches a constant value for large t. If in the case of a capacitance the voltage and the current are both constant, then from the voltage-current relation

$$i_C = C \frac{dv_C}{dt} \tag{3-33}$$

it follows that the current in the capacitance must be zero. Hence the capacitance can be replaced by an open circuit as far as its behavior for large t is concerned. Likewise the v-i relation for an inductance, i.e.,

$$v_L = L \frac{di_L}{dt}, \tag{3-34}$$

indicates that $v_L = 0$ for large t, if i_L is constant. Thus as far as the asymptotic response for large t is concerned, the inductance can be replaced by a short circuit. We conclude, therefore, that for networks of the type we are considering the response a long time after a step excitation is applied can be found by determining the voltages and currents in the resistance network that results when all inductances are replaced by short circuits and all capacitances are replaced by open circuits.

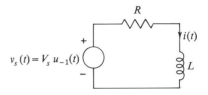

FIG. 3-26. Series RL network used to illustrate the inspection procedure for finding the asymptotic value of the response $i(t)$ for large t.

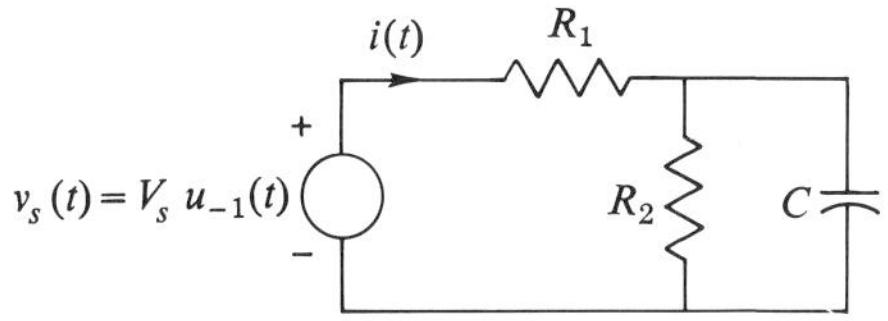

$v_s(t) = V_s \, u_{-1}(t)$

FIG. 3-27. RC network used to illustrate the inspection procedure for finding the response to a step excitation. The current response $i(t)$ is to be found in this case.

Thus, for example, in the RL network of Fig. 3-26 the current response for large t, obtained by replacing L by a short circuit, is V_s/R (as we have seen earlier when we obtained the response for this network by the formal methods). Likewise, if we are interested in the current response $i(t)$ in the resistance R_1 of the network of Fig. 3-27, we obtain the asymptotic value of $i(t)$ for large t by examining the network that results when C is replaced by an open circuit. Thus we find

$$i(t) = \frac{V_s}{R_1 + R_2} \tag{3-35}$$

for large t.

The remaining step in the inspection procedure we are developing for finding the total response is to establish the time constant of the network. If the basic network has been reduced to one of the forms shown in Fig. 3-24c and d, then we can immediately write down the time constant. As we have seen, the root of the characteristic equation for the RL network of Fig. 3-24c is $s = -R/L$, and hence the time constant is $\tau = L/R$.

Likewise for the RC network of Fig. 3-24d the root of the characteristic equation is $s = -1/RC$, and therefore the time constant is $\tau = RC$.

As an example of the application of inspection procedures to obtain the total response of a network to step excitation, we shall determine the current response $i(t)$ for the RC network of Fig. 3-27. The basic network in this case reduces to a capacitance C connected to the parallel combination of the two resistances R_1 and R_2. Thus we can immediately write down the time constant of the network as

$$\tau = \frac{R_1 R_2 C}{R_1 + R_2}. \qquad (3\text{-}36)$$

For this network we use the inspection procedure to find that the initial value of the current $i(t)$ in the resistance R_1 is V_s/R_1. We have already shown that the asymptotic value of $i(t)$ for large t is

$$i(t) = \frac{V_s}{R_1 + R_2}. \qquad (3\text{-}37)$$

Thus we can sketch the entire response $i(t)$ in the manner shown in Fig.

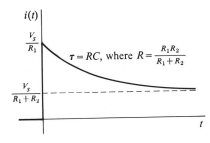

FIG. 3-28. Current response $i(t)$ for the network of Fig. 3-27 obtained by the inspection procedures developed in the text; τ is the time constant of the exponential component of the response.

3-28. The expression for the response is

$$i(t) = V_s u_{-1}(t) \left[\frac{1}{R_1 + R_2} - \left(\frac{1}{R_1 + R_2} - \frac{1}{R_1} \right) e^{-t/\tau} \right]$$

$$= \frac{V_s}{R_1 + R_2} u_{-1}(t) \left(1 + \frac{R_2}{R_1} e^{-t/\tau} \right). \qquad (3\text{-}38)$$

In summary, therefore, we have demonstrated that the response for step excitation of any network whose basic network can be reduced to the RL or RC combination of Fig. 3-24c or d can be determined by inspection of the network without writing down the differential equation for the response. The response is characterized by three numbers: (1) the initial value at $t = 0+$, which is determined from the resistance network that results when the capacitance is short-circuited or the inductance is open-circuited; (2) the asymptotic value of the response for large t, which is determined by solving the resistance network that results when the capacitance is replaced by an open circuit or the inductance is replaced by a short circuit; and (3) the time constant of the network, which is determined by reducing the basic network to a simple RL or RC network.

Problem 3-13

The network of Fig. 3-29 is initially at rest. Determine $v_R(t)$ and $i_L(t)$ by inspection.

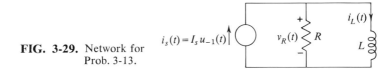

FIG. 3-29. Network for
Prob. 3-13.

Problem 3-14

For the network of Fig. 3-30 determine the current $i(t)$ by inspection. The network is at rest for $t < 0$.

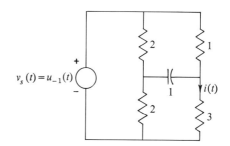

FIG. 3-30. Network for
Prob. 3-14.

Problem 3-15

Determine and sketch the impulse responses $v(t)$ and $i(t)$ for each of the

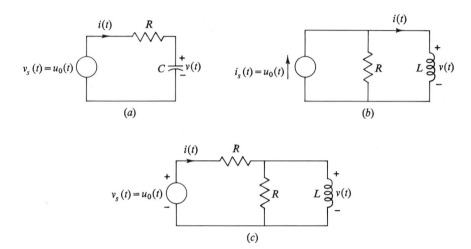

FIG. 3-31. Networks for which the impulse responses are to be determined (Prob. 3-15).

networks of Fig. 3-31. The networks are initially at rest.

Problem 3-16

a. The network shown in Fig. 3-32a is at rest for $t < 0$. Network A contains only resistances and step sources. The current $i(t)$ is as shown in Fig. 3-32b. Determine a network that has the same terminal v-i relation as that of network A.

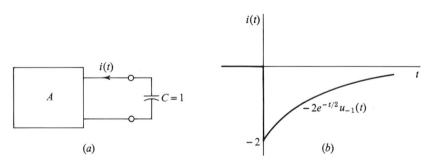

FIG. 3-32. Unknown network with a specified current response. The network A is to be determined (Prob. 3-16).

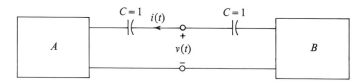

FIG. 3-33. Network for Prob. 3-16*b*.

b. Network *A* is now connected as shown in Fig. 3-33. Network *B* is
known to contain only resistances and step sources. The current $i(t)$
is the same as that shown in Fig. 3-32*b*. Determine a network that has
the same terminal *v-i* relation as that of network *B*.

Superposition of singularity functions to form more general functions

In many examples that we shall encounter, the excitation of a network
can be represented by a superposition of several time functions, such as
impulses, steps, or other singularity functions, each of which starts at a
different time. It is appropriate, therefore, for us to consider how the
representation of a time function is altered when it is shifted along the
time axis. Suppose we are given a function $f(t)$, such as that shown in
Fig. 3-34, and we then define a new function $g(t)$ that is the same as $f(t)$
but delayed by an amount t_0; i.e., $g(t)$ is obtained by shifting $f(t)$ to the
right by an amount t_0 as shown. Then the value of $g(t)$ at a particular
time t is equal to the value of $f(t)$ at time $t - t_0$; i.e., $g(t) = f(t - t_0)$.
Thus if any function $f(t)$ is delayed by t_0, then the delayed function is

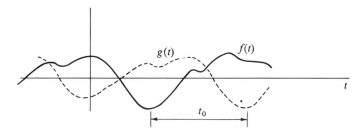

FIG. 3-34. Plot of a function $f(t)$ and the same function delayed by time t_0. The
delayed function is given by $g(t) = f(t - t_0)$.

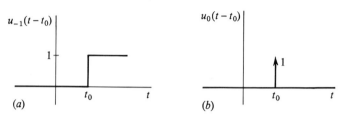

FIG. 3-35. Graphical representations of the delayed step and impulse $u_{-1}(t - t_0)$ and $u_0(t - t_0)$.

obtained by replacing the argument t by $t - t_0$. A step function that occurs at $t = t_0$ can be written, therefore, as $u_{-1}(t - t_0)$; an impulse occurring at $t = t_0$ is written as $u_0(t - t_0)$. These functions may be considered as steps or impulses that are delayed from their positions at $t = 0$ by a time t_0. Graphical representations of these functions for positive t_0 are shown in Fig. 3-35.

For the systems with which we are concerned, it is a simple matter to find the response to an excitation $x(t - t_0)$ if we know the response to an excitation $x(t)$. We make use of the property (shown in Prob. 2-24e) of systems that are initially at rest and are characterized by linear constant-coefficient differential equations that, if the response to an excitation $x(t)$ is $y(t)$, then the response to $x(t - t_0)$ is $y(t - t_0)$; i.e., the response is simply the original response shifted the same amount as the excitation. If a source voltage or current for such a system is represented by a sum of several time functions, each of which may start at a different time, we can use the superposition property to find the response.

Many source voltages $v_s(t)$ or source currents $i_s(t)$ can be approximated with sufficient accuracy by a continuous function consisting of a series of straight-line segments. A particularly simple method is available for finding the response of networks to such sources. An example of such a "piecewise-linear" source voltage is shown in Fig. 3-36. Suppose we wish to find the response of an RLC network to this source voltage. Differentiation of $v_s(t)$

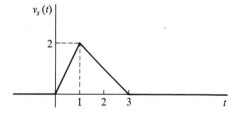

FIG. 3-36. Example of a piecewise-linear source voltage.

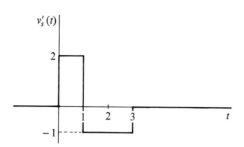

FIG. 3-37. Derivative of the piecewise-linear source voltage of Fig. 3-36. The derivative of a piecewise-linear continuous time function can be represented as a sum of step functions.

yields the time function shown in Fig. 3-37, which can be represented by the sum of step functions

$$v'_s(t) = 2u_{-1}(t) - 3u_{-1}(t - 1) + u_{-1}(t - 3) .$$ (3-39)

If the step response of the network is known, then the response to $v'_s(t)$ can be written down by inspection. Integration of this result yields the response to the original piecewise-linear source voltage $v_s(t)$.

An alternative way of approximating source voltages or currents of arbitrary waveforms is in terms of polynomials in t. If the source of excitation for a network is zero for $t < 0$ and can be expressed as a polynomial in t for $t > 0$, then the response can be determined by summing the responses associated with each term in the polynomial. Each term in the polynomial can be represented by one of the singularity functions $u_{-j}(t)$. Suppose, for example, that a particular source voltage is zero for $t < 0$ and can be approximated by a third-order polynomial for $t > 0$, such as

$$v_s(t) = \tfrac{1}{2}t - t^2 + \tfrac{1}{5}t^3 .$$ (3-40)

The source voltage can then be written as a sum of singularity functions as follows:

$$v_s(t) = \tfrac{1}{2}u_{-2}(t) - 2u_{-3}(t) + \tfrac{6}{5}u_{-4}(t) .$$ (3-41)

To obtain the total response, the response to each term in the expression for the source voltage is found and the separate responses are added. The response to a source voltage $\tfrac{6}{5}u_{-4}(t)$, for example, is obtained by finding the response to a unit step voltage source, integrating the result three times and multiplying by 6/5. Thus we see that the response of a network to an input describable by a polynomial function of time can be determined from the step response.

The examples we have given demonstrate that, once we have determined the response of an RLC network to a unit step excitation, we are immediately in a position to write down the response to a wide variety of excitations, simply through operations involving addition, integration, and shifting of the step response. The same statement could, of course, be made with respect to the response to a unit impulse, which is simply the derivative of a step response. As a matter of fact, once the step or impulse response of an RLC network is known, it is possible to find the response to an excitation of arbitrary waveform, as shown below in Prob. 3-23.

Problem 3-17

A function $f(x)$ assigns to each value of the argument x, say $x = x_0$, the value $f(x_0)$. If the argument x depends on a parameter t, then $f(x)$ can be considered to define a new function $g(t)$. For example, suppose that x is related to a parameter t by $x = t - 1$. Then $f(x)$ assigns to each value of t, say $t = t_0$, the value $f(t_0 - 1) = g(t_0)$. The function $g(t)$ can be written as $g(t) = f(t - 1)$, meaning that the value assigned to $g(t)$ at $t = t_0$ is equal to the value assigned to $f(x)$ at $x = t_0 - 1$.

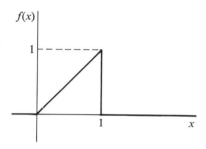

FIG. 3-38. Pulselike waveform for Prob. 3-17.

a. A function $f(x)$ is sketched in Fig. 3-38. Sketch $g(t) = f(x)$ as a function of t if x is given in each of the following ways:
   1. $x = t - 2$.
   2. $x = -t$.
   3. $x = t + 2$.
   4. $x = 2t$.
   5. $x = 3t - 2$.
b. Sketch each of the following as functions of t:
   1. $u_0(t + 2)$.
   2. $u_{-1}(4 - t)$.
   3. $u_{-2}(-3t)$.

Problem 3-18

a. Sketch $g(t) = \sum_{k=1}^{3} f(t - 2k)$ as a function of t, if $f(t)$ is as shown in Fig. 3-39.

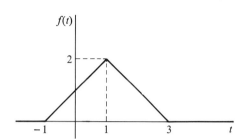

FIG. 3-39. Pulselike waveform
for Prob. 3-18*a.*

b. Express each of the following functions as a linear combination (with constant coefficients) of singularity functions:

1. $f_1(t) = \begin{cases} 0, & t < -1; \\ 1, & t > -1, \end{cases}$ as shown in Fig. 3-40.

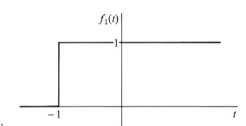

FIG. 3-40. Waveform for
Prob. 3-18*b*(1).

2. $f_2(t) = \begin{cases} 1, & t < -1; \\ 0, & t > -1, \end{cases}$ as shown in Fig. 3-41.

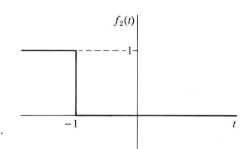

FIG. 3-41. Waveform for
Prob. 3-18*b*(2).

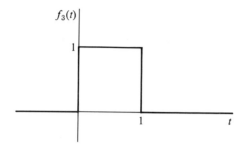

FIG. 3-42. Waveform for Prob. 3-18b(3).

3. $f_3(t) = \begin{cases} 0, t < 0; \\ 1, 0 < t < 1; \\ 0, t > 1, \end{cases}$ as shown in Fig. 3-42.

4. $f_4(t) = \begin{cases} 0, t < 0; \\ t, 0 < t < 2; \\ 2, t > 2, \end{cases}$ as shown in Fig. 3-43.

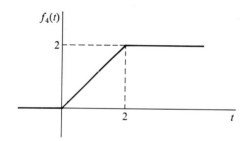

FIG. 3-43. Waveform for Prob. 3-18b(4).

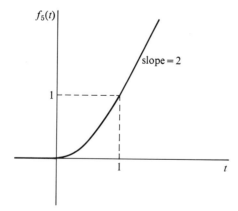

FIG. 3-44. Waveform for Prob. 3-18b(5).

5. $f_5(t) = \begin{cases} 0, t > 0; \\ t^2, 0 < t < 1; \\ 2t - 1, t > 1, \text{ as shown in Fig. 3-44.} \end{cases}$

Problem 3-19

The impulse response of a given *RLC* network is

$$y(t) = u_{-1}(t)e^{-t} .$$

Determine the response of the same network to each of the excitations $x(t)$ shown in Fig. 3-45, assuming initial-rest conditions.

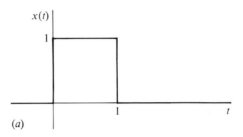

(a)

FIG. 3-45. Waveforms for
Prob. 3-19.

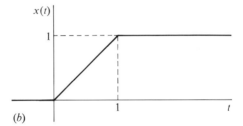

(b)

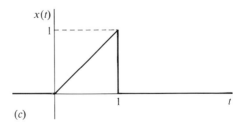

(c)

Problem 3-20

Network *N* in Fig. 3-46a contains no sources and at most one resistance, one inductance, and one capacitance. It is at rest prior to $t = 0$. The

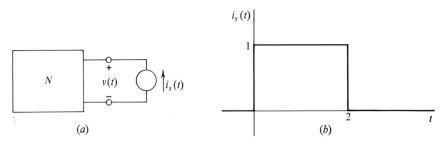

(a)   (b)

FIG. 3-46. An unknown network N with a specified current excitation. Network N is to be determined for each of the voltage responses of Fig. 3-47 (Prob. 3-20).

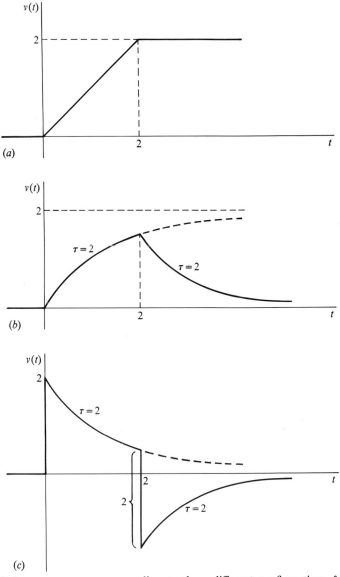

(a)

(b)

(c)

FIG. 3-47. Voltage responses corresponding to three different configurations for the network N of Fig. 3-46 (Prob. 3-20).

excitation $i_s(t)$ is shown in Fig. 3-46b. For each of the voltage responses
shown in Fig. 3-47, determine the network N.

Problem 3-21

A parallel RC network in series with a network N_1, as shown in Fig. 3-48a,
is excited with a current source with the waveform shown in Fig. 3-48b.
The voltage $v(t)$ is to be that shown in Fig. 3-48c.

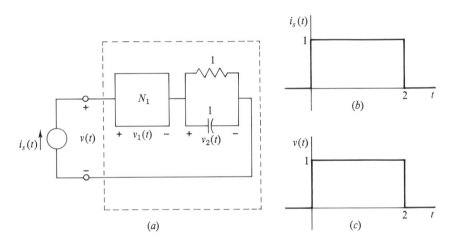

FIG. 3-48. Network for Prob. 3-21 with current excitation and voltage response
shown. The voltage $v_1(t)$ and the network N_1 are to be determined.

a. Sketch $v_1(t)$ for $t \geq 0$.
b. Determine the network N_1.

Problem 3-22

In a particular satellite communication problem, data in the form of a
sequence of binary numbers "one" and "zero" are to be coded in such a
way that a "one" is represented by four cycles of a sinusoid and a "zero"
by the absence of a signal. As one part of the transmitter in the satellite,
a network with the following specifications is required:
1. The excitation is a current source $i_s(t)$ that is a pulse of amplitude B
   starting at $t = 0$ and ending at $t = t_0$, as shown in Fig. 3-49.

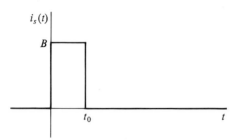

FIG. 3-49. Current excitation waveform for Prob. 3-22.

2. The response is a voltage $v(t)$. It is to be zero for $t < 0$ and must be given by $v(t) = A \sin \omega_0 t$ for four complete cycles starting at $t = 0$ and be zero thereafter.

   Design a network that meets the above specifications, using only inductances and capacitances. Determine the width of the input current pulse t_0 and values of the inductances and capacitances in terms of ω_0, A, and B.

Problem 3-23

Figure 3-50 illustrates how a time function $f(t)$ can be approximated by the sum of a large number of small steps occurring at times spaced Δt apart. This sequence of steps becomes a better and better approximation to the curve as the time interval Δt is made smaller and smaller. The jth step occurs at time t_j, and the height of this step is $f(t_j) - f(t_j - \Delta t)$. If Δt is sufficiently small, this difference is approximately equal to $f'(t_j)\Delta t$. Thus at time t_j a step function equal to $u_{-1}(t - t_j)f'(t_j)\Delta t$ is superposed on the time function that exists at time $t_j - \Delta t$. Consequently the approximation to the entire time function $f(t)$ can be written as the sum of a number of such steps, to give

$$f(t) \cong \sum_{\text{all } j} u_{-1}(t - t_j)f'(t_j)\Delta t . \tag{3-42}$$

We shall now proceed to determine the response $y(t)$ of a linear time-invariant system to an arbitrary excitation $x(t)$ by using the approximation given in Eq. (3-42) to represent the excitation. We shall define a time-invariant linear system as a linear system which has the property that the relation between the excitation and the response is independent of a time shift in the excitation; i.e., if $y(t)$ is the response to an excitation $x(t)$, then $y(t - t_1)$ is the response to an excitation $x(t - t_1)$.

a. Let the response of a time-invariant linear system to a unit step excitation applied at $t = 0$ be $s(t)$; i.e., when $x(t) = u_{-1}(t)$, then $y(t) = s(t)$.

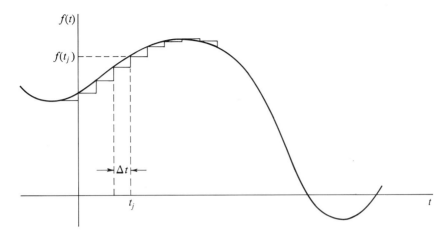

FIG. 3-50. Approximation of a curve by a sequence of small steps occurring at time intervals Δt (Prob. 3-23).

Determine the system response at time t_0 when the excitation is a unit step applied at time t_j, i.e., when $x(t) = u_{-1}(t - t_j)$.

b. An arbitrary excitation $x(t)$ is approximated by a sequence of steps as in Eq. (3-42). Determine the response of the system at time t_0 due to the step that is added to the excitation at time t_j. Express this response in terms of the response to a unit step.

c. Using superposition and your answer to (b), determine the response at time t_0 when the excitation is given by the entire sequence of steps in Eq. (3-42).

d. Find the limit of the response determined in (c) as $\Delta t \to 0$. Your result should be expressed in terms of an integral involving the unit step response $s(t)$ and the derivative of $x(t)$.

The expression derived in (d) is a basic result for time-invariant linear systems. It enables us to determine the response $y(t)$ to an arbitrary excitation $x(t)$ and it shows that a knowledge of the step response is sufficient to determine the response to any excitation.

In Chap. 2 we have seen that for a system governed by a constant-coefficient linear differential equation with initial-rest conditions, if the response to an excitation $x(t)$ is $y(t)$ then the response to $x'(t)$ is $y'(t)$. This result can be shown to hold for all time-invariant linear systems. Therefore if the step response of a time-invariant linear system is $s(t)$, the impulse response $h(t)$ is $h(t) = s'(t)$.

e. Apply integration by parts to the result derived in (d) to express the response at time t_0 in terms of an integral involving the excitation $x(t)$ and the impulse response $h(t)$. Assume that $x(t) = 0$ for $t = -\infty$.

Integral relations of the form derived in (d) and (e) are sometimes called *convolution* or *superposition integrals*. They play an important role in the analysis of linear systems and will be the subject of later studies.

Problem 3-24

The network of Fig. 3-51 contains only resistances, inductances, and capacitances and is initially at rest. If the excitation is $v_1(t) = u_{-1}(t)$, then the response is $v_2(t) = Au_{-1}(t)$, where A is a real constant.

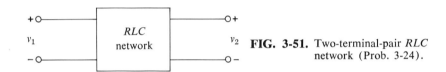

+O   RLC   O+
v_1 network v_2 **FIG. 3-51.** Two-terminal-pair *RLC*
−O   O−   network (Prob. 3-24).

a. If the excitation is $v_1(t) = u_0(t)$, what is the response?

b. Using the superposition integral (refer to Prob. 3-23), show that for any excitation $v_1(t) = f(t)$, the response is $v_2(t) = Af(t)$.

Remark. In this problem you have shown the very useful result that, if the response of an *RLC* network to a unit step excitation is a step of amplitude A, then the response of the network to any input is A times that input.

Problem 3-25

An *RLC* network has the response $y(t) = u_{-1}(t)e^{-t}$ when the excitation $x(t)$ is a unit impulse. Using the superposition integral, determine the response to the excitation $x(t) = tu_{-1}(t)$.

Problem 3-26

The network of Fig. 3-52 is initially at rest. We wish to determine $v(t)$. Since this network has only one natural frequency, one is tempted to use inspection techniques. However, there is a capacitive path across the voltage source $v_s(t)$, and hence the inspection technique developed on pages 108 to 113 for finding $v(0+)$ cannot be used. It is still possible to find $v(t)$ by inspection, using some special arguments. These arguments will not be

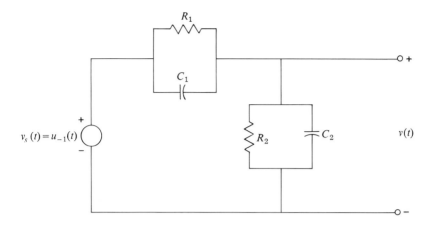

FIG. 3-52. Network for Prob. 3-26. Note that this network has a capacitive path across the voltage source.

developed, however, because they have only limited application. Instead it is recommended that this problem be solved by the formal methods that have been studied previously.

a. Write a differential equation relating $v(t)$ to $v_s(t)$ in Fig. 3-52. Solve this equation for $v(t)$ for initial-rest conditions, with $v_s(t) = u_{-1}(t)$.

b. What should be the relation among R_1, R_2, C_1, and C_2 such that $v(t)$ is a step? What is the height of this step in terms of R_1 and R_2?

The equivalent input network of a voltage-measuring device, such as a cathode-ray oscilloscope, is a parallel RC network, as shown in Fig. 3-53. The elements R_2 and C_2 are called the input resistance and capacitance, respectively, of the device.

One normally desires a measuring device to have as little effect as possible on the voltage to be measured. Suppose, for example, the Thevenin

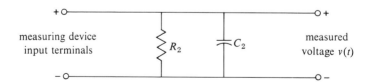

FIG. 3-53. Equivalent input network of a voltage-measuring device, such as a cathode-ray oscilloscope (Prob. 3-26).

equivalent network seen at the terminals of the network whose open-circuit voltage is to be measured is as shown in Fig. 3-54. When no measuring device is connected to the terminals, the voltage $v_0(t)$ is equal to the open-circuit voltage $v_s(t)$ that is to be measured.

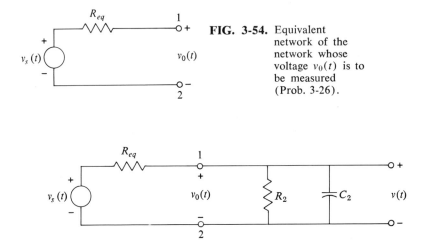

FIG. 3-54. Equivalent network of the network whose voltage $v_0(t)$ is to be measured (Prob. 3-26).

FIG. 3-55. Connection of the network whose voltage is to be measured and the voltage-measuring device (Prob. 3-26).

In order to measure $v_0(t)$ using the measuring device, we connect the output terminals 1 and 2 in Fig. 3-54 to the input terminals of the device, as shown in Fig. 3-55. In this case, however, the voltage $v(t)$ is not $v_s(t)$, because $v_0(t)$ has been changed, owing to the fact that the current in R_{eq} is no longer zero. In order that $v_0(t)$ shall be as nearly equal to $v_s(t)$ as possible, it is important that as little current as possible flow into the terminals of the measuring device.

One way to reduce the current flowing into the terminals of the measuring device is to connect a large resistance R_1 in series with the terminals as shown in Fig. 3-56. However, the voltage $v(t)$ is still not a faithful reproduction of $v_s(t)$. Since the oscilloscope displays a waveform proportional to $v(t)$, it is important that the waveform of $v(t)$ be the same, within a constant multiplier, as that of $v_s(t)$. (The constant multiplier, as long as it is known, can be corrected for in the amplitude scales of the oscilloscope.) From (b) we know that, if a capacitance C_1 is connected across R_1, then for a step input $v_s(t)$ a step output $v(t)$ is obtained by a suitable choice of the component values. It follows from Prob. 3-24 that the output $v(t)$

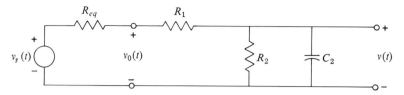

FIG. 3-56. Illustrating the addition of a large resistance R_1 in series with the terminals of the voltage-measuring device (Prob. 3-26).

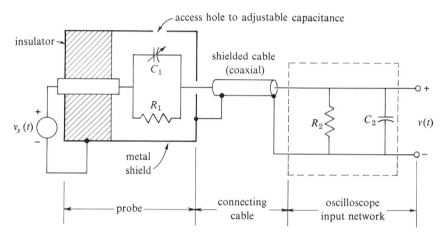

FIG. 3-57. Schematic diagram of an oscilloscope probe, shielded connecting cable, and oscilloscope input network. Capacitance C_2 includes the capacitance of the connecting cable. The voltage to be measured is $v_s(t)$, shown as a source at the left (Prob. 3-26).

will then be identical to $v_s(t)$ for any input $v_s(t)$, except for a constant multiplier. In oscilloscopes the resistance R_1 and the capacitance C_1 are usually placed inside the measuring probe, as shown in Fig. 3-57.

c. For a typical oscilloscope the input resistance is $R_2 = 10^6$, and the input capacitance is $C_2 = 18 \times 10^{-12}$. Assume that the input voltage to the probe is $v_s(t)$. What should be the values of R_1 and C_1 such that $v(t) = \frac{1}{10}v_s(t)$?

d. Let the value of C_1 found in (c) be $C_{1\,\text{crit}}$. Assuming R_1, R_2, and C_2 remain unchanged, sketch $v(t)$ when $v_s(t) = u_{-1}(t)$ and:

1. $C_1 > C_{1\,\text{crit}}$.
2. $C_1 < C_{1\,\text{crit}}$.
3. $C_1 = C_{1\,\text{crit}}$.

Excitation of a network by two or more sources; superposition

We have demonstrated previously that the principle of superposition can be applied to a linear differential equation under initial-rest conditions. As discussed below, when an RLC network is excited by more than one source, the resulting differential equation for the response contains the different source voltages and currents as separate terms on the right-hand side. As a consequence, application of the principle of superposition to the differential equation amounts to finding the response to each source separately, with all other sources set to zero, and adding these responses. This property is particularly useful, since it reduces the problem of finding the response of a network with a complex configuration of sources to a series of simpler problems each of which involves only one source.

The fact that the differential equation contains the different source voltages and currents as separate terms on the right-hand side can be seen by examining the steps involved in the formulation and reduction of the basic network equilibrium equations. When equilibrium equations are written for any network excited by more than one source, the voltage sources appear as separate terms in the KVL equations, and the current sources appear as separate terms in the KCL equations. When these equations, in combination with linear v-i relations for the elements, are reduced to a single equation in any one variable, only linear operations are involved. In the resulting equation, therefore, each source voltage and current still appears as a separate term that can be shifted to the right-hand side in order to put the equation in standard form.

As an example of the application of the principle of superposition to a network with more than one source, consider the network shown in Fig. 3-58a. We wish to solve for the voltage response $v(t)$ across the capacitance. The response v is obtained by first finding the response v_1 to the source i_s

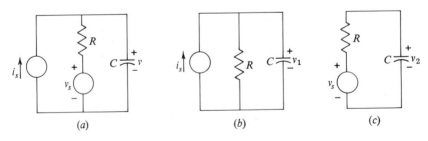

(a)　　　　　　　　(b)　　　　　　　　(c)

FIG. 3-58. (a) Example of a network with two sources of excitation. The voltage response v is determined by adding the response v_1 with v_s set to zero, as in network (b), and the response v_2 with i_s set to zero, as in network (c).

with v_s set to zero, as in Fig. 3-58b, and then finding the response v_2 to the source v_s with i_s set to zero, as in Fig. 3-58c. The total response v with both sources operating is then equal to the sum $v_1 + v_2$.

Response of networks not initially at rest

In our discussion to this point we have dealt exclusively with networks that are at rest before $t = 0$. We shall now turn our attention to networks in which there are nonzero voltages and currents for $t < 0$ due to some excitation or excitations that existed prior to $t = 0$. We are interested in finding the behavior of such networks for $t \geq 0$. We shall show that the response for $t \geq 0$ can be determined if we know (1) the state of the network at $t = 0$ due to excitations that existed prior to $t = 0$ and (2) the excitations for $t \geq 0$.

In order to investigate how the past behavior of a network influences its future response, let us examine the basic equations that govern network equilibrium. It is recalled that three sets of equations are necessary to describe equilibrium conditions in a network: KCL equations, KVL equations, and v-i relations for the elements. The KCL and KVL equations apply at all instants of time regardless of the elements and the values of the excitation, and they say nothing about the relation between past and present values of the voltages and currents. The voltage-current relations for the elements, on the other hand, can provide a connection between the present and the past. For a network composed of R, L, and C elements, the voltage-current relations for the three types of elements can be written:

$$R: \qquad v = Ri . \tag{3-44}$$

$$C: \qquad v(t) = \frac{1}{C} \int_{t_0}^{t} i(\tau) \, d\tau + v(t_0) . \tag{3-45}$$

$$L: \qquad i(t) = \frac{1}{L} \int_{t_0}^{t} v(\tau) \, d\tau + i(t_0) . \tag{3-46}$$

The relation for a resistance simply expresses the fact that the instantaneous value of current is proportional to the instantaneous value of voltage. The v-i relations for capacitances and inductances, however, indicate that these elements have memory; i.e., the present state of such an element depends on its past history.

The v-i relation for a capacitance can be written in the form

$$v(t) = v(0-) + \frac{1}{C} \int_{0-}^{t} i(\tau) \, d\tau . \tag{3-47}$$

The first term in Eq. (3-47) is the voltage across the capacitance at $t = 0-$, and the second term can be interpreted as the voltage that would exist across the capacitance if $i(t)$ were zero before $t = 0$. Thus as far as the behavior for $t \geq 0$ is concerned, the v-i relation (3-47) implies that a capacitance with arbitrary past history can be represented by a voltage source of value $v(0-)$ in series with a capacitance C across which there is no initial voltage. Consequently the v-i relation for a capacitance (Fig. 3-59a), valid for $t \geq 0$, is identical to that of the equivalent network shown

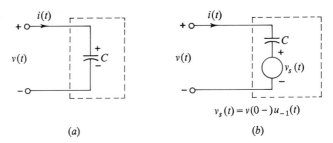

(a)   (b)

FIG. 3-59. Part (a) shows a capacitance C for which the voltage-current relation $v(t) = \dfrac{1}{C} \displaystyle\int_{t_0}^{t} i(\tau)\, d\tau + v(t_0)$ is valid for all t. The voltage across this capacitance at $t = 0-$ is $v(0-)$. Part (b) is an equivalent network for which the voltage-current relation, for $t \geq 0$, is identical to that of the capacitance in (a). The voltage across the capacitance C in the equivalent network must be zero for $t < 0$.

in Fig. 3-59b. In order to ensure that the voltage across the capacitance in the equivalent network of Fig. 3-59b be zero before $t - 0$, there must be no current flowing through the capacitance when it is connected in a network. It is therefore necessary to set $v_s(t)$ to zero for $t < 0$. This is accomplished in the equivalent network by multiplying the source voltage $v(0-)$ by $u_{-1}(t)$.

In the case of an inductance, the v-i relation (3-46) can be written

$$i(t) = i(0-) + \frac{1}{L} \int_{0-}^{t} v(\tau)\, d\tau . \qquad (3\text{-}48)$$

The first term in Eq. (3-48) is the current through the inductance at $t = 0-$, and the second term can be interpreted as the current that would exist in the inductance if it were at rest prior to $t = 0$. Following a procedure analogous to that used in the case of the capacitance, we can represent an inductance L (Fig. 3-60a) with arbitrary past history by the equivalent network in Fig. 3-60b. This network gives a valid representation of the

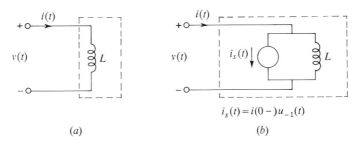

$$i_s(t) = i(0-)u_{-1}(t)$$

(a)   (b)

FIG. 3-60. Part (a) shows an inductance L for which the voltage-current relation $i(t) = \dfrac{1}{L}\displaystyle\int_{t_0}^{t} v(\tau)\,d\tau + i(t_0)$ is valid for all t. The current in this inductance at $t = 0-$ is $i(0-)$. Part (b) is an equivalent network for which the voltage-current relation, for $t \geq 0$, is identical to that of the inductance in (a). The current in the inductance L in the equivalent network must be zero for $t < 0$.

behavior of the inductance for $t \geq 0$. In the network of Fig. 3-60b there must be no current in the inductance for $t < 0$, in accordance with the second term in Eq. (3-48), and thus the parallel current source must be zero for $t < 0$.

Having shown how we can use equivalent networks to account for the past history of inductances and capacitances that are not at rest for $t < 0$, we are now in a position to state procedures for obtaining the response of a network for $t \geq 0$ when the network is not at rest for $t < 0$. Suppose there is one source of excitation[1] $x(t)$ for the network, and this takes the form shown in Fig. 3-61a. This excitation can be considered to be the sum of two parts—a component $x_1(t)$ that is equal to $x(t)$ for $t < 0$ and zero for $t \geq 0$, and a component $x_2(t)$ that is equal to $x(t)$ for $t \geq 0$ and zero for $t < 0$. Thus the response of the network for $t \geq 0$ can be obtained by adding two responses:[2] (1) the response for $t \geq 0$ when the excitation is $x_1(t)$, i.e., when the excitation is set to zero for $t \geq 0$; and (2) the response when the network is at rest for $t < 0$ and an excitation $x_2(t)$ is applied. The second of these components is obtained simply by the methods we have already developed for finding the response of a network that is initially at rest. The first component is obtained by setting all applied sources to zero for $t \geq 0$. Since, however, there will generally

---

[1] If there is more than one source, superposition methods can, of course, be used to obtain the total response by finding the reponse to each source separately, including the sources that account for nonrest conditions, and adding the results.

[2] We shall assume that before the application of any of the sources in the past the network was originally at rest. As a result, we can apply the principle of superposition to the network.

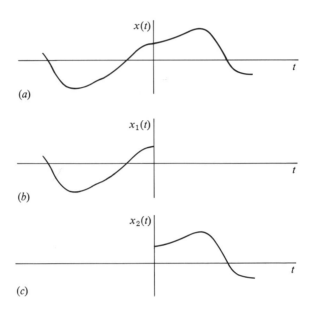

FIG. 3-61. The excitation $x(t)$ in (a) can be considered to be the sum of the two components $x_1(t)$ and $x_2(t)$, shown in (b) and (c) respectively.

he voltages across the capacitances and currents in the inductances at $t = 0-$, we can replace these elements by the equivalent networks of Figs. 3-59b and 3-60b. In these equivalent networks the capacitance and inductance elements are at rest for $t < 0$, and the step voltage and current sources start at $t = 0$. The first component of the response is, therefore, the response to these equivalent sources for $t \geq 0$.

In summary, then, when a network is not at rest for $t < 0$, we can find its response for $t \geq 0$ by setting all sources to zero for $t < 0$ and by replacing all inductances and capacitances by equivalent networks that are at rest for $t < 0$. These equivalent networks summarize the past history of the network prior to $t = 0$. Since the network that is obtained in this way is at rest for $t < 0$, we can use the methods we have already developed to find the response to each source separately, including the sources in the equivalent networks, and we can then apply the principle of superposition to find the total response for $t \geq 0$.

In order to illustrate these procedures, let us find the current response, for $t \geq 0$, of the RL network of Fig. 3-62, when the voltage source $v_s(t)$ is of the form shown at the left of the figure. We assume that $v_s(t)$ has remained at the constant value V_1 for a long time prior to $t = 0$. At

$t = 0-$, the current in the inductance is, by inspection, $i(0-) = V_1/R$. Thus, as far as the response for $t \geq 0$ is concerned, the inductance can be replaced by an inductance that is initially at rest, in parallel with a current source of value $(V_1/R)u_{-1}(t)$. Following the procedures we have developed, the total response for $t \geq 0$ is the sum of the responses $i_1(t)$ and $i_2(t)$ for the two situations shown in Fig. 3-63. In both cases, the network is at rest for $t < 0$. Using inspection methods, we can write the two parts of the response as follows:

$$i_1(t) = u_{-1}(t) \frac{V_1}{R} e^{-(R/L)t}, \qquad (3\text{-}49)$$

and

$$i_2(t) = u_{-1}(t) \frac{V_2}{R} (1 - e^{-(R/L)t}). \qquad (3\text{-}50)$$

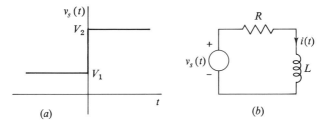

(a)   (b)

FIG. 3-62. Series RL network used to illustrate procedures for finding the response of a network that is not at rest for $t < 0$. The waveform of voltage source $v_s(t)$ is shown at the left.

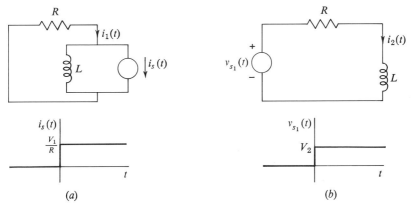

(a)   (b)

FIG. 3-63. Superposition of the responses $i_1(t)$ and $i_2(t)$ of the networks in (a) and (b) gives the total response of the network of Fig. 3-62, for $t \geq 0$.

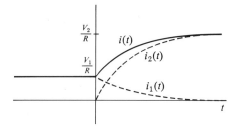

FIG. 3-64. Response of the *RL* network of Fig. 3-62. The dashed lines represent the two components of the response for $t \geq 0$, corresponding to the two situations depicted in Fig. 3-63.

The total response for $t \geq 0$ is given by $i(t) = i_1(t) + i_2(t)$ and is plotted in Fig. 3-64.

Problem 3-27

Using superposition, determine the current $i_1(t)$ for the network shown in Fig. 3-65. The network is at rest for $t < 0$.

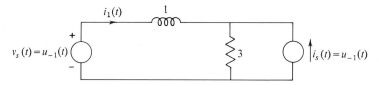

FIG. 3-65. Network for Prob. 3-27.

Problem 3-28

The resistive network N in Fig. 3-66 has two terminal pairs. When the network is excited as shown, the currents i_1 and i_2 are each equal to 1. When the voltage source at terminal pair *a-a'* is increased to 15, the current at terminal pair *b-b'* becomes zero.

What value of voltage source at *b-b'* would cause the current at *b-b'* to be zero if the voltage source at terminals *a-a'* has the value 10?

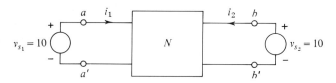

FIG. 3-66. Two-terminal-pair resistive network with a specified excitation (Prob. 3-28).

Problem 3-29

The voltage source in the network of Fig. 3-67 is $v_s(t) = e^{-2t}$ for $t \geq 0$, and the inductance current at $t = 0-$ is $i_L(0-) = 3$. Determine $i_L(t)$ for $t > 0$.

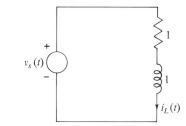

FIG. 3-67. Network for
Prob. 3-29.

Problem 3-30

In the network of Fig. 3-68, the capacitance voltage at $t = 0-$ is $v_C(0-) = 2$. If the source voltage is given by $v_s(t) = 6e^{-4t}$ for $t \geq 0$, determine the capacitance current $i_C(t)$ for $t > 0$, accounting for the initial conditions through the use of an equivalent source.

FIG. 3-68. Network for
Prob. 3-30.

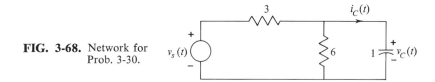

Problem 3-31

In many networks encountered in practice, an exact analytic expression for the excitation is not available. The excitation may be specified, for example, by an oscilloscope trace. If the network response is to be calculated, an analytic approximation to the excitation must be made.

Any waveform that can be generated in the laboratory has a Taylor's series representation and hence can be approximated arbitrarily closely in any given interval by a polynomial. An approximation in this form is particularly convenient, for it is readily expressible as a linear combination of singularity functions.

The network of Fig. 3-69, initially at rest, is excited by the voltage source waveform shown by the solid line in Fig. 3-70. This waveform can be

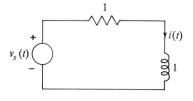

FIG. 3-69. *RL* network initially at rest. The voltage excitation $v_s(t)$ is shown in Fig. 3-70 (Prob. 3-31).

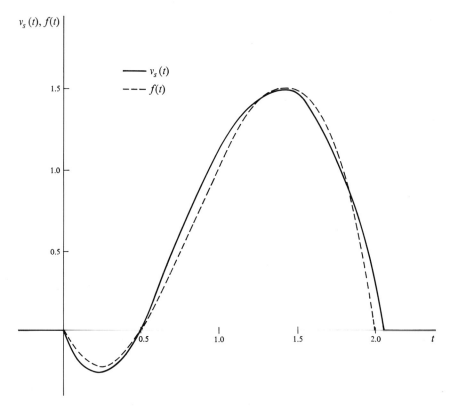

FIG. 3-70. Voltage excitation and polynomial approximation for the network of Fig. 3-69 (Prob. 3-31).

approximated by the dotted curve of Fig. 3-70, the exact expression for which is

$$f(t) = \begin{cases} -2t + 5t^2 - 2t^3 , & 0 < t \le 2 ; \\ 0 & , \text{ elsewhere .} \end{cases}$$

a. Determine the current $i(t)$ for $0 < t \le 2$ by using $f(t)$ as the source voltage $v_s(t)$.

b. Determine $i(t)$ for $t > 2$ by accounting for the inductance current at $t = 2$ by an equivalent source.

Problem 3-32

Several methods for determining the response of networks to simple excitations have been developed in the text. Let us determine the voltage response of the network shown in Fig. 3-71 by three different methods. The network is at rest for $t < 0$.

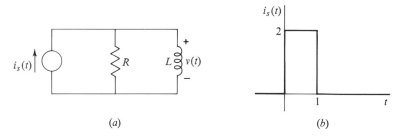

(a)   (b)

FIG. 3-71. Network and associated excitation used in Prob. 3-32 to illustrate three different methods of determining the response of networks to simple excitations.

a. *Method 1.* Find the differential equation relating $v(t)$ to $i_s(t)$. Solve this equation without referring back to the network, using the following method:

1. The right-hand side of the differential equation contains impulse functions. Replace the right-hand side by its integral in order that the right-hand side of the differential equation have only finite discontinuities.

2. Determine the solution to the resulting differential equation in each of the three regions $t < 0$, $0 \leq t < 1$, $t \geq 1$, using continuity arguments to evaluate the arbitrary constants.

3. Differentiate the result so obtained in order to find the solution for the actual excitation given (rather than its integral). Sketch the final result.

b. *Method 2.* Decompose the excitation into a linear combination of step functions. Determine the step response by inspection, and find the total solution as a linear combination of step responses. Sketch the result.

c. *Method 3.* Write the solution in the region $0 \leq t < 1$ as the response to a step applied at $t = 0$. Find the solution for $t \geq 1$ by replacing the inductance current at $t = 1-$ by an equivalent source. Sketch the result.

Networks with switches

In practice one frequently encounters systems that can be modeled by an interconnection of R, L, and C elements and sources together with switches. A switch has two states: it is a short circuit when it is closed and an open circuit when it is open. A network containing switches has the property, not previously encountered in our work, that the basic network may change depending on the switch positions, and consequently the differential equation governing the response may be altered when a switch is opened or closed. During a time interval within which the switch positions are fixed, however, the basic network is well defined, and the differential equation for the response can be readily determined.

Suppose, for example, that a switch were opened or closed at $t = 0$. Following the procedures we have already discussed for networks that are not initially at rest, we can consider the response starting at $t = 0$ to be the superposition of two responses: (1) the response for $t > 0$, assuming the excitation to be zero for $t > 0$, and (2) the response that would be obtained if the network configuration that exists for $t > 0$ were at rest for $t < 0$ and if all sources of excitation started at $t = 0$. The second component of the response can be obtained by the usual methods that apply to networks initially at rest. To determine the first component, i.e., the response of the source-free network for $t > 0$, we need to know the voltages across the capacitances and the currents through the inductances that would exist at $t = 0+$ if all sources were set to zero starting at $t - 0$. From the integral v-i relations for capacitances and inductances we know that the voltage across a capacitance cannot change instantaneously at $t = 0$ if the current through it is finite at $t = 0$, and the current through an inductance cannot change instantaneously at $t = 0$ if the voltage across it is finite at $t = 0$. If the voltages and currents are finite, therefore,[1] the initial values of the voltages across the capacitances and the currents

---

[1] The conditions under which the currents through the capacitances and the voltages across the inductances are finite when the switch is operated are similar to the conditions discussed on page 110 for networks with suddenly applied sources. As a matter of fact, it can be shown that, as far as the network behavior for $t > 0$ is concerned, a switch that is closed at $t = 0$ can be replaced by a step voltage source that changes instantaneously from the voltage existing across the switch at $t = 0-$ to zero voltage; likewise, a switch that is opened at $t = 0$ can be replaced by a step current source that changes instantaneously from the current in the switch at $t = 0-$ to zero current. In the former case, we can use the results derived on page 110 to show that an infinite current will exist in a capacitance at $t = 0$ only if there is a path through the network from one end of the source (or, in our case, the switch) to the other, which contains only capacitance branches. In the latter case, we can likewise show that an infinite voltage will exist across an inductance at $t = 0$ only if there is an inductance in all paths that can be drawn in the network from one end of the source (or, in our case, the switch) to the other. We shall not, however, consider these special cases in which infinite capacitance currents or inductance voltages arise.

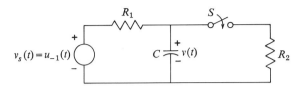

FIG. 3-72. Network used to illustrate the procedure for finding the response of a network containing a switch. The network is at rest for $t < 0$, and switch S is closed at $t = T$.

through the inductances for this first component of the response are equal to the values at $t = 0-$, i.e., just prior to the operation of the switch.

Let us examine the application of this procedure to the network of Fig. 3-72. We wish to find the voltage $v(t)$ across the capacitance, assuming the network to be at rest for $t < 0$. Switch S is closed at time $t = T$, where $T > 0$. Before the switch is closed, we have a simple series RC network with unit step voltage excitation applied at $t = 0$. The voltage response is given by

$$v(t) = u_{-1}(t)(1 - e^{-t/R_1C}).\qquad(3\text{-}51)$$

After the switch is closed, i.e., for $t > T$, we have seen that the response $v(t)$ can be considered to be the superposition of two responses: (1) the response $v_1(t)$, assuming the source to be zero for $t > T$, but with an initial voltage $v(T)$ across the capacitance, and (2) the response $v_2(t)$, assuming the network is at rest for $t < T$ and the source starts at $t = T$. The value of $v(t)$ is obtained by setting $t = T$ in Eq. (3-51). (We note that the voltage across the capacitance is the same immediately before and immediately after the switch is closed, since infinite current does not flow in the capacitance upon closing the switch.) Thus the two components $v_1(t)$ and $v_2(t)$ are the responses corresponding to the two situations shown in Fig. 3-73. The response $v_1(t)$ for the network in Fig. 3-73a for $t > T$

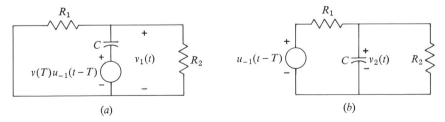

(a)   (b)

FIG. 3-73. These networks are used to find the response of the network in Fig. 3-72 after the switch S is closed at $t = T$. The total response for $t > T$ is the sum of the responses $v_1(t)$ and $v_2(t)$ of the networks in (a) and (b) respectively. Both networks are at rest for $t < T$.

is given by

$$v_1(t) = v(T)e^{-(t-T)/RC} , \qquad (3\text{-}52)$$

or, substituting the value of $v(T)$ from Eq. (3-51),

$$v_1(t) = (1 - e^{-T/R_1C})e^{-(t-T)/RC} . \qquad (3\text{-}53)$$

For the network of Fig. 3-73b the response for $t > T$ is given by

$$v_2(t) = \frac{R_2}{R_1 + R_2} (1 - e^{-(t-T)/RC}) , \qquad (3\text{-}54)$$

where $R = R_1R_2/(R_1 + R_2)$. The total response for $t > T$ is, therefore,

$$v(t) = \frac{R_2}{R_1 + R_2} (1 - e^{-(t-T)/RC}) + (1 - e^{-T/R_1C})e^{-(t-T)/RC}$$

$$= \frac{R_2}{R_1 + R_2} + \left(\frac{R_1}{R_1 + R_2} - e^{-T/R_1C}\right)e^{-(t-T)/RC} . \qquad (3\text{-}55)$$

The response for all $v(t)$ is plotted in Fig. 3-74.

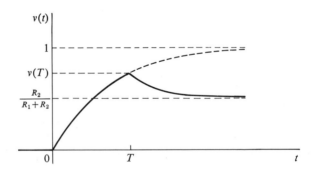

FIG. 3-74. The solid line shows the response $v(t)$ of the network of Fig. 3-72, in which switch S is closed at $t = T$. The dashed line indicates what the response would be if switch S remained open for all t.

Problem 3-33

The network shown in Fig. 3-75 is at rest for $t < 0$. The switch is open until $t = 1$, at which time it is closed. Determine and sketch the current $i_L(t)$ in the inductance for all t.

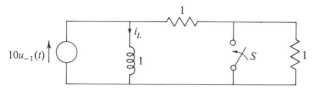

FIG. 3-75. Network for Prob. 3-33.

Problem 3-34

For the network shown in Fig. 3-76 the excitation i_s has been 2 amp for a very long time prior to $t = 0$, and the switch has been closed for a very long time prior to $t = 0$ (i.e., a time very long compared with the time constant of the network that exists with the switch closed). The switch is opened at $t = 0$ and closed again at $t = 1$.

Determine and sketch the response $i(t)$ for $t > -1$.

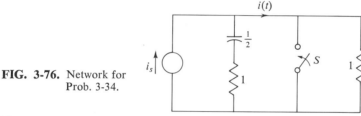

FIG. 3-76. Network for Prob. 3-34.

Problem 3-35

a. The network of Fig. 3-77 is at rest for $t < 0$ with switch S open. Find $i(t)$ with switch S open.

b. Assume that switch S has remained open for a long time, such that the homogeneous solutions for $i_1(t)$ and $i_2(t)$ are negligible compared with the particular integrals. Switch S is now closed at time T. Find $i(t)$ for $t \geq T$.

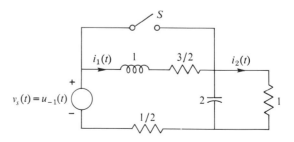

FIG. 3-77. Network for Prob. 3-77.

4

The Particular Integral; Steady-state Response of *RLC* Networks

The particular integral, and conditions under which it dominates the homogeneous solution

In our development to this point we have examined in some detail the behavior of *RLC* networks when excitations are suddenly applied at $t = 0$. We have seen that the response $y(t)$ of a network consisting of R, L, and C elements is the solution of a linear differential equation with constant coefficients, which can be written generally in the form

$$a_n \frac{d^n y}{dt^n} + a_{n-1} \frac{d^{n-1} y}{dt^{n-1}} + \cdots + a_1 \frac{dy}{dt} + a_0 y$$

$$= b_m \frac{d^m x}{dt^m} + b_{m-1} \frac{d^{m-1} x}{dt^{m-1}} + \cdots + b_1 \frac{dx}{dt} + b_0 x, \qquad (4\text{-}1)$$

where $x(t)$ is the excitation function. If the excitation function for the region $t > 0$ is of the form $x(t) = Xe^{s_p t}$, then the differential equation for this region can be written

$$a_n \frac{d^n y}{dt^n} + a_{n-1} \frac{d^{n-1} y}{dt^{n-1}} + \cdots + a_1 \frac{dy}{dt} + a_0 y \qquad (4\text{-}2)$$

$$= (b_m s_p^m + b_{m-1} s_p^{m-1} + \cdots + b_1 s_p + b_0) X e^{s_p t}.$$

Following the methods we developed in Chap. 2 for finding the solution of a linear constant-coefficient differential equation with an exponential excitation function, we try a solution of the form

$$y(t) = Ye^{s_p t}, \qquad (4\text{-}3)$$

where Y is a constant. Substituting this into Eq. (4-2), we find that (4-3) is a solution if Y is given by

$$Y = \frac{b_m s_p{}^m + b_{m-1} s_p{}^{m-1} + \cdots + b_1 s_p + b_0}{a_n s_p{}^n + a_{n-1} s_p{}^{n-1} + \cdots + a_1 s_p + a_0} X.$$ (4-4)

We have called the solution (4-3) the particular integral. The general solution of a differential equation is the sum of the particular integral and the homogeneous solution, i.e., the solution of the equation with the right-hand side set to zero. We have seen that the homogeneous solution for Eq. (4-1) for $t > 0$ is given by

$$y(t) = \sum_{k=1}^{n} A_k e^{s_k t},$$ (4-5)

where the A_k are arbitrary constants and the s_k are the roots of the characteristic equation; i.e., the s_k are the natural frequencies of the network. Thus the general solution for $t > 0$ can be written

$$y(t) = \sum_{k=1}^{n} A_k e^{s_k t} + Y e^{s_p t}.$$ (4-6)

In this chapter we shall focus our attention on the *particular integral* of the response of *RLC* networks to exponential excitations. We shall attempt to provide some insight into the relations between the analytical form of the particular integral and certain properties of the network response.

Our special interest in the particular integral stems from the fact that, in many situations that are encountered in practice, the homogeneous solution becomes arbitrarily small relative to the particular integral when t is sufficiently large. In these situations, therefore, the particular integral forms, in effect, the total response when the excitation has been applied for a sufficiently long time. For example, when an electric appliance is plugged into the a-c power outlet, the current that flows in the appliance after a fraction of a second has elapsed is determined entirely by the particular integral of the response, the homogeneous solution having decayed to a negligible value.

The conditions under which the particular integral forms the major component of the response can be examined by referring to Eq. (4-6.) Both the homogeneous solution and the particular integral are constructed from exponential functions of the form $B e^{s t}$, where B and s are constants that may be complex. If we write $s = \text{Re}\,(s) + j\,\text{Im}\,(s)$, then

$$e^{s t} = e^{[\text{Re}(s)] t} e^{j [\text{Im}(s)] t},$$ (4-7)

and hence the magnitude of the exponential function e^{st} is equal to $e^{[\mathrm{Re}(s)]t}$. If a response $y(t)$ consists of the sum of several exponential functions with different complex frequencies, the magnitude of the ratio between any two of these functions, say $B_a e^{s_a t}$ and $B_b e^{s_b t}$, is given by

$$\left|\frac{B_a e^{s_a t}}{B_b e^{s_b t}}\right| = \left|\frac{B_a}{B_b}\right| \left|e^{(s_a - s_b)t}\right| = \left|\frac{B_a}{B_b}\right| e^{[\mathrm{Re}(s_a - s_b)]t}, \tag{4-8}$$

which approaches zero as t is increased if $\mathrm{Re}\,(s_a) < \mathrm{Re}\,(s_b)$. Thus when t is sufficiently large, the response $y(t)$ must approach the exponential function whose complex frequency has (algebraically) the largest real part. With reference to Eq. (4-6), therefore, we can state that the particular integral will dominate the homogeneous solution for large t provided that $\mathrm{Re}\,(s_p) > \mathrm{Re}\,(s_k)$ for all s_k. When and if the particular integral can be considered to form the total solution, the network response is said to have reached the *steady state*.

It is often convenient to represent the complex frequencies s_k associated with the homogeneous solution (i.e., the natural frequencies of the network) and the complex frequency s_p of the excitation function as points in the complex plane. This plane is sometimes called the *complex-frequency plane*, or the *s plane*; if the complex frequency is given by $s = \sigma + j\omega$, then the abscissa is the real part σ and the ordinate is the imaginary part ω. The requirement that the particular integral dominate the homogeneous solution for large t can be interpreted as the requirement that the point in the s plane representing the complex frequency s_p of the excitation be located to the right of all points s_k.

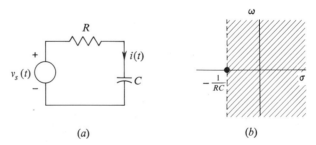

(a) (b)

FIG. 4-1. The natural frequency of the network in (a) is shown in (b) as a point in the s plane. The shaded area designates the region in which the complex frequency s_p of an exponential excitation must lie if the particular integral is to dominate the homogeneous solution for large t.

For the network of Fig. 4-1a, for example, the differential equation for the current $i(t)$ is

$$R\frac{di}{dt} + \frac{1}{C}i = \frac{dv_s}{dt}, \tag{4-9}$$

and the root of the characteristic equation is $s_1 = -1/RC$. This value of complex frequency is represented by a point on the negative real axis of the s plane, as shown in Fig. 4-1b. If the excitation function is an exponential of the form $V_s e^{s_p t}$, then for large t the particular integral dominates the homogeneous solution if Re $(s_p) > -1/RC$. If the complex frequency of the excitation is represented by a point in the s plane shown in Fig. 4-1b, then steady-state conditions are reached for large t if this point lies to the right of a vertical line passing through the point $-1/RC$, i.e., in the shaded area of the figure.

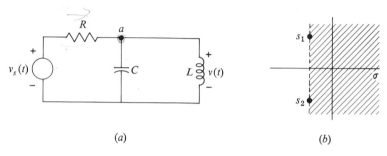

(a)   (b)

FIG. 4-2. The complex frequencies representing the solutions of the characteristic equation for the network in (a) are shown in (b) as s_1 and s_2 in the s plane. The shaded area has the same meaning as that in Fig. 4-1.

As a second example, consider the network shown in Fig. 4-2a. The equation for the voltage response $v(t)$ is obtained by applying Kirchhoff's current law to connection point a, giving

$$\frac{v - v_s}{R} + C\frac{dv}{dt} + \frac{1}{L}\int_{-\infty}^{t} v(\tau)d\tau = 0. \tag{4-10}$$

Rearranging terms and differentiating, we obtain

$$\frac{d^2v}{dt^2} + \frac{1}{RC}\frac{dv}{dt} + \frac{1}{LC}v = \frac{1}{RC}\frac{dv_s}{dt}. \tag{4-11}$$

There are two solutions of the characteristic equation which can be written in the form

$$s_1, s_2 = -\frac{1}{2RC} \pm j\sqrt{\frac{1}{LC} - \left(\frac{1}{2RC}\right)^2}. \tag{4-12}$$

These complex frequencies are shown in Fig. 4-2b as points in the s plane for the case where $1/LC > (1/2RC)^2$. Again we can state that, if the excitation is of the form $V_s e^{s_p t}$, then for large t the particular integral dominates the homogeneous solution if the point representing the complex frequency s_p lies in the shaded area of the figure to the right of a vertical line passing through the points s_1 and s_2.

Problem 4-1

The roots of the characteristic equation of a certain RLC network are plotted in Fig. 4-3. The excitation is of the form $u_{-1}(t)e^{s_p t}$.

a. Indicate the region in the s plane where the excitation frequency s_p can be located such that, for large time, (1) the particular integral dominates the homogeneous solution; (2) the homogeneous solution dominates the particular integral.

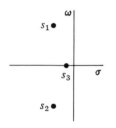

FIG. 4-3. Points in the s plane designating roots of the characteristic equation for Prob. 4-1; s_1 and s_2 are complex conjugates.

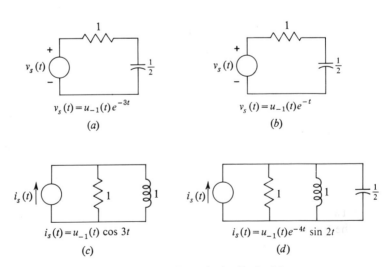

$v_s(t) = u_{-1}(t)e^{-3t}$

(a)

$v_s(t) = u_{-1}(t)e^{-t}$

(b)

$i_s(t) = u_{-1}(t) \cos 3t$

(c)

$i_s(t) = u_{-1}(t)e^{-4t} \sin 2t$

(d)

FIG. 4-4. Networks for Prob. 4-1.

b. For each of the networks shown in Fig. 4-4, indicate the positions in the complex plane of the natural frequencies of the network and the complex frequency or frequencies of the excitation. In each case determine the complex frequency or frequencies of the component of the solution that dominates for large t.

The system function

Definition.   From Eqs. (4-3) and (4-4), we can write the particular integral of the response of a system characterized by Eq. (4-1) as

$$y_p(t) = \frac{b_m s_p^m + b_{m-1} s_p^{m-1} + \cdots + b_1 s_p + b_0}{a_n s_p^n + a_{n-1} s_p^{n-1} + \cdots + a_1 s_p + a_0} X e^{s_p t} . \qquad (4\text{-}13)$$

If we now let

$$B(s_p) = b_m s_p^m + b_{m-1} s_p^{m-1} + \cdots + b_1 s_p + b_0 , \qquad (4\text{-}14)$$

and

$$A(s_p) = a_n s_p^n + a_{n-1} s_p^{n-1} + \cdots + a_1 s_p + a_0 , \qquad (4\text{-}15)$$

then the particular integral becomes

$$y_p(t) = \frac{B(s_p)}{A(s_p)} X e^{s_p t} . \qquad (4\text{-}16)$$

The complex amplitude of the particular integral is $[B(s_p)/A(s_p)] X$; i.e., it is obtained by multiplying the complex amplitude of the excitation by $B(s_p)/A(s_p)$.

The rational function $B(s_p)/A(s_p)$ plays a very significant role in network theory. It is the ratio of the complex amplitude of the particular integral of the response of an *RLC* network to the complex amplitude of the exponential excitation function. The general name that is applied to this ratio is *system function.* The system function $B(s_p)/A(s_p)$ is often designated by $H(s_p)$. When and if steady-state conditions are reached in the network, the particular integral forms the total response, and then the system function relates the complex amplitude of the total response to the complex amplitude of the excitation.

In general the system function is a function of the complex frequency s_p of the excitation function. For a given complex frequency s_p of the excitation, the system function $H(s_p)$ is simply a complex number; it can be specified either by its real and imaginary parts or by its magnitude and angle. Since the complex amplitude Y of the response[1] is given by

---

[1] Since in this chapter we are concerned primarily with the particular integral of the response, we shall for convenience use the term "response" to refer to this component unless otherwise noted.

$$Y = H(s_p)X, \qquad\qquad (4\text{-}17)$$

we see that the magnitude of the complex amplitude of the response is equal to the magnitude of the system function multiplied by the magnitude of the complex amplitude of the excitation function; its angle is equal to the angle of the system function plus the angle of the complex amplitude of the excitation function.

Types of system functions.   Various names are assigned to the system function, depending on the excitation and response variables that it relates. These names are summarized in Table 4-1. Two types of impedances and admittances are usually distinguished: *driving-point* impedances and admittances and *transfer* impedances and admittances. A system function is designated as a driving-point impedance or admittance when the pertinent current and voltage are measured at the same pair of terminals; the term transfer impedance or transfer admittance is used when the excitation and response variables are measured at two different pairs of terminals.

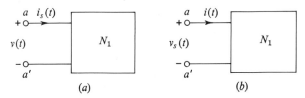

FIG. 4-5. Illustrating the definition of (*a*) driving-point impedance and (*b*) driving-point admittance. The driving-point impedance in (*a*) is $Z = V/I^s$, and the driving-point impedance in (*b*) is $Y = I/V^s$, where the quantities I_s and V_s represent complex amplitudes of excitations, and V and I represent complex amplitudes of responses.

Thus in Fig. 4-5*a*, if the excitation of the *RLC* network N_1 is a current $i_s(t) = I_s e^{s_p t}$ and the particular integral of the voltage response $v(t)$ is $V e^{s_p t}$, then $Z = V/I_s$ is the driving-point impedance at the terminals *a-a'*. Likewise, for the same network in Fig. 4-5*b*, the driving-point admittance at terminals *a-a'* is $Y = I/V_s$, where V_s is the complex amplitude of the

TABLE 4-1   Types of system functions

Name	Symbol	Excitation	Response
Impedance	Z	current	voltage
Admittance	Y	voltage	current
Transfer ratio		both voltage or both current	

excitation and I is the complex amplitude of the current response. We have already established (pages 23 to 25), however, that for a network connected to the external environment through only one terminal pair the relation between the current at the terminal pair and the voltage across the terminal pair is independent of the external environment. Thus the differential equation relating the voltage $v(t)$ and the current $i(t)$ at the terminals a-a' of network N_1, shown in Fig. 4-6, is the same independent

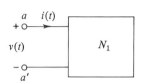

FIG. 4-6. The differential equation relating $v(t)$ and $i(t)$ for network N_1 is independent of the external network that is connected to terminals a-a'.

of whether v is the excitation and i the response or vice versa. In general, this equation is of the form shown in (4-1); when v is the excitation, the equation would normally be written

$$a_n \frac{d^n i}{dt^n} + a_{n-1} \frac{d^{n-1} i}{dt^{n-1}} + \cdots + a_0 i = b_m \frac{d^m v}{dt^m} + b_{m-1} \frac{d^{m-1} v}{dt^{m-1}} + \cdots + b_0 v, \quad (4\text{-}18)$$

and when i is the excitation, the equation is the same except the left- and right-hand sides would be interchanged if the convention of keeping the excitation on the right is maintained. It follows, therefore, that the system function when v is the excitation is the reciprocal of the system function when i is the excitation. Thus for the particular case of driving-point impedances and admittances,[1] we have the relation

$$Z = \frac{1}{Y} . \qquad (4\text{-}19)$$

A driving-point impedance, therefore, can be viewed simply as the ratio of the complex amplitude of the voltage to the complex amplitude of the current at the terminal pair independent of how the exponential excitation is applied.

The definitions of transfer impedance and admittance are illustrated in Fig. 4-7a and b. In Fig. 4-7a, a current excitation of complex amplitude I_a is applied at terminals a-a', and a voltage response of complex amplitude V_b is obtained across terminals b-b' in the network as shown. The transfer impedance Z_{ba} is then defined as the ratio V_b/I_a. Likewise in Fig.

---

[1] The reader should determine why the above derivation does not lead to a similar reciprocal relation in the case of transfer impedances.

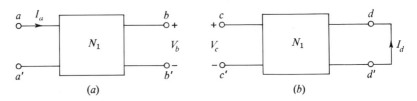

FIG. 4-7. Illustrating the definition of (*a*) transfer impedance and (*b*) transfer admittance. The transfer impedance in (*a*) is $Z_{ba} = V_b/I_a$, and the transfer admittance in (*b*) is $Y_{dc} = I_d/V_c$. The quantities I_a and V_c represent the complex amplitudes of the excitations $i_a(t)$ and $v_c(t)$, and V_b and I_d represent the complex amplitudes of the responses $v_b(t)$ and $i_d(t)$.

4-7*b* a voltage excitation of complex amplitude V_c is applied at terminals *c-c'*, and a current response of complex amplitude I_d is obtained in the short circuit connecting terminals *d-d'* of the network as shown. The transfer admittance Y_{dc} is then defined as the ratio I_d/V_c.

Problem 4-2

a. Each of the following differential equations relates the excitation $x(t)$ and the response $y(t)$ of some linear system. Find the corresponding system functions:

1. $\dfrac{dy}{dt} + 3y = 2x.$

2. $\dfrac{d^2y}{dt^2} + 4\dfrac{dy}{dt} + y = 2\dfrac{dx}{dt} + x.$

3. $\dfrac{d^3y}{dt^3} + 6\dfrac{d^2y}{dt^2} + 11\dfrac{dy}{dt} + 6y = \dfrac{d^2x}{dt^2} + x.$

b. Find the differential equation relating the excitation $x(t)$ and the response $y(t)$ for the system characterized by each of the following system functions:

1. $H(s_p) = \dfrac{s_p + 2}{s_p^2 + 2s_p + 2}.$

2. $H(s_p) = \dfrac{(s_p + 1 + j)(s_p + 1 - j)}{(s_p + 1)(s_p + 2)(s_p + 3)}.$

3. $H(s_p) = \dfrac{s_p + 2}{(s_p + 1)(s_p + 3)}.$

c. In each of the examples of (*b*), what is the homogeneous solution for $y(t)$, expressed in terms of arbitrary constants?

Problem 4-3

The driving-point impedance of a certain two-terminal network is given by

$$Z(s_p) = \frac{V}{I} = \frac{s_p^2 + 2s_p + 2}{s_p^2 + s_p + 1}.$$

Assuming that the current excitation is $i_s(t) = u_{-1}(t)$, find the asymptotic value of the voltage response $v(t)$ as $t \to \infty$.

Problem 4-4

In a model for a certain d-c voltmeter, the relation between the pointer deflection $\theta(t)$ and the input voltage $v(t)$ can be described by a linear constant-coefficient differential equation with a corresponding system function

$$\frac{\Theta}{V} = H(s_p) = \frac{K}{s_p + a},$$

where Θ and V are the complex amplitudes of $\theta(t)$ and $v(t)$, respectively, and K and a are real positive constants whose values depend on the structure of the voltmeter.

a. If the input voltage is $v(t) = Au_{-1}(t)$, where A is a real constant, what is the final value of $\theta(t)$, i.e., the value of $\theta(t)$ as $t \to \infty$?

b. We want to design the voltmeter such that $\theta(t)$ reaches at least 99 per cent of its final value $1/10$ sec after a step voltage has been applied (assuming that the meter is initially at rest). What is the permissible range for the constant a?

Impedance and admittance of R, L, and C elements. In order to determine the impedances or admittances of R, L, and C elements, we need to return to the differential equation relating v and i in each case.

Inductance. The differential equation relating v and i is

$$v = L\frac{di}{dt}.$$

For $v = Ve^{s_pt}$ and $i = Ie^{s_pt}$, we have
$$Ve^{s_pt} = Ls_pIe^{s_pt}.$$

Therefore,

$$Z(s_p) = \frac{V}{I} = Ls_p, \tag{4-20}$$

and

$$Y(s_p) = \frac{I}{V} = \frac{1}{Ls_p}. \tag{4-21}$$

Capacitance. The differential equation relating v and i is

$$i = C \frac{dv}{dt}.$$

For $v = Ve^{s_p t}$ and $i = Ie^{s_p t}$, we have
$$Ie^{s_p t} = Cs_p Ve^{s_p t}.$$

Therefore,
$$Z(s_p) = \frac{V}{I} = \frac{1}{Cs_p}, \tag{4-22}$$

and
$$Y(s_p) = \frac{I}{V} = Cs_p. \tag{4-23}$$

Resistance.　The voltage-current relation is

$$v = iR.$$

For $v = Ve^{s_p t}$ and $i = Ie^{s_p t}$, we have
$$Ve^{s_p t} = RIe^{s_p t}.$$

Therefore,
$$Z(s_p) = \frac{V}{I} = R, \tag{4-24}$$

and
$$Y(s_p) = \frac{I}{V} = G = \frac{1}{R}. \tag{4-25}$$

In the case of a resistance, we see that the impedance is a constant independent of the complex frequency s_p and is identical with the resistance R. For an inductance or capacitance, on the other hand, the impedance is a function of s_p.

Determination of the system function by algebraic methods.　Having determined the impedance of the basic elements, we shall now establish procedures for evaluating system functions for networks that consist of interconnections of these elements. One method that can always be used to obtain the system function is to set up the differential equation for the network response and then to write down $B(s_p)/A(s_p)$ by inspection of that equation. We shall now show, however, that the system function can be computed by direct algebraic methods that are analogous to the techniques used for solving resistive networks. Those techniques were based on Kirchhoff's laws, which apply to the distributions of voltages and currents in a network. The procedure we shall describe is based on the result that the complex amplitudes of the voltages and currents in a network also obey Kirchhoff's laws, and hence we shall first prove this result.

Consider the set of equilibrium equations for an *RLC* network, consisting of KCL equations, KVL equations, and voltage-current relations for the elements, and suppose that the excitation is a complex exponential with complex frequency s_p. We have required that these equilibrium equations be satisfied for real or complex time functions. For the case in which the roots of the characteristic equation are distinct from each other and from s_p, each voltage in the network can be written, for $t > 0$, in the form

$$v_j(t) = A_{1j}e^{s_1 t} + A_{2j}e^{s_2 t} + \cdots + A_{1j}e^{s_l t} + V_j e^{s_p t}. \qquad (4\text{-}26)$$

In this expression we have included all the natural frequencies $s_1, s_2, \ldots, s_l$ that are associated with all the voltage variables in the network. (For a given voltage, some of the constants $A_{1j}, A_{2j}, \ldots, A_{1j}$ may, of course, be zero.) Since the $v_j(t)$ are solutions of the network equilibrium equations they satisfy KVL, and hence for any closed path we can write

$$\sum_{\substack{\text{around} \\ \text{closed path}}} v_j(t) = 0. \qquad (4\text{-}27)$$

Using the expression for $v_j(t)$ given in Eq. (4-26), we can write this KVL equation as

$$\left(\sum A_{1j}\right)e^{s_1 t} + \left(\sum A_{2j}\right)e^{s_2 t} + \cdots + \left(\sum A_{1j}\right)e^{s_l t} + \left(\sum V_j\right)e^{s_p t} = 0, \qquad (4\text{-}28)$$

where each summation is around the closed path indicated by the summation in Eq. (4-27). If Eq. (4-28) is to hold for all time, it can be shown[1] that the coefficient of each exponential time function must be zero. In particular, the coefficient of $e^{s_p t}$ is zero, and we conclude that

$$\sum_{\substack{\text{around} \\ \text{closed path}}} V_j = 0. \qquad (4\text{-}29)$$

Following a similar argument, we can verify that the sum of the complex amplitudes of the currents entering any connection point is zero; i.e.,

$$\sum_{\substack{\text{into connection} \\ \text{point}}} I_j = 0. \qquad (4\text{-}30)$$

We have thus established that, for the particular integrals of responses to exponential excitations, the complex amplitudes of the voltages and currents in a network satisfy Kirchhoff's voltage and current laws. We have also seen that the relations between the complex amplitudes of the voltages and currents at the terminals of the R, L, and C elements are of the form $V = ZI$, or $I = YV$. Thus a set of simultaneous algebraic equations can be written for the complex amplitudes of the voltages and

---

[1] See W. Kaplan, *Ordinary Differential Equations*, Addison-Wesley Publishing Company, Inc., Reading, Mass., 1958, p. 143.

currents in an *RLC* network, and these are completely analogous to the equilibrium equations relating the voltages and currents for resistive networks. For comparison, the relevant quantities and relations are summarized in Table 4-2. Both sets of equations are algebraic. The only

TABLE 4-2   **Analogous quantities and relations used to establish equilibrium equations for complex amplitudes of voltages and currents in *RLC* networks and voltages and currents in resistive networks**

RLC networks	Resistive networks
V	v
I	i
$V = ZI$	$v = Ri$
KCL and KVL applied to complex amplitudes of voltages and currents	KCL and KVL applied to voltages and currents

difference between them is that one set involves complex amplitudes of exponential voltages and currents (designated by capital letters), and the other involves the voltages and currents themselves (designated by small letters).

We conclude, therefore, that we can solve for the complex amplitudes of the voltages and currents in a network in the same manner as we solved for voltages and currents in a resistive network. In effect, for the particular integrals of the responses associated with exponential excitations, we have reduced a set of differential equations relating the voltages and currents in a network containing R's, L's and C's to a set of algebraic equations relating the complex amplitudes of the voltages and currents. We are able to do this because, as we have seen, an exponential excitation for an *RLC* network yields an exponential response[1] (particular integral) with the same complex frequency. Once we have solved the algebraic equations for the complex amplitude of a given response, the response is obtained simply by multiplying by $e^{s_p t}$.

Since for an exponential excitation the complex amplitude of the response is the quantity that is of direct concern to us when we are focusing our attention on the particular integral, it is convenient to specify exponential voltages and currents in network diagrams simply by their complex amplitudes, which we designate by capital letters.

---

[1] As before, we assume that the complex frequency of the excitation is distinct from the natural frequencies of the network.

Determination of system functions for some simple networks. To illustrate the application of Kirchhoff's laws to the complex amplitudes of the voltages and currents in a network, let us determine the voltage-current relations for several simple connections of impedances. Consider first a series connection of two impedances Z_1 and Z_2, as shown in Fig. 4-8.

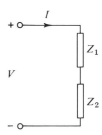

FIG. 4-8. Two impedances
in series.

From Kirchhoff's current law (applied to the complex amplitudes of the currents) we conclude that the complex amplitude of the current is the same in each impedance, and is equal to I. By Kirchhoff's voltage law and the *V-I* relations of impedances, the complex amplitude V of the voltage across the series combination is

$$V = Z_1 I + Z_2 I .\qquad(4\text{-}31)$$

The impedance of the series combination is then

$$\frac{V}{I} = Z = Z_1 + Z_2 ;\qquad(4\text{-}32)$$

i.e., series impedances combine additively in the same way as series resistances. This result could have been predicted without any computations, since the algebraic equilibrium equations for an interconnection of impedances are entirely analogous to those for the corresponding resistive network.

For the parallel impedances shown in Fig. 4-9, a voltage with complex amplitude V appears across both impedances, and the current I is

$$I = \frac{V}{Z_1} + \frac{V}{Z_2}.\qquad(4\text{-}33)$$

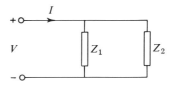

FIG. 4-9. Two impedances
in parallel.

Therefore the impedance of the parallel combination is

$$\frac{V}{I} = Z = \frac{1}{1/Z_1 + 1/Z_2} = \frac{Z_1 Z_2}{Z_1 + Z_2}. \tag{4-34}$$

By inverting this Z or by using admittances in Eq. (4-33), we obtain

$$Y = Y_1 + Y_2, \tag{4-35}$$

where $Y_1 = 1/Z_1$ and $Y_2 = 1/Z_2$. Thus parallel admittances combine additively in the same way as parallel conductances, a result that again could have been predicted from the similarity of the basic equilibrium equations listed in Table 4-2.

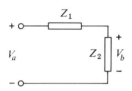

FIG. 4-10. Connection of impedances to illustrate the computation of a transfer function.

As another example, let us determine the transfer ratio V_b/V_a for the network of Fig. 4-10. We recognize this to be analogous to a resistive voltage divider network, and hence we can immediately write

$$\frac{V_b}{V_a} = \frac{Z_2}{Z_1 + Z_2}. \tag{4-36}$$

Figure 4-11 shows a somewhat more complicated network containing two meshes. The source is labeled simply by its complex amplitude V_s, and the complex amplitudes of the currents in the various branches are also labeled. Application of Kirchhoff's voltage laws to the two meshes

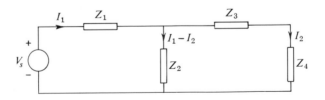

FIG. 4-11. Example of an impedance network with two meshes.

and substitution of the V-I relations for the elements in the resulting equations give the two equations

$$Z_1 I_1 + Z_2(I_1 - I_2) = V_s, \tag{4-37}$$

and
$$Z_3 I_2 + Z_4 I_2 - Z_2(I_1 - I_2) = 0, \tag{4-38}$$

from which the complex amplitudes I_1 and I_2 can be determined. Again the equations relating the complex amplitudes of the currents and the source voltage are algebraic and are exactly analogous to the equilibrium equations that would be obtained in terms of the actual currents and source voltage if the elements were resistances.

Problem 4-5

For each of the networks in Fig. 4-12 determine the driving-point impedance. Express your answers as ratios of polynomials in s_p.

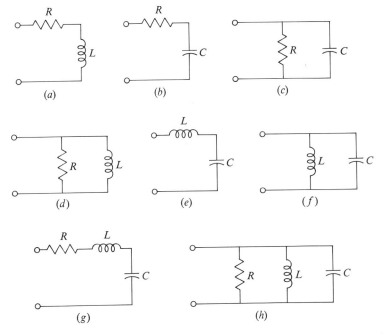

FIG. 4-12. Networks for which driving-point impedances are to be determined (Prob. 4-5).

Problem 4-6

For each of the networks of Fig. 4-13 determine the system function relating the indicated response to the excitation. Your answers should be expressed as ratios of polynomials in s_p.

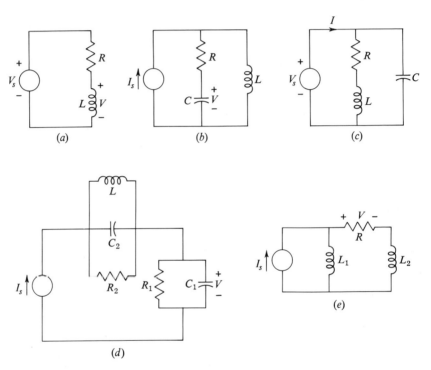

FIG. 4-13. Networks for which system functions are to be determined (Prob. 4-6).

Use of the system function to determine network responses

General approach. To illustrate the use of the system function to determine the particular integral of a network response, let us consider an *RLC* network excited by a source that is constructed from complex exponential building blocks of the form $Xe^{s_p t}$. The particular integral of the response corresponding to this excitation function is of the form $y(t) = Ye^{s_p t}$. If we represent the system function Y/X by $H(s_p)$, then the response is given by

$$y(t) = H(s_p)Xe^{s_p t} . \tag{4-39}$$

Suppose, for example, that the excitation is the real exponential function

$$x(t) = Ae^{\sigma t}, \tag{4-40}$$

where A and σ are real. The particular integral of the response is then

$$y(t) = H(\sigma)Ae^{\sigma t}. \tag{4-41}$$

Thus the response to a single real exponential excitation of complex frequency σ is simply the product of the excitation function and the system function, the latter being evaluated at the excitation frequency $s_p = \sigma$.

Very often we are interested in real source currents or voltages that can be expressed as the sum of two conjugate complex exponential building blocks. For example, if the excitation is the real time function

$$x(t) = Ae^{\sigma t} \cos{(\omega t + \phi)}, \tag{4-42}$$

then, as we have seen on pages 61 to 62, this can be expressed in terms of exponential building blocks as

$$x(t) = \tfrac{1}{2}Xe^{s_p t} + \tfrac{1}{2}X^* e^{s_p^* t}, \tag{4-43}$$

or, alternatively, as

$$x(t) = \text{Re}\,[Xe^{s_p t}], \tag{4-44}$$

where $X = Ae^{j\phi}$, and $s_p = \sigma + j\omega$. In order to determine the response to the excitation $x(t)$, we can proceed in either of the following ways: (1) find the response due to each exponential function in (4-43) separately, and then add the responses; or (2) find the response due to the single exponential function $Xe^{s_p t}$ and take the real part of the result.[1] Using the second method we can immediately write the response to the given excitation as

$$y(t) = \text{Re}\,[H(s_p)Xe^{s_p t}]. \tag{4-45}$$

Responses to sinusoidal excitations. An excitation that is of special interest in network theory is the sinusoidal excitation with constant amplitude. The principal reasons for the importance of sinusoids stem from the facts that (1) sinusoidal signals or combinations of them are easy to generate; (2) sinusoidal signals have the convenient property, in common with exponentials, that they preserve their form under linear time-invariant operations, e.g., a sinusoidal excitation of an *RLC* network yields a sinusoidal response of the same frequency; and (3) as will be seen in later

---

[1] This procedure was justified for the total response (homogeneous solution plus particular integral) in Prob. 2-24 but can readily be justified for the particular integral alone.

studies, a very broad class of functions can be represented as sums of sinusoids. Thus if we can determine the response of an *RLC* network to sinusoidal excitations, we can use superposition to determine the response to any member of this broad class of functions.

As an example of a sinusoidal excitation, let us suppose that the excitation of an *RLC* network is

$$x(t) = A \cos (\omega t + \phi), \qquad (4\text{-}46)$$

where A, ω, and ϕ are real constants. In terms of exponential building blocks, this can be written

$$x(t) = \tfrac{1}{2}Xe^{j\omega t} + \tfrac{1}{2}X^*e^{-j\omega t}, \qquad (4\text{-}47)$$

or, equivalently,

$$x(t) = \text{Re}\, [Xe^{j\omega t}], \qquad (4\text{-}48)$$

where $X = Ae^{j\phi}$. The angle ϕ is sometimes called the *phase* of the excitation. The response to the excitation (4-48) is given by

$$y(t) = \text{Re}\, [H(j\omega)Xe^{j\omega t}], \qquad (4\text{-}49)$$

which can be expressed in the sinusoidal f..rm

$$y(t) = |H(j\omega)|\, |X| \cos [\omega t + \phi + \Theta(j\omega)], \qquad (4\text{-}50)$$

where $\Theta(j\omega)$ is the angle of the system function $H(j\omega)$; i.e., $H(j\omega) = |H(j\omega)|e^{j\Theta(j\omega)}$. Since $|X| = A$, Eq. (4-50) can be written

$$y(t) = |H(j\omega)|A \cos [\omega t + \phi + \Theta(j\omega)]. \qquad (4\text{-}51)$$

From the sinusoidal form of the response (4-51), the following useful properties of the response of *RLC* networks to sinusoidal excitations are brought into evidence: (1) the response to a sinusoidal excitation of frequency $\omega/2\pi$ is a sinusoid with the same frequency but in general with a different amplitude and phase; (2) the amplitude of the sinusoidal response is the product of the amplitude of the excitation and the magnitude of the system function evaluated at the complex frequency $j\omega$; (3) the phase of the response [in our case $\phi + \Theta(j\omega)$] is the sum of the phase ϕ of the excitation and the angle Θ of the system function evaluated at the complex frequency $j\omega$.

EXAMPLES. We shall now apply the principles just discussed to the computation of the particular integral of the response of some simple networks that are excited either by a real exponential excitation or by a sinusoidal excitation. As a first example, consider the network shown in

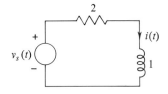

FIG. 4-14. Series *RL* network excited by a voltage source. The particular integral of the current $i(t)$ is to be determined for various excitations $v_s(t)$.

Fig. 4-14; we wish to find the particular integral of the current response $i(t)$ to the excitation $v_s(t)$.

Let us assume initially that the source voltage is a real exponential time function, given by

$$v_s(t) = 3e^{-(1/2)t}.$$ (4-52)

The admittance of the series *RL* network is

$$Y = \frac{1}{R + s_pL} = \frac{1}{2 + s_p},$$ (4-53)

which, for $s_p = -\frac{1}{2}$, reduces to $Y = \frac{2}{3}$. The particular integral of the current response is, therefore,

$$i(t) = 3Ye^{-(1/2)t} = 2e^{-(1/2)t}.$$ (4-54)

We note that steady-state conditions are achieved for large t in this example, since the excitation frequency $s_p = -\frac{1}{2}$ is algebraically greater than the root of the characteristic equation of the network, which is $s = -2$.

Let us now consider the problem of finding the response of the network of Fig. 4-14 when the voltage source is sinusoidal, say[1]

$$v_s(t) = 4 \cos (3t + \angle 30°).$$ (4-55)

This function can be written as a sum of exponentials or, alternatively, as

$$v_s(t) = \text{Re} [4\angle 30° \, e^{j3t}].$$ (4-56)

Following the procedure noted above, we obtain the response function corresponding to the exponential excitation $4 \quad 30° \, e^{j3t}$ and then take the real part of the result. The admittance, evaluated at $s_p = j3$, is given by

$$Y = \frac{1}{2 + j3} = \frac{1}{\sqrt{13}} \angle -56.3°.$$ (4-57)

---

[1] For purposes of computation it is often convenient to express numerical values of phase angles in degrees rather than in radians. When an angle is in degrees the symbol ° will always be used.

Thus the response is

$$i(t) = \text{Re}\left[\frac{4}{\sqrt{13}} \angle -26.3°e^{j3t}\right]$$

$$= \frac{4}{\sqrt{13}} \cos(3t - 26.3°). \tag{4-58}$$

We could, of course, have written down the response (4-58) directly from the result given previously in Eq. (4-51), once we had determined the magnitude and angle of the system function at the complex frequency $s_p = j3$. Graphical representations of the source voltage and of the steady-

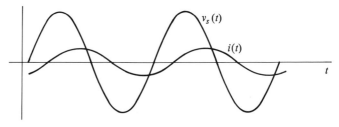

FIG. 4-15. Source voltage and steady-state current response of the network in Fig. 4-14 for a sinusoidal excitation $v_s(t) = 4 \cos(3t+30°)$.

state current response, which are displayed in Fig. 4-15, clearly demonstrate the change in amplitude and shift in phase of the response relative to the excitation.

As another example, consider the network shown in Fig. 4-16, in which

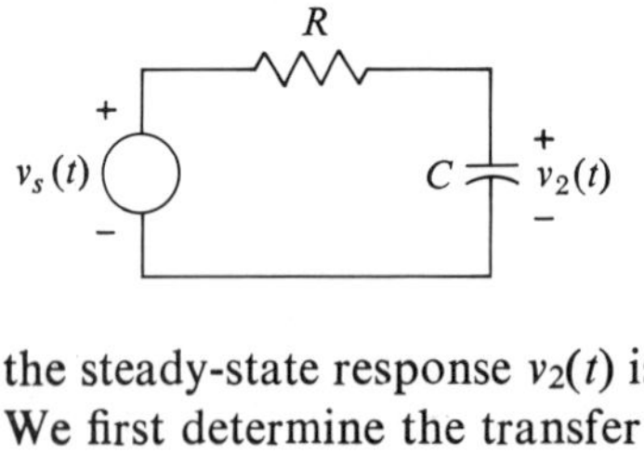

$v_s(t)$ R C $v_2(t)$

FIG. 4-16. Series RC network excited by a sinusoidal voltage source $v_s(t) = \cos \omega t$.

the steady-state response $v_2(t)$ is desired for a source voltage $v_s(t) = \cos \omega t$. We first determine the transfer ratio V_2/V_s by inspection:

$$\frac{V_2}{V_s} = \frac{1/s_pC}{R + 1/s_pC} = \frac{1}{RC} \cdot \frac{1}{s_p + 1/RC}. \tag{4-59}$$

Recognizing that the source voltage can be written as

$$v_s(t) = \text{Re}[V_s e^{j\omega t}],$$

we first evaluate the transfer ratio at $s_p = j\omega$, giving

$$\frac{V_2}{V_s} = \frac{1}{RC} \cdot \frac{1}{j\omega + 1/RC}, \qquad (4\text{-}60)$$

or, in polar form,

$$\frac{V_2}{V_s} = \frac{1}{RC} \frac{1}{\sqrt{\omega^2 + (1/RC)^2}} e^{j\theta}, \qquad (4\text{-}61)$$

where $\theta = -\tan^{-1} \omega RC$. Using this result, we can immediately write down the particular integral of the response as

$$v_2(t) = \mathrm{Re} \left[\frac{1}{RC} \frac{1}{\sqrt{\omega^2 + (1/RC)^2}} e^{j\theta} e^{j\omega t} \right]$$

$$= \frac{1}{RC} \frac{1}{\sqrt{\omega^2 + (1/RC)^2}} \cos(\omega t + \theta). \qquad (4\text{-}62)$$

Problem 4-7

The excitations in the networks of Fig. 4-17 are sinusoidal. In each case find the steady-state response for the indicated variable.

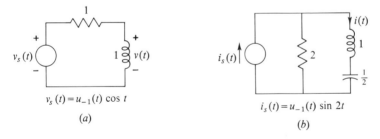

$v_s(t) = u_{-1}(t) \cos t$

(a)

$i_s(t) = u_{-1}(t) \sin 2t$

(b)

FIG. 4-17. Networks for which system functions are to be determined (Prob. 4-6).

Problem 4-8

For the network shown in Fig. 4-18, the transfer impedance $Z_{21}(s_p)$ is

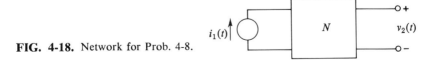

FIG. 4-18. Network for Prob. 4-8.

$$Z_{21}(s_p) = \frac{V_2}{I_1} = \frac{s_p}{s_p^2 + 3s_p + 2}.$$

For each of the excitations given below, determine whether steady state exists. Assuming that the network is at rest for $t < 0$, determine that part of $v_2(t)$ which dominates for large t in each case:

1. $i_1(t) = u_{-1}(t) \cos 2t$.
2. $i_1(t) = u_{-1}(t)e^{-t/2}$.
3. $i_1(t) = u_{-1}(t)e^{-3t}$.

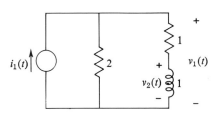

FIG. 4-19. Network for Prob. 4-9.

Problem 4-9

Consider the network shown in Fig. 4-19.
a. Determine the transfer impedance $Z_{21}(s_p) = V_2/I_1$.
b. When $i_1(t) = u_{-1}(t)e^{-2t}$, determine the term in $v_2(t)$ that dominates for large t if (1) the network is initially at rest, (2) $v_1(0-) = 2$ volts, owing to some excitation that occurred prior to $t = -1$.
c. Determine the complete solution for $v_2(t)$ for $t \geq 0$ when $i_1(t) = u_{-1}(t)e^{-2t}$ and the network is initially at rest.

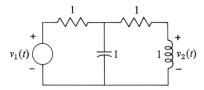

FIG. 4-20. Network for Prob. 4-10.

Problem 4-10

a. For the network of Fig. 4-20, find the voltage transfer ratio V_2/V_1.
b. Assuming $v_1(t) = \sin t + 2 \sin (\sqrt{2}t + \pi/3)$, for $t > 0$, find the steady-state solution for $v_2(t)$.

Problem 4-11

In the network of Fig. 4-21, $v_1(t)$ is the excitation and $v_2(t)$ is the response. The impulse response of the system is proportional to e^{-2t} for $t > 0$. Consider now an exponential excitation with complex frequency s_p. As s_p

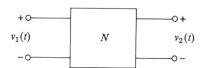

FIG. 4-21. Network for Prob. 4-11.

tends to zero, the voltage transfer function V_2/V_1 also tends to zero. As s_p approaches infinity, the transfer function approaches unity.

a. Determine the transfer function V_2/V_1.

b. If $v_1(t) = u_{-1}(t)e^{-4t}$, find the particular integral of $v_2(t)$ for $t > 0$.

c. For the same $v_1(t)$ as in (*b*), and if $v_2(0-) = 0$, find the dominant solution of $v_2(t)$ for large t.

Problem 4-12

The system function of a certain *RLC* network is of the form

$$H(s_p) = K \frac{s_p + a}{s_p^2 + bs_p + c},$$

where K, a, b, and c are real constants. When the excitation is $x(t) = u_{-1}(t) \cos t$, the response is

$$y(t) = \left[Ae^{-2t} \cos (t + \theta) + \sqrt{2} \cos \left(t + \frac{\pi}{4} \right) \right] u_{-1}(t),$$

where A and θ are real constants. Find values for K, a, b, and c.

Problem 4-13

Let $x(t)$ be the excitation of a given network that contains only resistances, capacitances, and inductances, and let $y(t)$ be its response. The excitation $x(t)$ is of finite amplitude for all time. This excitation may consist of the sum of more than one component. For $t > 0$, one component of the excitation is

$$x_1(t) = \sqrt{2} \cos \left(\omega_1 t + \frac{\pi}{4} \right),$$

and there is no other component of the excitation at frequency $j\omega_1$. The state of the system before $t = 0$ is not known. The system response for $t > 0$ is

$$y(t) = 2e^{-t} + \text{Re} \left[\frac{5 - \omega_1 + j(5 + \omega_1)}{-\omega_1^2 + 6 + j5\omega_1} (e^{-2t} + e^{j\omega_1 t}) \right].$$

a. Determine the system function $H(s_p) = Y/X$.

b. Was the system at rest for $t < 0$? Explain.

c. Determine, for $t > 0$, two different excitation functions that could give rise to this response.

Vector Diagrams

As we have seen, it is convenient to represent a sinusoidal signal $x(t) = A \cos(\omega t + \phi)$ in the form $x(t) = \text{Re}(Xe^{j\omega t})$, where $X = Ae^{j\phi}$. In this representation the complex amplitude X specifies both the amplitude and the phase of the sinusoidal signal. This complex amplitude can be represented by a vector in the complex plane, the length of the vector designating the amplitude of the sinusoidal signal and the angle of the vector from the horizontal designating the phase of the signal. A convenient visualization of the relations among the amplitudes and phases of the various steady-state sinusoidal voltages and currents in a network can be obtained by plotting on a single diagram the vectors corresponding to each of the voltages and currents. Such a diagram is called a vector diagram.

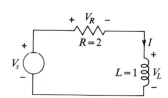

FIG. 4-22. Series *RL* network used to illustrate the construction of a vector diagram.

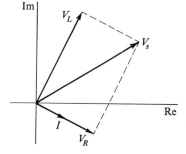

FIG. 4-23. Vector diagram showing relations among the complex amplitudes V_s, V_R, V_L, and I in Fig. 4-22.

To illustrate the construction of a vector diagram, let us consider the series *RL* network that we discussed previously in connection with Fig. 4-14. The network is shown again in Fig. 4-22, and a vector diagram for the network is given in Fig. 4-23. The source voltage is $v_s(t) = 4 \cos(3t + 30°)$, and hence if we use the representation $v_s(t) = \text{Re}[V_s e^{s_p t}]$, then the vector V_s associated with the voltage source is 4 units long and is at an angle of 30° with the horizontal. From Eq. (4-58), the vector I

representing the amplitude and phase of the current response is $4/\sqrt{13}$ = 1.11 units[1] long and is at an angle of $-26.3°$. On the same diagram we have drawn vectors representing the complex amplitudes V_R and V_L associated with the voltages across R and L in Fig. 4-22. From the voltage-current relations for the elements we have $V_R = RI = 2.22 \angle -26.3°$ and $V_L = j\omega LI = j3.33 \angle -26.3° = 3.33 \angle 63.7°$. We observe that the vectors V_R and V_L must add to give V_s, since Kirchhoff's laws have been shown to apply to these complex amplitudes.

As a further example, let us consider the series *RC* network of Fig. 4-16, shown again in Fig. 4-24. The source voltage is $v_s(t) = \cos \omega t$, and hence the complex amplitude associated with the source voltage is $V_s = 1 \quad 0°$. A vector diagram showing the relations among the amplitudes and phases

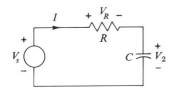

FIG. 4-24. Series *RC* network used to illustrate the construction of a vector diagram.

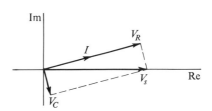

FIG. 4-25. Vector diagram showing complex amplitudes associated with the voltages and current for the *RC* network of Fig. 4-24.

of the voltages and current in Fig. 4-24 for the numerical values $R = 2$, $C = 1$, and $\omega = 2$ is given in Fig. 4-25. The vectors I, V_R, and V_2 are related to V_s through the following equations:

$$I = \frac{V_s}{Z} = \frac{V_s}{2 + 1/j2} = 0.485 V_s \angle 14.0° \; ;$$

$$V_R = RI = 0.970 V_s \angle 14.0° \; ;$$

$$V_2 = \frac{V_s}{1 + j4} = 0.243 V_s \angle -76.0° \; .$$

---

[1] The current vectors need not, of course, be drawn to the same scale as the voltage vectors.

Since the source voltage is $v_s(t) = \cos 2t$, the time functions corresponding to these complex amplitudes are

$$i(t) = 0.485 \cos (2t + 14.0°) \;;$$
$$v_R(t) = 0.970 \cos (2t + 14.0°) \;;$$
$$v_2(t) = 0.243 \cos (2t - 76.0°) \;.$$

In the next example we shall illustrate the relations that exist between the amplitudes and phases of the sinusoidal currents and voltages in the parallel RLC network of Fig. 4-26. The network is excited by a sinusoidal

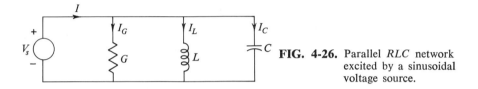

FIG. 4-26. Parallel RLC network excited by a sinusoidal voltage source.

voltage source $v_s(t) = \text{Re}\,[V_s e^{j\omega t}]$. Since $I_G = GV_s$, the vector I_G is parallel to V_s. The complex amplitude associated with the current in the inductance is $I_L = V_s/(j\omega L)$, and hence the vector I_L is at an angle of $-90°$ relative to V_s; the current in an inductance is said, therefore, to lag the voltage across it by 90°. The vector I_C, on the other hand, is at an angle of $+90°$ relative to V_s, since $I_C = j\omega C V_s$; thus the current in a capacitance is said to lead the voltage across it by 90°. Figure 4-27a shows a vector diagram for the RLC network for a particular value of ω, assuming that the complex amplitude V_s associated with the voltage source is real. In Fig. 4-27b the vector diagram is redrawn in order to draw attention to the KCL relation that exists among the complex amplitudes associated with the currents.

Since the angle of each sinusoidal voltage and current response in an RLC network is equal to the sum of the angle of the appropriate system function and the phase angle of the excitation, it is clear that shifting the angle of the excitation simply effects a rotation of the entire vector diagram for the network. For example, if the voltage source in Fig. 4-26 is given by $v_s(t) = |V_s| \cos (\omega t - 45°)$, then the vector diagram showing the complex amplitudes associated with various voltages and currents in the network would be obtained by rotating the diagram of Fig. 4-27a through an angle of $-45°$, as shown in Fig. 4-27c.

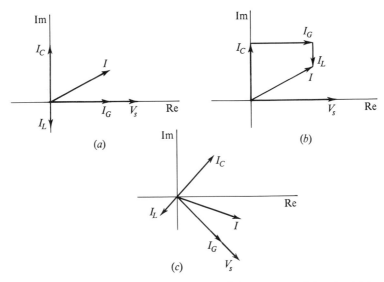

FIG. 4-27. Vector diagrams corresponding to the parallel *RLC* network in Fig. 4-26. Part (*a*) shows each vector originating at the origin; part (*b*) shows the vectors I_C, I_G, and I_L drawn in such a way as to demonstrate that their vector sum is equal to I; part (*c*) shows the vector diagram that results if the phase angle of the voltage source is −45° instead of 0°.

Problem 4-14

a. In the network of Fig. 4-28, the steady-state resistance voltage $v_R(t)$ is given by $v_R(t) = \cos t$, which can be expressed in the form $v_R(t) = \text{Re} \ (V_R e^{jt})$. Sketch on a vector diagram the complex amplitude V_s associated with the source $v_s(t)$ and the complex amplitudes V_R, I, and V_C associated with the steady-state components of the responses $v_R(t)$, $i(t)$, and $v_C(t)$ respectively.

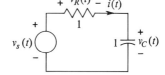

FIG. 4-28. Network for which the vector diagram is to be drawn (Prob. 4-14).

b. For the network of Fig. 4-28, assume now that the steady-state capacitance voltage $v_C(t)$ is given by $v_C(t) = 2 \cos (t + \pi/3)$, which can be expressed in the form $\text{Re} \ (V_C e^{jt})$. The resistance voltage is not necessarily that given in (*a*). By referring only to the vector diagram obtained in (*a*), sketch on a new vector diagram the complex amplitudes V_R, I, V_C, and V_s for this case.

c. For the network of Fig. 4-28, assume now that the voltage source $v_s(t)$ is given by $v_s(t) = 2 \cos (t + \pi/3) = \text{Re}\ (V_s e^{jt})$. By referring only to the vector diagram of (*a*), sketch on a new vector diagram the complex amplitudes V_R, I, V_C, and V_s for this case.

Problem 4-15

a. Draw a vector diagram relating the complex amplitudes V, I, I_R, and I_L, for the network shown in Fig. 4-29, assuming the complex frequency of the excitation to be $s_p = j\omega$.

b. Use the vector diagram of (*a*) to determine the value of a single element (*R*, *L*, or *C*) that, when connected in parallel with the elements shown in Fig. 4-29, will yield a real driving-point impedance at $\omega = 2$.

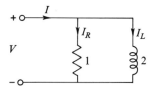

FIG. 4-29. Network for Prob. 4-15.

Frequency response

One way of summarizing a voltage or current response of a network for sinusoidal excitation with different values of ω is to display the system function in graphical form for a range of values of ω. Since the system function is complex, we represent it by two curves—the magnitude as a function of ω and the angle as a function of ω, and we call these curves *frequency-response curves*.[1] Figure 4-30 shows a typical pair of frequency-response curves, representing the magnitude and angle of the system function for the network of Fig. 4-16, which, from Eq. (4-61), is

$$\frac{V_2}{V_s} = \frac{1}{RC} \frac{1}{\sqrt{\omega^2 + (1/RC)^2}}\ e^{j\theta}, \tag{4-63}$$

---

[1] Strictly speaking, the term "frequency" is used to designate the number of cycles per second of a sinusoid, i.e., $\omega/2\pi$. However, when we refer to frequency-response curves, we usually designate the ordinate by ω and speak loosely of this quantity as frequency. This procedure should not lead to confusion, since the meaning of the term should always be clear from the context.

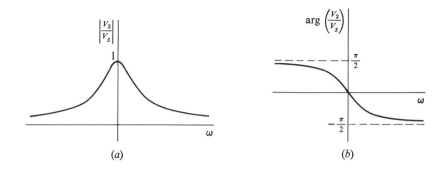

FIG. 4-30. Frequency-response curves depicting (a) magnitude and (b) angle of the transfer ratio V_2/V_s for the network in Fig. 4-16.

where $\theta = -\tan^{-1} \omega RC$. The graphs are plotted for both positive and negative values of ω because it is often convenient to think of sinusoidal signals as composed of two exponential functions with complex frequencies $j\omega$ and $-j\omega$.

As we have seen, the system function evaluated at $s_p = j\omega$ for positive values of ω can be interpreted directly in terms of the amplitude and phase of the sinusoidal response relative to the sinusoidal excitation. If in the example of Fig. 4-30 the excitation is written as $E \cos (\omega t + \phi)$ and the response as $R \cos (\omega t + \phi + \theta)$, then Fig. 4-30a, for positive ω, can be interpreted as the ratio R/E as a function of ω, and Fig. 4-30b, for positive ω, shows the phase angle θ as a function of ω.

Representation of system functions in terms of poles and zeros

We have observed on page 153 that the system function is the quotient of two polynomials in s_p; i.e.,

$$\frac{B(s_p)}{A(s_p)} = \frac{b_m s_p^m + b_{m-1} s_p^{m-1} + \cdots + b_1 s_p + b_0}{a_n s_p^n + a_{n-1} s_p^{n-1} + \cdots + a_1 s_p + a_0}. \qquad (4\text{-}64)$$

This is a suitable form in which to express the system function if our task is simply to calculate the value of the function for some numerical value of s_p. Frequently, however, we are not interested in the system function just for a single value of s_p but in its behavior as s_p is varied through some prescribed range of values. Of particular interest are frequency-response curves of the type shown in Fig. 4-30, which represent the magnitude and angle of the system function as s_p takes on imaginary values from $-j\infty$ to

$j\infty$. The behavior of the system function when it is expressed as a quotient of polynomials, as in Eq. (4-64), depends in a rather complicated and indirect way on the values of the coefficients b_0, b_1, $\ldots$, b_m and a_0, a_1, $\ldots$, a_n. It is difficult, for example, to formulate simple rules that state how each of these coefficients exerts an influence on the system function as s_p is varied in some prescribed manner. We shall now show, however, that it is possible to express the system function in a different form in which its behavior as a function of s_p can be visualized graphically without detailed analysis. This method of expressing the system function will also shed light on certain relations that exist between the frequency response of a network and its source-free behavior, as reflected by the homogeneous solution. Furthermore, it will be a convenient representation for approaching the synthesis problem, i.e., the problem of synthesizing a network to realize a prescribed frequency response.

A basic theorem of algebra[1] states that, if $f(x)$ is a polynomial of degree m, the equation $f(x) = 0$ has m roots, x_1, x_2, $\ldots$, x_m. Hence $f(x)$ can be factored into a product of m terms of the form $(x - x_1)(x - x_2)\cdots(x - x_m)$. Using this result, we can write the system function (4-64) as

$$\frac{B(s_p)}{A(s_p)} = K\frac{(s_p - {}_1s)(s_p - {}_2s)\cdots(s_p - {}_ms)}{(s_p - s_1)(s_p - s_2)\cdots(s_p - s_n)}, \qquad (4\text{-}65)$$

where K is a constant equal to b_m/a_n. The m complex constants ${}_1s$, ${}_2s$, $\ldots$, ${}_ms$ are called *zeros* of the system function; they are roots of the equation $B(s_p) = 0$. The n complex constants s_1, s_2, $\ldots$, s_n are called *poles* of the system function; they are roots of the equation $A(s_p) = 0$. When the complex frequency s_p of the excitation coincides with a zero of the system function, the system function is zero; when s_p coincides with a pole of the system function, the system function is infinite. From Eq. (4-65) we see that the system function is completely determined for any s_p if its poles and zeros are known and if the multiplying constant K is specified.

Each pole or zero is a complex number and can be represented by a point in the complex-frequency plane, or s plane. It is conventional to plot poles as x's and zeros as o's in the s plane, as shown in the plot of poles and zeros in Fig. 4-31. In this example there are four zeros, denoted by ${}_1s$, ${}_2s$, ${}_3s$, and ${}_4s$, and three poles s_1, s_2, and s_3.

In the general system function (4-64) the coefficients in the polynomials $B(s_p)$ and $A(s_p)$ are real, since they are combinations of values of R, L,

---

[1] See, for example, G. Birkhoff and S. MacLane, *A Survey of Modern Algebra*, The Macmillan Company, New York, 1941, pp. 113–116.

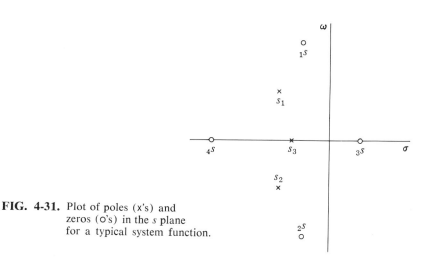

FIG. 4-31. Plot of poles (x's) and
zeros (o's) in the *s* plane
for a typical system function.

and *C* elements, and it follows[1] that the roots of the polynomials occur either on the real axis or as conjugate-complex pairs. Hence the poles and zeros of system functions are always arranged in this manner, as illustrated in Fig. 4-31.

The numerator and the denominator of the expression for the system function given in Eq. (4-65) contain a number of factors of the form $s_p - {}_ks$ and $s_p - s_k$, respectively. Each of these factors is a complex number that can be described by its magnitude and angle and can be represented by a vector in the *s* plane. If, for example, s_p and s_k are the two complex numbers shown in the *s* plane of Fig. 4-32, then the difference $s_p - s_k$ is a complex number whose *magnitude* is equal to the length of the vector from

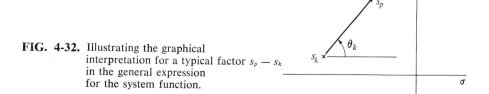

FIG. 4-32. Illustrating the graphical
interpretation for a typical factor $s_p - s_k$
in the general expression
for the system function.

[1] See Prob. 2-10.

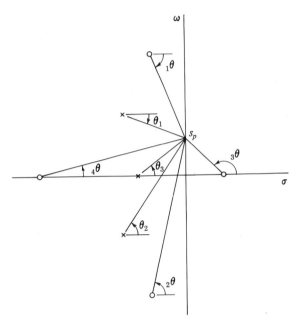

FIG. 4-33. Graphical construction illustrating the computation of a system function that is characterized by several poles and zeros. The complex frequency of the excitation is $s_p = j\omega$.

s_k to s_p. The *angle* of $s_p - s_k$ is equal to the angle θ_k ($-\pi < \theta_k \leq \pi$) measured from the positive real axis to the vector, with the counterclockwise direction taken as positive.

In Fig. 4-33, all the vectors for the pole-zero configuration of Fig. 4-31 are shown for the case in which the complex frequency of the excitation is $s_p = j\omega$. Since the numerator and the denominator of the system function are products of complex numbers, the magnitude of either numerator or denominator is the product of the magnitudes of the factors, and the angle is the sum of the angles of the factors. Thus if we represent the system function (4-65) as

$$\frac{B(s_p)}{A(s_p)} = H(s_p) = |H(s_p)|e^{j\Theta(s_p)}, \qquad (4\text{-}66)$$

then the magnitude of the system function is given by

$$|H(s_p)| = |K| \frac{\text{product of magnitudes of vectors from zeros to } s_p}{\text{product of magnitudes of vectors from poles to } s_p}, \qquad (4\text{-}67)$$

and the angle of the system function is given by

$$\Theta(s_p) = \sum \text{angles of vectors from zeros to } s_p$$
$$- \sum \text{angles of vectors from poles to } s_p \quad (4\text{-}68)$$
$$+ \text{ angle of the constant K.}$$

Since the coefficients in the polynomials $B(s_p)$ and $A(s_p)$ that form a system function are real, then the constant K, which, from Eq. (4-64), equals b_m/a_n, is a real number, and hence the angle of K is zero or π, depending on the sign of K. For the example shown, the angle of the system function is $\Theta = {}_1\theta + {}_2\theta + {}_3\theta + {}_4\theta - \theta_1 - \theta_2 - \theta_3$, where the angles are marked on the figure; the magnitude of the system function is the product of the lengths of the four vectors to $s_p = j\omega$ from ${}_1s$, ${}_2s$, ${}_3s$, and ${}_4s$ divided by the product of the lengths of the three vectors to $s_p = j\omega$ from s_1, s_2, and s_3. Note that the vectors depicted in the graphical construction represent only the factors in the numerator and denominator of Eq. (4-65). The constant multiplier K is not involved in this construction and hence cannot be determined from it.

A graphical construction such as that shown in Fig. 4-33 is helpful in visualizing the behavior of the system function for a network as a function of the complex frequency of the excitation. The magnitude and angle of the system function, plotted as a function of ω for $s_p = j\omega$, specify the frequency response of the network. As ω increases, the point at which the vectors terminate moves up the ω axis, and the lengths and angles of all the vectors change. Thus once the pattern of poles and zeros has been plotted in the s plane, the frequency-response curves can be determined (except for the effect of the constant multiplier K) simply from geometrical considerations. We shall illustrate this procedure by determining the frequency response for some system functions characterized by simple patterns of poles and zeros.

Consider first the system function

$$H(s_p) = K \cdot \frac{1}{s_p + \alpha}, \quad (4\text{-}69)$$

which is characterized by a single real-axis pole at $s = -\alpha$, as shown in Fig. 4-34*a*. The frequency-response curves can be determined by examining how the length and angle of the vector from the pole to the excitation frequency $s_p = j\omega$ vary as a function of ω. When $\omega = 0$, the vector lies along the real axis; its length is α and its angle is zero. Hence if K is assumed to be positive, the system function at $\omega = 0$ has a magnitude of K/α and an angle of zero. When ω is increased from $\omega = 0$, the length and angle of the vector increase. Hence the magnitude and angle of the system function decrease, since the vector is from a pole and represents a

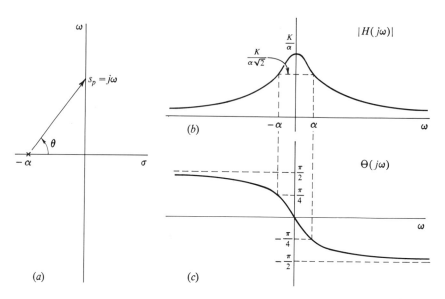

FIG. 4-34. Pole-zero representation and plots of magnitude $|H(j\omega)|$ and angle $\Theta(j\omega)$ of the system function versus frequency for a system function characterized by a single real-axis pole. (The constant multiplier K is assumed to be positive.)

factor in the denominator of the system function. At $\omega = \alpha$, i.e., $s_p = j\alpha$, the vector is at an angle $\theta = 45°$, and its magnitude is $\sqrt{2}$ times its magnitude at $\omega = 0$. Thus the magnitude of the system function at $\omega = \alpha$ is $1/\sqrt{2}$ times its magnitude at $\omega = 0$. As we shall see later, the electric power entering a pair of terminals in a network is proportional to the square of voltage or current at the terminals, and consequently the power at $\omega = \alpha$ is one-half the power at $\omega = 0$. For this reason, $\omega = \alpha$ is often called the *half-power frequency* or half-power point. For large positive values of ω, the vector is almost vertical, and its length is approximately ω. Thus the magnitude of the system function is asymptotic to K/ω, and its angle is asymptotic to $-\pi/2$. The complete frequency-response curves are shown in Fig. 4-34b and c.

Figure 4-35 shows several other pole-zero patterns that are frequently encountered, together with the corresponding plots of the magnitude of the system function versus ω. By visualizing the vectors from the poles and zeros to the point $s_p = j\omega$ as ω changes from zero to infinity, we can verify the shape of each frequency-response curve. Some of the values labeling the curves were obtained using approximations that are discussed in the next section.

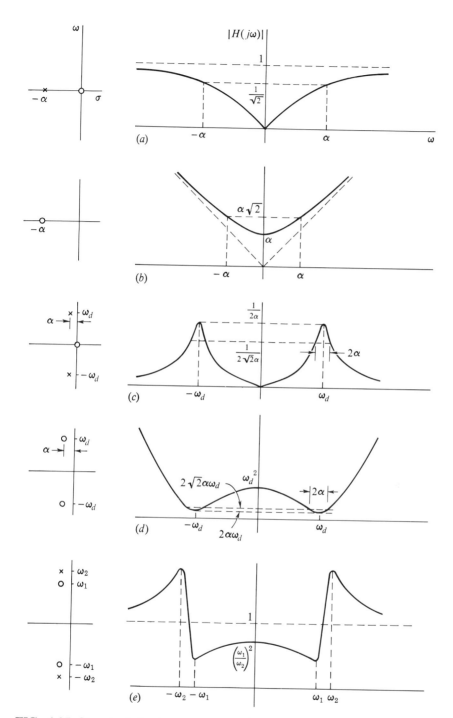

FIG. 4-35. Some typical pole-zero representations and corresponding plots of magnitude of system function versus ω. The constant K that multiplies the system function—see Eq. (4-65)—is taken as unity in these examples.

Resonance

When the complex frequency s_p of the excitation of a network passes sufficiently close to a pole (or zero) of the system function, there is a sharp peak (or valley) in the magnitude of the system function, since the length of the vector from that pole or zero to the point s_p becomes very small in this region. This type of behavior is called *resonance*, and the frequencies in the immediate vicinity of the pole or zero are said to be in the *resonance region*. For excitation frequencies $s_p = j\omega$, i.e., for sinusoidal excitation, resonance is exhibited for any network whose system function is characterized by a conjugate pair of poles or zeros that are close to the ω axis. Examples of pole-zero patterns of this type are those in Fig. 4-35c, d, and e.

The response of a network in the resonance region can be analyzed in a simple manner by inspection of the pole-zero pattern, if certain approximations are made. The approximations are based on the fact that, as the excitation frequency moves through the resonance region, the vectors from poles and zeros in this region exhibit large percentage changes in magnitude and angle while the percentage changes in the magnitudes and angles of vectors from poles and zeros far removed from this region remain relatively small.

We shall illustrate this method of analysis for the pole-zero pattern shown in Fig. 4-35c, which is a pattern frequently encountered in practice. The system function corresponding to this pole-zero pattern is

$$H(s_p) = \frac{s_p}{(s_p - s_1)(s_p - s_1^*)}, \tag{4-70}$$

where the constant multiplier is taken to be unity and s_1 and s_1^* are the locations of the conjugate pair of poles. The pole-zero pattern, together with vectors to the excitation frequency $s_p = j\omega$, is shown in Fig. 4-36. We shall use the notation $s_1 = -\alpha + j\omega_d$, and we shall consider the case

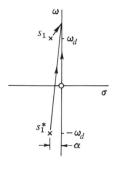

FIG. 4-36. Pole-zero pattern for the system function (4-70). The vectors from the poles and zeros to $s_p = j\omega$ are drawn to aid in the visualization of the frequency response.

in which $\alpha \ll \omega_d$; i.e., the distance of the poles s_1 and s_1^* from the ω axis is small compared with the distance ω_d from the poles to the real axis. (Inspection of the pole-zero pattern shows that this condition results in a frequency-response curve that has a large peak in the vicinity of ω_d.) The region of the s plane in the vicinity of s_1 is reproduced in magnified form in

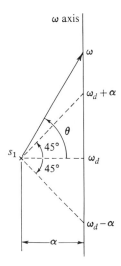

FIG. 4-37. Magnified version of the s plane of Fig. 4-36 in the resonance region associated with the pole s_1.

Fig. 4-37, and the vector from s_1 to a point $s_p = j\omega$ is shown. As ω is varied over this small resonance region, the percentage changes of the lengths and angles of the vectors from the zero at the origin and from the pole at s_1^* to the point $j\omega$ are very small compared with the corresponding percentage changes of the vector from s_1 to $j\omega$. Thus as ω moves through the resonance region, the vector from s_1 to $j\omega$ is responsible for the changes in the system function, and the other two vectors are relatively constant. The vector from the zero at the origin is approximately $j\omega_d$, and the vector from the pole at s_1^* is approximately $2j\omega_d$. Within the resonance region, therefore, the system function is given approximately by

$$H(j\omega) \cong \frac{j\omega_d}{2j\omega_d(j\omega - s_1)} = \frac{1}{2} \cdot \frac{1}{j\omega - s_1}. \qquad (4\text{-}71)$$

Thus to this approximation the magnitude of the system function is $\frac{1}{2}$ multiplied by the reciprocal of the length of the vector from s_1 to $j\omega$ in Fig. 4-37; the angle of the system function is the negative of the angle θ of this vector.

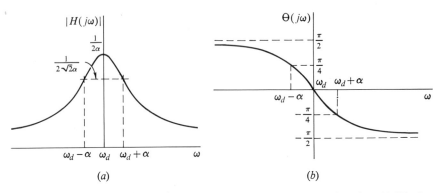

(a)   *(b)*

FIG. 4-38. Magnitude $|H(j\omega)|$ and angle $\Theta(j\omega)$ of the system function (4-70) for values of ω in the resonance region. The multiplying constant K is assumed to be unity.

Plots of the magnitude and angle of the system function in the resonance region are shown in Fig. 4-38. The half-power points, i.e., the frequencies for which the magnitude of the system function is $1/\sqrt{2}$ times its maximum value, occur at complex frequencies approximately equal to $j(\omega_d - \alpha)$ and $j(\omega_d + \alpha)$, since the magnitude of the vector from s_1 to each of these points (shown in Fig. 4-37) is $\sqrt{2}$ times the magnitude for $\omega = \omega_d$. The angles of the system function for these half-power points are approximately 45° and −45° respectively. The difference between the two half-power frequencies, usually called the half-power bandwidth, is 2α in this case.

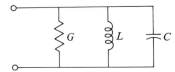

FIG. 4-39. An *RLC* network whose driving-point impedance is characterized by the pole-zero pattern given in Fig. 4-36.

Figure 4-39 shows a network for which the driving-point impedance is characterized by a pole-zero configuration of the form given in Fig. 4-36. The driving-point impedance is

$$Z = \frac{1}{Y} = \frac{1}{1/s_p L + G + s_p C}$$

$$= \frac{1}{C}\frac{s_p}{s_p^2 + s_p(G/C) + 1/LC}$$

$$= \frac{1}{C}\frac{s_p}{(s_p - s_1)(s_p - s_1^*)}, \qquad (4\text{-}72)$$

where s_1, $s_1^* = -G/2C \pm j\sqrt{1/LC - (G/2C)^2}$. Thus we can associate the constants α and ω_d in Fig. 4-36 with the elements G, C, and L as follows:

$$\alpha = \frac{G}{2C}, \qquad (4\text{-}73)$$

and

$$\omega_d = \sqrt{\omega_0^2 - \alpha^2}, \qquad (4\text{-}74)$$

where

$$\omega_0^2 = \frac{1}{LC}. \qquad (4\text{-}75)$$

Likewise, we can associate $1/C$ with the constant K that multiplies the system function. We have observed that a system function of the form given in Eq. (4-72) will exhibit resonance behavior if the poles s_1 and s_1^* are close to the ω axis, i.e., if $\alpha \ll \omega_d$. This requirement implies certain constraints on the element values for the network of Fig. 4-39. From Eqs. (4-73) and (4-74), the approximation $\alpha \ll \omega_d$ implies $\omega_d \approx \omega_0$; hence $\alpha \ll \omega_0$, and we have the requirement $G/2C \ll 1/\sqrt{LC}$, or $G \ll 2\sqrt{C/L}$.

It is of interest to observe that at the frequency ω_0, which is in the resonance region, the admittance $j\omega_0 C$ of the capacitance and the admittance $1/(j\omega_0 L)$ of the inductance are equal in magnitude but opposite in sign, since $\omega_0^2 = 1/LC$. Consequently at this frequency the sum of the admittances of the capacitance and the inductance is zero, leaving G as the total admittance of the network; i.e., the network looks like a resistance at the frequency $\omega = \omega_0$. This result can also be seen from Fig. 4-38, which shows that the phase angle at $\omega = \omega_d$ is zero.

Problem 4-16

a. For the network of Fig. 4-40 plot the pole-zero pattern corresponding to the system function V_2/V_1.

b. What must be the relative positions of the pole and zero in the plot determined in (*a*) in order that the system function V_2/V_1 be a constant?

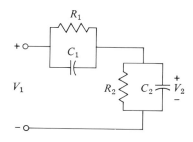

FIG. 4-40. Network for Prob. 4-16.

c. Determine the relation between the time constants of the two parallel *RC* networks in the network of Fig. 4-40 such that the system function V_2/V_1 is a constant. Compare this result with the result obtained in Prob. 3-26.

Problem 4-17

a. Construct the pole-zero plots for the following functions:

1. $H(s_p) = \dfrac{6}{s_p{}^3 + 2s_p{}^2 + 2s_p}$.

2. $H(s_p) = \dfrac{s_p{}^2 + 4}{2s_p{}^2 + 6s_p + 4}$.

b. Determine the system functions corresponding to the pole-zero plots of Fig. 4-41.

c. The poles and zeros of a certain driving-point impedance are as shown in Fig. 4-42. The driving-point impedance behaves like a 2-ohm resistance as $s_p \to 0$. Find this driving-point impedance as a function of s_p.

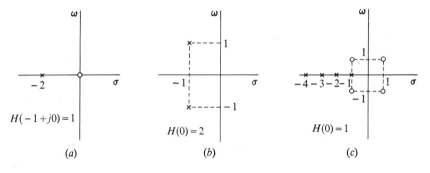

(a)   (b)   (c)

FIG. 4-41. Pole-zero plots for which system functions $H(s_p)$ are to be determined in Prob. 4-17*b*. The value of the system function at a particular s_p is given in each case.

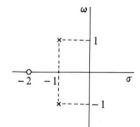

FIG. 4-42. Pole-zero plot for which the driving-point impedance is to be determined in Prob. 4-17*c*.

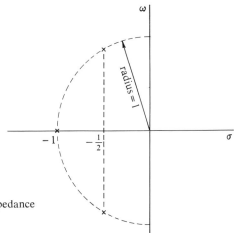

FIG. 4-43. Pole-zero plot
for which the transfer impedance
is to be determined
in Prob. 4-17*d*.

d. A transfer impedance $Z_{21}(s_p)$ has the pole-zero pattern shown in Fig. 4-43. As $s_p \to \infty$, $Z_{21}(s_p) \to 1/s_p{}^3$. Find $Z_{21}(s_p)$.

Problem 4-18

a. For each of the networks of Fig. 4-44, determine and plot the pole-zero pattern of the system function indicated.

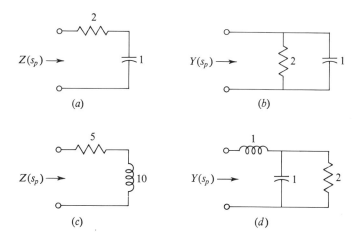

FIG. 4-44. Networks for which the pole-zero patterns are to be determined for the indicated driving-point impedance or admittance (Prob. 4-18).

b. By referring to the pole-zero patterns in (*a*), describe the behavior of each of the system functions for high and low frequencies; i.e., determine an approximate expression for the system function for large and for small ω. (Note that you are *not* asked for the value of the system function at $\omega = \infty$ and $\omega = 0$.)

c. Explain how the answers to (*b*) can be obtained by inspection of the network. Use your knowledge of the element impedances.

Problem 4-19

a. Construct on the *s* plane the vectors representing the function

$$s_p - (-2 - j),$$

for each of the points s_p indicated below. In each case, find the length *L* and the angle θ of the vector:

1. $s_p = 0$.
2. $s_p = j$.
3. $s_p = -1 + j2$.
4. $s_p = 4 + j2$.

b. Given that

$$H(s_p) = \tfrac{1}{2} \frac{s_p{}^2 - s_p}{(s_p + 1)(s_p{}^2 + 4)},$$

plot the poles and zeros of $H(s_p)$ in the *s* plane. Use this plot to determine the magnitude and angle of $H(s_p)$ when the complex frequency s_p of the excitation takes on each of the following values:

1. $s_p = j$.
2. $s_p = -j$.
3. $s_p = 2$.
4. $s_p = -2$.

c. We have seen that, for an *RLC* network, the system function relating the complex amplitudes of any pair of voltage or current variables is a ratio of polynomials with real coefficients, and hence the poles and zeros occur in complex conjugate pairs. Show that for such system functions the magnitude of $H(j\omega)$ is an even function of ω, i.e., $|H(j\omega)| = |H(-j\omega)|$, and that the angle of $H(j\omega)$ is an odd function of ω, i.e., $\arg H(j\omega) = -\arg H(-j\omega)$.

Problem 4-20

Many loudspeaker systems consist of two loudspeakers: the woofer, which reproduces the low-frequency part of the signal, and the tweeter, which

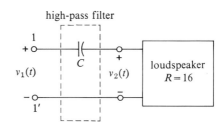

high-pass filter

FIG. 4-45. High-pass filter
(enclosed by dashed lines)
connected to loudspeaker
(Prob. 4-20).

reproduces the high-frequency part of the signal. A network is used to
select the high-frequency part of the signal and feed it into the tweeter.
Such a network is called a high-pass filter. Figure 4-45 shows a simple
high-pass filter connected to a tweeter. The entire audio signal is applied
at the terminals 1-1'.

a. Assuming that the equivalent network for the tweeter consists of just a
resistance R, plot the pole-zero pattern of the voltage transfer ratio
$H(s_p) = V_2/V_1$, and sketch the frequency-response curves (magnitude
and angle).

b. Suppose the equivalent resistance of the tweeter is 16 ohms. Find the
value of the capacitance C such that the half-power frequency of the
high-pass filter is

$$f_h = \frac{\omega_h}{2\pi} = 5 \times 10^3 \text{ cps} .$$

Problem 4-21

a. Sketch the pole-zero pattern for the driving-point impedance of the
network shown in Fig. 4-46.

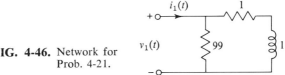

FIG. 4-46. Network for
Prob. 4-21.

b. Sketch the magnitude and angle of the driving-point impedance as functions of ω.

c. Determine the steady-state response $v_1(t)$ to a current excitation $i_1(t) =$
$\sin (t + \pi/4)$.

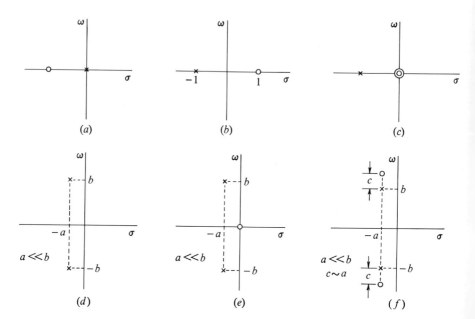

FIG. 4-47. Pole-zero plots to be paired with frequency-response curves in Prob. 4-22.

Problem 4-22

For each of the pole-zero plots of Fig. 4-47 determine which, if any, of the sketches of magnitude versus frequency in Fig. 4-48 and the sketches of phase versus frequency in Fig. 4-49 could result. You should be able to solve this problem by visualizing the appropriate vectors in the s plane.

Problem 4-23

For the parallel RLC network shown in Fig. 4-50, let us assume that $1/(2RC) \ll 1/\sqrt{LC}$.

a. Determine the frequency ω_1 at which the magnitude of the driving-point impedance of the network is a maximum. In this problem we shall define ω_1 as the resonant frequency of the network.

b. Assume that $R = 10$, $L = 1$, and $C = 1$. Determine an equivalent network, containing at most two elements, that has the same impedance as the network of Fig. 4-50 at the resonant frequency.

c. Repeat (b) for a frequency of twice the resonant frequency.

d. Repeat (b) for a frequency of one-half the resonant frequency.

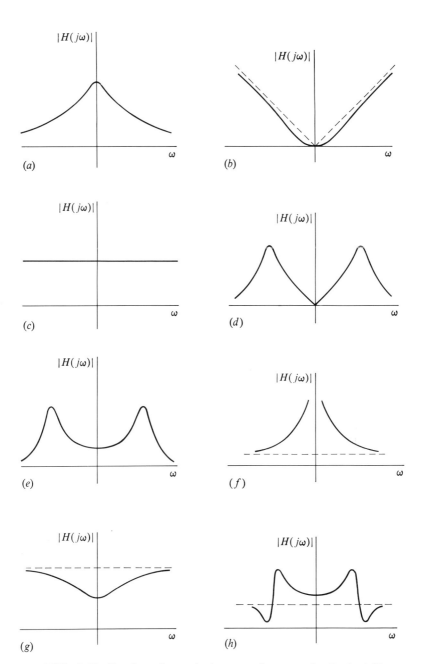

FIG. 4-48. Sketches of magnitude versus frequency for Prob. 4-22.

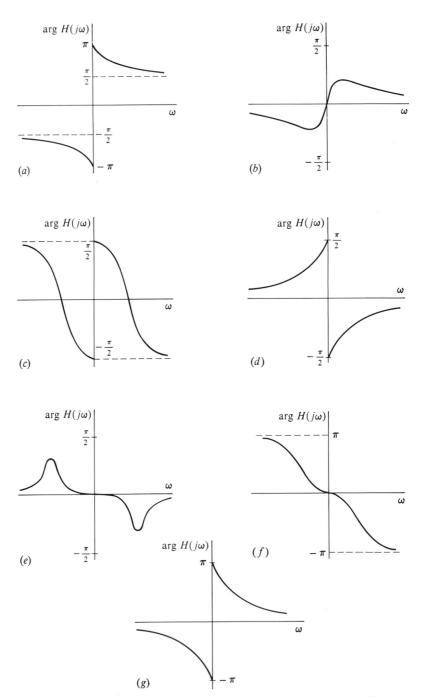

FIG. 4-49. Sketches of phase versus frequency for Prob. 4-22.

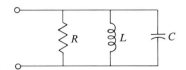

FIG. 4-50. Parallel *RLC* network
discussed in Prob. 4-23.

Note that the equivalent networks in (*b*), (*c*), and (*d*) are valid only at the frequencies for which they were derived.

Problem 4-24

The first stage of an ordinary radio receiver serves the function of rejecting the signals whose frequencies correspond to transmitters other than the one to which the radio is tuned. Only frequencies near the tuned frequency are sent to succeeding stages to be amplified. The heart of this first stage is often an *RLC* network of the type shown in Fig. 4-51, in which $R/2L \ll 1/\sqrt{LC}$.

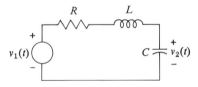

FIG. 4-51. Series *RLC* network
discussed in Prob. 4-24.

a. Determine the voltage transfer ratio $H(s_p) = V_2/V_1$ and plot its poles and zeros in the *s* plane.

b. For an *s*-plane plot such as shown in Fig. 4-52, it is sometimes convenient to define the quantities α, ω_d, and ω_0, where $\alpha = -\text{Re}(s_1)$, $\omega_d = \text{Im}(s_1)$, and ω_0 is the distance from the origin to s_1. Thus $\omega_0^2 = \alpha^2 + \omega_d^2$. For the pole-zero plot in (*a*), determine the parameters α, ω_d, and ω_0 in terms of the element values for the network.

c. Find the frequency at which $|H(j\omega)|$ is a maximum. This frequency is sometimes called the resonant frequency. Also determine the half-power frequencies.

d. Sketch the magnitude and angle of $H(j\omega)$ by inspection of the pole-zero pattern, again assuming that $R/2L \ll 1/\sqrt{LC}$.

e. The bandwidth of a system function $H(j\omega)$ that exhibits resonance is usually defined as the frequency difference between the two half-power frequencies. A good measure of the "selectivity" or "sharpness" of the peak in a resonant system is the ratio of the resonant frequency to the bandwidth. When this ratio is large, it is called the quality factor, *Q*,

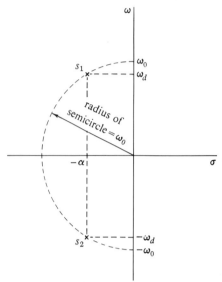

FIG. 4-52. Pole-zero plot for the network of Fig. 4-51 (Prob. 4-24).

of the network. For the network of Fig. 4-51 find the approximate bandwidth and Q. Express the bandwidth and the Q in terms of α, ω_0, and ω_d.

f. Determine the response $v_2(t)$ for the network of Fig. 4-51 when the excitation $v_1(t)$ is a unit impulse. Describe qualitatively how the impulse response changes as the Q of the network is changed, keeping the resonant frequency constant.

Recall that the homogeneous solution for the response of a network having two complex conjugate natural frequencies s_1, $s_2 = -\alpha \pm j\omega_d$ can be written in the form

$$ke^{-\alpha t} \cos (\omega_d t + \phi) .$$

In this expression the parameter α indicates how fast the response decays, and ω_d indicates the frequency of the oscillations. The parameters α and ω_d are therefore often called the damping factor and the damped natural frequency, respectively. If α is zero, the frequency of the oscillations is ω_0. This frequency is called the undamped natural frequency.

Problem 4-25

The purpose of this problem is to illustrate how the frequency response varies with changes in the positions of the poles and zeros for a simple but very useful system function. Consider the system function

$$H(s_p) = \frac{s_p}{s_p^2 + ks_p + 1},$$

where k is a positive constant.

a. Sketch the pole-zero plots for:

1. $k = 0.1$.
2. $k = 1.9$.
3. $k = 10.1$.

b. Sketch the magnitude and angle of $H(j\omega)$ as a function of ω for the three cases considered in (a).

c. Let the excitation for the system be

$$x(t) = \sin t + \sin 2t.$$

The steady-state response will then be of the form

$$y(t) = A \sin (t + \beta) + B \sin (2t + \gamma),$$

where A, B, β and γ are constants. From the pole-zero plots or the curves of magnitude and angle versus ω, determine which of the three values of k considered in (a) you would select if you wanted:

1. $|A| \gg |B|$.
2. $|A| \approx |B|$.
3. $\beta = 0$.

d. Determine a network that has the system function $H(s_p)$ as its driving-point impedance for each of the values of the parameter k given in (a).

Problem 4-26

A typical coupling network between two successive intermediate stages in a radio receiver is represented by Fig. 4-53. The approximate pole-zero pattern of the transfer impedance $Z_{21} = V_2/I_1$ is shown in Fig. 4-54. The values of ω_a, ω_b, and α are determined by the values of the network elements.

a. Assuming that $\omega_a \gg \alpha$ and $\omega_b \gg \alpha$ and that $(\omega_a - \omega_b) \ll \omega_b$, sketch $|Z_{21}(j\omega)|$ in the vicinity of ω_a and ω_b, i.e., in the region $(\omega_b - 2\alpha) < \omega < (\omega_a + 2\alpha)$, for each of the three cases listed below:

1. $\omega_a - \omega_b > \alpha$.
2. $\omega_a - \omega_b < \alpha$.
3. $\omega_a - \omega_b = 2\alpha$.

Argue from geometry in the s plane. Case (3) is called the critically-coupled case and provides a frequency response that we call maximally

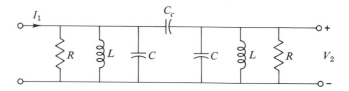

FIG. 4-53. Coupling network discussed in Prob. 4-26.

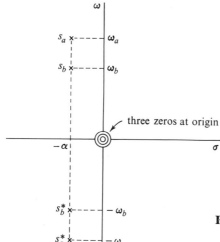

three zeros at origin

FIG. 4-54. Pole-zero pattern of the transfer impedance for the network of Fig. 4-53 (Prob. 4-26).

flat. Note that in all three cases the frequency-response curve is centered approximately at $\omega = \frac{1}{2}(\omega_a + \omega_b)$.

b. Determine the parameters α, ω_a, and ω_b for a typical radio receiver application in which the maximum of the frequency response is centered at 455 kcps with a half-power bandwidth of approximately 20 kcps, and the frequency response is maximally flat.

Relation of natural frequencies to impedance

Our study of *RLC* networks has consisted of an examination of the properties of the two parts of the solution of the differential equation that describes the behavior of a network: the particular integral and the homogeneous solution. The complex amplitude of the particular integral of the response of a network to an exponential excitation is obtained by multiplying the complex amplitude of the excitation by the system function, which is characterized by a set of poles and zeros. The homogeneous solution consists of the sum of a number of exponential terms with different complex frequencies; these complex frequencies are determined from the basic network, i.e., the network that results when the sources are set to zero. We shall now show that a close relation exists between the behavior of a network in the absence of sources and the system function of the network.

We shall restrict our discussion initially to the voltage-current relations at a single terminal pair of source-free *RLC* network. Consider the network

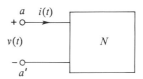

FIG. 4-55. Source-free two-terminal *RLC* network relevant to the discussion of relations between the natural frequencies and the system function of a network.

shown in Fig. 4-55, in which a voltage $v(t)$ exists at the terminal pair a-a' and a current $i(t)$ flows into the network at terminal a and out at terminal a'. We have observed previously (pages 23 to 25) that the relation between $v(t)$ and $i(t)$ at the terminal pair of a network is independent of the source or sources that give rise to $v(t)$ or $i(t)$. The general differential equation relating v and i can be written

$$a_n \frac{d^n v}{dt^n} + a_{n-1} \frac{d^{n-1} v}{dt^{n-1}} + \cdots + a_1 \frac{dv}{dt} + a_0 v$$

$$= b_m \frac{d^m i}{dt^m} + b_{m-1} \frac{d^{m-1} i}{dt^{m-1}} + \cdots + b_1 \frac{di}{dt} + b_0 i, \quad (4\text{-}76)$$

and the driving-point impedance of the network is given by

$$\frac{V}{I} = Z(s_p) = \frac{B(s_p)}{A(s_p)} = \frac{b_m s_p^m + b_{m-1} s_p^{m-1} + \cdots + b_1 s_p + b_0}{a_n s_p^n + a_{n-1} s_p^{n-1} + \cdots + a_1 s_p + a_0}. \quad (4\text{-}77)$$

Let us now determine the open-circuit voltage that could exist at terminals a-a' as a result of some past excitation. The current $i(t)$ is thus constrained to be zero, and we have

$$a_n \frac{d^n v}{dt^n} + a_{n-1} \frac{d^{n-1} v}{dt^{n-1}} + \cdots + a_1 \frac{dv}{dt} + a_0 v = 0. \quad (4\text{-}78)$$

As we have seen before, the solution of this homogeneous equation is

$$v(t) = \sum_{k=1}^{n} C_k e^{s_k t}, \qquad (4\text{-}79)$$

where the C_k are constants and $s_1, s_2, \ldots, s_n$ are roots of the characteristic equation

$$a_n s^n + a_{n-1} s^{n-1} + \cdots + a_1 s + a_0 = 0. \qquad (4\text{-}80)$$

These roots are the complex frequencies of the voltage that can exist across the open-circuited terminal pair of the network. They are often called the *open-circuit natural frequencies* of the network with respect to the given terminal pair.

The left-hand side of Eq. (4-80) is identical with $A(s)$, i.e., with the denominator of $Z(s_p)$ in Eq. (4-77) with s_p replaced by s. The roots of the equation $A(s_p) = 0$ are, we recall, poles of the impedance. We conclude, therefore, that *the open-circuit natural frequencies of a network with respect to a given terminal pair are the poles of the driving-point impedance at that terminal pair.* Equivalently, the open-circuit natural frequencies are the *zeros* of the driving-point admittance, since $Z(s_p) = 1/Y(s_p)$.

When the terminals $a\text{-}a'$ are short-circuited, the voltage $v(t)$ is constrained to be zero, and we have

$$b_m \frac{d^m i}{dt^m} + b_{m-1} \frac{d^{m-1} i}{dt^{m-1}} + \cdots + b_1 \frac{di}{dt} + b_0 i = 0. \qquad (4\text{-}81)$$

The solution of this homogeneous equation is

$$i(t) = \sum_{k=1}^{m} D_k e^{(_k s\, t)}, \qquad (4\text{-}82)$$

where the D_k are constants and $_1 s, _2 s, \ldots, _m s$ are roots of the characteristic equation

$$b_m s^m + b_{m-1} s^{m-1} + \cdots + b_1 s + b_0 = 0. \qquad (4\text{-}83)$$

These roots $_1 s, _2 s, \ldots, _m s$ are the *short-circuit natural frequencies* of the network with respect to the given terminal pair, since they are the complex frequencies of the current that can exist in the short-circuited terminal pair of the network.

The left-hand side of Eq. (4-83) is identical with $B(s)$, i.e., with the numerator of $Z(s_p)$ in Eq. (4-77) with s_p replaced by s. The roots of the equation $B(s_p) = 0$ are, we recall, zeros of the impedance. We conclude, then, that *the short-circuit natural frequencies of a network with respect to a given terminal pair are the zeros of the driving-point impedance at that terminal pair.* Equivalently, the short-circuit natural frequencies are the poles of the driving-point admittance.

The relations just described suggest that, if the driving-point impedance $Z(s_p)$ at the terminal pair of a network is known, then the open- and short-circuit natural frequencies of the network for that terminal pair can be written down immediately. To illustrate this procedure, we shall write down the impedances of several simple networks that consist of only one or two elements, and we shall determine the open- and short-circuit natural frequencies for the networks directly from the expressions for the impedances.

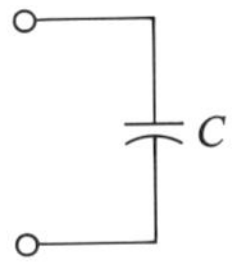

FIG. 4-56. A capacitance has an open-circuit natural frequency at $s = 0$.

As a first example, consider a capacitance (Fig. 4-56), the impedance of which is

$$Z(s_p) = \frac{1}{s_p C} . \tag{4-84}$$

The impedance $Z(s_p)$ has no zeros and has a pole at $s_p = 0$. Thus the capacitance has no short-circuit natural frequencies and has an open-circuit natural frequency at zero frequency. The fact that there is an open-circuit natural frequency at zero frequency means that a d-c voltage can exist across a capacitance in which there is no current—a familiar result that follows directly from the *v-i* relation $i = C\dfrac{dv}{dt}$. As a matter of fact, the same reasoning indicates that we would expect an open-circuit natural frequency at zero frequency for any network in which there is a capacitance in series with either terminal.

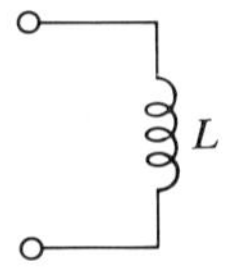

FIG. 4-57. An inductance has a short-circuit natural frequency at $s = 0$.

From the expression for the impedance of an inductance (Fig. 4-57),

$$Z(s_p) = s_p L , \tag{4-85}$$

we see that an inductance has no open-circuit natural frequencies, since there are no poles of the impedance. There is a zero of impedance at $s_p = 0$, showing that the inductance has a short-circuit natural frequency at zero frequency. This result indicates that a d-c current can exist in a short-circuited inductance, as we would expect by setting $v = 0$ in the v-i relation $v = L \dfrac{di}{dt}$. Similar short-circuit behavior would be expected for any two-terminal network in which an inductance is connected directly across the terminals, and hence such a network always exhibits a short-circuit natural frequency at zero frequency.

FIG. 4-58. Parallel RC network. The open-circuit natural frequency is at $s = 1/RC$.

For the parallel RC network in Fig. 4-58, the impedance is

$$Z(s_p) = \frac{1}{1/R + s_p C}$$

$$= \frac{1}{C} \frac{1}{s_p + 1/RC}. \tag{4-86}$$

The impedance has a pole at $s_p = -1/RC$, and hence this represents an open-circuit natural frequency of the RC network. The open-circuit behavior of the network could, of course, also have been obtained from the homogeneous differential equation for the voltage,

$$C \frac{dv}{dt} + \frac{1}{R} v = 0. \tag{4-87}$$

The solution of this equation is

$$v(t) = A e^{-t/RC}, \tag{4-88}$$

where A is an arbitrary constant. As expected, either method leads to the same complex frequency $s = -1/RC$ for the open-circuit voltage.

As a further example, consider the series RC network of Fig. 4-59. The impedance at the terminals is

$$Z(s_p) = R \frac{s_p + 1/RC}{s_p}. \tag{4-89}$$

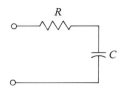

FIG. 4-59. Series *RC* network. The open-circuit natural frequency is at $s = 0$; the short-circuit natural frequency is at $s = -1/RC$.

There is a pole of impedance at zero frequency, and hence there is an open-circuit natural frequency at $s = 0$, as we would expect for a network in which there is a capacitance in series with the terminals. The zero of impedance at $s_p = -1/RC$ indicates that there is a short-circuit natural frequency of this value. Thus the short-circuit natural frequency for the series *RC* network of Fig. 4-59 is identical to the open-circuit natural frequency of the parallel network of Fig. 4-58. This result is to be expected, however, since short-circuiting the terminals of the series network gives the same configuration of elements as the parallel network with the terminals open.

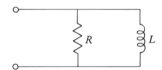

FIG. 4-60. Parallel RL network. The short-circuit natural frequency is at $s = 0$; the open-circuit natural frequency is at $s = -R/L$.

For the parallel *RL* network, shown in Fig. 4-60, the impedance is

$$Z(s_p) = R\,\frac{s_p}{s_p + R/L}. \tag{4-90}$$

The zero of impedance at $s_p = 0$ corresponds to a short-circuit natural frequency and reflects the fact that a steady current can flow through the short-circuited terminals. The pole of impedance at $s_p = -R/L$ corresponds to an open-circuit natural frequency and reflects the fact that the source-free behavior of the *RL* network is characterized by an exponential of the form $e^{-(R/L)t}$.

As a further example, consider the parallel *LC* network of Fig. 4-61, the impedance of which is

$$Z(s_p) = \frac{1}{s_pC + 1/s_pL}$$
$$= \frac{1}{C}\,\frac{s_p}{s^2 + 1/LC}. \tag{4-91}$$

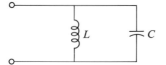

FIG. 4-61. Parallel LC network. The open-circuit natural frequencies are at $s = \pm j/\sqrt{LC}$; the short-circuit natural frequency is at $s = 0$.

This impedance has a zero at zero frequency and a conjugate pair of poles at $s_p = \pm j/\sqrt{LC}$. The zero corresponds to a short-circuit natural frequency at $s = 0$. The pure imaginary open-circuit natural frequencies indicate that the homogeneous solution for the voltage across the parallel LC network is sinusoidal.

The examples we have just discussed illustrate a useful and convenient method for determining the natural frequencies of a network with respect to a given terminal pair when the impedance at that terminal pair is known. The relations upon which this method is based, viz., the relations between open- and short-circuit natural frequencies and poles and zeros of impedance, can often be used, however, to accomplish the reverse objective, i.e., to determine the impedance at a terminal pair when the open- and short-circuit natural frequencies are known. Such a procedure, which permits the impedance to be determined to within a constant factor, is especially convenient for networks whose open- and short-circuit natural frequencies can be readily recognized as those belonging to simple structures. In these cases the natural frequencies and hence the driving-point impedance (except for a constant factor) can be determined directly from the few simple results discussed above for the basic one- and two-element networks.

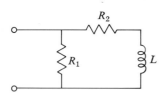

FIG. 4-62. Network used to illustrate the computation of impedance by finding natural frequencies.

To illustrate the method of determining impedance from natural frequencies, consider the network shown in Fig. 4-62. We note that a simple RL network results when the terminals are either open- or short-circuited. Recalling that the natural frequency for a network consisting of an R connected across an L is $s = -R/L$, we can immediately write down the open-circuit natural frequency for the network of Fig. 4-62 as $s = -(R_1 + R_2)/L$ and the short-circuit natural frequency as $s = -R_2/L$. Consequently the impedance is

$$Z(s_p) = K \frac{s_p + R_2/L}{s_p + (R_1 + R_2)/L}, \tag{4-92}$$

where K is a constant.

Once we have determined the locations of the poles and zeros from the natural frequencies, we need only evaluate the constant K in order to obtain a complete specification of the impedance. This constant can be determined if the value of the impedance for a given s_p or its asymptotic behavior as a function of s_p is known. It is frequently possible, simply by inspecting the network, to evaluate the impedance as s_p approaches infinity or as s_p approaches zero, since the impedances of capacitances and inductances approach zero or infinity at these limiting frequencies. In the network of Fig. 4-62, the impedance of the inductance becomes infinite as s_p approaches infinity, and hence the impedance Z approaches R_1. If we let s_p approach infinity in Eq. (4-92), we find that $Z(s_p)$ approaches K, and we conclude that K must be equal to R_1. Thus we have

$$Z(s_p) = R_1 \frac{s_p + R_2/L}{s_p + (R_1 + R_2)/L}. \tag{4-93}$$

As a check, we note from the network that, as s_p approaches zero, the impedance of the inductance becomes zero; i.e., the inductance becomes a short circuit, and hence the impedance of the network approaches $R_1 R_2/(R_1 + R_2)$. From Eq. (4-93), we verify that this is the impedance of the network when $s_p = 0$.

As an example of a network with a different form of asymptotic behavior, consider the network of Fig. 4-63. By inspection, we observe that the open-circuit natural frequency is $s = -R/(L_1 + L_2)$, and there are short-circuit natural frequencies at $s = 0$ and $s = -R/L_2$. Thus the impedance is

$$Z(s_p) = K \frac{s_p(s_p + R/L_2)}{s_p + R/(L_1 + L_2)}, \tag{4-94}$$

where K is a constant to be determined from the asymptotic behavior.

FIG. 4-63. Network used to illustrate the computation of impedance by finding natural frequencies. The asymptotic behavior of the impedance of this network at high and low frequencies is that of an inductance.

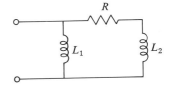

As s_p approaches zero, we see from the network that the impedance approaches that of an inductance L_1; i.e., $Z(s_p)$ approaches $s_p L_1$. But the expression for the impedance given in Eq. (4-94) approaches $K s_p (L_1 + L_2)/L_2$ as s_p approaches zero. Consequently we can write $K = L_1 L_2/(L_1 + L_2)$, and the impedance is given by

$$Z(s_p) = \frac{L_1 L_2}{L_1 + L_2} \frac{s_p(s_p + R/L_2)}{s_p + R/(L_1 + L_2)}. \qquad (4\text{-}95)$$

We can verify the value of the multiplying constant by noting from the network that the impedance approaches that of the parallel combination of the two inductances L_1 and L_2 for high frequencies. This is in agreement with Eq. (4-95), since if we let s_p approach infinity in the expression for $Z(s_p)$, we observe that $Z(s_p)$ approaches $[L_1 L_2/(L_1 + L_2)]s_p$.

Problem 4-27

Determine the driving-point impedance Z or admittance Y that is indicated in each of the networks of Fig. 4-64 by finding the open-circuit and short-circuit natural frequencies of the networks. In each case explain how the constant multiplier is found. Sketch and dimension the pole-zero plot corresponding to each system function.

Problem 4-28

Figure 4-65 represents an RLC network with two accessible terminal pairs, 1-1' and 2-2'. All the open- and short-circuit natural frequencies of the network are excitable from both terminal pairs. The network is at rest for $t < 0$. The following data are known about the network:

1. If $i_1(t) = u_{-1}(t)$, and terminal pair 2-2' is open-circuited, then

$$v_1(t) = u_{-1}(t)[1 + A e^{-t} \sin (t + \phi)],$$

where A and ϕ are constants.

2. If $i_2(t) = u_0(t)$, and terminal pair 1-1' is short-circuited, then

$$v_2(t) = u_{-1}(t) B e^{-t} \cos (2t + \theta),$$

where B and θ are constants.

a. Determine the driving-point impedance $Z_1(s_p)$ at terminal pair 1-1' with terminal pair 2-2' open-circuited, as a rational function of the complex frequency s_p.

b. Carefully outline all the steps necessary to determine A and ϕ in the expression for $v_1(t)$ above. Do not evaluate A and ϕ.

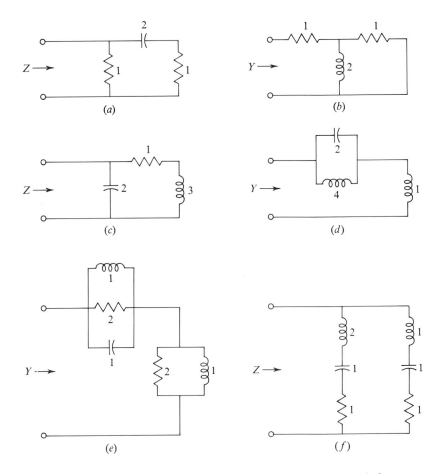

FIG. 4-64. Networks for which the driving-point impedances or admittances are to be found by computing natural frequencies (Prob. 4-27).

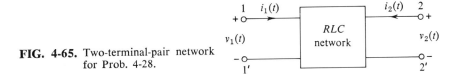

FIG. 4-65. Two-terminal-pair network for Prob. 4-28.

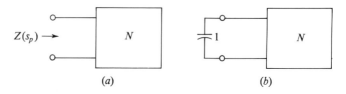

FIG. 4-66. (*a*) Two-terminal network *N* whose impedance is to be determined; (*b*) network *N* with a capacitance connected across its terminals (Prob. 4-29).

Problem 4-29

Determine the driving-point impedance $Z(s_p)$ for the two-terminal network *N* of Fig. 4-66*a* from the following information:

1. As $s \to \infty$, $Z(s_p) \to 2/s_p$.
2. With the terminal pair open, the natural frequencies of *N* are the roots of the equation

$$s^4 + 4s^2 + 2 = 0 .$$

3. When a 1-farad capacitance is connected to the terminals, as shown in Fig. 4-66*b*, the natural frequencies of the resulting network are the roots of the equation

$$s^4 + 2s^2 + \tfrac{2}{3} = 0 .$$

4. In both Fig. 4-66*a* and *b* all natural frequencies are excitable and observable from the terminal pair shown.

Problem 4-30

Two identical two-terminal *RLC* networks N_1 are connected together at their terminals, as shown in Fig. 4-67. The driving-point impedance seen at the terminals of one of the networks alone is Z_1.

a. Show that, in the absence of sources, the natural frequencies observable in the voltage *v* across the common terminal pair are the poles of Z_1, and the natural frequencies observable in the current *i* at one of the terminals are the zeros of Z_1.

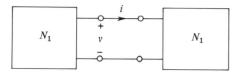

FIG. 4-67. Two identical two-terminal networks connected together (Prob. 4-30).

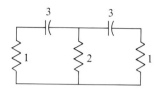

FIG. 4-68. Network whose natural frequencies
are to be determined (Prob. 4-30).

b. Apply the results of (*a*) to determine the two natural frequencies for the
network of Fig. 4-68. Indicate your reasoning.

Problem 4-31

From your knowledge of the analysis of two-terminal networks you should
now be able to recognize networks that realize simple prescribed driving-
point impedances or admittances. Consider, for example, the procedure
for determining a network with driving-point impedance

$$Z(s_p) = \frac{s_p + 1}{s_p}.$$

When the terminals of the network are open-circuited, the natural frequency
must be $s_p = 0$. This suggests a capacitance in a series with the terminals
of the network. When the terminals of the network are short-circuited,
the natural frequency must be $s_p = -1$. Since this natural frequency is
negative and real, we recognize it as the natural frequency of a resistance
in parallel with an inductance or capacitance. Thus the given impedance
can be realized by a network of the form shown in Fig. 4-69. The values

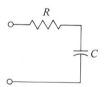

FIG. 4-69. Two-terminal *RC* network
illustrating a method of recognizing
networks that realize simple prescribed
driving-point impedances (Prob. 4-31).

of *R* and *C* are easily determined by consideration of the natural frequencies
and asymptotic behavior of the network.

For each of the following cases, determine a network with the specified
driving-point impedance or admittance:

1. $Z(s_p) = \dfrac{s_p}{s_p + 1}.$

2. $Y(s_p) = \dfrac{s_p + 1}{s_p + 2}.$

3. $Z(s_p) = 2\,\dfrac{s_p{}^2 + 2s_p + 2}{s_p(s_p + 1)}.$

4. $Y(s_p) = \dfrac{s_p(s_p{}^2 + 2)}{s_p{}^2 + 1}.$

Problem 4-32

Determine a two-terminal-pair network having the voltage transfer ratio

$$\frac{V_2}{V_1} = H(s_p) = \frac{\alpha_1 \alpha_2}{(s_p + \alpha_1)(s_p + \alpha_2)},$$

where α_1 and α_2 are positive real numbers.

Problem 4-33

It is often convenient to represent a system in terms of a block diagram that expresses the relation between the system input and output. For example a linear system with input $x(t)$, output $y(t)$, and system function $H(s_p)$ can be represented symbolically, as shown in Fig. 4-70. Block diagrams are symbolic representations of interconnections between systems and should not be confused with network diagrams.

a. The block diagram of Fig. 4-71 represents a system for which the input $x(t)$ is the excitation to both of the linear systems $H_1(s_p)$ and $H_2(s_p)$. The

FIG. 4-70. Block diagram for a simple linear system (Prob. 4-33).

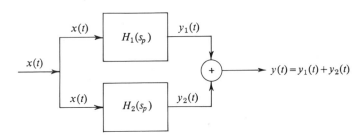

FIG. 4-71. Block diagram of system whose system function is to be determined in Prob. 4-33.

outputs of these linear systems are added to form the output of the over-all system. Determine the system function Y/X in terms of the system functions $H_1(s_p)$ and $H_2(s_p)$, and determine the impulse response $h(t)$ of the over-all system in terms of the impulse responses $h_1(t)$ and $h_2(t)$ of the systems characterized by $H_1(s_p)$ and $H_2(s_p)$, respectively.

b. By first constructing the differential equation, find the impulse response of a system whose system function is

$$H(s_p) = \frac{1}{s_p + \alpha},$$

given that the system is initially at rest and that α is any real or complex constant.

c. By studying the results of (*a*) and (*b*), you should be able to develop a procedure to determine the system function from the impulse response for any linear system whose impulse response is zero before $t = 0$ and can be represented in terms of exponential building blocks for $t \geq 0$. Describe this procedure, and then apply it to determine the system function for a system whose impulse response is

$$h(t) = u_{-1}(t) \left[2e^{-t} + e^{-3t} \cos 2t \right].$$

Problem 4-34

You have learned how to find the impulse response of a system from the system function by first constructing the differential equation. The purpose of this problem is to develop an alternative approach to finding the impulse response from the system function for system functions having only simple poles (i.e., having only distinct roots of the denominator polynomial).

a. Determine the impulse response of a system having the system function

$$H(s_p) = s_p{}^n,$$

where n is a nonnegative integer.

b. From knowledge of the partial fraction expansion,[1] and using the results of (*a*) above and (*b*) of Prob. 4-33, develop and describe a procedure by which the impulse response of a network can be determined directly from the system function without first constructing the differential equation.

c. Apply the procedure developed in (*b*) to determine the impulse response corresponding to each of the system functions given below:

---

[1] See, for example, G. B. Thomas, *Calculus and Analytic Geometry*, 3rd ed., Addison-Wesley Publishing Company, Inc., Reading, Mass., 1960, p. 359.

1. $H(s_p) = \dfrac{s_p}{s_p^2 + 1}$.

2. $H(s_p) = \dfrac{s_p^2 + s_p + 1}{2s_p}$.

3. $H(s_p) = \dfrac{s_p + 1}{s_p^2 + 5s_p + 6}$.

Problem 4-35

In Prob. 4-34 you saw how the impulse response of a linear system can be determined directly from the system function without first determining and solving the differential equation. The purpose of this problem is to extend that procedure to the determination of the response of a linear system to an excitation that is expressible as a linear combination of exponential signals.

When the output of one system constitutes the input to a second system, then the two systems are said to be cascaded. The cascade of two linear systems with system functions $H_1(s_p)$ and $H_2(s_p)$ respectively can be represented by a block diagram in the manner shown in Fig. 4-72.

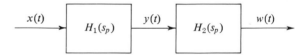

FIG. 4-72. Block diagram of the cascade of two linear systems (Prob. 4-35).

a. Determine the system function W/X of the system of Fig. 4-72 in terms of the system functions $H_1(s_p)$ and $H_2(s_p)$.

b. Consider a linear system with system function $H(s_p)$ and excitation $v(t)$. Show that the response of this system is identical to the impulse response $h_3(t)$ of the cascaded system in Fig. 4-73.

c. Using the results of (*a*) and (*b*) together with the results of Probs. 4-33 and 4-34, determine the response of a linear system with system function

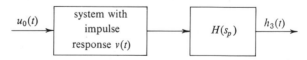

FIG. 4-73. The impulse response of this system is identical to the response of a linear system with system function $H(s_p)$ and excitation $v(t)$—(Prob. 4-35).

$$H(s_p) = \frac{1}{s_p + 1}$$

to each of the excitations below:

1. $v(t) = u_{-1}(t)2e^{-2t}$.
2. $v(t) = u_{-1}(t)(1 - e^{-2t})$.
3. $v(t) = u_{-1}(t)\sin t$.

A method for synthesis of networks with prescribed pole-zero patterns; dependent sources

Our discussion to this point has been concerned primarily with the *analysis* of the behavior of a prescribed network. A problem that is of equal if not greater importance is that of the design or *synthesis* of a network that exhibits a prescribed behavior. The behavior of the network to be synthesized is often specified in terms of a required frequency response for sinusoidal excitation. A typical problem would be to design an *RLC* network with two terminal pairs, as shown in Fig. 4-74*a*, such that the magnitude of the transfer ratio, $|V_2/V_1|$, has a given form as a function of frequency, say that shown in Fig. 4-74*b*.

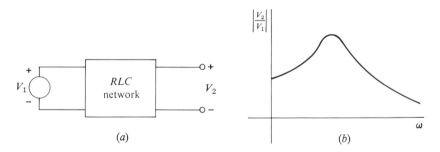

(*a*)   (*b*)

FIG. 4-74. Example of a network synthesis problem. A two-terminal-pair network (*a*) is to be synthesized to give the frequency-response curve shown in (*b*).

Methods are available for approximating a given frequency-response curve by appropriately locating a set of poles and zeros in the *s* plane (subject to certain constraints—for example, the constraint that poles and zeros occur either on the real axis or as conjugate-complex pairs). This task of finding suitable pole-zero locations that can be realized by an *RLC* network and that give a best approximation to a specified frequency-response curve is an important aspect of network synthesis. In the present discussion, however, we shall not concern ourselves with this problem. We shall assume that a suitable pattern of poles and zeros has already been derived by some means, and we shall describe one method for realizing a network configuration for which the system function is characterized by this given set of poles and zeros.

We have already computed (or we can determine by inspection) the pole-zero patterns for the system functions of a number of simple networks. Through our analysis of networks, therefore, we have developed an ability to recognize network configurations that correspond to certain simple pole-zero patterns. The system functions corresponding to these pole-zero patterns may represent driving-point impedances or admittances, transfer impedances or admittances or transfer ratios. Consider, for example, the s plane representation consisting of a simple real-axis pole, as shown in Fig. 4-75a. If this representation is to be associated with a driving-point imped-

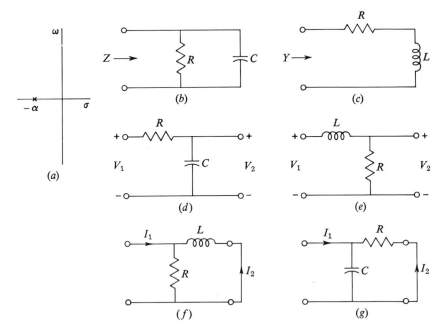

FIG. 4-75. For each of the networks in (b) to (g), the system function is characterized by a single real-axis pole, as shown in (a). For networks (b) and (c) the pertinent system functions are the driving-point impedance and admittance, respectively; for networks (d) and (e) the pertinent system function is the voltage transfer ratio V_2/V_1; for networks (f) and (g) the pertinent system function is the current transfer ratio I_2/I_1. In all RC networks, the values of R and C must satisfy the relation $1/RC = \alpha$. For all RL networks, the relation is $R/L = \alpha$.

ance, then the network shown in Fig. 4-75*b* would give the required real-axis pole; for the case of a driving-point admittance, the network in (*c*) of the figure would be appropriate. Two networks for which the voltage transfer ratios have single real-axis poles are those in (*d*) and (*e*) of the figure; Fig. 4-75*f* and *g* show networks whose current transfer ratios are each characterized by such a pole.

Figure 4-76 shows some simple pole-zero configurations for which the appropriate networks can be realized on the basis of our experience with network analysis. For example, it is possible to construct networks whose driving-point impedances or admittances match each of these pole-zero patterns by making use of the relations between the open- and short-circuit natural frequencies and the poles and zeros of the driving-point impedance. It is also possible to recognize other simple networks having transfer functions that are characterized by the pole-zero patterns of Fig. 4-76.

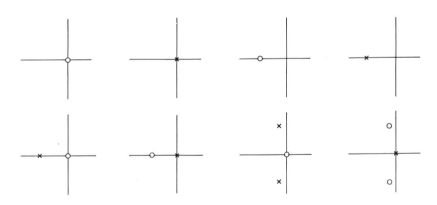

FIG. 4-76. Examples of pole-zero patterns that can be realized by simple network configurations.

When the pole-zero patterns are more complex than those given in Fig. 4-76, it becomes difficult to determine the appropriate network by inspection, and formal methods of synthesis are required. We shall now describe a simple and practical synthesis procedure that can often be applied in such cases. The essence of the method is to construct the required network from several components or building blocks, each of which has a system function corresponding to a simple subset of the prescribed configuration of poles and zeros.

We shall illustrate the procedure by realizing a two-terminal-pair network whose voltage transfer ratio has two real-axis poles, as shown in

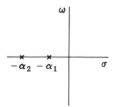

FIG. 4-77. Pole-zero pattern for the transfer ratio of a network that is to be synthesized.

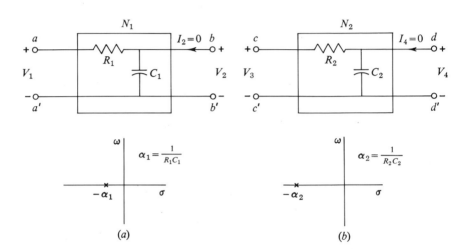

FIG. 4-78. Two component networks that are used to synthesize a network whose transfer ratio is characterized by the pole-zero pattern of Fig. 4-77. The pole-zero pattern of the voltage transfer ratio for each network is shown.

Fig. 4-77. From the networks of Fig. 4-75 we could without difficulty realize a network whose system function is characterized by just one of the real-axis poles of Fig. 4-77. Thus, as shown in Fig. 4-78, we can realize a network (network N_1) whose voltage transfer ratio, with output terminals b-b' open-circuited, is[1]

$$H_1(s) = \frac{V_2}{V_1} = \frac{1}{R_1 C_1} \cdot \frac{1}{s + 1/R_1 C_1} = \frac{\alpha_1}{s + \alpha_1}, \tag{4-96}$$

where $\alpha_1 = 1/R_1 C_1$, and another network (N_2) whose voltage transfer

---

[1] Throughout the remainder of the text the context should always serve to distinguish between a variable that designates an excitation frequency and a variable that designates a natural frequency. Hence we shall simplify our notation by using s instead of s_p to represent the complex frequency variable in a system function.

ratio, with output terminals d-d' open-circuited, is

$$H_2(s) = \frac{V_4}{V_3} = \frac{1}{R_2C_2} \cdot \frac{1}{s + 1/R_2C_2} = \frac{\alpha_2}{s + \alpha_2}, \qquad (4\text{-}97)$$

where $\alpha_2 = 1/R_2C_2$. If, now, a network (say N_3) is to be characterized by both real-axis poles, then the voltage transfer ratio $H(s)$ must be proportional to the product of $H_1(s)$ and $H_2(s)$; i.e.,

$$H(s) = K_3 H_1(s) H_2(s)$$

$$= K_3 \frac{\alpha_1}{s + \alpha_1} \cdot \frac{\alpha_2}{s + \alpha_2}, \qquad (4\text{-}98)$$

where K_3 is a constant. If we wish to realize network N_3 by using the two simpler networks N_1 and N_2, we must find a way of connecting N_1 and N_2 together such that the system function for the combination is the product of the system functions for the individual components. We cannot simply connect the output terminals b-b' of N_1 to the input terminals c-c' of N_2, since in general such a connection would allow current to flow at the output terminals of N_1. This flow of current would alter the transfer ratio V_2/V_1, which was calculated for an open-circuited output terminal pair. Thus any connection we make to terminals b-b' must not cause current to flow; in other words, the input impedance of the network that is connected across the terminals must be infinite.

In order to make a connection between terminals b-b' and c-c', we require, therefore, a two-terminal-pair device that has the following properties: (1) it must have infinite input impedance, and (2) the voltage across its output terminals must be proportional to the voltage across its input terminals. Such a device is sometimes called an isolating network and can be depicted in the manner shown in Fig. 4-79. When this network is used to join the networks of Fig. 4-78, the complete network of Fig. 4-80 is obtained. The over-all voltage transfer ratio is given by

$$\frac{V_4}{V_1} = \frac{V_2}{V_1} \cdot K \cdot \frac{V_4}{V_3}$$

$$= K \cdot \frac{\alpha_1}{s + \alpha_1} \cdot \frac{\alpha_2}{s + \alpha_2}. \qquad (4\text{-}99)$$

The two-terminal-pair network shown in Fig. 4-79 is one of four types of devices that can be used to provide isolation between two networks. These isolating networks are shown in Fig. 4-81. Network (a) is the same as that shown previously in Fig. 4-79; like network (a), network (b) has infinite

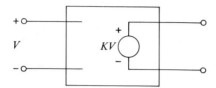

FIG. 4-79. Two-terminal-pair isolating network with infinite input impedance and a dependent voltage source at the output.

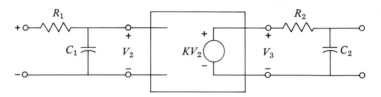

FIG. 4-80. Network arrangement that provides a voltage transfer ratio V_4/V_1 with the pole pattern given in Fig. 4-77.

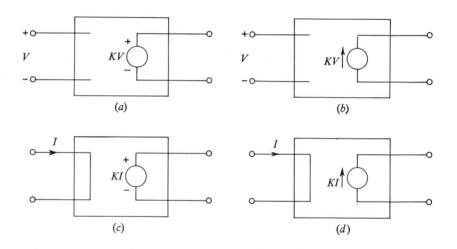

FIG. 4-81. Four ideal isolating networks.

input impedance, but the output is now a current source whose value is proportional to the voltage across the input terminals. The ideal isolating networks of Fig. 4-81c and d have zero input impedance, and the output voltage or current source has a value proportional to the current at the input terminals.

The voltage or current source contained within each of the isolating networks of Fig. 4-81 is called a *dependent source*. By definition, it has the property, not previously encountered in our study of networks, that its value is not fixed by a prescribed time function but is dependent on a voltage or current that exists at some point in the network. In our later studies we shall see that dependent sources are idealizations of certain electronic devices, such as vacuum tubes and transistors, and that models for the actual devices can be realized through interconnections of these sources and other network elements.

The availability of several types of isolating networks, i.e., several types of dependent sources, provides considerable freedom in the way in which a network can be realized for a given pole-zero pattern. To synthesize the network of Fig. 4-80, for example, we used the isolating network of Fig. 4-81a, although other networks in Fig. 4-81 could have been selected. If, for example, we were to use the isolating network of Fig. 4-81b, then the network connected across the dependent source would have to take a different form, since the excitation for this network would now be a current source rather than a voltage source. The complete network in this case

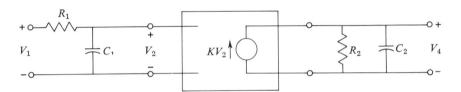

FIG. 4-82. Alternative realization of a network whose transfer ratio V_4/V_1 is characterized by the configuration of poles shown in Fig. 4-77.

could be synthesized in the form shown in Fig. 4-82. The over-all transfer ratio is now

$$\frac{V_4}{V_1} = K \frac{1}{R_1 C_1} \frac{1}{s + 1/R_1 C_1} \cdot \frac{1}{C_2} \frac{1}{s + 1/R_2 C_2}, \qquad (4\text{-}100)$$

which has the required two real-axis poles if we set $1/R_1 C_1 = \alpha_1$ and $1/R_2 C_2 = \alpha_2$. Still other networks could be realized for the same pole pattern by using the other types of isolating networks together with appropriate input and output networks.[1]

The example given above is illustrative of a general method for synthesizing a network whose system function has a prescribed pattern of poles or zeros of the form

---

[1] A network with the pole pattern of Fig. 4-77 can also be realized without the use of isolating networks. See Prob. 4-32.

$$H(s) = K \frac{(s - {}_1s)(s - {}_2s) \cdots (s - {}_ms)}{(s - s_1)(s - s_2) \cdots (s - s_n)}. \qquad (4\text{-}101)$$

The first step in the synthesis procedure is to factor this expression into a product of several smaller expressions, each of which may have only one or two of the poles or zeros and is sufficiently simple that a corresponding network can be synthesized by inspection. The networks corresponding to each of the component expressions are then connected together through appropriate isolating networks. The result is a network whose system function is proportional to the given $H(s)$. A given system function can be achieved with a number of different network configurations of varying degrees of complexity, since there are clearly many ways to factor the system function into smaller components, and several types of networks are available for isolating these components from one another.

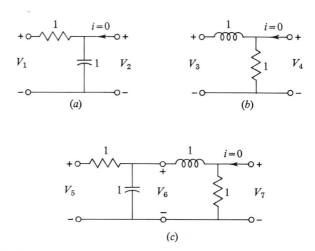

FIG. 4-83. The networks in (a) and (b) are combined to give the network in (c) —(Prob. 4-36).

Problem 4-36

Let the voltage transfer ratios of the two networks of Fig. 4-83a and b be $H_1(s) = V_2/V_1$ and $H_2(s) = V_4/V_3$, respectively, and let the over-all transfer ratio of the combination of the two networks shown in Fig. 4-83c be $H(s) = V_7/V_5$.
a. Find $H_1(s)$ and $H_2(s)$.
b. Find $H(s)$.
c. Explain why $H(s)$ is not equal to $H_1(s)H_2(s)$.

Problem 4-37

a. Determine the pole-zero pattern of $H(s)$ for each of the networks shown in Fig. 4-84.

b. Synthesize a network for each of the pole-zero patterns given in Fig. 4-85. The excitation variable (subscript 1) and response variable (subscript 2)

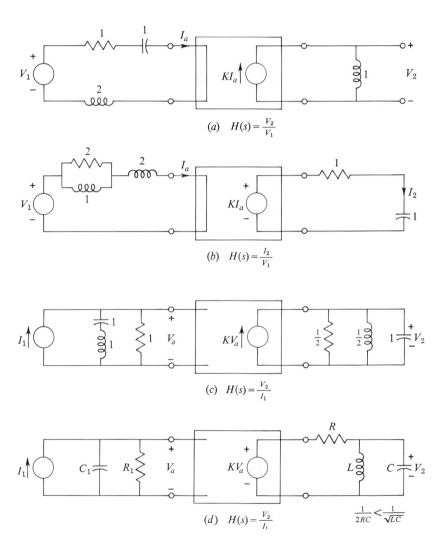

FIG. 4-84. Networks for which the pole-zero patterns of the indicated system functions $H(s)$ are to be determined (Prob. 4-37).

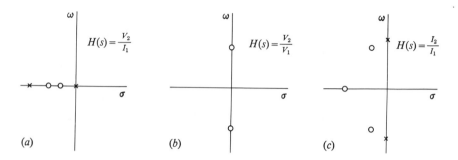

FIG. 4-85. Pole-zero patterns for which networks with the indicated system functions $H(s)$ are to be synthesized (Prob. 4-37).

associated with each pole-zero pattern are indicated on the figure. Use only resistances, inductances, and capacitances together with one or more isolating networks. Specify the form of the network, but do not determine element values.

Problem 4-38

In a certain space vehicle it is known that the relation between the throttle position $x(t)$ and the vehicle acceleration $y(t)$ is given by the differential equation

$$\frac{d^2y}{dt^2} + 2\frac{dy}{dt} + 2y = \frac{d^2x}{dt^2} + \frac{dx}{dt}.$$

It is desired to study the vehicle acceleration in response to various changes in the throttle position. Instead of performing costly experiments with the vehicle directly, it is decided to build an electrical analogue of the system so that the study can be carried out conveniently in the laboratory. We wish, therefore, to design an electrical network whose input voltage $v_1(t)$ is the analogue of the throttle position $x(t)$ and whose output voltage $v_2(t)$ is the analogue of the vehicle acceleration $y(t)$. That is, we wish to synthesize a network governed by the differential equation

$$\frac{d^2v_2}{dt^2} + 2\frac{dv_2}{dt} + 2v_2 = \frac{d^2v_1}{dt^2} + \frac{dv_1}{dt},$$

where v_1 is the input voltage and v_2 is the output voltage.

Synthesize such a network, and determine all the element values. Label the terminals associated with the voltages v_1 and v_2. Dependent sources may be used if desired.

Magnitude and frequency scaling

In previous sections of this chapter we showed how impedances can be computed for a given interconnection of R, L, and C elements, and we indicated how the frequency response of a network is related to the system function. We shall now develop certain simple procedures whereby a given network can be modified to yield a new network having properties that are the same as those of the given network except for a change in scale of impedance or frequency. Suppose, for example, the magnitude of the impedance as a function of frequency for a given network had the form shown in Fig. 4-86a. A change in scale of impedance such that the impedance is multiplied by one-half at all frequencies would lead to the frequency response curve shown by the solid line in Fig. 4-86b. Figure 4-86c demonstrates the effect of a change in the frequency scale by a factor of two, the impedance scale being the same as in Fig. 4-86a. In this case the value of the new impedance at frequency $\omega/2$ is the same as the value of the original impedance at frequency ω.

The scaling techniques we shall derive are useful in problems of network analysis and synthesis, since they indicate that, having solved one network

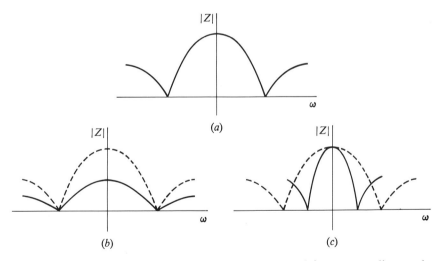

FIG. 4-86. Demonstration of the effect of impedance and frequency scaling on the magnitude of an impedance. The original $|Z|$ is shown as a function of frequency in (a) and by dashed lines in (b) and (c). In (b) the impedance scale is changed such that the impedance is multiplied by one-half at all frequencies; in (c) the frequency scale is changed such that the frequency at which each point on the original impedance curve occurs is multiplied by one-half.

problem, we can write down the solutions for many other problems simply by appropriate application of constant multiplying factors.

The scaling procedures stem from the fundamental network equilibrium equations—KCL equations, KVL equations, and the voltage-current relations for the elements. When applied to complex amplitudes of voltages and currents, these equations take the form

$$\sum_{\substack{\text{into connection} \\ \text{point}}} I_j = 0 , \tag{4-102}$$

$$\sum_{\substack{\text{around} \\ \text{closed path}}} V_j = 0 , \tag{4-103}$$

and
$$V_j = Z_j I_j , \tag{4-104}$$

where Z_j is the impedance of element j. A system function such as a driving-point impedance for a given network is computed by solving such a set of equations to determine the ratio of the appropriate voltage and current.

Suppose now that we wish to realize a new network with a driving-point impedance whose magnitude is M times as large as that for the given network. If we attempt to devise such a network simply by using the same network geometry and adjusting the values of the elements, then the KCL and KVL equations for the currents and voltages in the new network will, of course, be the same as those for the given network. The voltage-current relations for the elements will, however, be different if the elements are adjusted to have new values. If we could adjust the element values in such a way that, for the same currents in the new network as in the original network, all voltages are M times those in the original network, then the driving-point impedance, and for that matter all impedances associated with the network, would be increased by the factor M. This distribution of currents and voltages is, of course, consistent with KCL and KVL and can be made consistent with the voltage-current relations by multiplying the impedance of each element by M. From the voltage-current relations for the R, L, and C elements, we see that multiplication of impedances by M implies multiplication of resistance and inductance values by M and division of capacitance values by M.

In the case of frequency scaling, our objective is to change the element values in a given network such that for the resulting network the value of the system function at an excitation frequency ks (where $k = $ constant) is equal to the value of the system function of the given network at the excitation frequency s. Since both networks have the same geometry, the same KCL and KVL equations apply. However, the excitation frequency does affect the voltage-current relations of the inductance and capacitance elements. For the excitation frequency s these relations are of the form $V = sLI$ and $V = (1/sC)I$. If the excitation frequency is changed to ks, the voltage-current relations for these elements become $V = ksLI$ and $V = (1/ksC)I$. If now all inductance and capacitance values are divided by k, then the voltage-current relations for the elements of the resulting network at excitation frequency ks become identical to the voltage-current relations for the elements of the original network at excitation frequency s. Consequently the complete set of equilibrium equations and hence their solutions are identical in the two cases. Thus if all the L's and C's in a network are divided by a constant k, the system function of the resulting network at excitation frequency ks will be identical to that of the original network at excitation frequency s.

Problem 4-39

a. For the network shown in Fig. 4-87, scale the element values such that the voltage response V_2 for a given current excitation I_1 is multiplied by a factor of 100.

b. How does the scaling of (*a*) affect the transfer ratio $H = V_2/V_1$? Explain your answer.

Problem 4-40

The network of Fig. 4-88*a* has an admittance whose magnitude plot in the

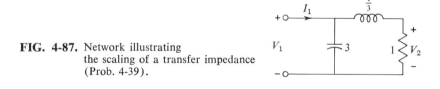

FIG. 4-87. Network illustrating the scaling of a transfer impedance (Prob. 4-39).

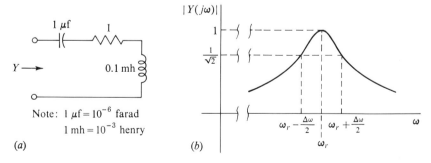

Note: $1 \mu f = 10^{-6}$ farad
$1 \text{ mh} = 10^{-3}$ henry

(*a*)

(*b*)

FIG. 4-88. Network with corresponding frequency-response curve, illustrating the scaling of frequency (Prob. 4-40).

resonance region is that of Fig. 4-88*b*. The magnitude of the admittance is a maximum for $\omega = \omega_r$.

a. Determine the values of ω_r, the bandwidth $\Delta\omega$, and the Q for the network shown in Fig. 4-88*a*. (See Prob. 4-24 for definition of Q.)

b. Using frequency scaling, determine a network for which $Y(j\omega)$ is as shown in Fig. 4-88*b* with $\omega_r = 10^3$.

c. Determine the bandwidth and Q for the modified network found in (*b*).

Problem 4-41

An *RLC* bandpass filter has been constructed to pass signals in a narrow frequency band centered about 1.0 kcps. The excitation and response of the filter are both voltages. After construction of this filter it has been decided to modify it for use on a different channel in which the signal frequency is centered at 1.1 kcps instead of 1.0 kcps. Since the inductances in the filter are very expensive relative to the resistances and capacitances, it is desired to use the same inductances in the modified filter and to change the values of the resistances and capacitances. The filter is to be modified by using a combination of frequency and impedance scaling.

a. Without referring to any specific network, describe how the resistance and capacitance values should be changed.

b. How will the bandwidth and the driving-point impedance of the filter be changed as a result of the modification that you propose?

Problem 4-42

a. Let $H(s)$ and $H_1(s)$ be the system functions of *RLC* networks N and N_1 respectively. Suppose the pole-zero pattern of $H_1(s)$ is the pole-zero pattern of $H(s)$ translated to the left by a distance α. Express $H_1(s)$ in terms of $H(s)$.

b. By reasoning directly from the basic equations that govern the network model, determine how to modify the elements of network N to obtain the network N_1.

c. The driving-point impedance $Z(s)$ of the network of Fig. 4-89*a* has the pole-zero plot of Fig. 4-89*b*. Modify the network so that the driving-point impedance of the modified network has the pole-zero plot of Fig. 4-89*c*.

Problem 4-43

The magnitude of the system function $H(s) = V_2/I_1$ for the network of Fig. 4-90*a* is shown in Fig. 4-90*b*. Such a network is an example of a low-pass filter.

a. Consider a system function $G(s)$ that is related to $H(s)$ as follows:

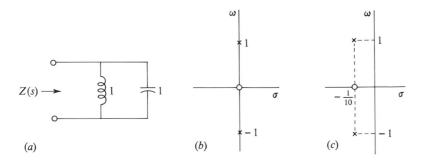

FIG. 4-89. The network in (a), with its corresponding pole-zero pattern in (b), is to be modified to give the pole-zero pattern in (c)—(Prob. 4-42c).

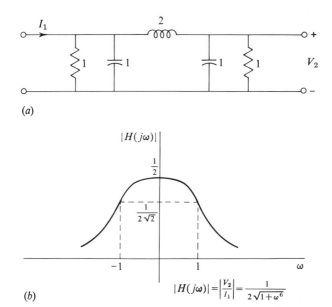

FIG. 4-90. Network, with corresponding frequency-response curve, illustrating low-pass-to-high-pass transformation (Prob. 4-43).

$$G(s) = H\left(\frac{1}{s}\right).$$ (4-105)

Sketch $|G(j\omega)|$ versus ω, labeling the half-power points. A network whose frequency response is of this form is called a high-pass filter.

b. By reasoning directly in terms of the *V-I* relations for the elements, determine how to alter the elements of any network such that its system function is transformed as indicated in Eq. (4-105).

c. Apply the general result that you have derived in (b) to the network of Fig. 4-90a to form the corresponding high-pass filter indicated in (a).

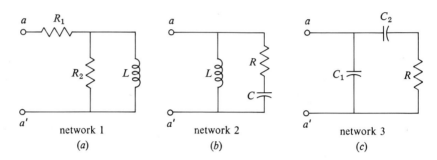

FIG. 4-91. Networks for Prob. 4-44.

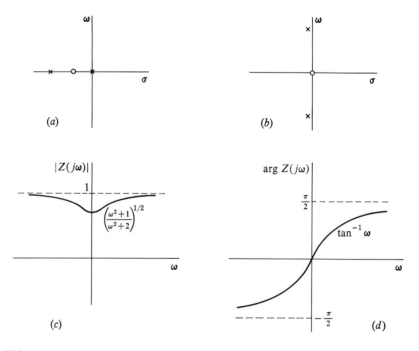

FIG. 4-92. Pole-zero patterns and frequency-response curves defining some of the properties listed in Prob. 4-44.

Problem 4-44

For each of the three networks shown in Fig. 4-91, determine which, if any, of the six properties listed below could belong to the network. The properties all refer to quantities measured at terminals a-a'. The network elements can have any positive real values excluding zero and infinity:

1. The driving-point impedance is characterized by the pole-zero plot in Fig. 4-92a.
2. The driving-point impedance is characterized by the pole-zero plot in Fig. 4-92b.
3. The voltage response to a unit step current source is $v(t) = Ae^{-3t} - Be^{-t}$ for $t > 0$, where A and B are nonzero constants. The state of the network is not specified for $t < 0$.
4. The magnitude of the driving-point impedance as a function of frequency has the form shown in Fig. 4-92c.
5. The angle of the driving-point impedance as a function of frequency has the form shown in Fig. 4-92d.
6. If the network is at rest for $t < 0$, the voltage response to a step current source at $t = 0$ has a finite discontinuity at $t = 0$.

5

General Equilibrium Equations
for Networks

Up to this point we have studied only simple networks in which the number of meshes or nodes is small. For these networks, the task of setting up an appropriate set of equilibrium equations is relatively simple. As we have seen, the equations are of three types: equations expressing Kirchhoff's voltage law (KVL) around a set of closed paths, equations expressing Kirchhoff's current law (KCL) at a set of nodes, and the voltage-current relations for the elements. The network need not be very elaborate, however, before the task of formulating and solving this set of equilibrium equations becomes unwieldy. In order to deal with networks of greater complexity, we need to develop systematic procedures for formulating equilibrium equations in such a way that many of the equations can be solved by inspection and the number of simultaneous equations that must be solved formally is as small as possible. Such systematic formulations of equilibrium equations for networks of arbitrary complexity will be developed in this chapter. The procedures we shall develop will be useful not only as a practical means for computing the response of specific networks but also as a basis for the study of general properties of networks.

The derivations in this chapter will be discussed mainly in terms of basic networks, i.e., networks with no voltage or current sources. We have shown previously that the equations expressing the constraints imposed by KVL and KCL on the element currents and voltages in a network with a given excitation can be so written that the left-hand sides of the equations are those of the basic network and hence are of the same form independent of the values of the source voltages and currents. The right-hand sides of the equations then reflect the particular source values and are, of course, zero for the case in which there is no excitation. Thus in order to examine the properties of the equilibrium equations involving the element currents and voltages, it is appropriate to focus our attention on the basic network, with the realization that the inclusion of sources simply adds known functions to the right-hand sides of certain of the Kirchhoff-law equations.

Some insight into the nature of the procedures we shall develop for formulating network equilibrium equations can, perhaps, be obtained if we view each of the three basic sets of equations—KCL equations, KVL equations, and voltage-current relations—as imposing constraints on the values that can be assumed by the b branch currents and the b branch voltages in a network. With no constraints applied, each of these $2b$ variables could, of course, assume any values whatever. If, however, we impose the requirement that the branch currents satisfy KCL, then we are no longer free to assign arbitrary values to all the b branch currents. We shall show that as a consequence of KCL we can assign arbitrary values only to a smaller number, say l, of branch currents, the remaining $b - l$ currents being expressible in terms of these l values by applying KCL. If we next impose the remaining constraints—the KVL equations and the voltage-current relations—then it is possible to formulate l equations in l current variables, and the solutions of these equations specify the values of these variables. All the voltages and currents in the network can be obtained from these l current variables by inspection. The method of solving for the network behavior when the constraints are applied in this order—first reducing the number of current variables through application of KCL and then solving for these currents by applying KVL and the voltage-current relations—forms the basis for the *loop method*.

An alternative procedure, on which the *node method* is based, is to impose, as a first step, the constraints that the b branch voltages satisfy KVL. As a consequence of KVL we are not free to assign arbitrary values to all b branch voltages, and we shall show that we can assign arbitrary values only to a smaller number $n - 1$ of such voltages, where n is the number of nodes in the network. The remaining $b - (n - 1)$ branch voltages can then be expressed in terms of these values by applying KVL. The next step in this procedure is to impose the remaining constraints—the KCL equations and the voltage-current relations—and to formulate thereby $n - 1$ equations in the $n - 1$ voltage variables. These equations can then be solved for the $n - 1$ voltage variables, and all the voltages and currents in the network can be obtained from these voltage variables by inspection.

In both the loop method and the node method the first step is to apply the constraints of either KCL or KVL and thereby to reduce the number of current or voltage variables to a set of so-called independent branch currents or voltages in terms of which the network behavior can be described. The mathematical concept of linear dependence plays a central role in this reduction process. Hence before proceeding to develop the loop and node methods, we shall define this concept and illustrate it in terms of a simple network.

The concept of linear dependence

Consider the basic network of Fig. 5-1, in which the four branch currents[1]

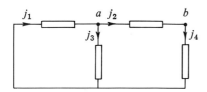

FIG. 5-1. Basic network used to illustrate the discussion of independent branch currents.

are denoted by j_1, j_2, j_3, and j_4. If no constraints were imposed on the branch voltages and currents, we would be free to choose arbitrary values for j_1, j_2, j_3, and j_4. If, however, we require that the branch currents satisfy KCL, we find[2]

at node a: $\qquad j_1 - j_2 - j_3 = 0$; $\hspace{4cm}$ (5-1)

at node b: $\qquad j_2 - j_4 = 0$. $\hspace{4.5cm}$ (5-2)

In this network, therefore, all branch currents could be specified, by means of KCL, in terms of the two branch currents j_1 and j_2, for example. The currents in branches 3 and 4 are simply linear combinations of the currents in branches 1 and 2. The branch currents j_3 and j_4 are said to be *linearly dependent* on the currents j_1 and j_2.

In general, a variable x_0 is defined to be *linearly dependent* on the variables $x_1, x_2, \ldots, x_n$ if and only if, for all values of x_k, it is possible to write

$$x_0 = \sum_{k=1}^{n} c_k x_k , \qquad (5-3)$$

where the c_k are constants. If such a relation cannot be written, then x_0

---

[1] In this chapter we shall introduce a new type of current variable, called a circulating current, and it will be convenient to maintain a distinction between circulating currents and branch currents. We shall use the symbol j to designate a branch current and reserve the symbol i to designate a circulating current.

[2] We saw in Prob. 1-4 that, if KCL is satisfied at all nodes but one, then it is automatically satisfied at the remaining node.

is said to be linearly independent of x_1, x_2, ..., x_n. The form of Eq. (5-3) suggests a convenient procedure for testing for linear dependence. In order to test whether x_0 is linearly dependent on x_1, x_2, ..., x_n, one simply sets $x_1 = x_2 = \cdots = x_n = 0$. If x_0 becomes zero, then it is linearly dependent[1] on x_1, x_2, ..., x_n; if x_0 does not become zero, then no such relation of the type given in Eq. (5-3) exists, and x_0 is independent[2] of x_1, x_2, ..., x_n. A set of variables x_1, x_2, ..., x_n is said to form an *independent set* if each member of the set is independent of the other members of the set.

Returning to the KCL equations (5-1) and (5-2) for the network of Fig. 5-1, we can readily see that j_3 and j_4 are linearly dependent on j_1 and j_2, since they are constrained to be zero when j_1 and j_2 are set to zero. Furthermore, j_1 and j_2 form an independent set, since setting either one to zero does not constrain the other to be zero. Another example of an independent set is the set j_1 and j_3; the three branch currents j_1, j_2, and j_3 do not, however, form an independent set.

Independent branch currents; trees and links

There exists a simple way of applying the test for linear dependence of branch currents by appealing directly to the geometrical structure of the network without reference to the algebraic KCL equations. As we have seen, the test for linear dependence of variables in algebraic equations requires that one or more variables be set to zero. If the variables are currents that flow in the branches of a network that is diagrammed as a geometrical structure, then a convenient way to set a branch current to zero is to cut the branch, as with a pair of scissors. From the definition of an independent set, the currents in a particular set of branches are independent if a current could flow in each one of the branches alone when all the other branches in the set are cut. Such a current (consistent with KCL) can flow in this one branch if it forms part of a closed path in the structure that remains after the cuts are made. Likewise the current in a particular branch is linearly dependent on the currents in a given set of branches if that current becomes zero when all the branches in the set are cut, i.e., if

---

[1] This test is only valid, of course, under the assumption that, if x_0 is related to the x_k's, then it is related in the linear fashion indicated by Eq. (5-3). Such an assumption is valid in the loop and node methods, since the variables are currents and voltages and the only constraints we are considering here are the linear constraints imposed by KCL and KVL. Hereafter the modifying adverb "linearly" will be understood, since the only type of dependence with which we are concerned is linear.

[2] *Ibid.*

that branch does not form part of a closed path after all the branches in the set are cut.

Since we are focusing our attention on the constraints imposed on the currents by KCL, we do not need to be concerned at this point with the values of the elements that form the branches. It is convenient, therefore, to redraw the basic network with each branch designated simply by a line connecting the appropriate pair of nodes, and with an arrow indicating the reference direction for the branch current. Such a representation of a basic network is called a *graph.*

For the network of Fig. 5-1 the graph can be drawn in the form shown in Fig. 5-2. Examination of this network graph shows that j_3 and j_4 are

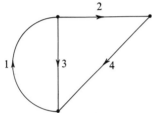

FIG. 5-2. Graph of network of Fig. 5-1.

forced to zero when branches 1 and 2 are cut, and consequently j_3 and j_4 must be linearly dependent on j_1 and j_2. Note also that j_1 and j_2 are independent, since after either branch is cut a closed path containing the other branch still remains. Thus either branch current can exist when the other is zero. Further examination of the network graph will show that there are other possible choices for independent sets, viz., j_1 and j_3, j_1 and j_4, j_2 and j_3, or j_3 and j_4.

The example of Fig. 5-1 has served to illustrate the two approaches that are available for finding an independent set of branch currents: one involves writing down a set of algebraic KCL equations and applying the test for linear dependence to the variables in these equations; the other examines the graph of the network and applies the test for linear dependence by cutting one or more branches in the graph. The latter approach has the advantage that it can be implemented simply by geometrical manipulations on the network graph without the necessity of writing down sets of equations. It is the approach we shall use in developing general procedures for finding sets of independent branch currents for networks of arbitrary complexity.

In general, suppose we start with the graph of a basic network and select a set of branches such that, if every branch in the set is cut, no closed paths remain, and such that the repairing of any one of the cuts creates a closed path. We shall denote the branches in this set as links. Then it follows that the currents in the links form an independent set and the remaining branch currents are dependent on the currents in the links. The structure formed by these remaining branches is called a *tree*. The tree clearly has the property that it joins any node in the network to any other node via one and only one path, since we stipulated that it has no closed paths and the addition of any branch to the tree will create a closed path. Figure 5-3 shows an example of a network graph with eight branches, together with two possible trees for the network.

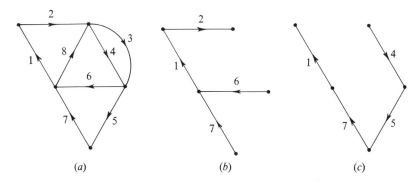

FIG. 5-3. Graph of a typical network, and two examples of trees for the network.

In order to determine the number of branches in a tree for a network, let us start at any one of the nodes and visualize the step-by-step construction of the tree. The first branch we draw terminates on two nodes. Since the tree connects all nodes, we can always arrange to draw each succeeding branch in such a way that one end of the branch terminates on one of the nodes used as the terminal for one or more of the branches already drawn and the other end terminates on a node that has not yet been used. Thus each additional branch uses up one more node. (A branch that terminates at both ends in nodes that have already been connected to other branches is inadmissible, since a closed path would be formed by such a branch.) The largest number of branches that can be connected to the nodes without creating a closed path, i.e., the number of branches in the tree, is therefore equal to $n - 1$, where n is the total number of nodes. The number of branches in the tree is seen to depend only on the number of nodes in the network, and consequently all trees that can be formed from a given network have the same number of branches. The number of links l is equal to the difference between the total number of branches b in the network and the number of branches in the tree; i.e.,

$$l = b - (n - 1). \tag{5-4}$$

In summary, then, given a tree for a network, the currents that flow in the l links form an independent set; the currents in the tree branches are linearly dependent on the link currents, and can be written, using KCL, as linear combinations of the link currents. Therefore, any arbitrary current distribution in a network (i.e., any set of values of all the branch currents consistent with KCL) can be realized by selecting an appropriate set of values for the l link currents.

Problem 5-1

a. Consider a set of variables $x_1, x_2, \ldots, x_n$ having the property that

$$\sum_{k=1}^{n} a_k x_k = 0,$$

independent of the values of the variables x_k, only when all the constants a_k are zero. Using the definitions in the text, show that the variables $x_1, x_2, \ldots, x_n$ form a linearly independent set.

b. Consider a linearly independent set of variables $x_1, x_2, \ldots, x_n$. Prove that

$$\sum_{k=1}^{n} a_k x_k = 0,$$

independent of the values of the variables x_k, only when all the constants a_k are zero.

Remark. The definition of a linearly independent set of variables is often stated in the following way: A set of variables $x_1, x_2, \ldots, x_n$ is linearly independent if

$$\sum_{k=1}^{n} a_k x_k = 0,$$

independent of the values of the variables x_k only when all the a_k are zero. In (a) and (b) of this problem you have shown that such a statement of the definition of a linearly independent set is equivalent to the one given in the text.

c. The two sets of variables x_1, x_2 and y_1, y_2, y_3 are related by the following equations:

$$x_1 = y_1 + 2y_2 + y_3,$$
$$x_2 = 2y_1 + y_2 + 3y_3.$$

If the variables x_1 and x_2 are linearly dependent, does it necessarily follow that the variables y_1, y_2, and y_3 are also linearly dependent?

Problem 5-2

For each of the network graphs shown in Fig. 5-4, determine:

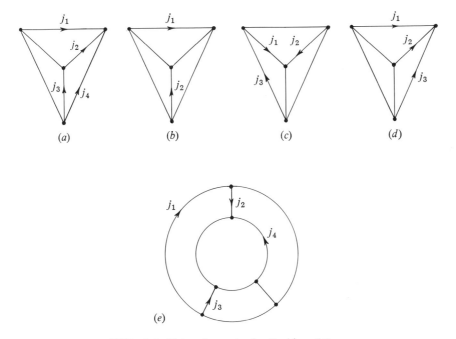

FIG. 5-4. Network graphs for Problem 5-2.

1. Whether the branch currents labeled form an independent set.
2. Whether all the remaining branch currents can be written in terms of the branch currents labeled, using KCL.

Problem 5-3

a. In the graph of Fig. 5-5 what is the maximum number m of branch currents that can be specified independently such that the resulting

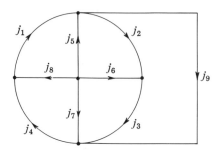

FIG. 5-5. Network graph for Problem 5-3.

current distribution is consistent with KCL? Does it follow that one can specify any set of m branch currents independently?

b. In Fig. 5-5 could the following sets of branch currents be consistent with KCL? Explain.

1. $j_1 = 3, j_3 = 1, j_5 = -1, j_6 = 1, j_8 = -1$;

2. $j_3 = 3, j_5 = 2, j_6 = 2, j_8 = 1, j_9 = 4$;

3. $j_1 = 1, j_4 = 2, j_5 = 2, j_7 = -1, j_8 = 2/3$;

4. $j_1 = 1, j_2 = 0, j_4 = -2, j_5 = -1, j_9 = 0$.

Loop method

Selection of a set of loop currents. We have just seen that as a result of the constraints imposed by KCL it is possible to specify all the currents in a network in terms of a set of l current variables, and we have shown that the link branch currents form a suitable set of such variables. The fact that l currents are sufficient to specify any distribution of branch currents consistent with KCL suggests the possibility that various linear combinations of these currents might yield other suitable sets of l variables. By appealing directly to the graph of the network, we can select an especially convenient set of such variables. We imagine the currents in the various branches of the network to be made up of a set of currents flowing around closed paths in the network. These currents are called *circulating currents* or *loop currents*. Loop currents have the following properties: (1) each branch current consists of a sum of loop currents that can be determined simply by inspection of the network graph, and (2) any set of branch currents that could result from loop currents must automatically satisfy

KCL, since a loop current leaves each node that it enters.

Before establishing that a set of loop currents is in fact capable of specifying any current distribution in a network, let us clarify the meaning of loop currents and their relation to branch currents by considering the example shown in Fig. 5-6. For the network of Fig. 5-6a we have arbitrarily chosen the loop currents to flow around the meshes, as indicated in

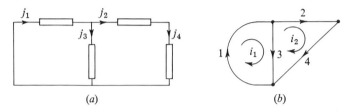

$$(a) \qquad\qquad\qquad\qquad (b)$$

FIG. 5-6. (a) Simple basic network, showing reference directions for branch currents. (b) Graph of network in (a), showing a set of two loop currents i_1 and i_2.

the graph of the network in Fig. 5-6b. The loop current i_1 flows through branch 1 and through branch 3, in the reference direction in both cases; loop current i_2 flows through branches 2 and 4 in the reference direction and through branch 3 in a direction opposite to the reference direction. Consequently we can write the branch currents in terms of these imagined loop currents as follows:

$$j_1 = i_1 ,$$
$$j_2 = i_2 ,$$
$$j_3 = i_1 - i_2 ,$$

and
$$j_4 = i_2 .$$

In general, a set of loop currents will be considered as the basic variables that describe the behavior of the network for the loop method of analysis. We shall develop a method for formulating a set of equations in these variables, the solution of which gives a complete description of the state of the network. It is pertinent, therefore, to ask the questions: How many loop currents are necessary for representing any arbitrary distribution of currents in a network (consistent, of course, with KCL), and how can such a set of loop currents be selected?

We have shown that a set of link currents can specify any distribution of branch currents consistent with KCL. Therefore if a set of loop currents is capable of representing arbitrary values for a set of link currents, then it must be capable of representing any distribution of branch currents in the network consistent with KCL. In other words, if arbitrary values are given for a set of link currents, then we must be able to find values for the loop currents that yield this distribution of link currents. Since there are l independent branch currents (i.e., l link currents), a set of loop currents that is to be capable of representing an arbitrary distribution of currents in the network must be at least l in number, and we shall show that l is sufficient.

Let us first discuss the conditions that must be imposed on the choice of an appropriate set of loop currents. We shall illustrate the discussion with the example of Fig. 5-3, and we shall tentatively select the set of four loop currents shown in Fig. 5-7a. By inspection of the figure, the eight branch currents are related to this set of loop currents by the following equations:

	i_1	i_2	i_3	i_4	
$j_1 = 1$		0	0	0	
$j_2 = 1$		0	0	0	
$j_3 = 0$		1	0	0	
$j_4 = 1$		0	0	1	(5-5)
$j_5 = 0$		0	1	0	
$j_6 = 1$		1	-1	1	
$j_7 = 0$		0	1	0	
$j_8 = 0$		1	0	1	

By listing the variables at the top of the columns, we arrange these equations in a form that focuses attention upon the array of coefficients. The numbers in the array represent the coefficients of the loop currents shown at the top. In other words, if the i above each column is placed beside the numbers in that column and $+$ signs are inserted between terms, then each row would form a simple algebraic equation. A property of this array (which follows immediately from its construction) that we shall make use of later is that each column identifies the branches in the path traversed by the loop current associated with that column, the signs indicating the direction of the loop current relative to the assigned directions for the branch currents. For example, looking at column 3, we see that i_3 flows through branches 5 and 7 in the positive direction and branch 6 in the negative direction.

Now if we focus our attention on the link branch currents associated,

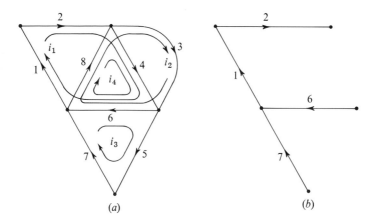

FIG. 5-7. (a) Example illustrating the selection of a set of loop currents; (b) a tree for the network of (a).

say, with the tree given in Fig. 5-7b, we have the following subset of Eq. (5-5):

	i_1	i_2	i_3	i_4	
$j_3 = 0$	1	0	0	
$j_4 = 1$	0	0	1	(5-6)
$j_5 = 0$	0	1	0	
$j_8 = 0$	1	0	1	

Our requirement is that, given arbitrary values for this set of link currents j_3, j_4, j_5, and j_8, we must be able to find loop currents i_1, i_2, i_3, and i_4 that yield these link currents. The theory of algebraic equations tells us that a necessary and sufficient condition for this requirement to be satisfied is that the determinant associated with the array of numbers in Eq. (5-6) is not zero. If the numbers in any column of the determinant were linear combinations of the numbers in any other column, then the determinant would be zero, and we could not solve the equations for the i's in terms of arbitrary values for the j's. In the above example, the determinant happens to be nonzero, indicating that we have selected an appropriate set of loop currents. If, however, we had selected for loop current i_4 the path through branches 1, 2, 4, 5, and 7, then the determinant would be zero, and it would not be possible in general to solve for the i's. (The student should verify this result for himself.)

Thus we can determine if any given set of l loop currents is an appropriate set for representing all possible distributions of branch currents consistent with KCL simply by writing the equations for any set of link branch currents in terms of the given loop currents and testing whether the determinant of the coefficients is nonzero. Alternatively we can derive a systematic procedure for selecting a set of loop currents in such a way that this determinant will always be nonzero. Then if this procedure is followed, we will always obtain an appropriate set of loop currents, and the determinant need not be tested. One way of selecting a suitable set of loop currents is to draw each loop current through one link only, closing the path through the tree branches. This procedure forces each link current to be identical to the corresponding loop current, and hence this set of loop currents can clearly represent arbitrary values of the link currents. The algebraic counterpart of this graphical argument is established by observing the equations relating the loop currents and the link currents—equations of the type shown in Eq. (5-6). If each loop current traverses one and only one link, then the array of coefficients in these equations has the property that each row contains only one entry and the column in which this entry occurs is different for each row. Consequently no column can be expressed as a linear combination of the remaining columns of the array, and the loop currents satisfy our requirement that the determinant be nonzero. The set of loop currents appropriate to the tree given in Fig. 5-7b is shown in Fig. 5-8.

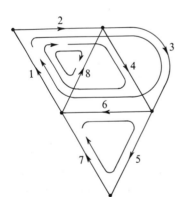

FIG. 5-8. Set of loop currents selected such that each loop current is equal to the current in one of the links corresponding to the tree shown in Fig. 5-7b.

We shall see shortly that in the case of planar networks (i.e., networks that can be mapped on a plane without any crossing branches) another set of paths that is appropriate for the loop currents consists of the paths around the meshes.

In the above discussion we established that, in order to test a given set of loop currents, it is only necessary to look at the equations relating the link branch currents to the loop currents. In the next section, however, we shall make use of properties of the entire array of coefficients associated with the equations relating all the branch currents to the loop currents, i.e., an array of the type (5-5). The properties of interest follow from the fact that the set of equations, of the type (5-6), involving only the link branch currents is a subset of the equations, of the type (5-5), involving all the branch currents. In the present discussion we shall refer to Eqs. (5-5) and (5-6) in order to indicate the full set and the link branch set of equations respectively; it should be clear, however, that the discussion applies to any such sets of equations and is in no way limited to the specific example for which these particular equations were written.

If the columns of the array of numbers associated with the link branch set of Eqs. (5-6) are independent, then clearly the columns of the larger set of Eqs. (5-5) involving all the branches are also independent. Thus a necessary condition that a set of loop currents be appropriate is that the columns of the full set (5-5) be independent.

That this condition is also sufficient is a consequence of the following result of algebra: for an $m \times l$ array of numbers (i.e., an array having m rows and l columns) in which $m \geq l$, if the l columns are independent, then at least one $l \times l$ determinant constructed from the array is nonzero. Hence there are l independent equations relating l of the branch currents to the loop currents, and these equations can be solved for the loop currents when arbitrary values are given for these l branch currents. But these l branch currents must correspond to link branches since the loop currents give rise to branch currents that satisfy KCL and since the only sets of l branch currents to which arbitrary values can be assigned consistent with KCL are link sets. We conclude. therefore, that, if the columns of the larger set of Eqs. (5-5) are independent, then there is a subset of l independent equations that relate link currents to loop currents—the condition we require if the loop currents are to be an appropriate set.

This same algebraic result can be used to show that we cannot choose more than l closed paths for loop currents such that the columns of the array of coefficients in the equations relating the branch currents to these loop currents are all independent. If more than l columns were independent, then this would imply, by the above result, that the same number of rows (i.e., more than l) were independent. Such a result would in turn imply that more than l branch currents can be specified arbitrarily—a result that we have shown to be false.

Problem 5-4

For the graph shown in Fig. 5-9, determine a set of loop current variables

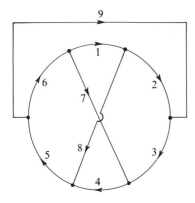

FIG. 5-9. Network graph
for Problem 5-4.

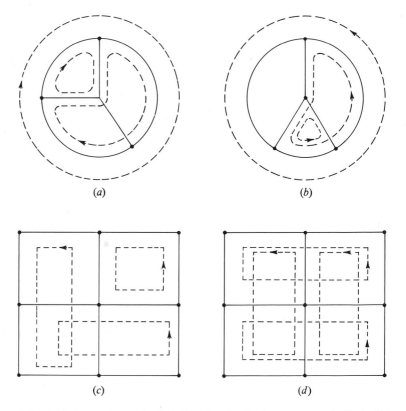

(a)

(b)

(c)

(d)

FIG. 5-10. Network graphs and closed paths for loop currents in Prob. 5-5.

capable of representing all possible current distributions that are consistent with KCL. Describe how you determine this set.

Problem 5-5

For each of the network graphs of Fig. 5-10 determine whether the loop currents shown constitute an appropriate set for the formulation of the network equilibrium equations.

Problem 5-6

Consider a basic network to which an appropriate set of l loop currents has been assigned. Show that, if an element is added between any pair of nodes, then an appropriate set of loop currents for the new network consists of the original set together with one loop current defined to flow through the added element and return through any path in the original basic network.

Applying KVL equations and the voltage-current relations for the elements. Having selected a set of loop currents which satisfy Kirchhoff's current law and which are capable of describing any current distribution consistent with KCL, we turn now to the basic relations that must be satisfied by the branch voltages, viz., Kirchhoff-voltage-law equations. In order to write the equations expressing Kirchhoff's voltage law, it is necessary to select a set of closed paths. In the example given above, let us tentatively select the l closed paths that were used for defining the loop currents in Fig. 5-7a. (In writing the KVL equations, we shall adopt the convention that voltage drops were added around the closed paths in the direction defined by the loop currents.) The KVL equations around these paths are as follows:

$$
\begin{array}{cccccccc}
v_1 & v_2 & v_3 & v_4 & v_5 & v_6 & v_7 & v_8 \\
1 & 1 & 0 & 1 & 0 & 1 & 0 & 0 & = 0 \\
0 & 0 & 1 & 0 & 0 & 1 & 0 & 1 & = 0 \\
0 & 0 & 0 & 0 & 1 & -1 & 1 & 0 & = 0 \\
0 & 0 & 0 & 1 & 0 & 1 & 0 & 1 & = 0
\end{array}
\qquad (5\text{-}7)
$$

Because of our particular choice of paths for writing KVL, the rows of numbers forming the coefficients in Eqs. (5-7) are identical to the columns of numbers forming the coefficients in Eqs. (5-5). This identity of the coefficients will always hold whenever the paths for evaluating KVL are chosen to be the same as the paths used for assigning loop currents, because each loop current passes through the same branches as those encountered in writing the corresponding KVL equation. If, therefore, the columns of

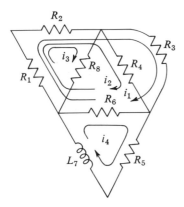

numbers in (5-5) are independent, then the rows of numbers in (5-7) are independent, and vice versa, and consequently the KVL equations are independent; i.e., no equation can be expressed as a linear combination of the other equations. Thus a set of closed paths that defines an appropriate set of l loop currents also leads to a set of independent KVL equations, and vice versa. Furthermore there are no more than l independent KVL equations in any network, since we have established (page 243) that there are no more than l paths for loop currents that result in independent columns in the equations for the branch currents of the type (5-5).

The usual procedure one follows in setting up the equilibrium equations on the loop basis is to select the same closed paths both for defining the loop currents and for writing down the KVL equations. This is not a necessary requirement, however; a different set of paths could be used for the KVL equations provided the set yielded independent equations. As before, the test for independence of the equations is that the rows in the array of numbers giving the coefficients in the equations, such as the rows in Eqs. (5-7), be independent.

Having established appropriate procedures for selecting current variables and for writing KVL equations, we are now in a position to formulate a set of network equilibrium equations which incorporate these procedures and which include the voltage-current relations for the elements. Each branch voltage in the KVL equations can be expressed as a function of the branch current simply by applying the voltage-current relation for the branch. Furthermore, each branch current can, by inspection, be expressed in terms of the l loop currents. Thus the l KVL equations can, by inspection, be written down with the l loop currents as variables.

Following the procedures just developed, let us write the equilibrium equations for the network of Fig. 5-11 by inspection. For this network,

FIG. 5-11. Network used to illustrate the formulation of equilibrium equations by the loop method.

an appropriate set of loop currents has already been selected in Fig. 5-8. The resulting equations for this basic network are:

$$(i_1 + i_2 + i_3)R_1 + (i_1 + i_2 + i_3)R_2 + i_1 R_3 + (i_1 + i_2 - i_4)R_6 = 0,$$

$$(i_1 + i_2 + i_3)R_1 + (i_1 + i_2 + i_3)R_2 + i_2 R_4 + (i_1 + i_2 - i_4)R_6 = 0,$$

$$(i_1 + i_2 + i_3)R_1 + (i_1 + i_2 + i_3)R_2 + i_3 R_8 = 0,$$

(5-8)

$$(i_4 - i_1 - i_2)R_6 + i_4 R_5 + L_7 \frac{di_4}{dt} = 0.$$

Planar networks. Most of the networks with which one is concerned have the special property that they are capable of being mapped on a plane in such a way that no branches cross each other. For such networks it is usually convenient to select as the current variables the set of currents circulating around each mesh, called mesh currents, and to write KVL equations around these closed paths defined by the meshes. We shall now show that this selection of closed paths yields a set of l independent KVL equations.

First let us establish that the number of meshes in a planar network is equal to l. Imagine that we start with some tree and add the links one by one. When the first link is added, a network with one mesh is formed. Addition of the second link either creates a second separate mesh or divides the original mesh into two. If this procedure is continued, the addition of each new link adds one to the number of meshes either by creating a new mesh or by dividing an existing one into two. Since the number of links is l, the number of meshes must also be l.

Thus we can write l KVL equations for the meshes, and, furthermore, from Prob. 1-5 it is clear that the KVL equation for any closed path can be obtained by adding (or subtracting) the equations for the meshes enclosed by the path. For example, for the network whose graph is shown in Fig. 5-12, the KVL equations for the four meshes A, B, C, and D, traversing

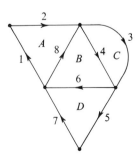

FIG. 5-12. Illustrating the selection
of meshes for writing KVL equations.

the paths in a clockwise direction, are, respectively,

$$v_1 + v_2 - v_8 = 0,$$
$$v_8 + v_4 + v_6 = 0,$$
$$v_3 - v_4 = 0,$$

and
$$v_5 + v_7 - v_6 = 0.$$

(5-9)

The sum of the voltage drops around the closed path defined by branches 1, 2, 4, and 6 in the figure is obtained simply by adding the equations for meshes A and B, giving

$$v_1 + v_2 + v_4 + v_6 = 0.$$ (5-10)

We observe, therefore, that by selecting meshes for writing KVL equations, we obtain l equations, and *from these l equations we are able to derive the KVL equations for any other closed path.* But we have previously shown (page 246) that there are l independent KVL equations for any network. Consequently the KVL equations for the meshes are an independent set of l equations.

We have also established previously that any set of paths that is appropriate for writing independent KVL equations is also appropriate for assigning loop currents, and vice versa. It follows, therefore, that the l mesh currents must be capable of representing the most general distribution of currents, consistent with KCL, in a planar network. We conclude that equilibrium equations for such a network can be formulated by assigning mesh currents and writing KVL equations around the meshes.

The network we have been using for an example is planar, and hence we can select the mesh currents as shown in Fig. 5-13. The KVL equations

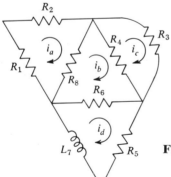

FIG. 5-13. Network used to illustrate the formulation of equilibrium equations in terms of mesh currents.

can be written by inspection as follows:

$$i_a R_1 + i_a R_2 + (i_a - i_b)R_8 = 0,$$

$$(i_b - i_a)R_8 + (i_b - i_c)R_4 + (i_b - i_d)R_6 = 0,$$

$$(i_c - i_b)R_4 + i_c R_3 = 0,$$
(5-11)

$$i_d R_5 + L_7 \frac{di_d}{dt} + (i_d - i_b)R_6 = 0.$$

From the solution of these four equations for i_a, i_b, i_c, and i_d, all the branch currents and voltages can be obtained by inspection.

Summary of development of loop method. The development of the loop method given above involves several steps as summarized below:

1. We showed that as a result of the constraints imposed by KCL the number of independent branch currents in a network is $l = b - (n - 1)$, where b is the number of branches and n the number of nodes.

2. If loop currents are selected to describe the behavior of a network, then KCL is automatically satisfied. We then derived a necessary and sufficient condition under which a given set of l loop currents is capable of representing a general distribution of currents in the network. This condition was that the columns of numbers forming the coefficients of the equations relating the b branch currents to the loop currents be independent. We showed that one way of guaranteeing that this condition is satisfied is to select each loop current to flow through only one link and to return through the tree branches.

3. Next we showed that, if KVL equations are written around a set of closed paths that are appropriate for selecting loop currents, then these KVL equations are independent, and vice versa.

4. The network equilibrium equations are formulated by applying the voltage-current relations for the elements and thereby writing the l KVL equations with the l loop currents as the variables.

5. For planar networks, a convenient procedure is to select the meshes as the closed paths for which loop currents are defined and for which the KVL equations are written. We showed that there are l meshes and that the KVL equations for these paths form an independent set.

Problem 5-7

a. Determine the maximum number of independent KVL equations that can be written for the network graph of Fig. 5-14.

b. Determine whether the KVL equations written for closed paths *abcd*,

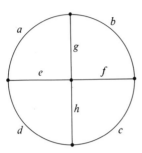

FIG. 5-14. Network for
Prob. 5-7.

abfe, aghd, and *bchg* in the graph of Fig. 5-14 are independent and contain all the KVL constraints that can be imposed on the graph.

Problem 5-8

a. Write a set of independent KVL equations that, when combined with
the *v-i* relations, are sufficient to find all branch currents in the network
of Fig. 5-15. Use any appropriate set of loop currents as the variables.

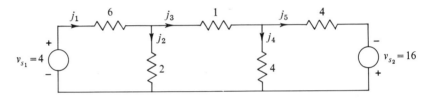

FIG. 5-15. Network for Prob. 5-8.

b. From your results in (*a*) determine the branch currents j_1, j_2, j_3, j_4,
and j_5.

Node method

The node method for writing network equilibrium equations is analogous
to the loop method, and many of the steps involved in the development of
the node method follow procedures similar to those used in connection
with the loop method. The first step is to select a set of voltage variables,
consistent with KVL, that are capable of representing any distribution of
branch voltages that is consistent with KVL. The second step is to impose
the constraints of KCL and the voltage-current relations for the elements,
and thereby to formulate a set of equations in the voltage variables.

Selection of a set of voltage variables.   In order to select a set of voltage variables consistent with KVL, we must consider the constraints that KVL imposes on the branch voltages. As a result of these constraints, not all branch voltages can be assigned independently. The KVL equations are, of course, a set of linear equations in the branch voltages, and hence we can apply the definition of linear dependence to derive procedures for finding an independent set of branch voltages. From this definition we recognize that a given set of branch voltages forms an independent set if and only if each of the voltages in the set could exist alone when all other branch voltages in the set are caused to be zero. Reference to the graph of the network suggests a convenient way of testing for linear dependence of branch voltages, since the setting of a branch voltage to zero is equivalent to replacing that branch by a short circuit. If all but one of the branches in a given set are replaced by short circuits, a voltage could exist (consistent with KVL) in the remaining branch only if that branch does not form a closed path when connected to the other branches in the set. Likewise, the voltage across a particular branch is linearly dependent on a given set of branch voltages if that voltage becomes zero when all the voltages in the set are caused to be zero. Such a situation would occur only if the branch in question formed a closed path with the branches in the set.

We recognize a similarity between the requirements that a set of branch voltages form an independent set and the requirement that the corresponding set of branches form a tree. We recall that, by definition, the branches of a tree do not form a closed path, but a closed path is formed by the addition of any one branch other than those in the tree. Thus the tree branch voltages form an independent set, and the voltages in the links are derivable from the tree branch voltages through application of KVL. Since the number of tree branches is $n - 1$, where n is the number of nodes in the network, then the number of independent branch voltages is $n - 1$.

As we have already noted, our first objective in the node method is to select for a given network a set of voltage variables that is capable of representing the most general distribution of branch voltages that can exist in the network consistent with KVL. One possible selection for this set of variables is a set of $n - 1$ tree branch voltages, since we have seen that such a set is an independent one and that all other branch voltages can be expressed in terms of this set through application of KVL. It is possible, however, to select other sets of voltage variables consisting of linear combinations of tree branch voltages, which may be more convenient from the point of view of formulating and solving the network equilibrium equations. The voltage across any pair of nodes in a network can, of course, be expressed as a linear combination of tree branch voltages. Thus we would expect that a properly selected set of $n - 1$ such node-pair volt-ages could form a suitable set of voltage variables. The requirement on this set of node-pair voltages is that it be capable of representing arbitrary values for a set of tree branch voltages (and thus be capable of representing an arbitrary distribution of branch voltages consistent with KVL). An algebraic test for the appropriateness of a set of node-pair voltages would be to write the set of equations for the tree branch voltages in terms of the given set of node-pair voltages and to determine whether the determinant of the coefficients is nonzero, i.e., determine whether we can find the node-pair voltages corresponding to any arbitrary specification of tree branch voltages. By appealing to the network graph, however, we can derive syste-matic procedures for selecting a set of voltage variables in such a way that this determinant will always be nonzero.

Let us consider the following procedure for selecting a set of node-pair voltages. Suppose we start with the n nodes of a given network and draw a treelike structure connecting all these nodes, without regard to whether the branches of this structure represent actual branches in the network. This fictitious tree will have $n - 1$ branches and will, of course, join any pair of nodes of the network with one and only one path. An example of this procedure is shown in Fig. 5-16. The graph of the original network is given

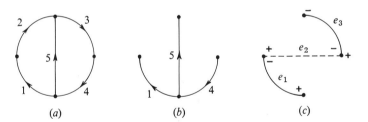

FIG. 5-16. (*a*) Graph of a network; (*b*) tree corresponding to the graph in (*a*); (*c*) fictitious tree formed from the nodes without regard to the configuration of branches in the graph of the network. The dotted path is used in this figure to designate a fictious tree branch that does not correspond to a branch in the network.

in (*a*) of the figure, and one tree corresponding to this graph is shown in (*b*). A fictitious tree connecting the nodes of the network (but in which all the branches do not necessarily represent branches in the network) is drawn in (*c*) of the figure.

Consider now the voltages across the $n - 1$ branches in a fictitious tree constructed in the manner just described. (In the example of Fig. 5-16*c*, these voltages[1] are designated e_1, e_2, and e_3.) We have seen that the voltages across the branches of any structure that forms a tree constitute an independent set, because the tree has no closed paths. Furthermore, the voltage between any pair of nodes can be determined from this set by application of KVL, since there is always a path through the tree connecting any pair of nodes. Consequently all branch voltages in the original network can be determined from this set, since each branch connects a pair of nodes. Thus the $n - 1$ node-pair voltages obtained from the construction of a fictitious tree constitute a set of voltages that are sufficient to describe any distribution of voltages in the network consistent with KVL.

For the example of Fig. 5-16 we can, by inspection, apply KVL to obtain the following relations between the branch voltages of the network and the node-pair voltages of (c) of the figure:

$$
\begin{array}{cccc}
& e_1 & e_2 & e_3 \\
v_1 = & 1 & 0 & 0 \\
v_2 = & 0 & 1 & 1 \\
v_3 = & 0 & 0 & -1 \\
v_4 = & -1 & -1 & 0 \\
v_5 = & 1 & 1 & 1
\end{array}
\tag{5-12}
$$

The equations for v_1, v_4, and v_5 constitute relations between the tree branch voltages of (b) and the node-pair voltages. As a check, we can readily verify that the coefficients in these three equations form an array of numbers in which the columns are independent, and hence the determinant of the coefficients is nonzero. This result is expected, since we know that e_1, e_2, and e_3, having been selected to represent branch voltages for a treelike structure, are capable of describing any distribution of branch voltages in the network.

There is one type of tree that is of particular interest in the node method, since selection of node-pair voltages corresponding to this tree always enables one to express any branch voltage simply as one of the node-pair voltages or as the difference between two of them. This tree is constructed by selecting one node as a so-called datum node and drawing lines from this node to each of the other $n - 1$ nodes of the network. The reference direction is usually selected so that the node-pair voltage variable is positive if the remote node is positive relative to the datum node. The node-

---

[1] When it is necessary to distinguish node-pair voltage variables from branch voltages, we shall use the symbol e to designate the former and reserve the symbol v for the latter.

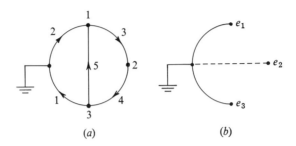

FIG. 5-17. (a) Graph of a network showing the selection of the leftmost node as the datum node; (b) fictitious tree corresponding to a node-to-datum set of voltages.

pair voltages for this tree (which may or may not be a fictitious tree) are often called *node-to-datum* voltages, and these form an appropriate and frequently used set of voltage variables for the node method.

For the network graph of Fig. 5-17a, suppose we select the leftmost node as the datum node and designate it by a ground symbol as shown. The appropriate fictitious tree is shown in Fig. 5-17b, where the nodes have been numbered as indicated. The equations relating the branch voltages to the node-to-datum voltages e_1, e_2, and e_3 are, by inspection,

$$
\begin{array}{cccc}
 & e_1 & e_2 & e_3 \\
v_1 = & 0 & 0 & 1 \\
v_2 = & -1 & 0 & 0 \\
v_3 = & 1 & -1 & 0 \\
v_4 = & 0 & 1 & -1 \\
v_5 = & -1 & 0 & 1
\end{array}
\qquad (5\text{-}13)
$$

Problem 5-9

a. Consider a network with b branches. Call the branch current and voltage of the kth branch j_k and v_k respectively. Show that, if $j_1, j_2, \ldots,$ j_r form an appropriate set of current variables (i.e., the currents are independent and all other branch currents can be expressed in terms of them), then $v_{r+1}, v_{r+2}, \ldots, v_b$ form an appropriate set of voltage variables (i.e., the voltages are independent and all other branch voltages can be expressed in terms of them).

b. For each of the network graphs of Fig. 5-18 determine whether the branch voltages labeled constitute an appropriate set.

c. For each of the network graphs in Fig. 5-19, determine whether the node-pair voltages labeled constitute an appropriate set.

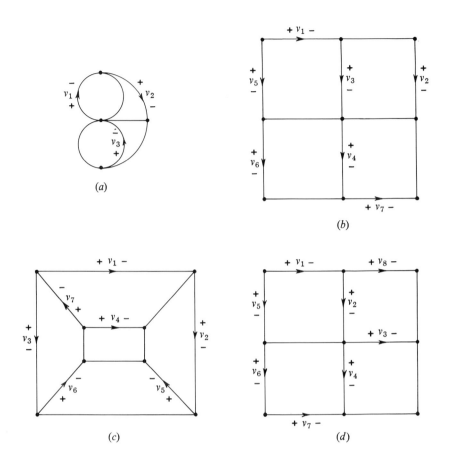

FIG. 5-18. Network graphs for Prob. 5-9*b*.

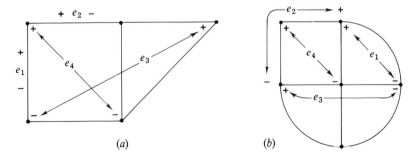

FIG. 5-19. Network graphs for Prob. 5-9*c*.

Problem 5-10

Consider a basic network to which an appropriate set of node-pair voltages has been assigned. Show that, if an element is added in series with any branch, then an appropriate set of node-pair voltages for the new network consists of the original set plus one node-pair voltage defined to be the voltage across the added element.

Applying KCL equations and the voltage-current relations for the elements. Having selected a set of voltage variables in a way that is consistent with Kirchhoff's voltage law and having noted that this set is capable of describing any voltage distribution that can exist consistent with KVL, we turn now to the basic relations that must be satisfied by the branch currents, viz., Kirchhoff's current law. In order to write the equations expressing Kirchhoff's current law it is necessary to select a set of nodes, or more generally, a set of closed surfaces encompassing groups of nodes, and to express the fact that the sum of currents entering or leaving each node (or closed surface) is zero.

The KCL equations for a network can take various forms, depending on the nodes or groups of nodes selected for writing them. For the network of Fig. 5-17a, let us tentatively select a set of $n - 1$ nodes consisting of all nodes except the datum node, and let us write the KCL equations in the form that states that the sum of the currents leaving each node is zero. These equations are:

$$
\begin{array}{ccccc}
j_1 & j_2 & j_3 & j_4 & j_5 \\
0 & -1 & 1 & 0 & -1 = 0 \\
0 & 0 & -1 & 1 & 0 = 0 \\
1 & 0 & 0 & -1 & 1 = 0
\end{array}
\qquad (5\text{-}14)
$$

By reasoning similar to that followed in connection with the loop method (page 245), we shall verify that the KCL equations written in this way form an independent set. In the KCL equations written for $n - 1$ nodes, such as Eqs. (5-14), let us examine one of the rows of coefficients, say the row corresponding to the kth node. We find a nonzero entry in this row for the current in each branch that connects to node k. Since we have written the KCL equations in a form that states that the sum of currents leaving each node is zero, an entry in row k is $+1$ if the reference arrow in the branch points away from node k and -1 if the reference arrow points toward the node. Consider now the set of equations relating the branch voltages to the node-to-datum voltages for the same $n - 1$ nodes as those used for writing the KCL equations—Eqs. (5-13) in the present example. Each equation in this set expresses one branch voltage as the node-to-datum voltage of the node that the branch leaves minus the node-to-datum voltage of the node that the branch enters. Hence if we look down the column of coefficients associated with the node-to-datum voltage e_k for node k, we shall always find a nonzero entry corresponding to each branch that is connected to node k. The entry is $+1$ if the reference arrow in the branch points away from the node and -1 if the reference arrow points toward the node. Consequently the coefficients of the j's in the KCL equations written for all nodes except the datum node form the same array of numbers (with rows and columns interchanged) as the coefficients of the e's in the equations that express branch voltages in terms of the node-to-datum voltages. We have previously established that the node-to-datum voltages form an independent set and hence that the columns of coefficients in the equations for the branch voltages are independent. Thus the rows of coefficients in the KCL equations are independent, and it follows that these KCL equations constitute a set of $n - 1$ independent equations in the branch currents. Furthermore, by following reasoning similar to that used in the loop method (page 246), it could be verified that there can be no more than $n - 1$ independent rows of coefficients in equations of the type given in (5-14), and hence no more than $n - 1$ independent KCL equations can be written for the nodes of a network. In other words, if KCL is satisfied at $n - 1$ nodes, then it is satisfied for all nodes—a fact that we saw in Prob. 1-4.

We have up to this point discussed the writing of KCL equations for individual nodes only, and we have noted that there are just $n - 1$ such independent equations. Other sets of equations can, of course, be derived by forming linear combinations of these node equations. An equation formed by adding several KCL equations for individual nodes can be interpreted as an equation that expresses KCL for a closed surface that encompasses these nodes.[1] Thus for example, if the first two equations of (5-14) are added, we obtain

$$-j_2 + j_4 - j_5 = 0 , \qquad (5\text{-}15)$$

which expresses KCL for a surface enclosing both nodes 1 and 2, as shown in Fig. 5-20. This equation together with the second and third equations of

---

[1] See Prob. 1-2.

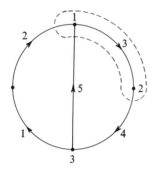

FIG. 5-20. Illustrating the writing of KCL equations for a surface enclosing more than one node. In this case the dashed line represents a surface enclosing nodes 1 and 2.

(5-14) forms an independent set of equations that guarantee that KCL is satisfied at all nodes in the network. Thus a set of equations expressing KCL for a network could consist of KCL equations for closed surfaces as well as for individual nodes. By following an argument parallel to that used in the loop method (page 243), we could show that we can write $n - 1$ independent KCL equations for nodes or surfaces in a given network, and no more. Hence, in order to guarantee that KCL is satisfied everywhere in a network, we must write a set of $n - 1$ KCL equations for nodes or surfaces and test that these are independent. Although a method that involves the writing of KCL equations for groups of nodes has great generality, we shall usually confine ourselves to the writing of KCL equations at $n - 1$ nodes, since this procedure is a simple one and since we have seen that it will always lead to a set of independent KCL equations.

Having indicated appropriate procedures for selecting voltage variables and writing KCL equations, we are now in a position to formulate a set of network equilibrium equations which incorporate these procedures and which include the voltage-current relations for the elements. Each branch current in the KCL equations can be expressed as a function of the branch voltage simply by applying the voltage-current relation for the branch. Likewise, each branch voltage can, by inspection, be expressed in terms of the $n - 1$ voltage variables. Thus the $n - 1$ KCL equations can, by inspection, be written down with the $n - 1$ voltages as variables. This process is carried out for the illustrative network, assuming resistance and capacitance elements as shown in Fig. 5-21. The datum node is the same as that given in Fig. 5-17, and the resulting equations are

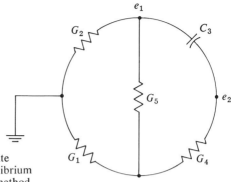

FIG. 5-21. Network used to illustrate
the formulation of equilibrium
equations by the node method.

$$e_1 G_2 + (e_1 - e_3)G_5 + C_3 \frac{d}{dt}(e_1 - e_2) = 0 \,,$$

$$C_3 \frac{d}{dt}(e_2 - e_1) + (e_2 - e_3)G_4 = 0 \,, \qquad (5\text{-}16)$$

$$e_3 G_1 + (e_3 - e_1)G_5 + (e_3 - e_2)G_4 = 0 \,.$$

In this particular example, it happens that the number of voltage variables, $n - 1 = 3$, is greater than the number of loop currents ($l = b - n + 1 = 2$) that would be selected as variables if the equilibrium equations for the network were to be written on the loop basis. Thus in this case, as in many situations that are encountered, the number of simultaneous equations required for the loop method is different from the number required for the node method. It is usually convenient to select the method (loop or node) that leads to the smaller number of equilibrium equations. Once these equations have been solved either for the l loop currents or for the $n - 1$ node-pair voltages, then the $2b$ branch currents and voltages can be written down by inspection without the necessity of further manipulation of equations.

Problem 5-11

Write a set of equilibrium equations for the network of Fig. 5-22. Use as variables the voltages e_1, e_2, and e_3 between the indicated connection points and datum. Do not solve the set of equations.

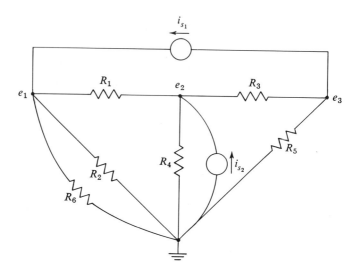

FIG. 5-22. Network for Prob. 5-11.

Equilibrium equations for networks with sources

The methods given above for writing general network equilibrium equations on the loop and node bases were derived for basic networks in which no sources were present. We have shown previously, however, that in the case of networks with sources the Kirchhoff-law equations written for connection points (or closed surfaces) and closed paths selected from the basic network are sufficient to guarantee that the Kirchhoff-law constraints on the element variables are satisfied. Furthermore, we observed that Kirchhoff-law equations for a network with sources can be written in such a way that their left-hand sides are characteristic of the basic network and their right-hand sides reflect the sources in the network. We shall now consider the application of these results to network equilibrium equations written on the loop and node bases, and we shall examine the general form of these equations for networks with sources.

Equations on the loop basis for networks with independent sources. When voltage and/or current sources are present, we have seen that the first step in setting up the equilibrium equations is always to form the basic network by setting all sources to zero. When the equilibrium equations are to be written on the loop basis, a set of l closed paths is chosen from the basic network for the assignment of loop currents, and a set of l closed paths is selected for writing KVL. (Usually the same closed paths are used for defining loop currents and for writing KVL.) With these closed paths assigned, the voltage and current sources are then reinserted into the network.

The voltage sources, which became short circuits when set to zero in the basic network, appear in the closed paths when reinserted into the network and thus contribute terms to the KVL equations for these closed paths.

The current sources, which became open circuits when they were set to zero in the basic network, now appear across nodes of that network. At the points where a current source is connected, KCL is clearly not satisfied by the loop currents assigned from the basic network. We can satisfy KCL simply by assigning, for each current source i_s, a loop current of value i_s that flows through the network in a closed path that includes the current source. (The addition of the loop current i_s does not influence the fact that the equations relating link currents to loop currents are independent. Hence the l loop currents assigned from the basic network together with the loop current i_s are capable of representing an arbitrary distribution of branch currents in the network consistent with KCL.)

Although new closed paths are formed by the reinsertion of current sources into the basic network, we saw in Chap. 1 that the paths containing current sources introduce no new KVL constraints on the element voltages, and hence it is not necessary to write new KVL equations beyond those already written for the closed paths selected from the basic network. When each KVL equation is written, it is customary to bring all the terms involving sources to the right-hand side so that the left-hand side remains charac- teristic of the basic network.

As an example, let us formally set up the equilibrium equations on the loop basis for the network shown in Fig. 5-23a. We first find the basic

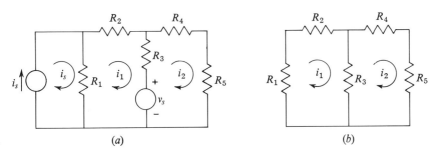

(a)   (b)

FIG. 5-23. (a) Network with a voltage and current source, used to illustrate the writing of equilibrium equations on the loop basis. (b) Basic network for the network in (a).

network, given in Fig. 5-23b, and then assign the loop currents i_1 and i_2. In order to satisfy KCL at connection points a and b, across which the current source is connected, we assign a loop current i_s, such as that shown in Fig. 5-23a. (Alternative paths could have been chosen for assigning the loop current i_s, such as the path that traverses the current source, R_2, and R_3, or the path that traverses the current source, R_2, R_4, and R_5.) The remaining steps are to select a set of closed paths from the basic network and to write KVL equations for these paths. In this example we shall follow the usual procedure of selecting from the basic network the same sets of paths for defining the loop current variables and for writing KVL equations. The KVL equations are written by inspection as follows:

$$(i_1 - i_s)R_1 + i_1 R_2 + (i_1 - i_2)R_3 + v_s = 0 , \qquad (5\text{-}17)$$

and
$$(i_2 - i_1)R_3 + i_2 R_4 + i_2 R_5 - v_s = 0 . \qquad (5\text{-}18)$$

Transferring the source terms to the right-hand sides of the equations and collecting the terms involving each of the current variables, we obtain

$$i_1(R_1 + R_2 + R_3) - i_2 R_3 = i_s R_1 - v_s , \qquad (5\text{-}19)$$

and
$$-i_1 R_3 + i_2(R_3 + R_4 + R_5) = v_s . \qquad (5\text{-}20)$$

When the equations are written in this form, the sources are accounted for by terms on the right-hand sides, and the left-hand sides are characteristic of the basic network.

When the terms on the left-hand sides of the equations are collected in the manner shown in Eqs. (5-19) and (5-20), each term can be interpreted as the component of the total voltage drop around a given closed path due to one of the loop currents. The first term in Eq. (5-19), i.e., $i_1(R_1 + R_2 + R_3)$, can be interpreted as the voltage drop around path 1 due to loop current i_1, and the second term, $-i_2 R_3$, is the voltage drop around path 1 due to i_2. Likewise, in the second equation the first term is the contribution of i_1 to the voltage drop around path 2, and the second term is the contribution of i_2 to the voltage drop around path 2.

This example suggests that there are, in general, two ways of grouping terms in the writing of loop equations, typified by Eqs. (5-17) and (5-18) on the one hand and (5-19) and (5-20) on the other. In the case of Eqs. (5-17) and (5-18) Kirchhoff's voltage law around each loop is expressed by evaluating separately the voltage drop across each element in the path and equating the sum of these voltage drops to the sum of the source voltages in the path. In the second method, exemplified by Eqs. (5-19) and (5-20), each term in a given KVL equation represents the contribution of one of the loop currents to the voltage drop around the path and can be evaluated by imagining all other loop currents to be zero.

Equations on the node basis for networks with independent sources. When sources are present in a network for which equilibrium equations are to be written on the node basis, the first step is again to form the basic network. From the basic network an appropriate set of node-pair voltages is assigned by the methods described previously, and a set of nodes is selected for writing KCL equations. (The most common procedure is to select a set of node-to-datum voltages, and the following argument will assume that this method is used. The argument may easily be modified, however, to apply to any other method of selecting node-pair voltages.) The voltage and current sources are then reinserted into the network.

Each current source, which became an open circuit when set to zero in the basic network, now appears across a pair of nodes and thus contributes terms to the KCL equations written for these nodes.

Each voltage source, which became a short circuit when set to zero in the basic network, now introduces two connection points (one at each end of the source) in place of one node in the basic network. The connection point at one end of the voltage source can be considered the "node" for which a node-to-datum voltage is assigned from the basic network. The voltage between the connection point at the other end of the source and the datum point is simply the algebraic sum of the assigned node-to-datum voltage variable and the source voltage. After the voltage sources have been reinserted in the basic network, therefore, the voltage between each connection point and the datum point, and hence, through KVL, the voltage between any pair of connection points, can be expressed in terms of the assigned node-to-datum voltage variables and the values of the voltage sources. We can then proceed to write the KCL equations for the $n - 1$ connection points or closed surfaces corresponding to nodes in the basic network, as we saw in Chap. 1.

Consequently the reinsertion of current and voltage sources in the basic network introduces new terms involving the source values into the equilibrium equations written on the node basis, in addition to the terms determined from the basic network. As before, it is customary to bring all source terms to the right-hand sides of the equations so that the left-hand sides remain characteristic of the basic network.

To illustrate this procedure, we shall select the same network given in Fig. 5-23a (and redrawn in Fig. 5-24a) and write the equilibrium equations on the node basis. In Fig. 5-24b we select a datum node as shown, and we assign the node-to-datum voltages e_1, e_2, and e_3. Notice that the voltage

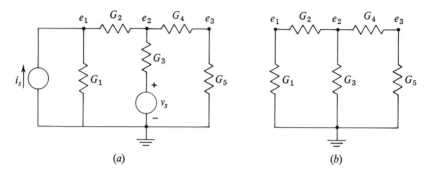

FIG. 5-24. (*a*) Network used to illustrate the writing of equilibrium equations on the node basis. (*b*) Basic network for the network in (*a*), showing the assigned node-to-datum voltages e_1, e_2, and e_3.

across element G_3 in Fig. 5-24a is $e_2 - v_s$ as a consequence of the presence of the voltage source, and hence the current flowing through G_3 is $(e_2 - v_s)G_3$. Writing the KCL equations for connection points corresponding to nodes 1, 2, and 3, we obtain

$$-i_s + e_1G_1 + (e_1 - e_2)G_2 = 0, \qquad (5\text{-}21)$$

$$(e_2 - e_1)G_2 + (e_2 - v_s)G_3 + (e_2 - e_3)G_4 = 0, \qquad (5\text{-}22)$$

and $$(e_3 - e_2)G_4 + e_3G_5 = 0. \qquad (5\text{-}23)$$

Transferring the source terms to the right-hand sides of the equations and collecting the terms involving each of the voltage variables, we obtain

$$e_1(G_1 + G_2) - e_2G_2 = i_s, \qquad (5\text{-}24)$$

$$-e_1G_2 + e_2(G_2 + G_3 + G_4) - e_3G_4 = v_sG_3, \qquad (5\text{-}25)$$

and $$-e_2G_4 + e_3(G_4 + G_5) = 0. \qquad (5\text{-}26)$$

Again we observe that the left-hand sides of the equations are associated with the basic network and the right-hand sides reflect the sources of excitation for the network.

Each term on the left-hand sides of the equilibrium equations written in the form (5-24) to (5-26) can be interpreted as the component of the total current leaving a given connection point due to one of the node-to-datum voltages, with all other node-to-datum voltages and all source voltages imagined to be zero. The first term in Eq. (5-24), i.e., $e_1(G_1 + G_2)$, is the current that would leave connection point 1 through all the branches connected to it if the voltage between this connection point and the datum point were e_1 and all other node-to-datum voltages and the source voltage were imagined to be zero. Likewise the second term is the current that would flow out of connection point 1 through the branch common to connection points 1 and 2 if e_2 were the only nonzero voltage. Similar interpretations can be made for each of the terms in Eqs. (5-25) and (5-26).

It is evident from this example that there are two ways of grouping terms in the writing of equilibrium equations on the node basis, typified by Eqs. (5-21) to (5-23) on the one hand and (5-24) to (5-26) on the other. In the case of Eqs. (5-21) to (5-23) Kirchhoff's current law for a connection point is expressed by evaluating separately the current that leaves the connection point through each element that is attached to the connection point and equating the sum of these currents to the sum of the source currents entering the connection point. In the second method, exemplified by Eqs. (5-24) to (5-26), each term in a given KCL equation represents the contribution of one of the node-to-datum voltages to the total current leaving a connection point.

Problem 5-12

Determine the voltage at each connection point in the network of Fig. 5-25 with respect to the indicated datum.

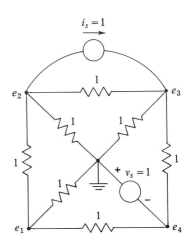

FIG. 5-25. Network for
Prob. 5-12.

Problem 5-13

a. For the network of Fig. 5-26 use the loop method to write a set of differential equations expressing network equilibrium.

b. For the network of Fig. 5-26 use the node method to write a set of

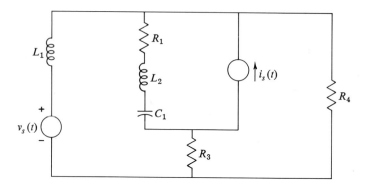

FIG. 5-26. Network for Prob. 5-13.

equilibrium equations in terms of the complex amplitudes of the voltage variables and the complex frequency s.

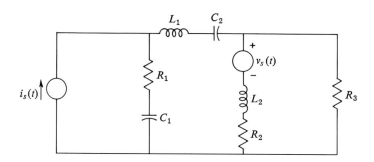

FIG. 5-27. Network for Prob. 5-14.

Problem 5-14

Using either the loop or node method, write a set of differential equations for the network of Fig. 5-27. It may be helpful to consider which method will yield the smaller set of equations. Do not solve the set of equations.

Problem 5-15

The set of equations

$$5y_1 - 2y_2 - y_3 = 2$$
$$-2y_1 + 4y_2 - y_3 = 1$$
$$-y_1 - y_2 + 5y_3 = 0$$

represents equilibrium equations for a particular network.

a. If the variables y_1, y_2, and y_3 are mesh currents and if the KVL equations are written for the closed paths corresponding to these currents, determine a network with appropriate sources that will lead to the set of equations above.

b. If the variables y_1, y_2, and y_3 are node-to-datum voltage variables, determine a network with appropriate sources that will lead to the set of equations above.

Problem 5-16

a. Determine a network, containing two nodes, that gives rise to the equilibrium equation

$$E_1 \left(\frac{1}{a_1} + \frac{1}{a_2 s} + a_3 s \right) = I_1 \, ,$$

where a_1, a_2, and a_3 are real constants, E_1 is the complex amplitude of the voltage of one node with respect to the other, and I_1 is the complex amplitude of the excitation. Express the element values in terms of a_1, a_2, and a_3.

b. Determine a network, containing two meshes, that gives rise to the equilibrium equations

$$\left(a + \frac{b}{s} + cs + d \right) I_1 - (cs + d)I_2 = V_s$$

$$-(cs + d)I_1 + (cs + d + e)I_2 = 0 \, ,$$

where a, b, c, d, and e are real constants, I_1 and I_2 are the complex amplitudes of the two mesh currents, and V_s is the complex amplitude of the excitation. Express the element values in terms of a, b, c, d, and e.

c. In (a), interchange E_1 and I_1, and assume that the equation now represents an equilibrium equation written on the loop basis, where I_1 is the mesh current. Determine a network that results in this loop equation, expressing the element values in terms of a_1, a_2, and a_3.

d. In (b), change I_1 and I_2 to E_1 and E_2 respectively, and change V_s to I_s. Assume that the equations now represent equilibrium equations written on the node basis, where E_1 and E_2 are the complex amplitudes of the node-to-datum voltages. Determine a network that results in these node equations, expressing the element values in terms of a, b, c, d, and e.

Remark. Networks for which the same equilibrium equations apply, but with the roles of current and voltage interchanged, are often called *dual* networks.

Networks with dependent sources. If one or more of the sources of excitation in a network are dependent sources,[1] the procedure that must be followed in writing the network equilibrium equations on the loop or node basis is in many respects similar to the method used when the sources are independent. We shall illustrate this procedure by first giving an example of a network for which the excitation consists only of independent sources. After setting up the equilibrium equations for this case, we shall then see how the equations are modified when one of the sources is made to be dependent on one of the currents or voltages in the network.

As our example, we shall use the network shown previously in Figs. 5-23 and 5-24 and drawn again in Fig. 5-28. As we have observed previously,

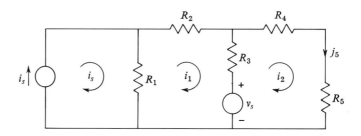

FIG. 5-28. Network used to illustrate the effect of dependent sources on the equilibrium equations. In the example discussed in the text, v_s is first regarded as an independent source and later as a dependent source with the constraint $v_s = Kj_5$.

the basic network is obtained by setting i_s and v_s to zero, i.e., by replacing the current and voltage sources by an open circuit and a short circuit, respectively. If we use the loop method, we can select the closed paths as indicated for defining the circulating currents, and we can write KVL equations for the paths defined by i_1 and i_2. The KVL equations are as follows:

$$i_1(R_1 + R_2 + R_3) - i_2R_3 = i_sR_1 - v_s ; \qquad (5\text{-}27)$$

$$-i_1R_3 + i_2(R_3 + R_4 + R_5) = v_s . \qquad (5\text{-}28)$$

Let us now suppose that the voltage source v_s is a dependent source whose value is constrained to be proportional to the current j_5 flowing through R_5; i.e.,

---

[1] Dependent sources were encountered previously in connection with the ideal isolating networks used in the synthesis of simple networks (see pages 217 to 219).

$$v_s = Kj_5 , \tag{5-29}$$

where K is a constant. This constraint equation can be written in terms of the loop current variables by noting that the branch current j_5 is equal to the loop current i_2, and hence Eq. (5-29) can be written

$$v_s = Ki_2 . \tag{5-30}$$

Equation (5-30) must now be solved simultaneously with Eqs. (5-27) and (5-28) in order to obtain the equilibrium conditions for the network.

The example just given demonstrates that the equilibrium equations for networks with dependent source are of two types: (1) a set of equations (either l loop equations or $n - 1$ node equations) that specify equilibrium conditions if all sources are imagined to be independent sources, and (2) a set of equations expressing the constraints for the dependent sources, consisting of one equation for each dependent source. In general the value of each dependent voltage or current source is proportional to some voltage or current in the network and can be written in the form of Eq. (5-29). We have seen, however, that this voltage or current can always be expressed as a linear combination of a set of loop currents (in the loop method) or node-pair voltages (in the node method), and hence each dependent source voltage or current in the second set of equations can always be expressed as a linear combination of the voltage or current variables used to formulate the first set of equations, in the manner shown in Eq. (5-30).

In order to interpret the effects of the dependent sources on the network behavior, a partial reduction of the set of equilibrium equations can be effected by substituting each equation of the second set into the first set, thereby eliminating the dependent source variables. In the example given above we substitute Eq. (5-30) into Eqs. (5-27) and (5-28) to obtain

$$i_1(R_1 + R_2 + R_3) - i_2 R_3 = i_s R_1 - Ki_2 , \tag{5-31}$$

and
$$-i_1 R_3 + i_2(R_3 + R_4 + R_5) = Ki_2 . \tag{5-32}$$

Bringing all terms in the variables i_1 and i_2 to the left-hand sides of the equations, we have

$$i_1(R_1 + R_2 + R_3) - i_2(R_3 - K) = i_s R_1 , \tag{5-33}$$

and
$$-i_1 R_3 + i_2(R_3 + R_4 + R_5 - K) = 0 . \tag{5-34}$$

When the equations are written in this fashion with only the terms corresponding to independent sources on the right-hand sides, then *the left-hand sides of the equations are characteristic of the network in the absence of independent sources but with the dependent sources present.*

A simple interpretation can be given to the individual terms in the equilibrium equations written in the manner shown in Eqs. (5-33) and (5-34), and this interpretation is basically the same as that noted previously for the case of networks with independent sources only. As before, each term in the KVL equation for a given closed path is evaluated by computing the total voltage drop around the closed path due to one loop current when all other loop currents are imagined to be zero. For example, the term $-i_2(R_3 - K)$ is equal to the voltage drop around path 1 due to the loop current i_2. This voltage drop has two parts: one due to i_2 flowing through the element R_3, which is common to paths 1 and 2, and the other due to the dependent voltage source in path 1, whose value is Ki_2.

It is evident that the equilibrium equations for a network with dependent sources can always be arranged as a set of linear constant-coefficient equations in the form indicated by Eqs. (5-33) and (5-34), since a dependent source voltage or current can always be expressed as a linear combination of the voltage or current variables in terms of which the equilibrium equations are written. Therefore the equations governing RLC networks that contain dependent sources are linear constant-coefficient equations of the same type as those encountered in the absence of dependent sources. Thus all the properties we have discussed for systems governed by linear constant-coefficient equations apply equally well when dependent sources are present.

Problem 5-17

a. Using either the loop or the node method, determine v_1 as a function of i_1 and i_s for the network in Fig. 5-29.

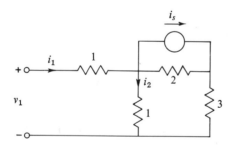

FIG. 5-29. Network for Prob. 5-17.

b. Let i_s be a dependent source of value $i_s = Ki_2$. Determine v_1 as a function of i_1.

c. For each part above, determine a network containing at most one independent source and one resistance that is equivalent to the given network with respect to the terminals.

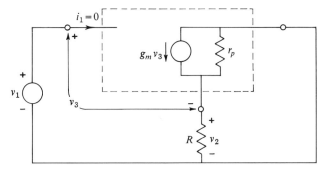

FIG. 5-30. Cathode-follower network for Prob. 5-18. The dashed line encloses an
equivalent network for a vacuum tube.

Problem 5-18

The network of Fig. 5-30 is a model for a *cathode follower*, a frequently
used vacuum-tube network. The input of the network is the voltage v_1,
and its output is the voltage v_2. The network inside the dashed line is a
linear model for a vacuum tube. Find the voltage gain (i.e., the voltage
transfer ratio V_2/V_1) in terms of the network parameters r_p, g_m, and R.

Problem 5-19

a. For the network of Fig. 5-31, find the voltage transfer ratio $H(s) = V_2/V_1$.
b. Plot the pole-zero pattern of $H(s)$.
c. Determine the impulse response of the network.
d. Explain why the network of Fig. 5-31 is sometimes called an *integrator*
when $K \gg 1$.

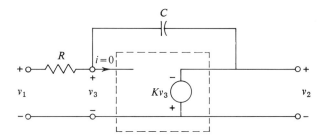

FIG. 5-31. Network for Prob. 5-19. The dashed line encloses a simplified model for
an amplifier.

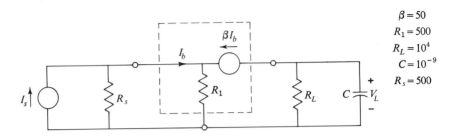

FIG..5-32. Network for Prob. 5-20. The dashed line encloses a simplified model for a transistor.

Problem 5-20

The network in the dashed box of Fig. 5-32 is a simple linear model for a transistor. The output of the network of Fig. 5-32 is V_L, and the input is I_s. Determine and sketch the frequency-response curves.

Natural frequencies of networks

The linear constant-coefficient equations written on the loop or node basis for an RLC network take the form of differential equations when the network contains inductance and capacitance elements. We have observed that in general we can reduce the set of simultaneous differential equations to a single linear constant-coefficient differential equation relating a specific response to the given excitations. From this differential equation we can formulate the characteristic equation for the response variable in question, and we have defined the roots of the characteristic equation as the natural frequencies associated with that variable. Alternatively we can obtain the natural frequencies associated with the response variable by writing an appropriate system function and finding its poles.

The natural frequencies of a network are defined to be the set of all the natural frequencies that can be observed in the network. We shall now proceed to discuss a method for determining the natural frequencies of a network directly from the set of equilibrium equations written on the loop or node bases.

In order to illustrate the procedure for a network containing independent sources only, we shall consider the network of Fig. 5-33, and we shall write the equilibrium equations for this network on the loop basis, with the mesh currents I_1 and I_2 as variables. These equations are

$$(R_1 + R_2 + Ls)I_1 - LsI_2 = 0, \qquad (5\text{-}35)$$

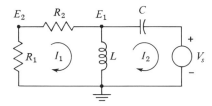

FIG. 5-33. Network used to illustrate the general procedure for finding natural frequencies.

and

$$-LsI_1 + \left(Ls + \frac{1}{Cs}\right)I_2 = -V_s. \qquad (5\text{-}36)$$

Using Cramer's rule, we can solve this set of equilibrium equations for the system functions I_1/V_s and I_2/V_s. Each of the system functions can be expressed as a ratio of determinants as follows:

$$\frac{I_1}{V_s} = \frac{\begin{vmatrix} 0 & -Ls \\ -1 & Ls + \dfrac{1}{Cs} \end{vmatrix}}{\begin{vmatrix} R_1 + R_2 + Ls & -Ls \\ -Ls & Ls + \dfrac{1}{Cs} \end{vmatrix}}, \qquad (5\text{-}37)$$

and

$$\frac{I_2}{V_s} = \frac{\begin{vmatrix} R_1 + R_2 + Ls & 0 \\ -Ls & -1 \end{vmatrix}}{\begin{vmatrix} R_1 + R_2 + Ls & -Ls \\ -Ls & Ls + \dfrac{1}{Cs} \end{vmatrix}}. \qquad (5\text{-}38)$$

We note that the expressions for both I_1/V_s and I_2/V_s involve the same denominator determinant. This denominator determinant will be the same for any configuration of current or voltage sources, provided the basic network remains unchanged, since the equilibrium equations have the same left-hand sides when the source terms are shifted to the right-hand sides. It should be evident that even in a more complicated network, involving many closed paths, the same denominator determinant would appear in the solution for each of the circulating currents. This fact is simply a consequence of Cramer's rule for the solution of simultaneous linear equations.

We have seen previously that the poles of a system function are the complex frequencies for which a response can exist with no excitations, i.e., are the natural frequencies associated with that response. It is evident that a zero of the denominator determinant of a system function is a pole of the system function provided that the numerator does not have a zero at the same frequency, and it can be shown that every pole of the system function must be a zero of the denominator determinant. It can also be shown that every zero in the denominator determinant obtained from a general set of equilibrium equations written on the loop basis is observable as a natural frequency in at least one of the current variables. Thus the roots of the equation obtained by setting the denominator determinant to zero can be considered as the natural frequencies for the currents in the network, and this equation is the characteristic equation associated with the current variables. In the present example, the characteristic equation is

$$(R_1 + R_2)Ls + \frac{L}{C} + \frac{1}{Cs}(R_1 + R_2) = 0 \,. \qquad (5\text{-}39)$$

Instead of writing equilibrium equations for the network of Fig. 5-33 on the loop basis, we could equally well have written a set of node equations, with node-to-datum voltages E_1 and E_2 as variables. Again these equations could be solved and each variable expressed as a ratio of determinants. The characteristic equation associated with the voltage variables would be obtained by setting the denominator determinant to zero, and the roots of this equation would be the natural frequencies associated with the voltage variables in the network. It can readily be verified that the characteristic equation obtained by this procedure is identical to Eq. (5-39).

In general, the natural frequencies observable in the current variables of a network are the same as those observable in the voltage variables, since the current and voltage variables are simply related by the v-i relations for the basic elements. The only exception is the case of a natural frequency at $s = 0$, since, from the v-i relations for capacitances and inductances, a constant voltage may exist across a capacitance with no current, or a constant current may exist in an inductance with no voltage. Except for this special case of a natural frequency at $s = 0$, therefore, we can state the following useful result: in order to obtain the natural frequencies of a network that contains only independent sources, write the equilibrium equations on either the node or loop basis, and find the zeros of the determinant of the coefficients of these equations.

In the case of a network with dependent sources we have observed that it is possible to eliminate the dependent-source variables and to obtain a set of equilibrium equations that have the same form as the equations for a network having only independent sources. In order to find the complex frequencies that can exist in the network with the independent sources set to zero, we follow the same procedure as that described above—we set the determinant of the coefficients on the left-hand sides of the equations to zero and determine the roots. These roots will be defined as the natural frequencies of a network with dependent sources. It is evident that the values of these roots are influenced by the dependent sources, since the

constraint equations for these sources are used to form the left-hand sides
of the equilibrium equations.

During our discussion of the formulation of equilibrium equations for
networks with dependent sources we observed that the procedure to be
followed in formulating the equations is first to establish appropriate closed
paths or connection points for writing KVL or KCL by examining the network that is formed by setting all sources to zero. On the other hand, we
have noted that the natural frequencies of the network are found by setting
only the independent sources to zero. In the case of networks with only
independent sources, the concept of the basic network, defined as the network with the sources set to zero, was useful both for the formulation of
equilibrium equations and for the determination of natural frequencies.
In the case of networks with dependent sources, however, it is clear that
we cannot define a basic network that will preserve both of these properties.
Consequently we shall choose not to attempt to extend the concept of the
basic network to networks containing dependent sources.

Problem 5-21

Determine the natural frequencies of the network shown in Fig. 5-34.

Problem 5-22

In the network of Fig. 5-35, v_s is a voltage-controlled voltage source given

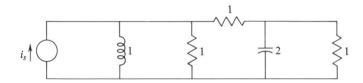

FIG. 5-34. Network for Prob. 5-21.

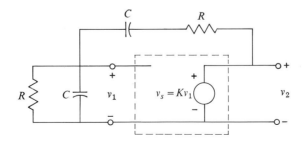

FIG. 5-35. Oscillator network for Prob. 5-22.

by $v_s = Kv_1$, where K is a real constant.   Determine the value of K for which the system can support a sustained sinusoidal oscillation; i.e., once started, the system will continue to produce a sinusoidal output $v_2(t)$. Determine the frequency ω_0 of this oscillation.   This network represents a model of an oscillator constructed by connecting resistances and capacitances to a voltage amplifier of gain K (shown inside the dotted box).

Problem 5-23

The block diagram of Fig. 5-36b is a symbolic representation of the network

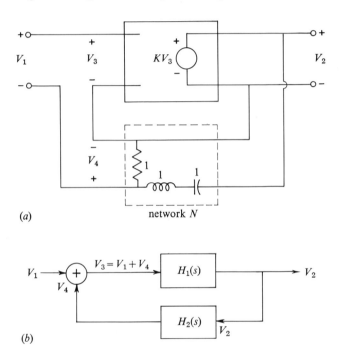

FIG. **5-36.** Network and block diagram for Prob. 5-23.

of Fig. 5-36a.   The relation $V_2 = KV_3$ is represented by the system $H_1(s)$. The voltage transfer ratio V_4/V_2 is represented by the system $H_2(s)$.

As indicated, the output V_2 is "fed back" to the input through the "feedback" network N, whose system function is $H_2(s)$.   The sum of V_4 (the output from the feedback network) and V_1 (the actual input to the over-all system) forms the input V_3 to the system $H_1(s)$.

a. Find the over-all voltage transfer ratio $H(s) = V_2/V_1$ in terms of $H_1(s)$ and $H_2(s)$.

b. Find expressions for $H_1(s)$ and $H_2(s)$ from the network of Fig. 5-36a and write $H(s) = V_2/V_1$ as a function of s and K.

c. Determine a value for K such that the system will operate as an oscillator with the input terminals short-circuited. What is the frequency of oscillation?

Problem 5-24

Two networks N_1 and N_2 with driving-point impedances $Z_1(s)$ and $Z_2(s)$, respectively, are connected as shown in Fig. 5-37.

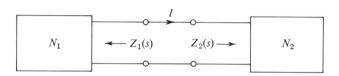

FIG. 5-37. Network for Prob. 5-24.

a. For the combined network write the equilibrium equation on the loop basis in terms of the current variable I.

b. From your result in (a) write an equation in terms of $Z_1(s)$ and $Z_2(s)$ whose solution yields the natural frequencies that are observable in the current i.

c. Apply the result of (b) to find the natural frequencies observable in the current i when

$$Z_1(s) = \frac{s + 7}{s(s + 5)},$$

and

$$Z_2(s) = \frac{s + 1}{s}.$$

d. Determine the frequency of oscillation of a network of the form of Fig. 5-37, when

$$Z_1(s) = \frac{s + 2}{s},$$

and

$$Z_2(s) = \frac{s - 2}{2}.$$

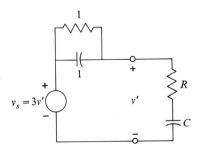

FIG. 5-38. Oscillator network for Prob. 5-24e.

e. Using the method developed above, determine values for R and C in the network of Fig. 5-38 that will allow a sustained oscillation at frequency $\omega_0 = 1$.

6

Networks with Terminals

As we indicated in Chap. 1, we are frequently interested in examining the behavior of some portion of a network and in writing equilibrium equations that are valid for this portion independent of the environment to which it is connected. We shall now show how the procedures that were developed in Chap. 5 for writing equilibrium equations on the loop and node bases can be applied to networks with terminals. These procedures will in general yield a set of equations that characterize the behavior of the network with respect to its terminals. These equations, which can be written in certain standard forms, will provide a means for characterizing devices having more than two terminals.

Equilibrium equations for *n*-terminal networks

We consider first a network N that is connected to the external environment through n terminals, as shown in Fig. 6-1. One of the terminals, say

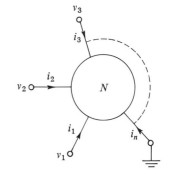

FIG. 6-1. An *n*-terminal network showing the assignment of voltage and current variables. Terminal *n* is selected as the reference terminal.

terminal n, is selected as a datum node, or reference terminal, and voltages v_1, v_2, . . . , v_{n-1} are assigned to the remaining terminals, representing the voltages between the respective terminals and the reference terminal. We also assign currents i_1, i_2, . . . , i_n to the terminals as shown. Our objective is to find the constraints that network N imposes on the values of the voltages and currents at the terminals.

In order to find these constraints we follow a procedure similar to that used in Chap. 1 in connection with the writing of equilibrium equations for networks with two terminals. We imagine that we have written the set of equilibrium equations for the complete network that includes network N and the environment to which it is connected, and we select from this set the equations that involve currents and voltages in N. We shall assume that the node method is used for writing the equilibrium equations. As we have seen, application of the node method involves several steps: assigning node-to-datum voltages, writing KCL equations for the nodes, and applying the v-i relations for the elements. For the n-terminal network of Fig. 6-1 we have already assigned voltages to the terminals, and we can readily assign node-to-datum voltages to the remaining nodes in the network. The equilibrium equations that involve currents and voltages in network N consist of KCL equations for all of the terminals except the reference terminal and for the remaining nodes in N, together with the v-i relations for the elements, where the voltages across the elements are expressed in terms of the node-to-datum voltage variables. The KCL equation for a terminal, say terminal k, expresses the fact that the sum of the currents leaving this terminal through branches that lie within N is equal to the sum of the currents from the external network entering through the terminal. But this latter sum is simply the current i_k that has been assigned to the terminal. The KCL equations for the terminals and for the remaining nodes that lie within N, when combined with the v-i relations for the elements, provide the complete set of equilibrium equations for network N, and these equations specify the constraints that network N imposes on the currents and voltages at the terminals.

As an example of the application of this procedure for writing equilibrium equations for an n-terminal network, let us determine the relations among the terminal currents and voltages for the interconnection of admittances that forms the three-terminal network shown in Fig. 6-2. We shall formulate the equations in terms of the complex amplitudes of exponential voltages and currents. We select one of the terminals as a datum node and assign currents I_1 and I_2 and node-to-datum voltages V_1 and V_2 to the other two terminals and node-to-datum voltage V_3 to the remaining node as shown. The equilibrium equations for the network consist of KCL

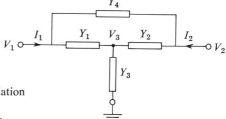

FIG. 6-2. Three-terminal network
used to illustrate the formulation
of equilibrium equations
for networks with terminals.

equations for the terminals and for the internal node, the *v-i* relations for the elements being incorporated in these equations in the manner discussed in connection with the development of the node method in Chap. 5. These equations are

$$(V_1 - V_2)Y_4 + (V_1 - V_3)Y_1 = I_1 , \qquad (6\text{-}1)$$

$$(V_2 - V_1)Y_4 + (V_2 - V_3)Y_2 = I_2 , \qquad (6\text{-}2)$$

and
$$(V_3 - V_1)Y_1 + (V_3 - V_2)Y_2 + V_3 Y_3 = 0 . \qquad (6\text{-}3)$$

From Eq. (6-3) we can express V_3 in terms of V_1 and V_2 as follows:

$$V_3 = \frac{Y_1}{Y_1 + Y_2 + Y_3} V_1 + \frac{Y_2}{Y_1 + Y_2 + Y_3} V_2 . \qquad (6\text{-}4)$$

Substituting this expression for V_3 into Eqs. (6-1) and (6-2) and rearranging terms, we obtain

$$V_1\left[Y_1 + Y_4 - \frac{Y_1{}^2}{Y_1 + Y_2 + Y_3} \right] - V_2\left[Y_4 + \frac{Y_1 Y_2}{Y_1 + Y_2 + Y_3} \right] = I_1 , \qquad (6\text{-}5)$$

and

$$-V_1\left[Y_4 + \frac{Y_1 Y_2}{Y_1 + Y_2 + Y_3} \right] + V_2\left[Y_2 + Y_4 - \frac{Y_2{}^2}{Y_1 + Y_2 + Y_3} \right] = I_2 . \qquad (6\text{-}6)$$

These equations involve only the voltages and currents at the terminals of the network and specify the constraints that the network imposes on these voltages and currents.

Equations (6-5) and (6-6) have the form

$$Y_{11}V_1 + Y_{12}V_2 = I_1 , \qquad (6\text{-}7)$$

and
$$Y_{21}V_1 + Y_{22}V_2 = I_2 , \qquad (6\text{-}8)$$

where the Y_{ij} are defined in terms of the admittances of the elements by comparison of Eqs. (6-5) and (6-6) with Eqs. (6-7) and (6-8). We could have expected the constraint equations among the terminal voltages and currents for any three-terminal RLC network to have the general form given in Eqs. (6-7) and (6-8). These equations simply express the fact that the current response I_1 or I_2 is a superposition of the response to an excitation V_1 and the response to an excitation V_2. For example, the contribution to I_1 of the excitation V_1 is $Y_{11}V_1$, i.e., the product of V_1 and the system function Y_{11}.

From Eqs. (6-7) and (6-8) an interpretation of the various admittances Y_{11}, Y_{12}, Y_{21}, and Y_{22} can be given in terms of measurements that can be made at the terminals of the network, as shown in Fig. 6-3: Y_{11} is the

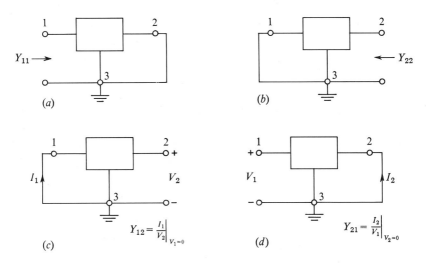

FIG. 6-3. Definition of short-circuit admittance parameters for a three-terminal network in terms of measurements at the terminals. Driving-point admittances Y_{11} and Y_{22} are defined as in (a) and (b) respectively; transfer admittances Y_{12} and Y_{21} are defined by the diagrams and relations shown in (c) and (d) respectively.

driving-point admittance between terminal 1 and the reference terminal with $V_2 = 0$, i.e., $Y_{11} = I_1/V_1$ with terminal 2 short-circuited to the reference terminal; Y_{22} is the driving-point admittance between terminal 2 and the reference terminal with $V_1 = 0$, i.e., $Y_{22} = I_2/V_2$ with terminal 1 short-circuited to the reference terminal; Y_{12} is the transfer admittance relating the short-circuit current between the reference terminal and terminal 1 to the voltage V_2 between terminal 2 and the reference terminal; and Y_{21} has a similar interpretation as the ratio of I_2 to V_1 with terminal 2 short-circuited to the reference terminal. The admittances Y_{ij} are called *short-circuit admittance parameters* since all measurements that are made to determine them require that the terminals, other than those associated with the excitation, be short-circuited.

If the determinant of the coefficients of Eqs. (6-7) and (6-8) is nonzero, we can invert the equations to obtain an alternative set of equations that characterize the three-terminal network. These equations are of the form

$$Z_{11}I_1 + Z_{12}I_2 = V_1, \tag{6-9}$$

and
$$Z_{21}I_1 + Z_{22}I_2 = V_2, \tag{6-10}$$

where $Z_{11} = Y_{22}/|Y|$, $Z_{22} = Y_{11}/|Y|$, $Z_{12} = -Y_{12}/|Y|$, and $Z_{21} = -Y_{21}/|Y|$. The symbol $|Y|$ is used to denote the determinant

$$|Y| = \begin{vmatrix} Y_{11} & Y_{12} \\ Y_{21} & Y_{22} \end{vmatrix} = Y_{11}Y_{22} - Y_{12}Y_{21}. \tag{6-11}$$

The equations written in the form (6-9) and (6-10) suggest that the voltage at each of the terminals of the network can be interpreted as a superposition of the responses to current excitations I_1 and I_2 applied at the terminals. For example, the term $Z_{11}I_1$ in Eq. (6-9) is the voltage that would appear between terminal 1 and the reference terminal if a current excitation I_1 were applied at terminal 1 with $I_2 = 0$, i.e., with terminal 2 open-circuited; the term $Z_{12}I_2$ is the open-circuit voltage that would appear between terminal 1 and the reference terminal if a current excitation I_2 were applied at terminal 2. Thus the impedances Z_{11} and Z_{12} can be interpreted in terms of observations that can be made at the terminals of the network, as shown in Fig. 6-4: Z_{11} is the driving-point impedance between terminal 1 and the reference terminal with terminal 2 open-circuited, and Z_{12} is the transfer impedance relating the open-circuit voltage

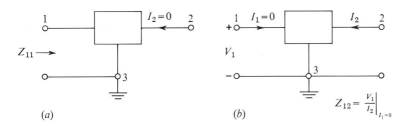

FIG. 6-4. Definition of open-circuit impedance parameters Z_{11} and Z_{12} for a three-terminal network in terms of measurements at the terminals. The driving-point impedance Z_{11} is defined as in (*a*), and the transfer impedance Z_{12} is defined by the diagram and relation shown in (*b*).

response at terminal 1 to a current excitation at terminal 2. Similar interpretations can be given to the impedances Z_{21} and Z_{22}. The impedances Z_{ij} are called *open-circuit impedance parameters* since all measurements that are made to determine them require that the terminals, other than those associated with the excitation, be open-circuited.

The characterization of a three-terminal network in terms of Eqs. (6-7) and (6-8) suggests the general form of the equations for an n-terminal network. In order to formulate these equations, one terminal is selected as the reference terminal, and a KCL equation for the current at each of the remaining $n - 1$ terminals is then written. The current I_k at any terminal k can be considered to be the superposition of the current responses due to voltage excitations applied between each terminal and the reference terminal. For example, the component of the current at terminal k due to voltage V_j applied between terminal j and the reference terminal can be written $Y_{kj}V_j$, where Y_{kj} is the transfer admittance relating the current response at terminal k to the voltage excitation at terminal j with all terminals other than j short-circuited to the reference terminal. Thus the equations that characterize the network with respect to its terminals can be written in the general form

$$Y_{11}V_1 + Y_{12}V_2 + \cdots + Y_{1,n-1}V_{n-1} = I_1,$$
$$Y_{21}V_1 + Y_{22}V_2 + \cdots + Y_{2,n-1}V_{n-1} = I_2, \tag{6-12}$$
$$\cdots\cdots\cdots\cdots\cdots\cdots\cdots\cdots\cdots\cdots\cdots\cdots$$
$$Y_{n-1,1}V_1 + Y_{n-1,2}V_2 + \cdots + Y_{n-1,n-1}V_{n-1} = I_{n-1}.$$

The admittances Y_{kj} are the short-circuit admittance parameters for the n-terminal network. For a given n-terminal network these parameters depend, of course, on the particular terminal that is selected as the reference terminal.

An alternative characterization for an n-terminal RLC network can be given in terms of open-circuit impedance parameters, as was done for a three-terminal network in Eqs. (6-9) and (6-10). If the determinant of the coefficients of Eqs. (6-12) is nonzero, the alternative form of the equations can be derived either by inverting the equations or by following an argument similar to that for the three-terminal network in connection with the interpretation of Eqs. (6-9) and (6-10). This argument recognizes that the voltage V_k between terminal k and the reference terminal can be considered to be the superposition of the voltage responses due to current excitations applied at each terminal. The general form of the equations written on this basis is as follows:

$$Z_{11}I_1 \quad + Z_{12}I_2 \quad + \cdots + Z_{1,n-1}I_{n-1} \quad = V_1,$$
$$Z_{21}I_1 \quad + Z_{22}I_2 \quad + \cdots + Z_{2,n-1}I_{n-1} \quad = V_2,$$
$$\cdots\cdots\cdots\cdots\cdots\cdots\cdots\cdots\cdots\cdots\cdots\cdots\cdots\cdots$$
$$Z_{n-1,1}I_1 + Z_{n-1,2}I_2 + \cdots + Z_{n-1,n-1}I_{n-1} = V_{n-1}. \tag{6-13}$$

The impedances Z_{ij} are the open-circuit impedance parameters for the n-terminal network for the particular selection of terminal n as the reference terminal. By comparing (6-12) with the inverted set (6-13) and using Cramer's rule, we find that the open-circuit and short-circuit parameters are related by the equations

$$Z_{ij} = \frac{|Y|_{ji}}{|Y|}, \tag{6-14}$$

where $|Y|$ is the determinant of the coefficients of Eqs. (6-12) and $|Y|_{ji}$ is the cofactor associated with the jth row and the ith column of this array of coefficients.

Problem 6-1

a. Determine the parameters Y_{11}, Y_{12}, Y_{21}, and Y_{22} associated with the three-terminal network of Fig. 6-5, with respect to the reference terminal indicated.

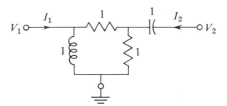

FIG. 6-5. Three-terminal network for Prob. 6-1.

b. By inverting the set of equations that relate the terminal variables of the network in Fig. 6-5, determine the parameters Z_{11}, Z_{12}, Z_{21}, and Z_{22} for this network, with respect to the reference terminal indicated.

Problem 6-2

The three-terminal network of Fig. 6-6 contains a dependent source. Find the Z parameters (Z_{11}, Z_{12}, Z_{21}, Z_{22}).

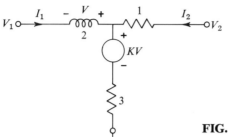

FIG. 6-6. Three-terminal network containing a dependent source (Prob. 6-2).

Problem 6-3

It is often convenient for the designer of transistor networks to know the Z or Y parameters that characterize a transistor when it is represented as a three-terminal network. However, it is inconvenient to measure either all the Z parameters or all the Y parameters for a transistor. Because of this difficulty, transistor specifications usually quote a set of parameters that are different from those we have met previously, called the *hybrid parameters,* or *H parameters*. These are defined by the following equations:

$$V_1 = H_{11}I_1 + H_{12}V_2 ; \qquad (6\text{-}15)$$

$$I_2 = H_{21}I_1 + H_{22}V_2 . \qquad (6\text{-}16)$$

Determine the Y parameters (Y_{11}, Y_{12}, Y_{21}, and Y_{22}) in Eqs. (6-17) and (6-18) below in terms of the H parameters in Eqs. (6-15) and (6-16):

$$I_1 = Y_{11}V_1 + Y_{12}V_2 ; \qquad (6\text{-}17)$$

$$I_2 = Y_{21}V_1 + Y_{22}V_2 . \qquad (6\text{-}18)$$

Problem 6-4

A three-terminal network N is characterized by the equations

$$i_1 = 2v_1 + v_2 ,$$

and

$$i_2 = 3v_1 + 2v_2 .$$

Determine the values of v_1 and v_2 when network N is connected in the manner shown in Fig. 6-7.

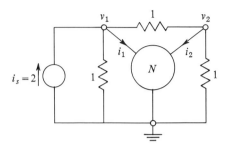

FIG. 6-7. Three-terminal network N embedded within a network (Prob. 6-4).

Problem 6-5

The short-circuit Y parameters and the open-circuit Z parameters are to be measured for a three-terminal network containing only resistances. The only equipment available to use for the measurement is: (1) a d-c voltage source of known value, (2) an ideal voltmeter, and (3) an ideal ammeter. (An ideal voltmeter measures voltage without drawing any current, whereas an ideal ammeter measures current without having any voltage drop across it.) Explain how you would measure the Z and Y parameters of the network, relative to a specified reference terminal.

Equilibrium equations for n-port networks

We frequently encounter networks with terminals that are connected to the external environment in pairs, such that the current entering one terminal of a pair is equal to the current leaving the other terminal of the pair. When the currents at a pair of terminals are constrained to be equal and opposite, the term *terminal pair* or *port* is used to describe the two terminals. Figure 6-8 shows an n-port network and indicates the convention that is used to assign the voltage and the current variable associated with each port.

In order to obtain equilibrium equations for an n-port network, we could treat the network like a $2n$-terminal network and write a set of equations following the procedures discussed in the previous section. To the equilibrium equations for the voltages and currents at the terminals we would then add equations that specify the constraints on the currents at each terminal pair. This procedure is rather cumbersome, however, and we shall use a more direct method for formulating the equations such that the constraints on the currents at each terminal-pair are automatically incorporated in the equations.

This alternative procedure takes advantage of the fact that, since the current entering one terminal of a pair is equal to the current leaving the

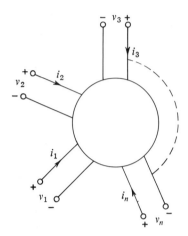

FIG. 6-8. An n-port network, showing the convention for assigning voltages and currents to the various terminal-pairs.

other terminal, the external network that is seen looking out from any port can be regarded as an element with an unspecified v-i relation. Thus the equilibrium equations that characterize an n-port network can be written as though an element were connected across each terminal pair, except that v-i relations for these elements are not specified. The procedures that we developed in Chap. 5 for selecting appropriate variables and for writing equilibrium equations in terms of these variables, either on the loop basis or the node basis, can then be applied directly to a network with ports. The equilibrium equations written in this manner can in most cases of interest be reduced to a set of equations relating the voltages and currents at the terminal pairs.

As an example, let us compute the relations among the voltages and currents at the terminals of the two-port network shown in Fig. 6-9. In order to write equilibrium equations for this network, we imagine elements to be connected across terminal pairs 1-1' and 2-2' respectively. If we use

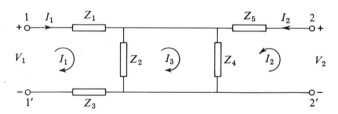

FIG. 6-9. Two-port network used to illustrate the writing of equilibrium equations for networks with terminals.

the loop method, we can assign loop currents, as shown in Fig. 6-9. (For convenience we assign loop currents I_1 and I_2 such that they are equal to the currents assigned at the terminals.) Following the usual procedure we write KVL equations around the closed paths defined by the three loop currents. The voltages across the elements are expressed in terms of the loop currents using the v-i relations for the elements. Similar substitutions are not made, however, for the terminal voltages, since v-i relations for the networks external to the two-port network are not specified. If the terminal voltage variables are shifted to the right-hand sides, the KVL equations for the three closed paths become

$$Z_1 I_1 + Z_2(I_1 - I_3) + Z_3 I_1 = V_1 , \tag{6-19}$$

$$Z_2(I_3 - I_1) + Z_4(I_3 + I_2) = 0 , \tag{6-20}$$

and
$$Z_5 I_2 + Z_4(I_2 + I_3) = V_2 . \tag{6-21}$$

In order to obtain relations among the voltages and currents at the terminals, we shall reduce Eqs. (6-19) to (6-21) by eliminating I_3. From Eq. (6-20) we can express I_3 in terms of I_1 and I_2 as follows:

$$I_3 = \frac{Z_2}{Z_2 + Z_4} I_1 - \frac{Z_4}{Z_2 + Z_4} I_2 . \tag{6-22}$$

Substituting this equation into (6-19) and (6-21), we obtain

$$\left[Z_1 + Z_2 + Z_3 - \frac{Z_2^2}{Z_2 + Z_4} \right] I_1 + \frac{Z_2 Z_4}{Z_2 + Z_4} I_2 = V_1 , \tag{6-23}$$

and
$$\frac{Z_2 Z_4}{Z_2 + Z_4} I_1 + \left[Z_4 + Z_5 - \frac{Z_4^2}{Z_2 + Z_4} \right] I_2 = V_2 . \tag{6-24}$$

These equations can be written in the form

$$Z_{11} I_1 + Z_{12} I_2 = V_1 , \tag{6-25}$$

and
$$Z_{21} I_1 + Z_{22} I_2 = V_2 , \tag{6-26}$$

where the Z_{ij} are defined in terms of the impedances of the elements by comparison of Eqs. (6-23) and (6-24) with Eqs. (6-25) and (6-26). We recognize that these equations have the same form as those for a three-terminal network. Thus we can call the impedances Z_{ij} in Eqs. (6-25) and (6-26) the open-circuit impedance parameters, and we can interpret them in the manner discussed above for the three-terminal network. We should note, however, that in the case of the three-terminal network, Eqs. (6-9) and (6-10) specify the terminal behavior for any external connection, whereas for the two-port network, Eqs. (6-25) and (6-26) apply only when the currents entering and leaving each port are constrained to be equal.

In a manner similar to that described above for the three-terminal network we can invert Eqs. (6-25) and (6-26), provided that the determinant of the coefficients is nonzero, to obtain the two equations

$$Y_{11}V_1 + Y_{12}V_2 = I_1 , \tag{6-27}$$

and
$$Y_{21}V_1 + Y_{22}V_2 = I_2 , \tag{6-28}$$

where the Y_{ij} are the short-circuit admittance parameters for the two-port network. These are related to the open-circuit impedance parameters by the equations $Y_{11} = Z_{22}/|Z|$, $Y_{22} = Z_{11}/|Z|$, $Y_{12} = -Z_{12}/|Z|$, and $Y_{21} = -Z_{21}/|Z|$, where the symbol $|Z|$ is used to denote the determinant

$$|Z| = \begin{vmatrix} Z_{11} & Z_{12} \\ Z_{21} & Z_{22} \end{vmatrix} = Z_{11}Z_{22} - Z_{12}Z_{21} . \tag{6-29}$$

An extension of the equations for a two-port network to those for an n-port network can easily be carried out following reasoning similar to that used for the case of the n-terminal network. The general form of the equations is that of Eqs. (6-12) or of Eqs. (6-13), depending on whether the characterization of the network is to be in terms of short-circuit admittance parameters or in terms of open-circuit impedance parameters. In the case of the n-port network, however, there are n equations for the terminal voltages and currents, whereas there are $n - 1$ such equations for the n-terminal network.

Problem 6-6

a. Write a set of equations, in terms of Z parameters, relating the voltages and currents at the terminals of the network shown in Fig. 6-10, taking terminal 4 as the reference terminal.

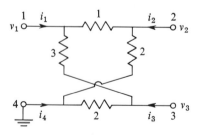

FIG. 6-10. Four-terminal network for Prob. 6-6.

b. Assume now that the external connection to the network imposes the constraints $i_1 = -i_4$ and $i_2 = -i_3$, such that terminal pairs 1-4 and 2-3 can be considered ports. Use the results of (a) to determine the equations characterizing this two-port network, in terms of Z parameters.

Problem 6-7

When a given four-terminal network N is characterized as a two-port network as shown in Fig. 6-11a, the variables V_1, V_2, I_1, and I_2 are related by the following equations:

$$V_1 = 2I_1 + I_2 ,$$
$$V_2 = I_1 + (s + 1)I_2 .$$

a. For the connection of Fig. 6-11b, find, if possible, the transfer voltage ratio V/V_s. If not possible, explain why.

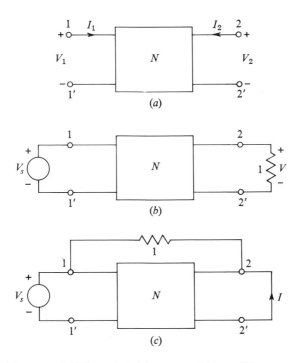

(a)

(b)

(c)

FIG. 6-11. The network N shown in (a) is connected in two different ways to a voltage source and a resistance in (b) and (c)—(Prob. 6-7).

b. For the connection of Fig. 6-11*c*, find, if possible, the transfer admittance I/V_s. If not possible, explain why.

Problem 6-8

Three completely enclosed networks are to be studied. On the outside of each "black box" there are four terminals, marked a, b, c, and d. One of the "black boxes" contains network N_1, another contains network N_2, and the other contains network N_3, as shown in Fig. 6-12.

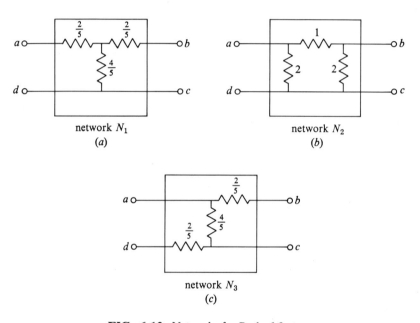

FIG. 6-12. Networks for Prob. 6-8*a* to *c*.

a. Choosing terminals *a-d* as one terminal pair and *b-c* as the other, determine the open-circuit impedance parameters for each of the networks.

b. If possible, devise a measurement that will enable you to determine which network is N_3.

c. If possible, devise a set of measurements that will permit you to differentiate between N_1 and N_2.

d. You are given two networks N_a and N_b, as shown in Fig. 6-13. These networks are equivalent with respect to terminal pairs 1-1' and 2-2'. Are they necessarily equivalent with respect to all measurements that can be made on the terminals shown? Why?

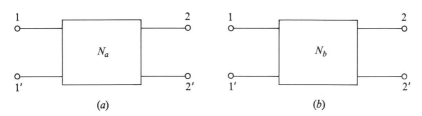

FIG. 6-13. Networks for Prob. 6-8d.

Problem 6-9

Characterize each of the four two-port networks of Fig. 6-14 in one of the forms given below. Determine all the coefficients in the set of equations selected for each network.

1. $V_1 = Z_{11}I_1 + Z_{12}I_2$,
   $V_2 = Z_{21}I_1 + Z_{22}I_2$.

2. $I_1 = Y_{11}V_1 + Y_{12}V_2$,
   $I_2 = Y_{21}V_1 + Y_{22}V_2$.

3. $V_1 = H_{11}I_1 + H_{12}V_2$,
   $I_2 = H_{21}I_1 + H_{22}V_2$.

4. $I_1 = G_{11}V_1 + G_{12}I_2$,
   $V_2 = G_{21}V_1 + G_{22}I_2$.

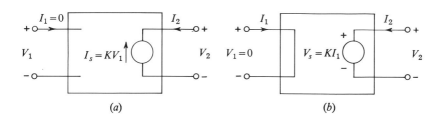

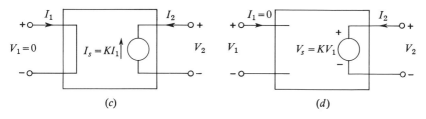

FIG. 6-14. Networks for which constraint equations for the terminal voltages and currents are to be written (Prob. 6-9).

Characterization of devices with more than two terminals

When we discussed the network model in Chap. 1, we restricted our consideration to elements with two terminals, recognizing that a large class of devices can be modeled in terms of such elements. Some devices, however, can be modeled only by networks with more than two terminals, and the behavior of these devices with respect to their terminals can frequently be characterized by a set of linear equations having the same form as the equations presented above for multiterminal networks.

In the case of a device with three or more terminals (as for the simpler two-terminal device) it must be emphasized that the equations characterizing it give an approximation to its behavior only with respect to its terminals and do not necessarily provide a representation of the physical events within the device. The only requirements on the multiterminal device are that KCL and KVL be satisfied by the terminal currents and voltages and that any other constraints imposed on these voltages and currents by the device be independent of the network to which it is connected.

Dependent sources. In a sense we have already introduced one type of device having more than two terminals, since one can consider the dependent source as a two-port network. Thus, for example, if we consider the dependent source shown in Fig. 6-15 as a two-port network for which the

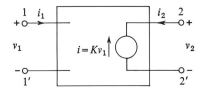

FIG. 6-15. Example of a dependent source.

driving-point impedance at terminals 1-1' is infinite, the constraint equations are

$$i_1 = 0, \tag{6-30}$$

and
$$i_2 = -Kv_1, \tag{6-31}$$

where K is a constant. These equations can be considered as special forms of the general equations (6-27) and (6-28) for a two-port RLC network. The other three types of dependent sources (given previously in Fig. 4-81) can be characterized in a similar fashion, as shown in Prob. 6-9.

Coupled inductances. One of the basic two-terminal elements introduced in Chap. 1 was the inductance, which is a model of a coil whose magnetic field can be assumed to link only itself. In practice the magnetic field for a given coil can in fact link another coil, and hence a current in the first coil can cause a voltage to exist across the second coil. This coupling between the two coils cannot be accounted for in terms of the v-i relations of two separate inductances, but the combination of the two coils can be modeled by a network with four terminals. Such a four-terminal network is called a coupled pair of inductances and is represented by the symbol given in Fig. 6-16. The current i_1 flowing into terminal 1 is constrained to be equal

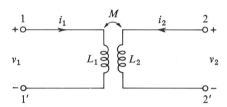

FIG. 6-16. Symbol for two coupled inductances.

to the current flowing out of terminal 1', and likewise the current i_2 flowing into terminal 2 is constrained to be equal to the current flowing out of terminal 2'. Hence the coupled inductances have the properties of a two-port network independent of the external network that may be connected to the inductances.

The relations between the voltages and currents at the terminals are by definition

$$v_1 = L_1 \frac{di_1}{dt} + M \frac{di_2}{dt}, \tag{6-32}$$

and

$$v_2 = M \frac{di_1}{dt} + L_2 \frac{di_2}{dt}, \tag{6-33}$$

where L_1 and L_2 are positive constants and M is a positive or negative constant subject to the constraint $M^2 \le L_1 L_2$. This two-port network, together with its constraint equations, makes no attempt, of course, to provide a representation of the electromagnetic fields that exist in the vicinity of a pair of coils but simply gives a description of the behavior of the two coils with respect to events that can be observed at their terminals. The first term in Eq. (6-32), for example, represents the voltage that would appear across terminal pair 1-1' with $i_2 = 0$, i.e., with terminal pair 2-2' open-circuited. The v-i relation at terminal pair 1-1' with $i_2 = 0$ is simply that of an inductance of value L_1. The second term on the right-hand side of

Eq. (6-32), i.e., $M \dfrac{di_2}{dt}$, represents the open-circuit voltage that would appear across terminal pair 1-1' with a current i_2 at terminal pair 2-2'. Likewise the term $M \dfrac{di_1}{dt}$ in Eq. (6-33) represents the open-circuit voltage that would appear across terminal pair 2-2' with a current i_1 at terminal pair 1-1'. Because M is the proportionality constant in the terms that specify the effect of the current at one terminal pair on the voltage at the other terminal pair, it is called the *mutual inductance*.

In terms of complex amplitudes of the terminal voltages and currents we can write the following relations for the coupled inductances:

$$V_1 = sL_1I_1 + sMI_2, \qquad (6\text{-}34)$$

and
$$V_2 = sMI_1 + sL_2I_2. \qquad (6\text{-}35)$$

We note that these equations have the same form as Eqs. (6-25) and (6-26) for a two-port network, and hence we can identify sL_1 with Z_{11}, sL_2 with Z_{22}, and sM with Z_{12} and Z_{21}, which are equal in this case.

It is of course possible to have more than two coupled inductances in a network. The equations defining the *v-i* characteristics for a set of n coupled inductances can be written down directly by extending Eqs. (6-34) and (6-35) to the case of n terminal pairs. The equations would have the same form as those for a general n-port network.

When coupled inductances are embedded in a network, it is always possible to write equilibrium equations for the larger network, treating the coupled inductances simply as an n-port network. If the *v-i* relations for the coupled inductances are given in the form of Eqs. (6-34) and (6-35), then it is convenient to use the loop method for writing these equilibrium equations rather than the node method, since in the loop method voltage drops across elements are expressed in terms of the currents through the elements.

As an example, we shall write equilibrium equations for the network of Fig. 6-17, which consists of a coupled pair of inductances connected to a simple external network. Assigning circulating currents I_1 and I_2 as shown, and using the relations for the coupled inductances given in Eqs. (6-34)

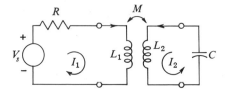

FIG. 6-17. Network containing coupled inductances.

and (6-35), we can by inspection write the equilibrium equations on the loop basis as follows:

$$RI_1 + sL_1I_1 + sMI_2 = V_s,\qquad(6\text{-}36)$$

$$sMI_1 + sL_2I_2 + \frac{1}{sC}I_2 = 0.\qquad(6\text{-}37)$$

These equations can easily be solved for I_1 and I_2.

Ideal transformer. The ideal transformer is a two-port network which can be considered to represent a limiting case of a coupled pair of inductances (as L_1 and L_2 become very large, with $M^2 = L_1L_2$) and which approximates the terminal behavior of some physical transformers over a limited frequency range. This network is represented by the symbol shown in Fig. 6-18, and, as in the case of coupled inductances, the currents enter-

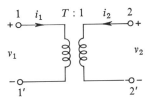

FIG. 6-18. Symbol for an ideal transformer.

ing and leaving a terminal pair are constrained to be equal. The relations between the voltages and currents at the terminals are defined as follows:

$$v_2 = \frac{1}{T}v_1,\qquad(6\text{-}38)$$

$$i_2 = -Ti_1,\qquad(6\text{-}39)$$

where T is a constant. If the ideal transformer is considered to approximate a physical transformer, the T can be interpreted as the ratio of the number of turns on the transformer primary (associated with terminals 1-1′) to the number of turns on the secondary (associated with terminals 2-2′).

For a network in which an ideal transformer is embedded, equilibrium equations cannot be formulated directly by the usual node or loop methods, since the v-i relations (6-38) and (6-39) are not in a form that permits the terminal voltages to be expressed in terms of the currents or the terminal currents to be expressed in terms of the voltages. It may sometimes be necessary to use the longer procedure of writing separately the KVL equations, the KCL equations, and the v-i relations rather than using the loop or node methods in which the v-i relations are applied by inspection.

An example of a simple network that includes an ideal transformer is the two-terminal network of Fig. 6-19. Equilibrium equations for this

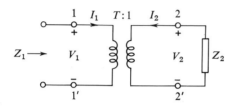

FIG. 6-19. Network illustrating the impedance transformation property of an ideal transformer. The input impedance is given by $Z_1 = T^2 Z_2$.

network are

$$V_2 = \frac{1}{T} V_1 , \tag{6-40}$$

$$I_2 = -T I_1 , \tag{6-41}$$

and
$$V_2 = -Z_2 I_2 . \tag{6-42}$$

Reduction of these equations leads to the relation

$$\frac{V_1}{I_1} = T^2 Z_2 ; \tag{6-43}$$

i.e., the impedance Z_1 at terminals 1-1′ is equal to the impedance Z_2 across terminals 2-2′ multiplied by the square of the "turns ratio" T.

Problem 6-10

Determine $v_1(t)$ for the network of Fig. 6-20. The network is at rest for $t < 0$.

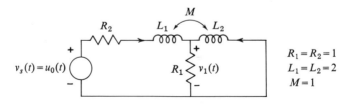

FIG. 6-20. Network containing coupled inductances (Prob. 6-10).

Problem 6-11

Determine $v_0(t)$ for the network of Fig. 6-21. The network is initially at rest.

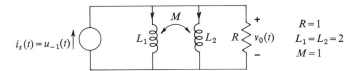

FIG. 6-21. Network for Prob. 6-11.

Problem 6-12

a. Two coupled inductances are connected together in each of the configurations shown in Fig. 6-22a and b. Determine the impedances Z_a and Z_b in terms of L_1, L_2, and M, where $Z_a = V_a/I_a$ and $Z_b = V_b/I_b$.

b. Determine M in terms of Z_a and Z_b.

Note. The method illustrated in this problem is one that is commonly used for measuring mutual inductance.

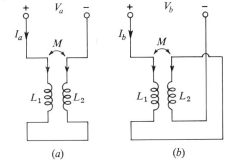

FIG. 6-22. Two different connections for a pair of coupled inductances (Prob. 6-12).

(a)   (b)

Problem 6-13

a. Determine the open-circuit Z parameters representing the network of Fig. 6-23 with respect to terminal pairs 1-1' and 2-2'.

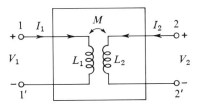

FIG. 6-23. Coupled inductances considered in Prob. 6-13.

b. Determine values for L_a, L_b, and L_c in terms of L_1, L_2, and M such that the networks of Fig. 6-23 and Fig. 6-24 are equivalent with respect to terminal pairs 1-1' and 2-2'.

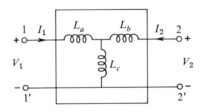

FIG. 6-24. Equivalent network for the coupled inductances of Fig. 6-23 (Prob. 6-13).

c. Is the network of Fig. 6-24 equivalent to the network of Fig. 6-23 with respect to all terminal pairs? Why?

d. Show that, by adding an ideal transformer to your network in (*b*), you can obtain a network that is equivalent to that of Fig. 6-23 with respect to all terminal pairs.

Problem 6-14

Find the driving-point admittance Y for the network of Fig. 6-25.

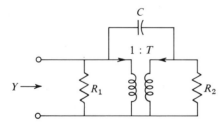

FIG. 6-25. Network containing an ideal transformer (Prob. 6-14).

7

Network Theorems

In the preceding chapters we have been concerned primarily with the formulation of equilibrium equations and with the solution of these equations for specific networks. We shall now focus our attention on certain general properties of networks.

Thevenin's theorem

Let us examine the general properties of the v-i relation for a two-terminal RLC network with sources. We shall express the v-i relation at the terminals in a form that will suggest a simple network that is equivalent to the given network with respect to the terminals.

The situation with which we are concerned is depicted in Fig. 7-1, which

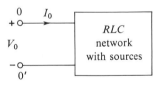

FIG. 7-1. Network to illustrate the application of Thevenin's theorem.

shows an RLC network with sources connected through the terminal pair 0-0' to some external network. The sources are exponential voltages or currents with the same complex frequency, and we shall focus our attention on the complex amplitudes V_0 and I_0 of the particular integrals of the voltage and current at the terminals.

Thevenin's theorem states that, as far as the effect on the external network is concerned, the RLC network with sources can be replaced by a so-called Thevenin equivalent network consisting of a voltage source in series with an impedance (or, alternatively, a current source in parallel with an impedance). We proceed now to prove this theorem and to determine the value of the voltage or current source and the impedance in the Thevenin equivalent network.

We consider first the situation in which there are no dependent sources in the network; i.e., the only sources are independent current and voltage sources. Since we are seeking a characterization of the network from the point of view of its terminals, our objective is to obtain a relation between V_0 and I_0. In order to derive this relation, it is convenient to account for the current I_0 at the terminals by imagining a current source of that value to be connected across the terminals. We shall proceed to find the voltage response V_0 across the terminal pair as a consequence of I_0 and of all the other sources in the network. Since the elements in the network are linear, we can use superposition to express the output voltage as the sum of the responses to all the sources and to I_0.

The contribution to V_0 from the jth current source can be written $Z_{0j}I_j$, where Z_{0j} is the transfer impedance from the jth current source to the output voltage with all other sources (including I_0) set to zero. For $j = 0$, $Z_{00}I_0$ is the component of V_0 due to I_0, where Z_{00} is the driving-point impedance at terminals 0-0' with all other sources set to zero. The contribution to V_0 from the kth voltage source can be written $H_{0k}V_k$, where H_{0k} is the system function from the kth voltage source to the output voltage with all other sources (including I_0) set to zero. By superposition,

$$V_0 = \sum_{\text{all } j} Z_{0j}I_j + \sum_{\text{all } k} H_{0k}V_k . \tag{7-1}$$

Since we are seeking a relation between V_0 and I_0, let us separate from the first summation in (7-1) the term corresponding to the current I_0 at the output terminals. Thus we have

$$V_0 = \sum_{j \neq 0} Z_{0j}I_j + \sum_{\text{all } k} H_{0k}V_k + Z_{00}I_0 . \tag{7-2}$$

The combination of the two summations on the right-hand side of Eq. (7-2) gives the voltage at terminals 0-0' with $I_0 = 0$, i.e., the open-circuit output voltage V_{oc}. Thus Eq. (7-2) can be written

$$V_0 = V_{oc} + Z_{00}I_0 . \tag{7-3}$$

This relation between the voltage V_0 and the current I_0 at the terminals of the network is the same as the voltage-current relation that would exist at the terminals of the equivalent network shown in Fig. 7-2. Thus if we were concerned only with the behavior of the network with respect to its termi-

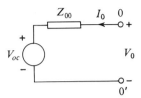

FIG. 7-2. Thevenin equivalent network.

nals, we could not tell if the components inside the network were replaced by the equivalent network in Fig. 7-2.

Equation (7-3) suggests methods whereby the Thevenin equivalent network for a given network can be determined either by calculation or, in the laboratory, by measurement. The open-circuit voltage can be measured directly or it can be calculated in a straightforward manner by finding the system functions Z_{0j} and H_{0k}. The Thevenin equivalent impedance Z_{00} can be determined by either of the following methods: (1) From Eq. (7-3) or from the equivalent network of Fig. 7-2 we see that, if we set $V_0 = 0$, i.e., if we short-circuit the terminals 0-0', then I_0 becomes the short-circuit current I_{sc} and is given by $I_{sc} = -V_{oc}/Z_{00}$. Thus the impedance is

$$Z_{00} = -\frac{V_{oc}}{I_{sc}}. \tag{7-4}$$

Consequently the Thevenin equivalent impedance is the negative of the ratio of the open-circuit voltage at the terminals to the short-circuit current. (2) The equivalent network or Eq. (7-3) indicates that Z_{00} is the impedance looking into terminals 0-0' with V_{oc} set to zero. Comparison of Eqs. (7-2) and (7-3) indicates that setting V_{oc} to zero is accomplished by setting all independent voltage and current sources inside the network to zero. With these sources set to zero, the impedance Z_{00} is evaluated by applying a source at terminals 0-0' and determining the resulting voltage V_0' and current I_0'. The impedance is then $Z_{00} = V_0'/I_0'$. It is usually convenient to apply a voltage source or a current source, but of course excitation from any external network is adequate.

Let us now examine how the above theorem is modified when we allow the network to contain dependent as well as independent sources. We shall illustrate the effect of dependent sources by assuming that there is only one such source—a voltage source V_d whose value is proportional to some node-pair voltage E_a; i.e., $V_d = K_1 E_a$, where K_1 is a constant. (The method used to obtain the result is the same when there is more than one independent source, although it is algebraically more complex.) The general nature of the result we shall develop will be the same regardless of the type of dependent source we use.[1]

The proof for this case is similar to that derived previously, except that we must now account for the dependent source V_d. If we assume for the moment that V_d is an independent source, then it contributes to Eq. (7-2) a term $T_{0d}V_d$, where T_{0d} is the transfer function from the source voltage V_d to the response V_0. Thus we have

$$V_0 = \sum_{j \neq 0} Z_{0j}I_j + \sum_k H_{0k}V_k + Z_{00}I_0 + T_{0d}V_d. \qquad (7\text{-}5)$$

But the source voltage V_d is in fact a dependent source and is proportional to a particular node-pair voltage E_a in the network. This voltage E_a, like V_0, can be expressed as a sum of terms representing contributions to E_a from each of the voltage and current sources in the network, including the current I_0 that exists at the external terminal pair and also including the voltage source V_d. Consequently we can express E_a as follows:

$$E_a = \sum_{j \neq 0} Z_{aj}I_j + \sum_k H_{ak}V_k + Z_{a0}I_0 + T_{ad}V_d, \qquad (7\text{-}6)$$

where the subscript a in the system functions Z_{aj}, H_{ak}, and T_{ad} indicates that each system function is a ratio of the voltage E_a to the appropriate source voltage or current. Substituting the dependent-source constraint $V_d = K_1 E_a$ into Eq. (7-6), we obtain

$$V_d = \frac{K_1}{1 - K_1 T_{ad}} \left[\sum_{j \neq 0} Z_{aj}I_j + \sum_k H_{ak}V_k + Z_{a0}I_0 \right] \qquad (7\text{-}7)$$

Substitution of (7-7) into (7-5) leads to the following expression for the output voltage:

$$V_0 = \sum_{j \neq 0} \left(Z_{0j} + \frac{K_1 T_{0d}}{1 - K_1 T_{ad}} Z_{aj} \right) I_j + \sum_k \left(H_{0k} + \frac{K_1 T_{0d}}{1 - K_1 T_{ad}} H_{ak} \right) V_k$$

$$+ \left(Z_{00} + \frac{K_1 T_{0d}}{1 - K_1 T_{ad}} Z_{a0} \right) I_0. \qquad (7\text{-}8)$$

The two summations in Eq. (7-8) combine to give the voltage at terminals 0-0' with $I_0 = 0$, i.e., the open-circuit voltage V_{oc}. Thus

$$V_{oc} = \sum_{j \neq 0} \left(Z_{0j} + \frac{K_1 T_{0d}}{1 - K_1 T_{ad}} Z_{aj} \right) I_j + \sum_k \left(H_{0k} + \frac{K_1 T_{0d}}{1 - K_1 T_{ad}} H_{ak} \right) V_k. \quad (7\text{-}9)$$

---

[1] The case of a current-controlled current source is considered in Prob. 7-1.

Let us define the coefficient of I_0 as Z'_{00}; i.e.,

$$Z'_{00} = Z_{00} + \frac{K_1 T_{0d}}{1 - K_1 T_{ad}} Z_{a0} \qquad (7\text{-}10)$$

Equation (7-8) then reduces to

$$V_0 = V_{oc} + Z'_{00} I_0 , \qquad (7\text{-}11)$$

which is of the same form as Eq. (7-3) derived previously. The equivalent network for which (7-11) is the voltage-current relation at the terminals is shown in Fig. 7-3. The network is the same as that given previously in

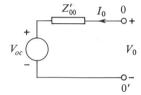

FIG. 7-3. Thevenin equivalent network for a network that includes a dependent source. The values of V_{oc} and Z_{00} are derived in the text.

Fig. 7-2, and we note that the result for the example with the dependent source is identical to the previous result if K_1 is set to zero.

For the equivalent network of Fig. 7-3, the value of the open-circuit voltage V_{oc} can be determined by direct measurement in the laboratory or by calculation of the appropriate system functions and use of Eq. (7-9). It follows directly from Eq. (7-10) or Fig. 7-3 that the internal impedance Z'_{00} can again be determined in two ways. One method is to find the open-circuit voltage V_{oc} and the short-circuit current I_{sc} and to use the relation $Z'_{00} = -V_{oc}/I_{sc}$. In the second method we set V_{oc} in Fig. 7-3 to zero and find the impedance at the terminals under this condition. From Eqs. (7-9) and (7-10) we note that, to set V_{oc} to zero without altering Z'_{00}, we must set *only the independent sources to zero.*

In the above development, Eqs. (7-3) and (7-11) have been written in a form that suggests the equivalent networks of Figs. 7-2 and 7-3. The equations can, however, be recast in a form that suggests an alternative equivalent network. From Eq. (7-11), the short-circuit current at the terminals is determined by setting V_0 to zero, yielding $I_{sc} = -V_{oc}/Z'_{00}$ or $V_{oc} = -I_{sc}Z'_{00}$. Thus Eq. (7-11) can be written

$$V_0 = -I_{sc}Z'_{00} + I_0 Z'_{00} ,$$

or

$$I_0 = I_{sc} + V_0 Y'_{00} , \qquad (7\text{-}12)$$

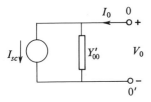

FIG. 7-4. Norton equivalent network.

where $Y'_{00} = 1/Z'_{00}$. We recognize this relation between V_0 and I_0 to be the voltage-current relation at the terminals of the network shown in Fig. 7-4. This equivalent network consisting of a current source in parallel with an internal admittance Y'_{00} is sometimes called a Norton equivalent network.

In summary, we have shown two simple networks that are equivalent, with respect to a given single terminal pair, to a network that contains RLC elements and sources. One equivalent network consists of a voltage source in series with an impedance. The value of the voltage source is the open-circuit voltage at the given terminal pair, and the equivalent impedance is the impedance seen at the terminals of the network with all independent sources set to zero (but with dependent sources, if any, still operating). The alternative equivalent network consists of a current source in parallel with an admittance. The value of the current source is the short-circuit current at the particular terminal pair, and the equivalent admittance is the reciprocal of the equivalent impedance defined above.

Problem 7-1

Consider a two-terminal network containing resistances, inductances, capacitances, independent voltage and current sources, and one current-controlled current source. Derive the Thevenin equivalent network for this case. Refer to the derivation given in the text for the case of a network containing a voltage-controlled voltage source (pages 303 to 305).

Problem 7-2

A two-terminal network N contains only resistances and d-c sources. With the terminals open-circuited, the terminal voltage is $v_{oc} = 20$ volts. A variable resistance R is connected across the terminals as shown in Fig. 7-5, and its value is adjusted until $v_1 = v_{oc}/2$. The value of this resistance is then measured and found to be 10 ohms. Determine the Thevenin equivalent network for N.

The method described above, using a variable resistance, is often used

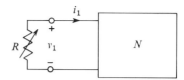

FIG. 7-5. Illustrating a method that can be used for finding the Thevenin equivalent network for a network N (Prob. 7-2).

in the laboratory to determine the Thevenin equivalent resistance of a network.

Problem 7-3

For the network of Fig. 7-6 determine the Thevenin equivalent network with respect to terminals 1-1′, assuming the responses to the two sources have reached steady state.

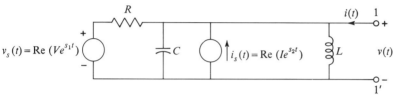

FIG. 7-6. Network for Prob. 7-3.

Problem 7-4

For the two-terminal RLC network N of Fig. 7-7a, it is observed that (1) the steady-state open-circuit voltage v is given by $v_{oc} = \cos t$, and (2) the steady-state short-circuit current i is given by $i_{sc} = -2 \sin t$.

The network N is now connected as shown in Fig. 7-7b. Is the given information sufficient for obtaining the steady-state current response i_1? If your answer is "yes," find i_1. If your answer is "no," state what additional information about the network N is necessary in order to obtain i_1.

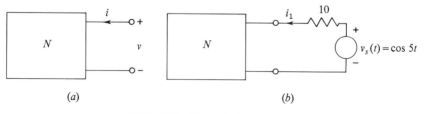

(a)   (b)

FIG. 7-7. Networks for Prob. 7-4.

Problem 7-5

The network inside the dashed line in Fig. 7-8 is a simplified linear model for a vacuum tube. The connection shown is often called a cathode follower. Find the Thevenin equivalent network at terminals 0-0′.

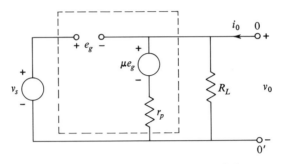

FIG. 7-8. The dashed line encloses an equivalent network for a vacuum tube. The Thevenin equivalent network with respect to terminals 0-0′ is to be found in Prob. 7-5.

Problem 7-6

The network inside the dashed box in Fig. 7-9 is a simplified linear model for a transistor. Find the Norton equivalent network seen looking to the left at the terminal pair 1-1′.

The network of Fig. 7-9 is commonly referred to as an emitter follower. It is the transistor equivalent of the vacuum-tube network of Prob. 7-5. A typical value for α is 0.98.

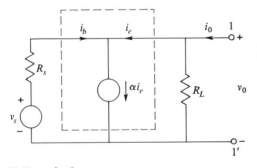

FIG. 7-9. The dashed line encloses a simplified equivalent network for a transistor. The Norton equivalent network with respect to terminals 1-1′ is to be found in Prob. 7-6.

Tellegen's theorem

Statement of theorem. Consider a network consisting of an interconnection of elements, where the term "element" is used in the most general sense to represent a terminal pair across which a voltage exists and through which a current flows.[1] As in Chap. 1, we shall use the sign convention that the positive direction of the current is from the + to the − terminal of the element, as shown in Fig. 7-10. Let us imagine a set of currents i_1,

FIG. 7-10. Symbol for a general electrical element with two terminals, showing the convention for assigning signs to the voltage v and the current i.

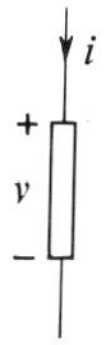

$i_2, \ldots , i_N$ associated with the N elements in a network, and let us assume that the only constraint on these currents is that they satisfy Kirchhoff's current law. We also imagine a set of voltages $v_1, v_2, \ldots , v_N$ associated with the elements in the network, and we assume that the only constraint on these voltages is that they satisfy Kirchhoff's voltage law. Tellegen's theorem[2] states that

$$\sum_{k=1}^{N} v_k i_k = 0 , \qquad (7\text{-}13)$$

where i_k is the current associated with the kth element, v_k is the voltage associated with the kth element, and the sum is over all the elements in the network.

Proof of theorem. Since the voltages v_k satisfy KVL, then for each connection point in the network we can specify a voltage with respect to some fixed reference or datum point. Let us designate the connection points in the network by the symbols $a, b, c, \ldots$, and let us denote the voltages between these points and the reference point as $e_a, e_b, e_c, \ldots$. The voltage across each element can then be expressed, using KVL, as the difference between two of these voltage variables. Thus if element 1 connects between points a and b, as shown in Fig. 7-11, then the voltage v_1 across the element is $e_a - e_b$. The term $v_1 i_1$ for element 1 in the sum (7-13) can then be written

---

[1] In our previous discussions of *RLC* networks, we restricted the use of the term "element" to resistances, inductances, and capacitances. In this section we shall apply the term in the more general sense defined here. We note that this definition includes a resistance, an inductance, a capacitance, and a dependent or independent source and also includes any port of an *n*-port network, such as a coupled inductance or a terminal pair of an ideal transformer.

[2] B. D. H. Tellegen, A general network theorem, with applications. Philips Research Reports 7, 259-269 (1952).

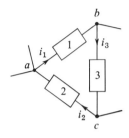

FIG. 7-11. Portion of a network used to illustrate the proof of Tellegen's theorem.

$$v_1i_1 = (e_a - e_b)i_1$$

$$= e_ai_1 - e_bi_1 . \tag{7-14}$$

The terms corresponding to other elements in the network have a form similar to that given in Eq. (7-14). For example, for the configuration shown in Fig. 7-11, the terms corresponding to elements 2 and 3 are, respectively,

$$v_2i_2 = (e_c - e_a)i_2$$

$$= e_ci_2 - e_ai_2 , \tag{7-15}$$

and

$$v_3i_3 = (e_b - e_c)i_3$$

$$= e_bi_3 - e_ci_3 . \tag{7-16}$$

Having written each of the products v_ki_k in the sum (7-13) as the sum of two terms, in the form shown in (7-14) to (7-16), we now rearrange these terms so that the terms associated with each voltage variable are grouped together. The terms associated with voltage variable e_a, for example, will be those corresponding to all elements that connect to point a in the network. For a given element of this set the term will have a positive sign if the reference arrow is directed away from point a and a negative sign if it is directed toward point a. If in our example we factor e_a from each term, then the sum of the terms in this group can be written

$$e_a \left[\sum_{\substack{\text{currents} \\ \text{leaving } a}} i_k - \sum_{\substack{\text{currents} \\ \text{entering } a}} i_k \right] . \tag{7-17}$$

Since the currents satisfy KCL, the factor in the brackets is zero. The same argument can be used to show that the group of terms associated with the voltage variable for each connection point sums to zero. Hence the sum of all terms is zero, and we have the result

$$\sum_{k=1}^{N} v_ki_k = 0 . \tag{7-18}$$

From the proof just given, we see that Tellegen's theorem is based only on the requirements that the voltages satisfy KVL and the currents satisfy KCL. The theorem places no restriction on the v-i relations for the elements and thus is valid for networks containing nonlinear as well as linear elements. Furthermore, there is no requirement that the voltages be associated with the same set of element values as the currents. For example, the v's in Eq. (7-18) could correspond to the voltages that exist in a network when the elements have one set of values, and the i's could correspond to the currents that exist when the elements have another set of values.

Networks with terminal pairs. In the proof of Tellegen's theorem, the only requirements we impose on an element are that it has two terminals through which a current is defined and across which a voltage is defined. For a network with ports, each port clearly satisfies this requirement, and hence we can apply Tellegen's theorem to an n-port network, treating each port as an element. We recall, however, that it is customary to define the positive senses of the voltages and currents at terminal pairs in the manner indicated in Fig. 7-12, and we note that this convention is opposite to the one used for internally connected elements in the network. Hence for a network with ports the terms $v_k i_k$ corresponding to the ports in Eq. (7-18) appear with negative signs, and we have

$$\sum_{\substack{\text{all internal} \\ \text{elements}}} v_k i_k - \sum_{\text{all ports}} v_k i_k = 0 . \qquad (7\text{-}19)$$

Thus we have the following basic relation for networks with ports:

$$\sum_{\text{all ports}} v_k i_k = \sum_{\substack{\text{all internal} \\ \text{elements}}} v_k i_k . \qquad (7\text{-}20)$$

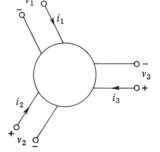

FIG. 7-12. Network with several ports, showing the usual convention for assigning currents and voltages at the terminal pairs.

Reciprocity relation

We shall now use Tellegen's theorem to derive certain basic relations among the voltages and currents at the terminals of two-port networks that contain only resistances, inductances, and capacitances. Such a network is illustrated in Fig. 7-13. Let us assume exponential excitations, and let

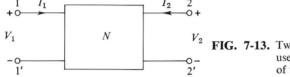

FIG. 7-13. Two-port RLC network used to illustrate the derivation of the reciprocity relation.

us represent the particular integrals of the voltages and currents by complex amplitudes in the usual manner. Consider two different sets of voltages and currents in the network, resulting from two different external connections at the terminal pairs. One set of voltages and currents will be denoted by unprimed symbols and the other by primed symbols. Applying Tellegen's theorem to one set of voltages (primed symbols) and the other set of currents (unprimed symbols), we can write[1]

$$V_1'I_1 + V_2'I_2 = \sum_{\substack{\text{all internal} \\ \text{elements}}} V_k'I_k . \qquad (7\text{-}21)$$

A similar equation can be written for the voltages designated by unprimed symbols and the currents designated by primed symbols as follows:

$$V_1I_1' + V_2I_2' = \sum_{\substack{\text{all internal} \\ \text{elements}}} V_kI_k' . \qquad (7\text{-}22)$$

Since we have stipulated that each element is a resistance, inductance, or capacitance, we can write for each element

$$V_k' = Z_kI_k' , \qquad (7\text{-}23)$$

and

$$V_k = Z_kI_k , \qquad (7\text{-}24)$$

where Z_k is the impedance of the element. Consequently the summation on the right-hand side of Eq. (7-21) can be written

---

[1] The proof that we have given for Tellegen's theorem was derived in terms of instantaneous values of the voltages and currents. The theorem also applies, however, to complex amplitudes of voltages and currents, since, as we have seen, these complex amplitudes obey Kirchhoff's laws.

$$\sum_k V_k' I_k = \sum_k Z_k I_k' I_k$$

$$= \sum_k V_k I_k' . \tag{7-25}$$

Hence we can equate the left-hand sides of Eqs. (7-21) and (7-22), giving

$$V_1' I_1 + V_2' I_2 = V_1 I_1' + V_2 I_2' . \tag{7-26}$$

This is the general form of the so-called *reciprocity relation* for two-port networks. Any two-port network to which this relation applies is said to be a *reciprocal network*.

Three special cases of this reciprocity relation, corresponding to three different forms of external connection for a two-port network, are of particular interest.

CASE 1: $I_2 = 0$ and $I_1' = 0$. Substituting these conditions into Eq. (7-26), we obtain

$$\left.\frac{V_2}{I_1}\right|_{I_2 = 0} = \left.\frac{V_1'}{I_2'}\right|_{I_1' = 0} \tag{7-27}$$

The condition $I_2 = 0$ corresponds to an open circuit at terminal pair 2-2', and hence the ratio V_2/I_1 can be interpreted as the transfer impedance Z_{21} of the network when the excitation is a current at terminals 1-1' and the response is the open-circuit voltage at terminals 2-2'. Likewise, the ratio V_1'/I_2' can be interpreted as the transfer impedance Z_{12} of the network when the excitation is a current at terminals 2-2' and the response is the open-circuit voltage at terminals 1-1'. Equation (7-27) states that these two open-circuit transfer impedances are equal.

The fact that $Z_{12} = Z_{21}$ enables us to establish properties of the network responses for excitation functions with arbitrary waveforms. Suppose we connect a current source $i(t)$ at terminal pair 1-1' of an *RLC* network and measure the voltage $v(t)$ with terminal pair 2-2' open-circuited, as shown in Fig. 7-14a. We now perform a second experiment in which we

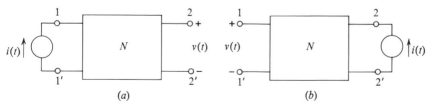

(a)   (b)

FIG. 7-14. Two-port *RLC* network *N* with a current excitation applied at one terminal pair and the open-circuit voltage response measured at the other. As a consequence of the reciprocity relation, the open-circuit voltage response $v(t)$ is the same in the two situations shown.

connect the same current source $i(t)$ at terminal pair 2-2' and measure the open-circuit voltage at terminal pair 1-1', as indicated in Fig. 7-14b. Since $Z_{12} = Z_{21}$, the differential equation relating excitation and response is the same in the two cases, and hence the open-circuit voltage at terminal pair 1-1' is again $v(t)$. Thus for a reciprocal network the positions of a current source and a voltage-measuring device (which draws no current) can be interchanged without altering the voltage reading.

CASE 2: $V_2 = 0$ and $V_1' = 0$. Substitution of these conditions into Eq. (7-26) yields

$$\left.\frac{I_2}{V_1}\right|_{V_2 = 0} = \left.\frac{I_1'}{V_2'}\right|_{V_1' = 0}. \tag{7-28}$$

The condition $V_2 = 0$ corresponds to a short circuit at terminal pair 2-2', and the ratio I_2/V_1 represents the short-circuit transfer admittance Y_{21}. Likewise the ratio I_1'/V_2' with $V_1' = 0$ represents the short-circuit transfer admittance Y_{12}. Equation (7-28) states that these two transfer admittances are equal.

As in the first case discussed above and illustrated by Fig. 7-14, we can interpret Eq. (7-28) in terms of measurements made at the terminals of the network with arbitrary time functions as the excitation functions. Suppose we connect a voltage source $v(t)$ at one terminal pair and measure the short-circuit $i(t)$ at the other. Then from Eq. (7-28) the point of application of the source and the point of measurement of the current can be interchanged, and the results of the experiment will be unchanged. This situation is illustrated by the two connections shown in Fig. 7-15.

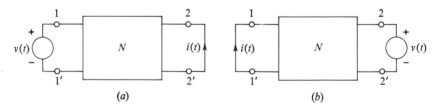

(a)   (b)

FIG. 7-15. Two-port RLC network N with a voltage excitation applied at one terminal pair and the short-circuit current response measured at the other. As a consequence of the reciprocity relation, the short-circuit current response $i(t)$ is the same in the two situations shown.

CASE 3: $I_2 = 0$ and $V_1' = 0$. If we substitute these conditions into the general reciprocity relation (7-26), we obtain

$$\left.\frac{V_2}{V_1}\right|_{I_2=0} = -\left.\frac{I_1'}{I_2'}\right|_{V_1'=0}. \tag{7-29}$$

The condition $I_2 = 0$ corresponds to an open circuit at terminal pair 2-2', and $V_1' = 0$ corresponds to a short circuit at terminal pair 1-1'. Eq. (7-29) states that the voltage transfer ratio for the situation depicted in Fig. 7-16a is equal to the negative of the current transfer ratio for the

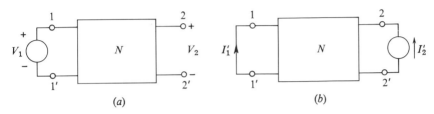

           (a)   (b)

FIG. 7-16. In (a) a voltage source is applied at terminal pair 1-1' of network N, and the response is the open-circuit voltage at terminal pair 2-2'. In (b) a current source is applied at terminal pair 2-2', and the response is the short-circuit current at terminal pair 1-1'. Application of the reciprocity relation to these situations gives $V_2/V_1 = -I_1'/I_2'$.

excitation and response conditions shown in Fig. 7-16b. As before, we can interpret Eq. (7-29) in terms of observations of voltages and currents at the network terminals.

A fourth case, corresponding to $I_1 = 0$ and $V_2' = 0$, could also be discussed, but this is equivalent to case 3 with terminal pairs 1-1' and 2-2' interchanged and hence gives rise to no new result.

Problem 7-7

For each of the parts below, prove the statement to be true or to be false.[1]
You may use any results already proved in the text:

1. The reciprocity relation applies to all two-terminal-pair networks containing only resistances, capacitances, inductances, and independent sources.

2. The reciprocity relation applies to all two-terminal-pair networks containing only capacitances, inductances, and positive and negative resistances.

3. The reciprocity relation applies to all two-terminal-pair networks con-

---

[1] When there is appreciable doubt as to the validity of a theorem, one can often save considerable time if, before attempting a proof, one searches for a counterexample, since a single counterexample is sufficient to prove the theorem false.

taining only resistances, capacitances, inductances, and dependent sources.

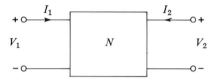

FIG. 7-17. Two-terminal-pair network for Prob. 7-8.

Problem 7-8

The two-terminal-pair network of Fig. 7-17 is described by the equations

$$V_1 = Z_{11}I_1 + Z_{12}I_2,$$

and

$$V_2 = Z_{21}I_1 + Z_{22}I_2.$$

a. The network has the property that

$$\left.\frac{V_2}{I_1}\right|_{I_2 = 0} = \left.\frac{V_1'}{I_2'}\right|_{I_1' = 0}, \tag{7-30}$$

where unprimed variables are associated with one experiment and primed variables with another. Show that the network has each of the following properties:

1. $$\left.\frac{V_2}{V_1}\right|_{I_2 = 0} = -\left.\frac{I_1'}{I_2'}\right|_{V_1' = 0}; \tag{7-31}$$

2. $$\left.\frac{I_2}{V_1}\right|_{V_2 = 0} = \left.\frac{I_1'}{V_2'}\right|_{V_1' = 0}. \tag{7-32}$$

b. Prove that, if the network is characterized by the given set of equations and has any one of the properties (7-30) to (7-32), then it must satisfy the general reciprocity relation, i.e.,

$$V_1I_1' + V_2I_2' = V_1'I_1 + V_2'I_2. \tag{7-33}$$

Problem 7-9

a. The two-terminal-pair RLC network of Fig. 7-18 is characterized by the equations

$$V_1 = Z_{11}I_1 + Z_{12}I_2,$$

and

$$V_2 = Z_{21}I_1 + Z_{22}I_2.$$

FIG. 7-18. Two-terminal-pair network for Prob. 7-9.

Apply the reciprocity relation to show that $Z_{12} = Z_{21}$.

b. The same two-terminal-pair *RLC* network of Fig. 7-18 can be characterized by the equations

$$I_1 = Y_{11}V_1 + Y_{12}V_2,$$

and $$I_2 = Y_{21}V_1 + Y_{22}V_2.$$

Show that $Y_{12} = Y_{21}$.

c. Consider the *n*-terminal-pair *RLC* network of Fig. 7-19. The terminal

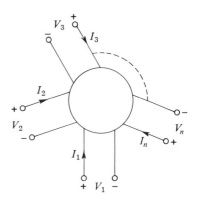

FIG. 7-19. Network with *n* terminal pairs (Prob. 7-9).

behavior of this network can be characterized by the set of equations

$$V_1 = Z_{11}I_1 + Z_{12}I_2 + \cdots + Z_{1n}I_n$$
$$V_2 = Z_{21}I_1 + Z_{22}I_2 + \cdots + Z_{2n}I_n$$
$$\cdots\cdots\cdots\cdots\cdots\cdots\cdots\cdots\cdots$$
$$V_n = Z_{n1}I_1 + Z_{n2}I_2 + \cdots + Z_{nn}I_n.$$

Show that $Z_{ij} = Z_{ji}$ for any i and j; i.e., show that the array of coefficients $(Z_{ij}\text{'s})$ is symmetrical about the principal diagonal.

We would now like to show that the Z and Y parameters for an *n*-terminal *RLC* network have the same symmetry properties as those just shown for an *n*-port *RLC* network; i.e., $Z_{ij} = Z_{ji}$ and $Y_{ij} = Y_{ji}$. The proof of this result for an *n*-terminal network follows immediately from the result derived in (c) above, since it can be shown that for any n-terminal network there exists an $(n - 1)$-port network whose Z and Y parameters are the same as those of the n-terminal network.

d. Consider an n-terminal network whose Z and Y parameters are defined with respect to a selected reference terminal. By making appropriate connections to the reference terminal of this network, construct an $(n - 1)$-port network whose terminal behavior is characterized by the same set of equations as those characterizing the n-terminal network.

Problem 7-10

A large number of electrical devices can be modeled by networks with three terminals. Since networks of this type are encountered frequently, it is convenient to be able to represent them by simple equivalent networks for which the relations between the voltages and currents at the terminals are the same as those for the given networks. Two equivalent representations, for three-terminal networks that satisfy the reciprocity relation, will be derived in this problem.

a. For the three-terminal *RLC* network of Fig. 7-20, the open-circuit

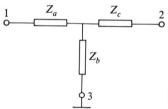

FIG. 7-20. T-equivalent network for a three-terminal *RLC* network.

Z parameters with terminal 3 as the reference terminal are Z_{11}, Z_{12}, and Z_{22}. (As we have seen in Prob. 7-9, $Z_{21} = Z_{12}$ as a consequence of reciprocity.) Express these Z parameters in terms of Z_a, Z_b, and Z_c. Also, express Z_a, Z_b, and Z_c in terms of Z_{11}, Z_{12}, and Z_{22}.

b. For the three-terminal *RLC* network of Fig. 7-21, the short-circuit Y parameters with terminal 3 as the reference terminal are Y_{11}, Y_{12}, and Y_{22}. Express these Y parameters in terms of Y_e, Y_f, and Y_g. Also, express Y_e, Y_f, and Y_g in terms of Y_{11}, Y_{12}, and Y_{22}.

c. Two three-terminal networks are called equivalent if they have the same Z parameters (or Y parameters). Determine Z_a, Z_b, and Z_c in terms of Y_e, Y_f, and Y_g such that the three-terminal networks of Figs. 7-20 and 7-21 are equivalent.

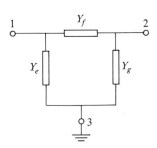

FIG. 7-21. π-equivalent network
for a three-terminal RLC network.

From the results of (*a*) and (*b*), it is clear that any given three-terminal
RLC network has an equivalent network of the form of Fig. 7-20 (referred
to as the T-equivalent), and also an equivalent network of the form of
Fig. 7-21 (referred to as the π-equivalent). However, it should be emphasized that in these equivalent networks the impedances Z_a, Z_b, Z_c and the
admittances Y_e, Y_f, Y_g are not always realizable by positive elements alone.
d. Find the T- and π-equivalent networks for the resistive network shown
in Fig. 7-22.

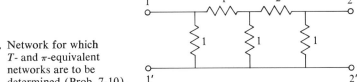

FIG. 7-22. Network for which
T- and π-equivalent
networks are to be
determined (Prob. 7-10).

Problem 7-11

The following information is given about the two-terminal-pair network
in Fig. 7-23:
1. The network contains only resistances.
2. The input resistance at terminals 1-1' with terminals 2-2' open-circuited
   is $R_{in} = 3$.
3. The input resistance at terminals 2-2' with terminals 1-1' open-circuited
   is $R_{in} = 4$.

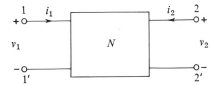

FIG. 7-23. Two-terminal-pair network
for Prob. 7-11.

4. $v_2/i_1 = 2$ when terminals 2-2' are open-circuited.

By using a T- or π-equivalent, determine the input resistance at terminals 1-1' if a resistance $R = 2$ is connected to terminals 2-2'.

Problem 7-12

a. Prove that the reciprocity relation holds for the pair of coupled inductances shown in Fig. 7-24.

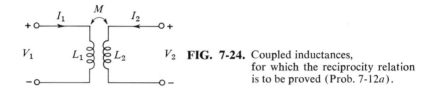

FIG. 7-24. Coupled inductances, for which the reciprocity relation is to be proved (Prob. 7-12*a*).

b. Consider a two-terminal-pair network containing only resistances, inductances, capacitances, and one pair of coupled inductances, as shown in Fig. 7-25. Using Tellegen's theorem and the results of (*a*), prove that the reciprocity relation holds for such a two-terminal-pair network.

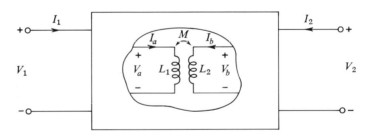

FIG. 7-25. Two-terminal-pair network containing a coupled pair of inductances (Prob. 7-12*b*).

c. Prove that the reciprocity relation holds for an ideal transformer, shown in Fig. 7-26.

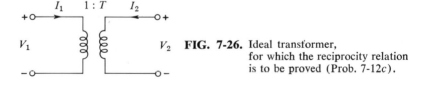

FIG. 7-26. Ideal transformer, for which the reciprocity relation is to be proved (Prob. 7-12*c*).

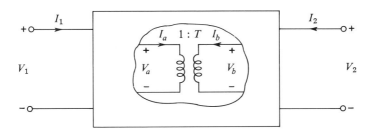

FIG. 7-27. Two-terminal-pair network containing an ideal transformer (Prob. 7-12*d*).

d. Consider a two-terminal-pair network containing only resistances, inductances, capacitances, and one ideal transformer, as shown in Fig. 7-27. Using Tellegen's theorem and the result of (*c*), show that the reciprocity relation holds for such a network.

Problem 7-13

A two-terminal-pair *RLC* network *N* is connected as shown in Fig. 7-28. When $i_s(t) = u_{-1}(t)$, the resulting current $i_2(t)$ is given by $i_2(t) = f(t)$. The network is now connected as shown in Fig. 7-29. The voltage source is $v_s(t) = u_0(t)$. The network is initially at rest in both cases. Find the voltage $v_1(t)$ in terms of $f(t)$.

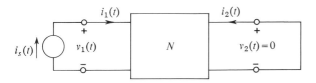

FIG. 7-28. Two-terminal-pair network for Prob. 7-13.

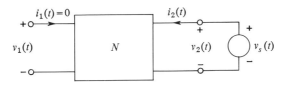

FIG. 7-29. Two-terminal-pair network of Fig. 7-28 with a voltage source connected at the right-hand terminal pair (Prob. 7-13).

Problem 7-14

The following information is given about the two-terminal-pair network in Fig. 7-30:

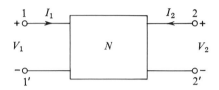

FIG. 7-30. Two-terminal-pair network for Prob. 7-14.

1. The input admittance at terminal pair 1-1' with terminal pair 2-2' open-circuited is

$$Y_a = \frac{1}{s+1}.$$

2. The input admittance at terminal pair 1-1' with terminal pair 2-2' short-circuited is

$$Y_b = \frac{s+1}{s^2+s+1}.$$

3. The input impedance at terminal pair 2-2' with terminal pair 1-1' open-circuited is

$$Z_c = \frac{s+1}{s}.$$

a. Express Y_a, Y_b, and Z_c in terms of the Y parameters of the network.
b. Determine the differential equation relating $v_1(t)$ to $i_2(t)$ if terminal pair 2-2' is short-circuited.

Problem 7-15

A two-terminal RLC network N_A is embedded within a two-terminal-pair RLC network N as indicated in Fig. 7-31. The following steady-state voltages and currents are observed:

$$v_1(t) = \sqrt{(2)^2 + 1} \cos (t + \tan^{-1} \tfrac{1}{2})$$
$$i_1(t) = \cos t$$
$$v_2(t) = 3 \cos t$$
$$i_2(t) = \cos t$$
$$v_3(t) = 2 \cos t$$
$$i_3(t) = 2 \cos t$$

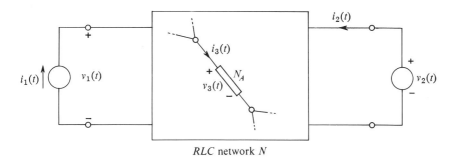

RLC network N

FIG. 7-31. Two-terminal-pair *RLC* network in which a two-terminal network N_A is embedded (Prob. 7-15).

The two-terminal *RLC* network N_A is now changed to a different two-terminal *RLC* network N_B, and the excitations are changed so that the values listed below for the voltages and currents are observed. (We shall use primed symbols in order to distinguish current and voltage values in this second experiment from those in the first experiment above.)

$$v_1'(t) = \sqrt{(5)^2 + (8)^2} \cos (t + \tan^{-1} \tfrac{8}{5})$$
$$i_1'(t) = 3 \cos t$$
$$v_2'(t) = \sqrt{(7)^2 + (5)^2} \cos (t + \tan^{-1} \tfrac{5}{7})$$
$$i_2'(t) = 2 \cos t$$
$$i_3'(t) = 5 \cos t$$

Determine the steady-state voltage $v_3'(t)$.

Uniqueness of responses of *RLC* networks

We have had occasion in our study of network responses, particularly in Chap. 3, to make use of the so-called uniqueness property of the responses of *RLC* networks to given excitations. This property, which was assumed without proof, states that the response of a network that is initially at rest and that consists of positive *R*, *L*, and *C* elements is unique for a given excitation. The uniqueness property is important because it assures us that, if we can determine a solution of the equilibrium equations by any means whatsoever, including guessing, this solution is the only one.[1] We are now in a position to prove the uniqueness property and hence to justify the use of inspection methods for finding network responses.

---

[1] We should note that the uniqueness property of networks does not imply that a solution of the equilibrium equations exists. It is, in fact, possible to imagine interconnections of sources and elements such that no solution exists.

The proof of the uniqueness property is carried out by showing that, for a network which is initially at rest and which consists of fixed sources and positive R, L, and C elements, there cannot exist two distinct sets of element voltages and currents both of which satisfy KCL, KVL, and the v-i relations for the elements. We begin by assuming that two sets of voltages and currents can exist in the network, and then we shall show that these two sets must be identical if the values of the sources are identical in the two cases. We shall designate one set of source and element voltages and currents in the network by the unprimed symbols v_k and i_k and the other set by primed symbols v'_k and i'_k, where the subscript denotes the kth element or source.

Consider now the sum

$$\sum_{s+e} (v_k - v'_k)(i_k - i'_k), \qquad (7\text{-}34)$$

where the symbol $s + e$ under the summation sign indicates that the summation is over all sources and elements in the network. This sum can be expanded to give

$$\sum_{s+e} v_k i_k - \sum_{s+e} v_k i'_k - \sum_{s+e} v'_k i_k + \sum_{s+e} v'_k i'_k. \qquad (7\text{-}35)$$

From Tellegen's theorem, each summation in Eq. (7-35) is zero, and therefore

$$\sum_{s+e} (v_k - v'_k)(i_k - i'_k) = 0. \qquad (7\text{-}36)$$

We now focus attention on the source terms in Eq. (7-36), and we impose the condition that the sources associated with the unprimed and primed conditions are the same. Hence for all voltage sources we have $v_k = v'_k$, and for all current sources we have $i_k = i'_k$, and thus all terms in the summation of Eq. (7-36) that correspond to sources are zero. Consequently,

$$\sum_{e} (v_k - v'_k)(i_k - i'_k) = 0, \qquad (7\text{-}37)$$

where the summation is now over the element voltages and currents only.

If we separate the terms in Eq. (7-37) into those associated with the R, L, and C elements, respectively, and if we designate the voltages across these elements by the respective subscripts l, m, and n, we obtain

$$\sum_{R} (v_l - v'_l)(i_l - i'_l) + \sum_{L} (v_m - v'_m)(i_m - i'_m)$$
$$+ \sum_{C} (v_n - v'_n)(i_n - i'_n) = 0, \qquad (7\text{-}38)$$

where the symbols under the summation signs indicate that the summations are over the resistance, inductance, and capacitance elements, respectively. Introducing the v-i relations for the elements, we can write

$$\sum_R R_l(i_l - i_l')^2 + \sum_L L_m(i_m - i_m')\frac{d}{dt}(i_m - i_m')$$

$$+ \sum_C C_n(v_n - v_n')\frac{d}{dt}(v_n - v_n'), \qquad (7\text{-}39)$$

where R_l, L_m, and C_n represent the lth resistance, the mth inductance, and the nth capacitance, respectively.

Since we have assumed that the network is initially at rest, let us select t_1 as an instant of time at which all the element voltages and currents are zero. We now integrate Eq. (7-39) with respect to time from t_1 to time t and make use of the fact that the inductance currents and capacitance voltages are zero at $t = t_1$. Thus we obtain

$$\sum_R R_l \int_{t_1}^{t}(i_l - i_l')^2 \, d\tau + \tfrac{1}{2}\sum_L L_m[i_m(t) - i_m'(t)]^2$$

$$+ \tfrac{1}{2}\sum_C C_n[v_n(t) - v_n'(t)]^2 = 0 . \qquad (7\text{-}40)$$

If all resistances, inductances, and capacitances are positive, then all terms on the left-hand side of Eq. (7-40) must be greater than or equal to zero. Thus the equation can only be satisfied if every term is zero, i.e., if $i_l = i_l'$, $i_m = i_m'$, and $v_n = v_n'$. Consequently the unprimed set of element voltages and currents is equal to the primed set, and hence there cannot be two different sets of element voltages and currents that both satisfy the equilibrium equations for the network. We conclude, therefore, that for a given excitation the response of an RLC network that is initially at rest is unique if the R's, L's, and C's are all positive.

Properties of driving-point impedances of RLC networks

We have seen that the driving-point impedance of an RLC network can be characterized by a number of poles and zeros in the complex-frequency plane, and we have observed that a large number of pole-zero patterns can be realized by such networks. It can be shown, however, that, when the element values in an RLC network are positive, there are certain restrictions on the form of the pole-zero patterns that characterize driving-point impedances; i.e., not all pole-zero patterns can be realized by networks with positive R, L, and C elements. Tellegen's theorem is useful in demonstrating the nature of some of these restrictions on the pole-zero patterns associated with certain types of networks.

As an example, let us consider a network consisting only of positive R and L elements, and let us examine the locations of the zeros of the driving-point impedance at a pair of terminals of such a network. We shall assume that a current excitation with complex amplitude I is applied at the terminals and that a voltage with complex amplitude V appears across the terminals. If $Z(s)$ is the driving-point impedance at the terminals, then we can write

$$VI^* = Z(s)|I|^2 . \qquad (7\text{-}41)$$

Thus the zeros of $Z(s)$ are the complex frequencies at which the product VI^* is zero. If we let V_k and I_k represent the complex amplitudes of the voltage and current associated with the kth element in the network, then we know that the V_k's in the network satisfy KVL and the I_k^*'s satisfy KCL. Consequently we can apply Tellegen's theorem to obtain

$$VI^* = \sum_{\substack{\text{all internal} \\ \text{elements}}} V_k I_k^*$$

$$= \sum_{R} R_l |I_l|^2 + \sum_{L} s L_m |I_m|^2 , \qquad (7\text{-}42)$$

where R_l and L_m represent the lth resistance and mth inductance, respectively. The symbols I_l and I_m represent the complex amplitudes of the currents in these respective elements, and the summations designated by R and L are over all the resistance and inductance elements, respectively. If we let $s = \sigma + j\omega$ and if we set $VI^* = Z(s)|I|^2$ as in Eq. (7-41), then Eq. (7-42) becomes

$$Z(s)|I|^2 = \sum_{R} R_l |I_l|^2 + \sigma \sum_{L} L_m |I_m|^2 + j\omega \sum_{L} L_m |I_m|^2 . \qquad (7\text{-}43)$$

At a zero of $Z(s)$, this expression is zero, and hence both real and imaginary parts of the right-hand side are zero. Since all R_l and L_m are positive, then all the summations in Eq. (7-43) are positive. Thus at a zero of $Z(s)$ we must have $\omega = 0$ and $\sigma < 0$. Consequently the zeros of the driving-point impedance of a network consisting of positive R and L elements are constrained to lie on the negative real axis of the s plane.

Several other properties of the pole-zero configurations of RL, RC, LC, and RLC networks with positive element values are considered in Prob. 7-16.

Problem 7-16

Consider a network with driving-point impedance $Z(s)$. By using Tellegen's theorem, show that:

1. If the network contains only positive R and L elements, then the poles of $Z(s)$ (or equivalently, the zeros of the driving-point admittance) lie on the negative real axis of the s plane.
2. If the network contains only positive R and C elements, then the poles and zeros of $Z(s)$ lie on the negative real axis of the s plane.
3. If the network contains only positive R, L, and C elements, then the poles and zeros of $Z(s)$ lie in the left half of the s plane.
4. If the network contains only L and C elements (of either positive or negative values), then the poles and zeros of $Z(s)$ lie on the imaginary axis of the s plane.

8

Energy and Power

Definition of energy and power

As we discussed in Chap. 1, it is not within the realm of network theory to provide a physical interpretation of the variables voltage and current. Such an interpretation requires the application of the concepts of electromagnetic fields. For the same reasons, network theory does not provide a physical interpretation of energy and power. Electromagnetic field theory shows that, when a voltage and a current can be defined at a terminal pair of a device or interconnection of devices, the energy flow into the terminal pair in a given time interval is the integral of the product of the voltage and current in this time interval. In network theory we shall take this result as our definition of energy.

Thus for a terminal pair that is characterized by a current $i(t)$ and a voltage $v(t)$, as shown in Fig. 8-1, we define the energy $W(t)$ that flows into the terminal pair from time t_0 to time t to be

$$W(t) = \int_{t_0}^{t} v(\tau)i(\tau)\, d\tau \, . \tag{8-1}$$

Note that the energy given by this equation is defined to flow into the terminal pair when the reference directions of $v(t)$ and $i(t)$ are those shown in Fig. 8-1.

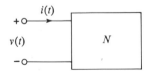

FIG. 8-1. Terminal pair of a network used to establish sign conventions for the definition of energy and power.

The power $p(t)$ flowing into the terminals at a given time t is defined as the rate of flow of energy into the terminals; i.e.,

$$p(t) = \frac{dW(t)}{dt} .\qquad(8\text{-}2)$$

Thus from Eqs. (8-1) and (8-2), we have

$$p(t) = v(t)i(t) ;\qquad(8\text{-}3)$$

i.e., the power is the product of the voltage and the current at the terminal pair.[1]

Conservation of energy

We now consider a network with n ports, as shown in Fig. 8-2, and we

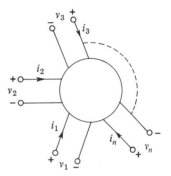

FIG. 8-2. Network with n ports, used to illustrate the law of conservation of energy for networks.

shall compute the total power flowing into the network at all the ports. The network consists of an arbitrary interconnection of sources and of linear or nonlinear elements. The usual sign conventions are observed in defining the voltage and current variables v_k and i_k both at the network terminals and for the elements and sources. From Tellegen's theorem applied to networks with terminal pairs [Eq. (7-20)] we can write

$$\sum_{\substack{\text{all ports}}} v_k i_k = \sum_{\substack{\text{all internal} \\ \text{elements and} \\ \text{sources}}} v_k i_k .\qquad(8\text{-}4)$$

Equation (8-4) states that the power flowing into the terminals of a network is equal to the power that flows into all elements and sources inside the network. Integration of Eq. (8-4) shows that, if a network is initially at

---

[1] When the units of current, voltage, and time are amperes, volts, and seconds, respectively, the unit of power is the watt, and the unit of energy is the watt-second, sometimes called the joule.

rest at some time t_1, then the energy flowing into the terminals from time t_1 to time t is equal to the energy flowing into all elements and sources in the network during the same time interval. This relation is a form of the law of conservation of energy for networks.

It is important to note that the law of conservation of energy for networks is derived directly from Tellegen's theorem, which is a consequence of Kirchhoff's voltage and current laws. Thus the law of conservation of energy is implied by Kirchhoff's laws and does not represent an additional constraint on the voltages and currents in a network. Indeed, if the network model defined in Chap. 1 provides an adequate representation of physical networks, we should expect that the properties we observe in such physical networks must be predictable from Kirchhoff's laws and the v-i relations without requiring additional constraints.

Energy and power in RLC networks

Expressions for the energy and power flow in resistance, inductance, and capacitance elements can be obtained from Eqs. (8-1) and (8-3), using the v-i relations for the elements.

Resistance.   For a resistance element, the power is given by

$$p(t) = vi = \frac{v^2}{R} = i^2R , \tag{8-5}$$

and the energy flow into a resistance in the time interval t_0 to t is

$$W(t) = \int_{t_0}^{t} Ri^2(\tau) \, d\tau . \tag{8-6}$$

From Eqs. (8-5) and (8-6) we observe that for positive resistances the power and the energy are always positive; i.e., energy always flows into a resistance and can never flow out. In the physical situation power is said to be "dissipated" in the resistance. The network model, of course, gives no indication of what happens to the power that flows into the resistance. It may be converted to such forms as thermal, electromagnetic, or mechanical energy.

Inductance. The power flowing into an inductance is given by

$$p(t) = vi = L \frac{di}{dt} i = \frac{d}{dt} [\tfrac{1}{2} Li^2(t)]. \tag{8-7}$$

Integration of this result gives the following expression for the total energy that flows into an inductance in the time interval t_0 to t:

$$W(t) = \int_{t_0}^{t} \frac{d}{d\tau} [\tfrac{1}{2} Li^2(\tau)] \, d\tau$$

$$= \tfrac{1}{2} Li^2(t) - \tfrac{1}{2} Li^2(t_0). \tag{8-8}$$

Since $p(t)$ and $W(t)$ in Eqs. (8-7) and (8-8) can be either positive or negative, the power flow into a positive inductance can be either positive or negative; i.e., power can flow into or out of the terminals of an inductance. From Eq. (8-8), the energy flow into an inductance in the time interval t_0 to t depends only on the values of the current at the ends of the interval and not on how the current varies within the interval. If we select the beginning of the interval as a time t_0 at which $i(t_0) = 0$, then the energy flow into the inductance up to time t is given by $\tfrac{1}{2} Li^2(t)$.

The energy that flows out of the inductance in the time interval from t to some later time t_1 is given by $\tfrac{1}{2} Li^2(t) - \tfrac{1}{2} Li^2(t_1)$. For a given time t, this expression has a maximum value when t_1 is selected such that $i(t_1) = 0$; this maximum value is $\tfrac{1}{2} Li^2(t)$. Consequently we see that all the energy that is put into the inductance in the time interval from t_0 to t can be extracted during a subsequent time interval. We are justified, therefore, in saying that the energy $\tfrac{1}{2} Li^2(t)$ is *stored* in the inductance at time t and that the inductance does not dissipate energy. From electromagnetic field concepts it can be shown that in an ideal coil energy is stored in the magnetic field, and hence the energy stored in an inductance in our network model is referred to as magnetic stored energy.

Capacitance. The power flowing into a capacitance is given by

$$p(t) = vi = vC \frac{dv}{dt} = \frac{d}{dt} [\tfrac{1}{2} Cv^2(t)]. \tag{8-9}$$

Integration of this expression in the time interval t_0 to t gives the energy that flows into the capacitance in this time interval:

$$W(t) = \int_{t_0}^{t} \frac{d}{d\tau} [\tfrac{1}{2} Cv^2(\tau)] \, d\tau$$

$$= \tfrac{1}{2} Cv^2(t) - \tfrac{1}{2} Cv^2(t_0) . \qquad (8\text{-}10)$$

As in the case of an inductance we can verify that a capacitance is capable of storing energy and that it does not dissipate energy. If a voltage $v(t)$ exists across a capacitance, then the energy stored in the capacitance at time t is $\tfrac{1}{2} Cv^2(t)$. From electromagnetic field concepts it can be shown that in an ideal capacitor the energy is stored in the electric field, and hence the energy stored in a capacitance in our network model is referred to as electric stored energy.

An interpretation of power flow in RLC networks. The concepts of dissipated energy and stored energy in R, L, and C elements can be introduced into the law of conservation of energy to obtain another interpretation of this law. Consider an *RLC* network with terminal pairs, and let us write Eq. (8-4) in such a way that the summation of vi products for internal elements is separated into three summations—one for the resistance elements, one for the inductance elements, and one for the capacitance elements. Thus we have

$$\sum_{\substack{\text{terminal} \\ \text{pairs}}} v_k i_k = \sum_{R} v_l i_l + \sum_{L} v_m i_m + \sum_{C} v_n i_n , \qquad (8\text{-}11)$$

where the subscripts l, m, and n refer to voltages and currents in the resistance, inductance, and capacitance elements, respectively, and the symbols R, L, and C under the summation signs indicate that the summations are over these respective groups of elements.

We now introduce the v-i relations for the elements to obtain

$$\sum_{\substack{\text{terminal} \\ \text{pairs}}} v_k i_k = \sum_{R} i_l^2 R_l + \sum_{L} i_m L_m \frac{di_m}{dt} + \sum_{C} v_n C_n \frac{dv_n}{dt} , \qquad (8\text{-}12)$$

which can be written

$$\sum_{\substack{\text{terminal} \\ \text{pairs}}} v_k i_k = \sum_{R} i_l^2 R_l + \frac{d}{dt} \sum_{L} T_m + \frac{d}{dt} \sum_{C} U_n , \qquad (8\text{-}13)$$

where T_m and U_n represent the energy stored in the mth inductance and in the nth capacitance respectively. The left-hand side of Eq. (8-13) represents the total power flowing into the network through the terminals. The first summation on the right-hand side, which we shall designate by p_d, represents the power dissipated in the network; the second and third terms can be interpreted as the rate of increase of magnetic and electric stored energy in the network, respectively. If we designate the total energy stored in the inductances (magnetic energy) as T and the total energy stored in the capacitances (electric energy) as U, then we can express the total power flowing into the network at its terminals as

$$p_{in} = p_d + \frac{d}{dt}(T + U).$$ (8-14)

Thus we have the result that the total power flowing into an RLC network is equal to the power dissipated within the network plus the rate of increase of stored energy in the network.

Problem 8-1

Show that an ideal transformer does not store or dissipate energy.

Problem 8-2

A power amplifier is to be used to drive a loudspeaker as shown in Fig. 8-3.

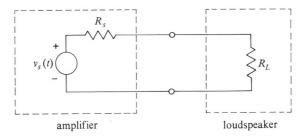

FIG. 8-3. Equivalent network for a power amplifier connected to a loudspeaker (Prob. 8-2).

The equivalent network of the amplifier as seen from its output terminals is a voltage source $v_s(t)$ in a series with a positive resistance R_s. Assume that the loudspeaker looks like a positive resistance R_L at its input terminals.
a. Assuming that the resistance R_s is fixed, sketch the curve of the power delivered to the loudspeaker as a function of R_L. Indicate on this

sketch the value of R_L in terms of R_s such that maximum power is delivered to the loudspeaker. Under this condition the loudspeaker is said to be "matched" to the amplifier.

b. Suppose now that the loudspeaker resistance R_L is fixed and the amplifier output resistance R_s is variable. Determine the value of R_s in terms of R_L such that maximum power is delivered to the loudspeaker.

c. In order to match the source and the load when both R_s and R_L are fixed, one can use an ideal transformer as shown in Fig. 8-4. Determine the turns ratio T such that maximum power is delivered to the loudspeaker.

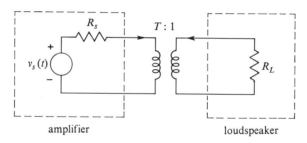

FIG. 8-4. Equivalent network for a power amplifier connected to a loudspeaker through an ideal transformer (Prob. 8-2).

Problem 8-3

The linear, resistive network of Fig. 8-5 is excited by the two voltage sources $v_{s_1}(t)$ and $v_{s_2}(t)$. The network contains no other sources.

a. Consider any resistance R in the network. How is the current in this resistance related to the voltage waveforms $v_{s_1}(t)$ and $v_{s_2}(t)$?

b. Derive a necessary and sufficient constraint between $v_{s_1}(t)$ and $v_{s_2}(t)$ in order that the total energy dissipated in any resistance R with both sources acting can be computed by adding the energies dissipated when each source acts alone.

c. In Fig. 8-6, three possible waveforms for $v_{s_1}(t)$ and three possible wave-

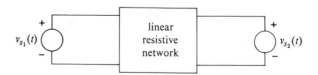

FIG. 8-5. Network excited by two voltage sources (Prob. 8-3).

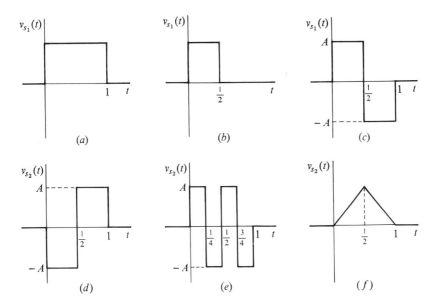

FIG. 8-6. Waveforms for $v_{s_1}(t)$ and $v_{s_2}(t)$ in the network of Fig. 8-5 (Prob. 8-3).

forms for $v_{s_2}(t)$ are given. For each of the waveforms for $v_{s_1}(t)$ determine which waveforms for $v_{s_2}(t)$ can be chosen such that the conditions of (b) are met.

Energy and power in the sinusoidal steady state

It is of particular interest to examine energy and power relations in networks with sinusoidal excitations, since there are many applications in which sinusoidal signals are used. As we have seen, it is usually convenient to determine the steady-state response of networks with sinusoidal excitations through the use of complex amplitudes, and it is appropriate, therefore, that we compute power relations in terms of complex amplitudes. Let us assume that the voltage and current at a pair of terminals of a network, shown in Fig. 8-7, are given by

$$v(t) = |V| \cos (\omega t + \phi), \qquad (8\text{-}15)$$

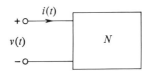

FIG. 8-7. Two-terminal network with sinusoidal voltage and current at the terminals.

$$i(t) = |I| \cos(\omega t + \eta), \qquad (8\text{-}16)$$

where $|V|$, $|I|$, ω, ϕ, and η are constants. These expressions can be written in terms of complex exponentials as

$$v(t) = \tfrac{1}{2}[Ve^{j\omega t} + V^*e^{-j\omega t}], \qquad (8\text{-}17)$$

and

$$i(t) = \tfrac{1}{2}[Ie^{j\omega t} + I^*e^{-j\omega t}], \qquad (8\text{-}18)$$

where $V = |V|e^{j\phi}$ and $I = |I|e^{j\eta}$. The power flowing into the terminals is the product of $v(t)$ and $i(t)$, and thus we have

$$p(t) = \tfrac{1}{4}[VI^* + V^*I + VIe^{j2\omega t} + V^*I^*e^{-j2\omega t}]. \qquad (8\text{-}19)$$

Combining terms, we can reduce this to

$$\begin{aligned}
p(t) &= \tfrac{1}{2}\,\mathrm{Re}\,[VI^*] + \tfrac{1}{2}\,\mathrm{Re}\,[VIe^{j2\omega t}] \\
&= \tfrac{1}{2}\,\mathrm{Re}\,[VI^*] + \tfrac{1}{2}\,\mathrm{Re}\,[|V||I|e^{j(2\omega t + \phi + \eta)}] \\
&= \tfrac{1}{2}\,\mathrm{Re}\,[VI^*] + \tfrac{1}{2}|V||I| \cos(2\omega t + \phi + \eta). \qquad (8\text{-}20)
\end{aligned}$$

The second term in this expression for the power is a sinusoid with a frequency 2ω, i.e., with a frequency twice that of the voltage and current. The average value of this second term is zero, and therefore the average power, which we shall denote by P_{av}, is given by the first term, i.e.,

$$P_{av} = \tfrac{1}{2}\,\mathrm{Re}\,[VI^*]. \qquad (8\text{-}21)$$

A sketch of the waveform of $p(t)$ is given in Fig. 8-8. The power flowing into the terminals is a sinusoid of frequency 2ω (or period π/ω) and of amplitude $\tfrac{1}{2}|V||I|$, superimposed on an average value of $\tfrac{1}{2}\,\mathrm{Re}\,[VI^*]$. Since $|\mathrm{Re}\,[VI^*]| \leq |V||I|$, the curve of $p(t)$ either becomes tangent to the horizontal axis or changes sign during each cycle. During the intervals of time indicated by the shaded regions in the figure energy flows out of the terminals of the network.

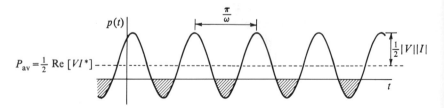

FIG. 8-8. Waveform of power at a pair of terminals with sinusoidal voltage and current.

Resistance. If the network N in Fig. 8-7 is simply a resistance element, then the complex amplitudes of the voltage and current are related by the equation $V = IR$, and therefore $v(t)$ and $i(t)$ are in phase, i.e., $\phi = \eta$ in Eqs. (8-15) and (8-16). Under these conditions Eq. (8-20) reduces to

$$p(t) = \tfrac{1}{2}|I|^2 R + \tfrac{1}{2}|I|^2 R \cos (2\omega t + 2\phi) . \tag{8-22}$$

Thus the average power dissipated in a resistance is $\tfrac{1}{2}|I|^2 R$. If R is positive, the maximum value of the power $p(t)$ is $|I|^2 R$, and the minimum value is zero.

Inductance. At the terminals of an inductance the complex amplitude of the voltage and current are related by the equation $V = j\omega L I$. If $I = |I| e^{j\eta}$, then $V = \omega L |I| e^{j(\eta + \pi/2)}$. In this case VI^* is imaginary, and hence the average power is zero. The expression (8-20) for the power becomes

$$p(t) = \tfrac{1}{2}\omega L |I|^2 \cos \left(2\omega t + 2\eta + \frac{\pi}{2} \right). \tag{8-23}$$

Thus the power flowing into an inductance is simply a sinusoid of frequency 2ω.

The energy stored in the inductance for a sinusoidal current $i(t) = |I| \cos (\omega t + \eta)$ is

$$T(t) = \tfrac{1}{2}L i^2 = \tfrac{1}{2}L|I|^2 \cos^2 (\omega t + \eta)$$
$$= \tfrac{1}{4}L|I|^2 [1 + \cos (2\omega t + 2\eta)] . \tag{8-24}$$

The average value of the stored energy is $\tfrac{1}{4}L|I|^2$, and there is again a sinusoidal component with frequency 2ω.

Capacitance. In the case of a capacitance, we have the V-I relation $I = j\omega C V$. If $V = |V| e^{j\phi}$, then $I = \omega C |V| e^{j(\phi + \pi/2)}$. From Eq. (8-20), the power flowing into a capacitance is, therefore,

$$p(t) = \tfrac{1}{2}\omega C |V|^2 \cos \left(2\omega t + 2\phi + \frac{\pi}{2} \right), \tag{8-25}$$

which is a sinusoid of frequency 2ω with zero average value.

For a voltage $v(t) = |V| \cos (\omega t + \phi)$ across the capacitance, the energy stored is

$$U(t) = \tfrac{1}{2}C v^2 = \tfrac{1}{2}C|V|^2 \cos^2 (\omega t + \phi)$$
$$= \tfrac{1}{4}C|V|^2 [1 + \cos (2\omega t + 2\phi)] , \tag{8-26}$$

which has an average value of $\tfrac{1}{4}C|V|^2$.

RLC networks.   Let us now consider the case in which network N in Fig. 8-7 is a one-port network containing only positive R, L, and C elements. For such a network we have shown previously [Eq. (8-14)] that the power flow into the terminals is given by

$$p_{in} = p_d + \frac{d}{dt}(T + U),$$ (8-27)

where p_d is the power dissipated in the resistances and T and U represent the energy stored in the inductances and capacitances, respectively. The second term on the right-hand side of Eq. (8-27) represents the power flow into the inductances and capacitances. We have seen that in the sinusoidal steady state this power flow is sinusoidal with an average value of zero. Hence the average power flowing into the network at the terminals is equal to the average power dissipated in the resistances; i.e.,

$$P_{av} = \tfrac{1}{2} \sum_R |I_l|^2 R_l,$$ (8-28)

where I_l is the amplitude of the sinusoidal current flowing in resistance R_l, and the summation is over all resistances in the network. For positive resistances this quantity is, of course, always positive.

Let us suppose now that the impedance at the terminals of the *RLC* network for complex frequency $s = j\omega$ is given by

$$Z = |Z|e^{j\theta}.$$ (8-29)

Thus if V and I are the complex amplitudes of the voltage and current at the terminals, we can write

$$VI^* = |Z||I|^2 e^{j\theta}$$

$$= |V||I|e^{j\theta},$$ (8-30)

and the expression for P_{av} in Eq. (8-21) becomes

$$P_{av} = \tfrac{1}{2} \operatorname{Re}[VI^*] = \tfrac{1}{2}|V||I|\cos\theta.$$ (8-31)

The power flowing into the network can then be written as

$$p(t) = \tfrac{1}{2}|V||I|\cos\theta + \tfrac{1}{2}|V||I|\cos(2\omega t + \phi + \eta),$$ (8-32)

where ϕ and η are the angles of V and I as before. The constant $\cos\theta$ in this equation determines the relative amount of energy that is returned to the source in each cycle, i.e., determines the relative size of the shaded areas in Fig. 8-8. If $\cos\theta = 1$, i.e., $\theta = 0$, corresponding to an impedance that is a pure resistance, then $P_{av} = \tfrac{1}{2}|V||I|$, and the amplitude of the sinusoidal component of the power is equal to the average value of the power, as we have seen for a resistance element. If, on the other hand, we have $\cos \theta = 0$, i.e., $\theta = \pm\pi/2$, then $P_{av} = 0$, and power flows into the terminals during one-half of each cycle and out of the terminals during the other half. The power flow in this case is like that at the terminals of an inductance or a capacitance. Since for a given voltage and current amplitude the constant $\cos \theta$ determines the power dissipated, it is often called the *power factor* of the network.

We have shown above that the average power flowing into the terminals of a network with positive R, L, and C elements is always positive, and hence for such a network the factor $\cos \theta$ must always be positive. Consequently the angle θ of the driving-point impedance must lie in the range $-\pi/2 \leq \theta \leq \pi/2$ for all ω.

Problem 8-4

In general, impedance or admittance can be written either in the polar form or in equivalent rectangular form. The imaginary part of an impedance is often called *reactance*. Similarly, the imaginary part of an admittance is called *susceptance*.

In power transmission applications it is often useful to modify a network so that its driving-point reactance or susceptance is zero at a given single frequency $s = j\omega_1$; i.e., its driving-point impedance is that of a resistance at that frequency. (An example is given in Prob. 8-5c.)

a. Given a network with impedance $Z = a + jb$ at a specified frequency $s = j\omega_1$, what is the susceptance at that frequency in terms of a and b?

b. What type of element (R, L, or C, with positive element values) should be connected in parallel with a network whose susceptance at a specified frequency $s = j\omega_1$ is (1) positive, (2) negative, in order that the resulting admittance shall be real at that frequency? What is the relation between the real part of the admittance before and after the parallel element is added?

c. What type of element (with positive element value) should be connected in series with a network whose reactance at a specified frequency $s = j\omega_1$ is (1) positive, (2) negative, in order that the resulting impedance shall be real at that frequency? What is the relation between the real part of the impedance before and after the series element is added?

d. Determine the value of the element that should be connected in (1) series, (2) parallel with the network shown in Fig. 8-9 such that the resulting impedance is real at $s = j2$. What is the value of the resulting impedance in each case?

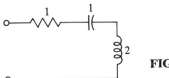

FIG. 8-9. Network for Prob. 8-4*d*.

Problem 8-5

The networks shown in Fig. 8-10 represent a system encountered in the generation and transmission of power.

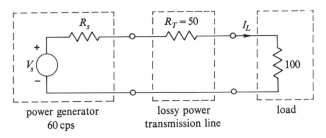

power generator
60 cps

lossy power
transmission line

load

FIG. 8-10. Equivalent network for a 60-cps power generator connected to a load through a transmission line (Prob. 8-5).

a. Determine the load current I_L and the average power that the generator must produce in order that the load receive 1,000 watts. Explain why the generator must deliver more than 1,000 watts of average power.
b. Suppose now that the load is changed to that shown in Fig. 8-11. Determine the load current and average power that the generator must produce in order that this new load receive an average power of 1,000 watts. Why must the generator produce more average power with the load of Fig. 8-11 than with the load of Fig. 8-10?
c. The load of Fig. 8-11 can be compensated to have unity power factor at the specified frequency by adding an element in parallel with the load. Determine the element value for this means of compensation.
d. Determine the average power that the generator must deliver if the

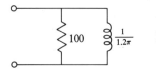

FIG. 8-11. Alternative load for the network of Fig. 8-10 (Prob. 8-5).

load is that of Fig. 8-11, compensated as in (c), in order that the load receive an average power of 1,000 watts.

Your results should suggest why the power companies wish to know the type of load to which they are delivering power before they fix the cost per watt to the consumer, and why it is desirable for the consumer to compensate for the power factor of a load.

Problem 8-6

The Thevenin equivalent network at terminal-pair a-a' for a sinusoidal generator is shown in Fig. 8-12. The figure shows the generator connected to a load with impedance $Z_L = R_L + jX_L$.

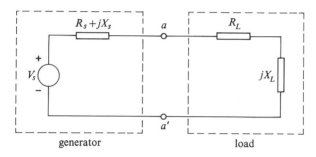

FIG. 8-12. Equivalent network for a sinusoidal generator connected to a load (Prob. 8-6).

a. If R_L is fixed and X_L is variable, determine X_L in terms of R_s, X_s, R_L, and V_s such that the average power delivered to the load is a maximum.

b. Determine in terms of V_s, R_s, and X_s the maximum average power available from the source at terminals a-a'. (Imagine that we are free to select any RLC network as a load.)

Problem 8-7

For RLC networks with two or more sources of excitation, we have seen that superposition can be applied to determine any voltage or current in the network. However in most situations it is not possible to use super-position in power calculations for a network since the power flowing into a pair of terminals is proportional to a product or square of voltage and current variables. A special case in which superposition can be applied in the calculation of power, illustrated in Fig. 8-13, is that of an RLC network excited by one sinusoidal voltage source and one sinusoidal current source with the same frequency and phase as the voltage source.

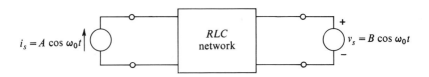

FIG. 8-13. Two-port network excited by a current source and a voltage source (Prob. 8-7).

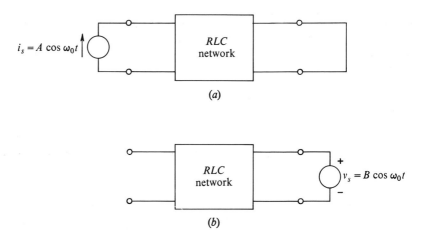

FIG. 8-14. Network of Fig. 8-13: (*a*) with voltage source set to zero; (*b*) with current source set to zero (Prob. 8-7).

Verify that the power dissipated in the two-port RLC network shown in Fig. 8-13 can be computed by superposing the power dissipated in the network due to each source acting separately; that is, the sum of the power dissipated in the network for the connection indicated in Fig. 8-14*a* and the power dissipated in the network for the connection indicated in Fig. 8-14*b* is equal to the power dissipated in the network for the connection shown in Fig. 8-13. [You may wish to make use of the reciprocity property (7-29) for two-port RLC networks.]

Problem 8-8

A network containing only L's and C's is terminated in a resistance R, as shown in Fig. 8-15. For a complex frequency $s = j\omega$, the impedance seen at terminal pair 1-1' is $Z_1(j\omega)$.

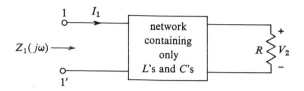

FIG. 8-15. Network for Prob. 8-8.

a. Express the average power flowing into terminal pair 1-1' in terms of the current I_1 and the impedance $Z_1(j\omega)$.

b. In terms of R and $Z_1(j\omega)$ determine the magnitude of the transfer impedance $Z_T(j\omega) = V_2/I_1$. It may be helpful to reason in terms of energy relations.

Problem 8-9

Let $f(t)$ be a periodic function of period T; i.e., $f(t + T) = f(t)$ for all t. The root-mean-square (rms) value, sometimes called the effective value, of $f(t)$ is defined as

$$F_{\text{rms}} = \sqrt{\frac{1}{T} \int_0^T f^2(\tau)\, d\tau} \ .$$

a. Suppose the voltage $v(t)$ across a resistance R is periodic (but not necessarily sinusoidal) with period T, and suppose the current through the resistance is $i(t)$. Find a relation between V_{rms} and I_{rms}, the rms values of $v(t)$ and $i(t)$ respectively.

b. Find expressions for the average power dissipated in R,

$$P_{\text{av}} = \frac{1}{T} \int_0^T p(\tau)\, d\tau = \frac{1}{T} \int_0^T v(\tau) i(\tau)\, d\tau \ ,$$

in terms of (1) V_{rms} and R; (2) I_{rms} and R; and (3) V_{rms} and I_{rms}, respectively.

c. A constant voltage is applied across the same resistance R. What should be the value of this voltage in terms of $v(t)$ so that the power dissipated in R is the same as P_{av} of (b)? Using your result, justify the use of the term "effective value."

d. Determine the rms values of the following waveforms:
1. $f(t) = A$, where A is a constant.
2. $f(t) = A \cos(\omega t + \theta)$.
3. $f(t)$ is the waveform shown in Fig. 8-16. It is periodic with period T.

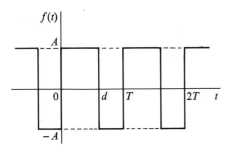

FIG. 8-16. Waveform of $f(t)$ in Prob. 8-9d, part (3).

e. Prove that, for any real periodic function $f(t)$:
1. $f(t)$, $-f(t)$, and $|f(t)|$ have the same rms value.
2. $f(t)$ and $f(t + a)$, where a is any constant, have the same rms value.

Problem 8-10

Two periodic functions $f_1(t)$ and $f_2(t)$, with periods T_1 and T_2 respectively, are said to be orthogonal to each other if

$$\frac{1}{T} \int_0^T f_1(\tau) f_2(\tau) \, d\tau = 0,$$

where T is a common multiple of T_1 and T_2.

Let $f(t) = f_1(t) + f_2(t)$. Show that $F_{\text{rms}}^2 = F_{1\text{rms}}^2 + F_{2\text{rms}}^2$ if and only if $f_1(t)$ and $f_2(t)$ are orthogonal. In other words, show that
1. if $f_1(t)$ and $f_2(t)$ are orthogonal, then $F_{\text{rms}}^2 = F_{1\text{rms}}^2 + F_{2\text{rms}}^2$;
2. if $F_{\text{rms}}^2 = F_{1\text{rms}}^2 + F_{2\text{rms}}^2$, then $f_1(t)$ and $f_2(t)$ are orthogonal.

Problem 8-11

a. Show that two sinusoidal signals $A \cos(\omega_1 t + \theta_1)$ and $B \cos(n\omega_1 t + \theta_2)$ are orthogonal if n is a positive integer and $n \neq 1$.
b. Show that two sinusoidal signals of the same frequency but different phase are orthogonal if and only if the phase difference is $\pm \dfrac{\pi}{2}$.
c. Find the rms values of the following functions:
1. $A + B \sin(\omega t + \theta)$.
2. $A \sin \omega t + B \sin(2\omega t + \theta)$.

3. $A \sin \omega t + B \cos \omega t$.
4. $A \sin \omega t + B \sin (\omega t + \pi/4)$.

Problem 8-12

Consider an RLC network excited by n sinusoidal sources. Each of the sources has a frequency that is a different integral multiple of some frequency ω_0. Show that the total average power delivered to the network by the n sources can be determined by adding the individual powers delivered by the n sources each acting separately.

Problem 8-13

Determine the average power dissipated in the resistance R in the network of Fig. 8-17 for each of the following sets of values for the two source currents:

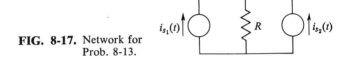

FIG. 8-17. Network for Prob. 8-13.

1. $i_{s_1}(t) = \cos 2\omega t$ and $i_{s_2}(t) = 3 \cos \omega t$.
2. $i_{s_1}(t) = i_{s_2}(t) = \sin \omega t$.
3. $i_{s_1}(t) = 2 \sin \omega t$ and $i_{s_2}(t) = 3 \cos \omega t$.
4. $i_{s_1}(t) = \cos 2\pi t$, and $i_{s_2}(t)$ is a square wave with period 1, as shown in Fig. 8-18.

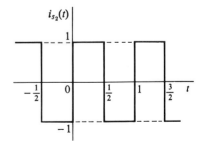

FIG. 8-18. One of the waveforms for $i_{s_2}(t)$ for the network of Fig. 8-17 (Prob. 8-13).

Vector power

The fact that the average power at the terminals of a network in the sinusoidal steady state is given by $\frac{1}{2} \operatorname{Re}[VI^*]$ suggests that one might define a *vector power* P by

$$P = \tfrac{1}{2} VI^* . \qquad (8\text{-}33)$$

(Since $P_{av} = \tfrac{1}{2} \operatorname{Re}[VI^*] = \tfrac{1}{2} \operatorname{Re}[V^*I]$, we could define vector power by either $\tfrac{1}{2}VI^*$ or $\tfrac{1}{2}V^*I$. We shall arbitrarily select the former of these as the definition.) We shall denote the imaginary part of P by Q_{av}, and we shall call this quantity the reactive power. Hence the vector power can be written

$$P = P_{av} + jQ_{av} . \qquad (8\text{-}34)$$

This procedure of mathematically defining the quantities P and Q_{av} has at first sight no obvious motivation. We shall shortly show, however, that the quantity Q_{av} is intimately associated with stored energy in much the same way that P_{av} is associated with dissipated energy.

In order to look for an interpretation of P and Q_{av}, let us compute the vector power flowing into the terminals of an RLC network. From Tellegen's theorem we can write

$$P = \sum_{\substack{\text{terminal} \\ \text{pairs}}} \tfrac{1}{2} V_k I_k^* = \sum_{\text{elements}} \tfrac{1}{2} V_k I_k^* . \qquad (8\text{-}35)$$

The summation over the elements can be expressed as three separate summations corresponding to the three types of elements in the network to give

$$P = \sum_R \tfrac{1}{2} V_l I_l^* + \sum_L \tfrac{1}{2} V_m I_m^* + \sum_C \tfrac{1}{2} V_n I_n^* , \qquad (8\text{-}36)$$

where the subscripts l, m, and n again refer to resistance, inductance, and capacitance elements respectively. Using the V-I relations for the elements, we obtain

$$P = \sum_R \tfrac{1}{2} R_l |I_l|^2 + \sum_L \tfrac{1}{2} j\omega L_m |I_m|^2 - \sum_C \tfrac{1}{2} j\omega C_n |V_n|^2$$

$$= \sum_R \tfrac{1}{2} R_l |I_l|^2 + j2\omega \left[\sum_L \tfrac{1}{4} L_m |I_m|^2 - \sum_C \tfrac{1}{4} C_n |V_n|^2 \right]. \qquad (8\text{-}37)$$

But we have already shown that the average energy stored in an inductance is $\tfrac{1}{4}L|I|^2$, and the average energy stored in a capacitance is $\tfrac{1}{4}C|V|^2$. Therefore in Eq. (8-37) the summations over the inductance and capacitance elements represent the average stored energy T_{av} and U_{av} in the inductances and capacitances, respectively. Likewise we have seen that the summation over the resistances represents the average power dissipated in the resistances, which we have designated as P_{av} in Eq. (8-28). Consequently the vector power can be written

$$P = P_{av} + jQ_{av} = P_{av} + j2\omega(T_{av} - U_{av}) . \qquad (8\text{-}38)$$

The reactive power, therefore, is 2ω times the difference between the average stored energy in the inductances (magnetic stored energy) and the average stored energy in the capacitances (electric stored energy).

Impedance in terms of energy

When Eq. (8-38) for the vector power is applied to an *RLC* network with one terminal pair, it is possible to derive an expression for the impedance of the network for a complex frequency $s = j\omega$ in terms of the power dissipated and the average electric and magnetic stored energy in the network. Let V and I represent the complex amplitudes of the voltage and current at the terminals, and let $Z(j\omega)$ be the impedance of the network for complex frequency $j\omega$. The vector power can be written

$$P = \tfrac{1}{2}VI^* = \tfrac{1}{2}Z(j\omega)|I|^2 , \qquad (8\text{-}39)$$

and hence $\qquad\qquad\qquad Z(j\omega) = \dfrac{2P}{|I|^2} . \qquad (8\text{-}40)$

Substituting the expression for P in Eq. (8-38) into this equation, we obtain

$$Z(j\omega) = \frac{1}{|I|^2} [2P_{av} + j4\omega(T_{av} - U_{av})] . \qquad (8\text{-}41)$$

Although the frequency ω only appears explicitly in the imaginary part of this expression, each of the terms P_{av}, T_{av}, and U_{av} is in general a function of frequency.

Several properties of *RLC* networks can be deduced from this expression for impedance in terms of dissipated and stored energy. For frequencies at which the average stored magnetic and electric energies are equal, it follows from (8-41) that the driving-point impedance is real; i.e., the terminal behavior of the network is that of a resistance. When the average stored magnetic energy is greater than the average stored electric energy, the imaginary part of the impedance is positive. The imaginary part of the impedance is negative when the average stored magnetic energy is less than the average stored electric energy.

As an illustration of the application of Eq. (8-41) and of other relations involving energy and power in the sinusoidal steady state, let us consider the series *RLC* network shown in Fig. 8-19. If we let $i(t) = |I| \cos \omega t$, then the stored magnetic energy, as a function of time, is given by

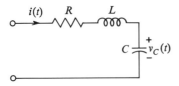

FIG. 8-19. Series *RLC* network used to illustrate energy and power relations in the sinusoidal steady state.

$$T = \tfrac{1}{2}L|I|^2 \cos^2 \omega t$$

$$= \tfrac{1}{4}L|I|^2(1 + \cos 2\omega t). \tag{8-42}$$

The voltage across the capacitance is $v_C(t) = (|I|/\omega C) \cos (\omega t - \pi/2)$, and hence the stored electric energy is

$$U = \tfrac{1}{2}(|I|^2/\omega^2 C) \cos^2 (\omega t - \pi/2)$$

$$= \tfrac{1}{4}(|I|^2/\omega^2 C)[1 + \cos (2\omega t - \pi)]. \tag{8-43}$$

The average magnetic and electric energies are $T_{av} = \tfrac{1}{4}L|I|^2$ and $U_{av} = \tfrac{1}{4}(|I|^2/\omega^2 C)$, respectively. At the frequency $\omega_0 = 1/\sqrt{LC}$, T_{av} and U_{av} are equal, and the driving-point impedance is therefore real. We observe from Eqs. (8-42) and (8-43) that under these conditions the total stored energy $T + U$ is a constant and is equal to the peak value of T and of U; i.e.,

$$T + U = \tfrac{1}{2}L|I|^2 = \tfrac{1}{2}\frac{|I|^2}{\omega_0^2 C}. \tag{8-44}$$

If we set $\omega = \omega_0$ in Eqs. (8-42) and (8-43), then at certain instants of time, i.e., at times t for which $\cos 2\omega_0 t = 1$, the energy stored in the inductance is a maximum and the energy stored in the capacitance is zero. At other instants of time, i.e., at times t for which $\cos 2\omega_0 t = -1$, all the stored energy is in the capacitance, and no energy is stored in the inductance. Thus the stored energy oscillates between electric stored energy in the capacitance and magnetic stored energy in the inductance, and the source does not participate in this interchange of stored energy. The source simply provides the energy that is dissipated in the resistance. (In the case of *RLC* networks that are more complex than the series *RLC* network of Fig. 8-19, however, it is not in general true that the total stored energy remains constant at frequencies for which $T_{av} = U_{av}$.)

We do not, of course, expect that introduction of the concepts of energy and power will enable us to derive new properties of networks that we could not already have derived from the Kirchhoff-law equations and the *v-i* relations for the elements, since the energy and power relations are derived from these basic network equations. However, certain energy and power concepts that we have discussed here can be applied not only to linear systems that are governed by constant-coefficient ordinary differential equations but also to systems that are governed by partial differential equations, such as those encountered in electromagnetic field problems. For example, the phenomenon of oscillation of stored energy between electric and magnetic forms is encountered frequently in systems that can be described in terms of electromagnetic fields distributed in space. Thus the interpretation of behavior of systems in terms of energy and power will turn out to be applicable beyond the scope of network theory problems.

Problem 8-14

In this problem, we shall introduce a definition of resonance in terms of energy. Following the argument given in the text for a driving-point impedance, it can be readily shown that for a two-terminal RLC network the driving-point admittance is given by

$$Y(j\omega) = \frac{2}{|V|^2}[P_{av} + j2\omega(U_{av} - T_{av})], \qquad (8\text{-}45)$$

where $|V|$ is the amplitude of the sinusoidal voltage across the terminals, and the remaining symbols have the same meaning as those in Eq. (8-41). The resonant frequency of a network is sometimes defined as the frequency at which $U_{av} = T_{av}$.

As a simple example, let us consider the parallel RLC network of Fig. 8-20.

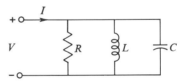

FIG. 8-20. Parallel RLC network for Prob. 8-14.

a. Verify the expression for Y given above in Eq. (8-45).
b. Find the resonant frequency ω_0 by setting $U_{av} = T_{av}$.
c. The bandwidth and quality factor Q are defined as in Prob. 4-24. Verify that

$$Q = 2\pi \left[\frac{\text{average energy stored at the resonant frequency}}{\text{energy dissipated per cycle at the resonant frequency}} \right].$$

Problem 8-15

a. Determine the driving-point impedance at the terminal pair a-a' of the network shown in Fig. 8-21.

b. For a voltage excitation $v(t) = \sin 2t$, calculate the average electric and magnetic stored energies and the average power dissipated.

c. From your answer to (*b*), determine $Z(j2)$, and check your answer with that of (*a*).

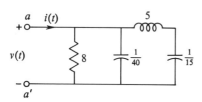

FIG. 8-21. Network for Prob. 8-15.

INDEX

353

Set in Monotype Times New Roman

Format by Frances Torbert Tilley

Composition by Westcott & Thomson, Inc.